D0020966

Devon &
Cornwall

WITHDRAWN

Exmoor &
North Devon
p120

Exeter &
East Devon
p46

Newquay &
North Cornwall
p180

Plymouth &
Dartmoor
p98

Bodmin &
East Cornwall
p140

South
Cornwall
p150

Torquay &
South Devon
p66

West Cornwall &
the Isles of Scilly
p204

Oliver Berry, Belinda Dixon

Contents

HOUND TOR, DARTMOOR
NATIONAL PARK P109

RICH LEGG / GETTY IMAGES ©

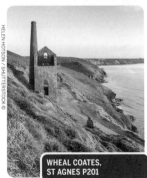

WHEAL COATES,
ST AGNES P201

HELEN HOTSON / SHUTTERSTOCK ©

ON THE ROAD

BEER P64

SAVO ILIC / SHUTTERSTOCK ©

Contents

Welcome to Devon & Cornwall

Welcome to the wild, wild west – a land of gorse-clad cliffs, booming surf, white sand and epic, widescreen skies.

World-Class Coastline

There's one aspect of the West Country that's impossible to miss – its epic coastline. Bordered on three sides by sea, the combined coastlines of Devon and Cornwall stretch for more than 530 miles, encompassing plunging cliffs, sandy bays, secluded coves, craggy headlands and postcard-pretty fishing villages aplenty. There's a beach to suit all tastes, whether you're here to laze in the sunshine, paddle in the blue or set out in search of the perfect wave. And with a good map and an adventurous spirit, solitude is never far away.

Living History

Whether it's the silhouette of a crumbling castle on a lonely hilltop, or the spectre of moody mine stacks spiking the horizon, the region's history plays out wherever you look. From its long legacy of fishing and seafaring to its illustrious mining heritage, Devon and Cornwall are crammed with fascinating reminders of the past. You could while away your days exploring ancient hillforts or mysterious stone circles, marvel at the ambition of the region's great gardens and country houses, or venture inside a decommissioned tin mine, an underground telegraph station or even a working lighthouse.

The Great Outdoors

Getting active is the best way to experience the region's landscapes. Hiking trails and cycling paths criss-cross the countryside, and the South West Coast Path winds its way through a kaleidoscope of coastal landscapes. But there are many more ways to get active: coasteering over rocky crags, kayaking down a wooded creek, paddleboarding to a remote cove or stargazing under pitch-black night skies. And there's a wealth of wildlife to spot too, from Exmoor's wild deer to the Lizard's red-billed choughs – and you'll never forget your first glimpse of a wild dolphin or basking shark.

Food Feasts

Fantastic fish and farm-made cheeses, small-batch beers and world-class wines, Michelin-starred bistros and quirky beach cafes: Devon and Cornwall can now proudly claim to be one of Britain's most exciting places to eat and drink. There's a good reason several of the UK's top chefs have decided to make their home here – some of Britain's best produce can be found right on their doorstep. Whether it's cracking open a fresh crab, barbecuing fish on the beach, picnicking on the cliffs or tucking into a traditional Cornish pasty, there's a wealth of foodie experiences waiting out west.

Why I Love Devon & Cornwall

By Oliver Berry, Writer

Cornwall is my home county, so it's the place I know better than anywhere. I've travelled all over the globe as a travel writer, but there's something special about the world out west, and I always find myself drawn back. I reckon I've visited pretty much every beach there is over the years, but there's always something new to see: the light, the weather and the changing seasons all bring out a different side to the landscape. For me, the Lizard and the Penwith coastline are every bit as spectacular as any of the more exotic places I've visited.

For more about our writers, see p288

Above: Clovelly (p138)

Devon & Cornwall

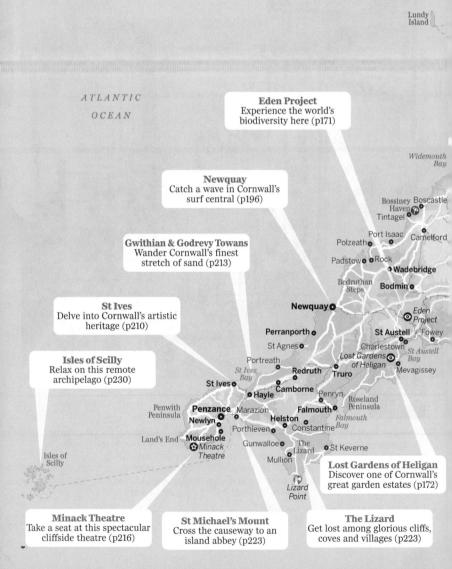

ATLANTIC
OCEAN

Lundy
Island

Eden Project
Experience the world's
biodiversity here (p171)

Widemouth
Bay

Newquay
Catch a wave in Cornwall's
surf central (p196)

Bossiney Boscastle
Haven
Tintagel

Port Isaac Camelford
Polzeath
Padstow Rock

Wadebridge

Bedruthan
Steps **Bodmin**

Gwithian & Godrevy Towans
Wander Cornwall's finest
stretch of sand (p213)

St Ives
Delve into Cornwall's artistic
heritage (p210)

Newquay

Eden
Project

Perranporth
St Agnes

St Austell Fowey

Charlestown
Lost Gardens *St Austell*
of Heligan *Bay*
Mevagissey

Isles of Scilly
Relax on this remote
archipelago (p230)

Portreath
St Ives
Bay **Redruth** **Truro**

St Ives

Hayle **Camborne**

Penwith
Peninsula **Penzance** Marazion

Penryn Roseland
Peninsula

Falmouth *Falmouth*
Bay

Newlyn

Helston

Land's End Porthleven Constantine

Mousehole
Minack
Theatre

Gunwalloe The
Lizard St Keverne

Isles of
Scilly

Mullion

Lizard
Point

Lost Gardens of Heligan
Discover one of Cornwall's
great garden estates (p172)

Minack Theatre
Take a seat at this spectacular
cliffside theatre (p216)

St Michael's Mount
Cross the causeway to an
island abbey (p223)

The Lizard
Get lost among glorious cliffs,
coves and villages (p223)

N 0 ——————— 50 km
0 ——————— 25 miles

Exmoor National Park
Watch red deer on a wildlife
safari (p126)

Clovelly
Devon's prettiest village?
Quite possibly (p138)

*Bristol
Channel*

Lynton Lynmouth
Porlock
Ilfracombe ○

Croyde ○
Braunton ○

*Barnstaple
Bay*
Appledore ○
Bideford ○

Heartland
Peninsula ○ Clovelly

*Severn
Estuary*

*Bridgwater
Bay*

Exmoor
National
Park
Dunster ○

Exford ○

Barnstaple ○

Dulverton ○

*The
Quantocks*

○ **Bude**

Okehampton ○

Tamar

Dartmoor
National
Park

Lydford ○

Chagford ○

Moretonhampstead ○

Widecombe-
in-the-Moor ○

*Tamar
Valley*
Princetown ○

Tavistock ○

*Bodmin
Moor*

○ **Liskeard**

Plymouth ○

○ Looe
Polperro ○ *Rame
Peninsula*

South West Coast Path
Amble through breathtaking
coastal scenery (p35)

◎ **Exeter**

Sidmouth ○ ○ Beer
Branscombe

*Lyne
Bay*

Exmouth

Teignmouth ○

*Start
Bay*

○ **Ashburton**

○ **Torquay**

*Tor
Bay*
Totnes ○
○ **Brixham**
○ **Dartmouth**

Exeter
Climb the Gothic towers
of the cathedral (p52)

Bigbury-
on-Sea ○
Bantham ○ ○ Thurlestone
Hope
Cove ○

○ Kingsbridge

○ Salcombe

Dartmoor National Park
Explore the wild tors and
hills of Dartmoor (p109)

*English
Channel*

ELEVATION

	500m
	400m
	300m
	200m
	100m
	0

Dartmouth
Soak up the history of
this seafaring port (p82)

Devon & Cornwall's
Top 16

Eden Project

1 Located inside a Cornish clay pit just outside St Austell, the futuristic biomes of the Eden Project (p171) have become an iconic symbol of Cornwall's renaissance. Housing an outlandish array of plants, trees and botanical curiosities from across the globe, they're the largest greenhouses on earth, and internationally famous (they even appeared in a Bond film). They're great to visit in all weather, and there's something going on whenever you come – whether it's a spring flower show, a summer gig, an autumn food fest or a wintertime ice-skate. Don't miss it.

Isles of Scilly

2 Scattered across the Atlantic, 28 miles from Land's End, this remote island archipelago (p230) is Cornwall's answer to the Caribbean. Of the 140-odd islands, only five are permanently inhabited, leaving the rest to seabirds, seals and the occasional basking shark. Blessed with a laid-back lifestyle, electric-blue water and some of Britain's best beaches, the islands are hard to leave – especially once your internal clock has switched over to Scilly time. You can visit them in a day, but they'll soak up as much time as you can spare.

Below: View of Bryher (p234) from Tresco (p233)

RUTH BROWN / GETTY IMAGES ©

NEIL DUGGAN / SHUTTERSTOCK ©

Dartmoor National Park

3 Bleakly bewitching, the heather-clad heaths and granite tors of Dartmoor (p109) have an edge of wildness about them that feels quite different from the rest of Devon. It's a place where nature still holds sway, and the only sign of human habitation is a few scattered farmhouses and drystone walls. Hiking and biking are the main draws here, and it's one of the few areas in Britain where wild camping is still legal, where you can pitch a tent just about anywhere and sleep out under wild skies.

St Ives

4 When it comes to seaside settings, St Ives (p210) is a world-beater. Tucked in beside a grand curve of coastline, with a jumble of slate roofs, narrow lanes and golden beaches, it's quite simply one of Cornwall's most beautiful sights. The town is famous for its artistic connections, too: Barbara Hepworth established an artists' colony here in the 1930s, and the town is also home to the Tate St Ives, the far-west wing of the renowned national gallery, which has recently been blessed with a multimillion-pound extension.

Exeter Cathedral

5 A heap of Gothic grandeur in the centre of Devon's oldest city, this mighty cathedral (p52) is the region's foremost house of worship, and its greatest sight. Largely built during the 13th century, its most notable features are the decorative facade and a fabulous vaulted ceiling – but it's the chance to climb up the towers that excites most visitors. Unsurprisingly, there's a wraparound view from the top, stretching right across Exeter; on a clear day, you might even spy Dartmoor and the Devon coast.

South West Coast Path

6 No matter where you go in Devon and Cornwall, you'll never be far from the South West Coast Path (p35). Winding through a string of cliffs, coves, villages, peninsulas and headlands, this fabulous footpath is one of the region's must-experience attractions. Hard-core hikers tackle the whole route, a truly epic ramble of more than 630 miles that also takes in the coastlines of Dorset and Somerset. Others focus just on the Devon or Cornwall sections, but really, an hour's stroll is every bit as stunning.

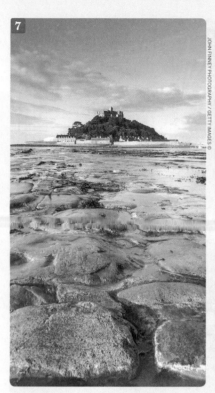

JOHN FINNEY PHOTOGRAPHY / GETTY IMAGES ©

KRU / SHUTTERSTOCK ©

ALLE CHARLES / SHUTTERSTOCK ©

St Michael's Mount

7 Cornwall's answer to Mont St-Michel occupies a rocky island opposite the old harbour of Penzance. The abbey (p223) was originally built by Benedictine monks, but has served many roles over the years (including a coastal fort, stately home and even an ammunition dump). It's now the family home of the St Aubyn family, although it's officially owned by the National Trust. Don't miss the chance to walk across to the island along its famous cobbled causeway, which only reveals itself at low tide.

Lost Gardens of Heligan

8 From colourful magnolias to rare rhododendrons, the West Country's gardens bloom with horticultural interest. Its temperate climate and subtropical valleys provide the perfect growing conditions for exotic trees, plants and flowers, including many species that can't survive anywhere else in Britain. Each has its own special attraction: the Lost Gardens of Heligan (p172) are particularly impressive, forgotten for decades and now stunningly restored by a team of dedicated gardeners, with kitchen gardens, trimmed lawns, outdoor artworks and wild jungle valleys to explore.

Exmoor National Park

9 Britain's smallest national park, Exmoor (p126) straddles the Devon–Dorset border. While it might not quite have the epic quality of Dartmoor, Exmoor has charms all of its own, from a unique water-powered railway at Lynton to the panoramic viewpoint of Dunkery Beacon. But, as always, it's the landscape that's Exmoor's selling point: it's a photogenic patchwork of medieval fields, ancient oak woods and plunging coombes (valleys), and is one of the best places in Britain to spot herds of wild red deer.

The Lizard

10 This peculiarly named peninsula (p223) juts out from Cornwall's southern coastline, and was notorious as one of Cornwall's most treacherous headlands – countless ships met their end on its hidden reefs and inky cliffs down through the centuries. These days it's a place to wander the cliffs, explore the remote coves and watch wildlife – if you're really lucky, you might spot Cornwall's symbolic bird, the red-billed chough, which is thriving again here after years of decline. Bring binoculars – and swimming gear.

Minack Theatre

11 Etched in the Penwith cliffs above a cauldron of booming surf, this eye-popping clifftop amphitheatre (p216) has to be one of the most memorable places to watch a play anywhere in the world. Pinch yourself and you could be forgiven for thinking you'd been transported back in time to ancient Greece, but it was actually a 20th-century project, dreamt up and built by a lady called Rowena Cade. Stone seats rise in steep tiers around the stage, and the backdrop is sea, sky and circling gulls. It's a dream.

14

Dartmouth

12 Nestled in the heart of the South Hams, this handsome port (p82) has a seafaring history stretching back more than eight centuries, and it's still home to Britain's top naval academy. It's a glorious setting, surrounded by green fields, rolling hills and a picturesque river, and a great base for exploring the rest of the South Hams – from Agatha Christie's holiday home to the alternative town of Totnes and the many pretty coves of the south coast. It even has its own paddle steamer.

Gwithian & Godrevy Towans

13 Cornwall's north coast is a non-stop string of golden beaches, stretching all the way from Bude to the very end of the land near Sennen. There's a reason to visit every one if you can: some are brash and breezy, others are quiet and secluded, and can only be reached via a walk along the coast path. For all-round scenic splendour, the side-by-side beaches of Gwithian and Godrevy (p213) are hard to beat: together they form more than 3 miles of sand, and are beloved by everyone from bodyboarders to dog-walkers. Bottom: Lighthouse on Godrevy Island

ALAN COPSON / GETTY IMAGES ©

JAMES PEARCE / SHUTTERSTOCK ©

Coastal Adventures

14 Devon and Cornwall have some of the finest coastline anywhere in Europe, so they're a great place for sea-themed adventures. Surfing is the traditional choice, with the epicentre in Newquay (p196), although Croyde, Bude, Padstow, Perranporth and Sennen are all prime spots too. And if you really get the watersports bug, there are plenty more activities to try, like stand-up paddleboarding, kayaking, coasteering and more. And yes, since you ask, the water's a bit cold – but with a decent wetsuit, you won't feel the chill. Above: Croyde (p136)

Clovelly

15 Tumbling down a formidably steep hillside on the north Devon coast, the improbably pretty village of Clovelly (p138) feels like a step back into a more pastoral time. Bisected by a cobbled street lined by cob houses and fishers' cottages, it's a vision of village life that could have been lifted straight out of a film set. It's a place that is awash with photo opportunities, especially in the late evening when the winding lanes are at their quietest and quaintest.

Cornish Pasties

16 Stuffed with beef, swede, potatoes and onions, wrapped in pastry and crimped on the side (not the top!), pasties are Cornwall's original takeaway snack, developed as a portable lunchbox for men working in the local fields and tin mines. Now awarded officially protected status, nothing tastes quite like a true pasty that's been made in Cornwall according to a time-honoured recipe. You'll find them for sale at bakeries and cafes all over the county. Everyone has their favourite, but for us, it's Ann's Pasties (p229) that takes the prize.

Need to Know

For more information, see Survival Guide (p265)

Currency
Pound (£)

Language
English & Cornish

Visas
Visas to enter the UK are not needed for stays of up to six months. The country is not a member of the Schengen Zone.

Money
ATMs are widely available; Visa and Mastercard credit cards are widely accepted, but other credit cards less so.

Mobile Phones
The UK uses the GSM 900/1800 network; it's compatible with Europe, Australia and New Zealand, but not with the North American GSM 1900. Check with your provider on compatibility issues.

Time
Greenwich Mean Time (GMT); British Summer Time (BST; GMT plus one hour, April to October)

When to Go

Exeter
GO Apr–Oct

Newquay
GO Jun–Sep

Penzance
GO May–Sep

Falmouth
GO Apr–Jun; Sep

Warm to hot summers, mild winters

High Season
(Jun–Aug)

➡ Prices are at their highest, and hotels, B&Bs and campsites are full.

➡ Traffic and crowds are to be expected, especially in July and August.

➡ Packed calendar of festivals and events.

Shoulder
(Mar–May & Sep–Oct)

➡ Peak prices drop and seasonal deals are available.

➡ Weather can be more settled than in summer.

➡ Quietest during school term; half-terms are always busy.

Low Season
(Nov–Feb)

➡ Rates for B&Bs and hotels are at their lowest.

➡ Some sights and attractions close or operate shorter hours.

➡ Accommodation and trains are booked out for Christmas and New Year.

Useful Websites

Lonely Planet (www.lonely planet.com) Destination information, hotel bookings, traveller forum and more.

Simply Scilly (www.visitislesof scilly.com) The lowdown on the Isles of Scilly.

Traveline SW (www.travelinesw. org.uk) Public transport info for the southwest.

Visit Cornwall (www.visitcorn wall.co.uk) The official tourist site: accommodation, activities and more.

Visit Devon (www.visitdevon. co.uk) Devon's official tourist site with accommodation listings, events, activities and more.

Important Numbers

England (and UK) country code	☑44
International access code	☑00
Emergency (police, fire, ambulance, moorland rescue or coastguard)	☑112 or ☑999

Exchange Rates

Australia	A$1	£0.61
Canada	C$1	£0.62
Eurozone	€1	£0.92
Japan	¥100	£0.71
New Zealand	NZ$1	£0.56
USA	US$1	£0.78

For current exchange rates, see www.xe.com.

Daily Costs

**Budget:
Less than £90**

➡ Hostel bed: £15–25

➡ Campsite pitch: £10–20

➡ Public transport: £5–10

➡ Pasty and a pint: £6–8

**Midrange:
£90–150**

➡ Double room in a B&B: £90–120

➡ Lunch and dinner in local restaurants: £20–30

➡ Admissions and activities: £10–20

➡ Petrol per day: £10–20

**Top End:
More than £150**

➡ Room in a luxury hotel: from £150

➡ Meals in top-end restaurants: £50–70

Opening Hours

Opening hours vary throughout the year, especially in rural and coastal areas.

Banks 9.30am to 4pm or 5pm Monday to Friday; some open 9.30am to 1pm Saturday.

Pubs and Bars Noon to 11pm Monday to Saturday (some till midnight or 1am Friday and Saturday), 12.30pm to 11pm Sunday.

Shops 9am to 5.30pm or 6pm Monday to Saturday, and often 11am to 5pm Sunday.

Restaurants Lunch is noon to 3pm, dinner 6pm to 9pm or 10pm.

Arriving in Devon & Cornwall

Exeter Airport (p272) Bus 56/56A/56B (£2.40, 30 minutes) runs to Exeter St David's train station, via the city centre and Exeter bus station, hourly between around 6.30am and 6.30pm. A taxi fare to the city centre typically costs around £35.

Newquay Cornwall Airport (p272) First Kernow bus 56 (£3, 30 minutes, hourly Monday to Saturday, three on Sunday) links Newquay with the airport. Services run from 7am to around 5.30pm. Bus 56 also runs between the airport and Padstow (£4, one hour, same frequency). A taxi will cost £15 to £25 from Newquay town centre.

Plymouth Ferry port Bus 34/34A (£1.20, four minutes, every 30 minutes) goes past the ferry port from the city centre. It runs from around 6am Monday to Saturday (7.30am Sunday) to 9.30pm (8.30pm on Sunday). A taxi will cost around £6.

Top Tips

Use public transport Traffic can be a problem, but there are some superb train lines and cycle tracks to explore – not to mention the coast path.

Consider National Trust membership Gets you free entry to many estates and gardens.

Pack sandals A pair of strapped multi-activity sandals are perfect for clambering over rocks and walking on hot sand.

Don't feed seagulls These birds are becoming a menace in many areas – don't feed them scraps, and beware dive-bombs.

Buy a wetsuit and snorkel If you're planning on a lot of beach time, having your own gear is a wise investment.

For much more on **getting around**, see p32 & p272

If You Like...

Views

For every knockout view in the southwest, there's another waiting just around the corner. Don't forget to pack the wide-angle lens.

Land's End As far west as you can get on mainland Britain: next stop, the Scilly Isles. (p215)

Brown Willy The highest hill in Cornwall, in the middle of Bodmin Moor. (p145)

Carn Brea Panoramic views from a craggy hilltop in the heart of Cornwall's mining country. (p203)

Exeter Cathedral Climb the spire for a bird's-eye perspective on Exeter. (p52)

Start Point A pocket of Devon wildness with a picturesque lighthouse. (p88)

Bedruthan Steps Look out over a panorama of rock towers. (p199)

The Jurassic Coast Rust-red, fossil-rich cliffs, best viewed between Beer and Branscombe. (p48)

Lizard Point The most southerly headland in Britain, craggy and spectacular. (p229)

Beaches

When it comes to beaches, few corners of Britain can match Devon and Cornwall. There are hundreds to explore, whether you're planning to paddle in the shallows, delve into the rock pools or don a wetsuit and brave the waves.

Sennen A far-west beach with a strong surfing culture – and quieter than Newquay. (p217)

Perranporth Over a mile of family-friendly sands on Cornwall's north coast. (p200)

Porthminster The biggest of three sandy beaches just a stone's throw from St Ives. (p212)

Kynance Cove The Lizard's postcard cove, framed by cliffs and islands. (p228)

Porthcurno A perfect pocket of sand beneath the Minack Theatre. (p216)

Croyde Surf-central in Devon, and just as exciting as Fistral. (p136)

Bantham South Devon's finest overlooks Burgh Island. (p95)

Crackington Haven A craggy, wild beach near Bude. (p186)

Gardens

The southwest's balmy temperatures mean many plant species flourish here that simply wouldn't survive anywhere else in Britain. Some gardens are well known, others a local secret.

Abbey Garden A horticultural wonderland on the faraway island of Tresco. (p233)

Trebah Garden Giant ferns, exotic trees and gunnera galore in a subtropical valley near Falmouth. (p164)

Tremenheere Sculpture Garden A peaceful garden near Penzance, dotted with sculptures and artworks. (p219)

RHS Rosemoor Showpiece garden covering 26 hectares, run by the prestigious Royal Horticultural Society. (p134)

Broomhill Sculpture Gardens Crazy artworks litter a 4-hectare valley near Barnstaple. (p137)

Dartington Estate This wonderful estate near Totnes encompasses formal gardens, woodlands and river walks. (p79)

Outdoor Adventures

Hiking, surfing and swimming are the most obvious ways to get out and active, but they're certainly not the only ones.

Kayaking Pilot a kayak down the tranquil Fowey River. (p174)

Snorkelling Swim with wild seals off the Isles of Scilly. (p238)

Stand-up paddleboarding Steer your board around the blue waters of Bantham. (p95)

Coasteering Clamber the north-coast cliffs, then plunge in for a dip. (p198)

Wild swimming Brave the Dartmoor cold in a stream, lake or pool. (p113)

Rock-climbing Climb up a quarry face near Falmouth, then abseil back down. (p157)

Zorbing Roll down a Cornish hillside in a plastic bubble. Repeat. (p199)

Zip-lining Reach breakneck speeds above a flooded quarry near Liskeard. (p148)

Eating Like a Local

Cornwall and Devon have forged ahead with their foodie fare, and there are scores of intriguing places where you can eat 100% locally.

Hidden Hut Dining on the beach courtesy of this WWII-era hut. (p170)

Cornish Food Box Company A one-stop shop for Cornish treats. (p166)

Trevaskis Farm Pick-your-own fruit, cream teas, local veg – this place does it all. (p214)

Top: Kynance Cove (p228)

Bottom: Start Point (p88)

PLAN YOUR TRIP IF YOU LIKE...

Philps Premier for pasties, according to the locals. (p212)

Glorious Oyster Never shucked an oyster? Now's your chance. (p139)

Crab Shed Try fresh-picked crab by the Salcombe seaside. (p94)

Jelbert's Ices This ice-cream maker is so good, it only makes one flavour. (p222)

W Harvey Pick up your own crab fresh off the Newlyn day-boats. (p222)

Historic Houses

Country houses litter the countryside, a reminder of the days when Devon and Cornwall were the playground of the landed gentry. These days, many are owned by the National Trust.

St Michael's Mount Cornwall's island abbey, star of a million postcards. (p223)

Lanhydrock Quintessential English Victoriana, from smoking rooms to cavernous kitchens. (p144)

Antony House Marvel at the outlandish garden topiary at this house on Cornwall's Rame Peninsula. (p178)

Godolphin This huge estate near the Lizard is currently a restoration work-in-progress. (p226)

Arlington Court A Regency house known for its fabulous collection of horse-drawn carriages. (p137)

Overbeck's Wander round the fantasy pad of wacky inventor Otto Overbeck. (p92)

Knightshayes Court The Middle Ages meets Victorian excess at this over-the-top country estate. (p61)

Coleton Fishacre Glorious art deco house in south Devon, with gardens to match. (p86)

Wild Places

If you're craving a bit of wildness far from the madding crowd, there are plenty of places where you can find solitude, even in the height of summer.

Penwith Moors Few people explore these wild western moors, with their hill forts and ancient monuments. (p214)

Scilly's Outer Islands The uninhabited islands of Scilly are 100% people-free. (p236)

Golitha Falls Seek out a fairytale cascade on the edge of Bodmin Moor. (p143)

Lundy Island Two hours from north Devon, this island is a paradise for wildlife-watchers. (p138)

Wistman's Wood This mysterious patch of ancient oak forest on Dartmoor is rich in myths and legends. (p116)

Braunton Burrows Well off the beaten track, this is Devon's largest dune system. (p137)

Looe Island A wildlife haven that's only a short boat-trip from Looe. (p176)

Helford River Steer a kayak downriver in search of Frenchman's Creek. (p157)

Camping & Glamping

Nothing beats a night under the stars, and you'll find superb campsites scattered all over Devon and Cornwall – from basic tap-and-toilet sites to glamping spectaculars.

Treloan (www.coastalfarm holidays.co.uk) Spacious camping on the rural Roseland.

Henry's (www.henryscampsite. co.uk) Wacky, wonderful, and just a walk from Lizard village.

Cornish Tipi Holidays (www. cornishtipiholidays.co.uk) The original tipi site in Cornwall, in a delightful wooded setting.

EkoPod (www.ekopod.co.uk) Bed down in a geodesic dome near Bodmin Moor.

Blackdown Yurts (www.black downyurts.co.uk) Posh camping, complete with wood burners and compost loos.

Wood Life (www.thewoodlife. org) Woodland camping in a luxury handmade tent.

Vintage Vardos (www.fisherton farm.com) Three restored gypsy wagons on a private Devon farm.

Dartmoor Wild Camping Pick your spot, pitch your tent, and you'll have Dartmoor to yourself. (p109)

Dartmoor is the only place in England where wild camping is legal, but even here there are rules – consult the Dartmoor National Park Authority website (www.dartmoor. gov.uk) for details.

Month by Month

January

Winter still has the southwest firmly in its grip; it's usually cold, wet and sometimes snowy, although the dreary days are often interspersed with the occasional cold, crisp bit of winter sunshine.

February

February tends to be a grim, grey month, and it's another likely time of the year for snowfall, especially on the high moors of Dartmoor, Exmoor and Bodmin Moor.

March

Daffodils and snowdrops in the hedgerows provide the first hint that winter might be on its way out, while Shrove Tuesday marks the beginning of the Easter festivities.

◉ St Columb Hurling

An ancient Cornish free-for-all in which the townsfolk of St Columb chase around town in pursuit of a silver ball. It kicks off on Shrove Tuesday and, yes, it's as dangerous as it looks.

🎏 St Piran's Day

Various events take place on 5 March in honour of Cornwall's patron saint, St Piran. One of the largest is a mass march across the sands of Perranporth to the tumbledown chapel known as St Piran's Oratory, buried among the dunes.

April

The weather's usually warming up by April, and there are often periods of spring sunshine. Roads and sights are busy around Easter.

🍴 Porthleven Food Festival

More than 30,000 people throng to this harbour town in south Cornwall for this big food fair, hosting chef's demos, discussions and local produce galore. It's grown from humble beginnings into one of the southwest's largest food fairs. (p227)

🏃 World Pilot Gig Championships

This racing regatta on Scilly in late April or early May revolves around pilot gigs, or long rowboats. Teams come from across the world to compete, and accommodation is booked out across St Mary's. (p232)

May

Light crowds and settled weather, as well as a couple of ancient festivals that date back to pagan times, make May one of the best months to visit.

🎏 'Obby 'Oss Day

Padstow's chaotic, colourful May Day festival involves two colourful 'osses' (blue and red) twirling around the town's streets. It's riotous, raucous, and royally good fun. (p191)

🎏 Flora Day

Townsfolk take to Helston's streets for their annual street fair, and enact the age-old Furry Dance – a waltz-like dance accompanied by its own special tune. (p226)

✪ Devon County Show

In mid-May Devon's farmers and food producers congregate for this annual agricultural show, a key event on the county calendar since 1872.

🏇 Polo on the Beach

In mid-May, professional polo players gallop across the sands of Watergate Bay, followed by late-night concerts and fireworks over the sea.

✪ Fowey Festival

This lit-fest began as the Daphne du Maurier Festival, but it's now a more general celebration of writing and writers. (p175)

June

Usually a good month to travel, with reliable weather, some interesting events and relatively few visitors – at least compared to next month.

✪ Royal Cornwall Show

Cornwall's biggest agricultural show (www.royalcornwallshow.org) happens in early June on a purpose-built showground just outside Wadebridge. Expect food stalls, cooking displays and parades of prize-winning livestock.

✪ Golowan Festival

Penzance's big summer party and arts festival runs over several days in mid-June. Music, parades, plays,

parties – and an almighty knees-up on Mazey Day. (p219)

◉ Falmouth International Sea Shanty Festival

Hooray, and up she rises... Sea shanties fill the air in Falmouth in this mid-June singing celebration. Bottles of rum and pieces of eight optional. (p157)

✪ The Great Estate

A new event at Scorrier House near Redruth, The Great Estate (www.great estatefestival.co.uk) hosts a silent disco, a gin garden and camel racing. Oh, and bands too.

July

Temperatures are hotting up by mid-July, and so are the crowds. The weather is usually quite fine, but there are no guarantees – cloudy days alternate with clear blue skies.

✪ Eden Sessions

Major music acts play against the backdrop of the biomes across several weekends during the Eden Sessions (www.edensessions. com). Elton John, Blondie and Madness are alumni.

✪ Port Eliot Festival

Blending literature, arts, dance, poetry and live music, this magical festival takes place in the sweeping grounds of a Cornish country house in St Germans, Cornwall. (p257)

✪ Tropical Pressure

Reggae and world music are the focus for Tropical Pres-

sure (www.tropicalpressure. co.uk) in July, hosted at the Mount Pleasant Eco Park near Porthtowan. (p202)

August

Peak season: on sunny days, it can seem as if half of Britain has descended on the southwest's shores. Expect heavy traffic, human and automotive, as well as unpredictable weather.

✪ Sidmouth Folk Week

Held in the first week of August since 1955, Sidmouth Folk Week attracts top names from the folk world. (p63)

✪ Boardmasters

Newquay's major music festival. Big-name bands take to various stages around Watergate Bay near Newquay, alongside surf and skate competitions. (p199)

✪ Dartmouth Royal Regatta

Yachties and sailing enthusiasts all make a beeline for Dartmouth's regatta, which also hosts a shopping marquee and music stage. (p85)

✪ Torbay Royal Regatta

Sailing boats, rowing races, a fun-run and a cracking fireworks display mark this water-focused regatta in late August. (p74)

◉ British Fireworks Championships

Plymouth's skies are filled with bursts of colour for this two-night fireworks contest in mid-August. It's spectacular, loud and best of all, completely free. (p106)

☆ Beer Regatta

The **Beer Regatta** (www. beer-regatta.co.uk) celebrates the Beer village's sea connections. The festival highlight is the Beer Lugger races, in which boats battle it out in the bay.

✕ Newlyn Fish Festival

The fish market and harbour overflow with food stalls during the Newlyn Fish Festival, and there's ample opportunity to sample the wares. (p219)

September

The summer hordes have mostly left for home by September, which makes this a good month to explore if you're allergic to crowds.

☆ St Ives September Festival

A lively mixed-arts festival encompassing literature, music, theatre and more, held in various venues around St Ives in early September. (p257)

✕ Great Cornish Food Festival

Culinary-themed celebration in a marquee on Truro's Lemon Quay. Watch chefs work their gastronomic magic, and meet some of Cornwall's top food producers. (p166)

☆ Looe Music Festival

From small beginnings, Looe Music Festival (www. looemusic.co.uk) has grown into a major event, attracting acts like The Jesus and Mary Chain, Happy Mondays and Bryan Ferry.

October

October paints the West Country in autumnal colours, making this a great month to visit the region's landscaped gardens and country estates.

✕ Falmouth Oyster Festival

Mass oyster eating on Falmouth's quayside, plus cookery demos, boat races and concerts. Held in late October. (p157)

November

There's nearly always a nip in the air by November, so wrap up warmly and bring a brolly.

◉ Bonfire Night

You'll be able to find a fireworks display wherever you are on or around 5 November: Plymouth, Exeter, Newquay and Truro all put on a decent show.

✼ Flaming Tar Barrels

The unhinged locals of Ottery St Mary carry flaming tar barrels through packed-out streets on 5 November, while paramedics and health-and-safety officials watch in horror.

December

Cold nights, late-night shopping and street processions mark the festive month of December: chestnuts and mulled wine are essential.

✼ City of Lights

Huge wicker lanterns are paraded through the streets of Truro to celebrate the start of the festive season at this community festival in early December. (p166)

✈ Time of Gifts

The Eden Project builds a giant ice-rink beside the biomes in December, and hosts a range of festive events, from food-tasting to wreath-making. (p171)

◉ Mousehole Christmas Lights

The tiny Cornish fishing village of Mousehole has a long tradition of lighting up the festive season in stunning style.

✼ Montol Festival

This pagan-themed festival in Penzance celebrates the winter solstice, with a masked parade overseen by the spooky Lord of Misrule.

Itineraries

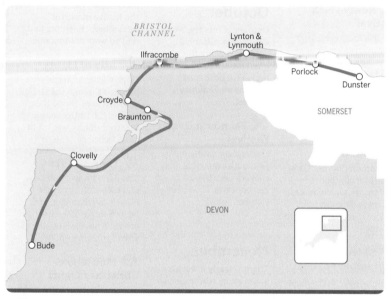

BRISTOL CHANNEL

Lynton & Lynmouth

Ilfracombe

Porlock

Dunster

Croyde

Braunton

SOMERSET

Clovelly

DEVON

Bude

5 DAYS North Coast Explorer

Wild views and sea-smacked shores characterise this coastal road trip, which starts on Exmoor and winds west onto Cornwall's stunning north coast.

Kick things off in **Dunster** with a visit to the ruby-red castle, then head west through the village of **Porlock** to take the spectacular hairpin road over Porlock Hill. Follow the road along the moor's north coast to the twin seaside towns of **Lynton and Lynmouth**, and factor in time for a walk along the beautiful Valley of the Rocks.

Continue west to take in some old-fashioned seaside atmosphere in **Ilfracombe**, a classic candy-floss resort known for its Victorian villas and busy beaches, as well as an unexpectedly arty side thanks to Damien Hirst, who owns a restaurant in town. Further west brings you to beachy **Croyde** and **Braunton**, where you can learn the surfing basics or just stroll through the dunes. Next comes **Clovelly**, a lost-in-time village lined with cob cottages and cobbled streets, before you cross the Cornish border to **Bude**, another seaside town that's surrounded by sandy beaches, including family-friendly Summerleaze and cliff-backed Crackington Haven.

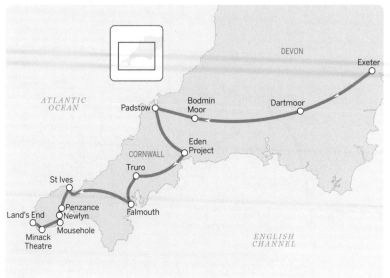

Southwest Classics

This end-to-end road trip factors in the must-see sights of Devon and Cornwall. Begin in the historic city of **Exeter**, where you can get a grandstand view from the top of the cathedral's towers before heading west into the wilds of **Dartmoor**. This strange, stark landscape of open heaths and twisted tors is prime hiking territory, but there are plenty of pretty villages to explore, such as Chagford and Widecombe-in-the-Moor. More wide-open scenery unfolds as you travel over windswept **Bodmin Moor**, another dramatic landscape that's also home to Cornwall's highest hill, Brown Willy. From here, it's not too far to **Padstow**, a former fishing port that has reinvented itself as Cornwall's culinary hotspot.

Southeast of Padstow, in a disused clay pit, loom the giant greenhouses of the **Eden Project**, which house an amazing array of trees and plants collected from across the globe, and have become one of Cornwall's most iconic attractions. Heading southwest brings you to **Truro** – the county's capital and its only city, centred around an impressive 19th-century cathedral. Along the Fal River lies the historic harbour of **Falmouth**, a lively university town where you can explore the county's seagoing heritage at the National Maritime Museum. Next comes arty **St Ives**, awash with galleries and crafts shops, as well as the renowned (and recently revamped) Tate St Ives, which houses works by the town's artistic luminaries. Take some time to explore the nearby beaches – especially the grand sweep of Gwithian and Godrevy, sprawling for three glorious golden miles to the west.

Head further west into Penwith for a visit to the old town of **Penzance**, where you'll find some excellent art galleries and plenty of handsome period architecture. Nearby **Newlyn** is also worth a stop if you're a fan of fish and seafood, but it can't compare to **Mousehole** when it comes to scenery; this old pilchard port is wonderfully photogenic, with its combination of seaside cottages, winding lanes and granite harbour. If time allows, take in a play at the clifftop **Minack Theatre**, and finish with a stroll along the headland at **Land's End** – last stop on mainland Britain before the Isles of Scilly, 28 miles out to sea.

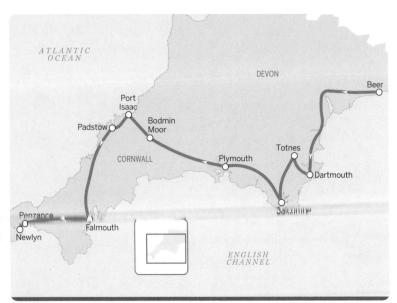

10 DAYS Epicurean West Country

Devon and Cornwall have rightly earned a reputation for fantastic food and drink. Begin in **Beer**, with top-quality fish sourced straight off the boats in Lyme Bay, and officially certified as 100% sustainable. Saunter west to **Dartmouth** for a meal at Mitch Tonks' seafood bistro, Seahorse, and a pint at one of the town's atmospheric harbour pubs. Along the river near **Totnes**, make time for an organic lunch at Riverford Field Kitchen, a fantastic location if you care about food provenance. Nearby, you can indulge in some fine wine and cheese-tasting at Sharpham winery, and take a tour of the vines above the Dart River. Continue onwards to chi-chi **Salcombe**, a town renowned for epicurean indulgences: our tip is to go for oysters and crustaceans at the Crab Shed. On your way west, it's well worth popping into **Plymouth** to sample the city's famous gin, visit the fish market and dine by the harbour on the Barbican – there are some great bistro and street-food stalls to discover here, and it's also a prime spot for some fish and chips.

Then it's on into Cornwall, with a detour over **Bodmin Moor** to visit the sublime St Tudy Inn, run by talented chef Emily Scott, and some wine-tasting at the renowned Camel Valley Vineyard. Continue on to **Port Isaac**, where seafood supremo Nathan Outlaw has made his base with a brace of restaurants – one for small plates, the other for seriously sophisticated dining (it's the only restaurant in Cornwall with two Michelin stars). From here, it's a short spin along the coast to **Padstow**, Cornwall's most famous foodie town, where you can dine at restaurants owned by celeb chefs Rick Stein and Paul Ainsworth, and taste beers at the up-and-coming Padstow Brewing Company. Finish with a bit more wine-tasting at Trevibban Mill, where you can also dine superbly at the vineyard's excellent bistro, Appleton's at the Vineyard.

Next, cut down to the south coast to **Falmouth** for some mussels and seafood at the Wheelhouse, before continuing all the way west to **Penzance** for a meal at Bruce Rennie's superb bistro, the Shore. Round the epicurean adventure off in **Newlyn** for the freshest crab, lobster and crustaceans you'll ever taste.

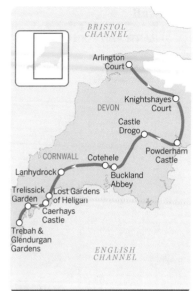

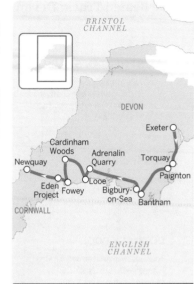

10 DAYS Great Estates

This tailored trip links some of the southwest's most impressive country houses and gardens. It begins with vintage carriages at **Arlington Court**, then heads southeast to visit the Victoriana-filled halls of **Knightshayes Court** and the battlements of **Powderham Castle**, both easy day trips from Exeter. To the west lies **Castle Drogo**, an architectural fantasy built during the early 20th century, while **Buckland Abbey** boasts an older heritage: it was Francis Drake's former home.

Over the Cornish border, **Cotehele** is a mostly Tudor manor with a wonderful old quay. On the edge of Bodmin Moor, **Lanhydrock** mixes 17th- and 19th-century styles: look out for the Great Hall and kitchens. To the south are the **Lost Gardens of Heligan**, forgotten for the best part of a century until they were rediscovered by Tim Smit, creator of the Eden Project. Nearby **Caerhays Castle** is famous for its rhododendrons, but is only open for a few months in spring. For year-round displays, head for the trio of extravagant gardens around Falmouth: the rolling hills and woodlands of **Trelissick**, the secret subtropical valley of **Trebah**, and the formal gardens of **Glendurgan** and its magnificent maze.

7 DAYS Family Fun

Many people have memories of happy family holidays to the West Country, but there's a lot more to it these days than just beaches and buckets and spades.

For this family-focused adventure, begin in **Exeter** with a spooky tour of the city's underground passages and a canoe down the river from Exeter Quay. Then factor in quality beach time in **Torquay** before visiting the predators and primates of **Paignton Zoo**, followed by a bit more beachtime at **Bantham** and **Bigbury-on-Sea**.

Over in Cornwall, brave the high-speed zip wires of **Adrenalin Quarry**, then head west to watch cute capucin monkeys at Wild Futures Monkey Sanctuary near **Looe**, cycle round the trails of **Cardinham Woods** and kayak along the river near **Fowey**. But whatever you do, there's one thing no one in the family will want to miss – and that's the amazing biomes of the **Eden Project**. Round things off with as much time as you can spare to explore the wonderful beaches of Cornwall's north coast. **Newquay** is an ideal location, as you can learn to surf and hand-plane at Watergate Bay, coasteer on Holywell Bay or get deliciously dizzy inside a zorb near Porth.

Off the Beaten Track: Devon & Cornwall

ATLANTIC OCEAN

ST NECTAN'S GLEN

Take a bracing dip in this secret pool on the north Cornish coast, shaded by trees and said to be frequented by fairies. (p187)

HARTLAND POINT

Drink in the drama from this out-of-the-way headland that most visitors never take time to explore. (p139)

BOSSINEY HAVEN

Find some coastal solitude on this remote north-coast beach, sheltered under sheer granite cliffs. (p180)

DOZMARY POOL

This windswept lake on Bodmin Moor is awash with legends: it's said by some to be where King Arthur received Excalibur from the Lady of the Lake. (p149)

GOLITHA FALLS

Trek to a gorgeous wooded waterfall near St Neot on the southern edge of Bodmin Moor: perfect picnic territory. (p148)

CLAY TRAILS

Cycle through an otherworldly landscape of turquoise mica pools and china clay remains. (p172)

LANTIC & LANSALLOS

Leave the crowds far behind on these hard-to-reach beaches on the south Cornish coast, or just explore the spectacular stretch of coast path. (p174)

ZENNOR HILL

Trek to the summit of this rock-strewn hill for an amazing 360-degree perspective of the wild Penwith Moors. (p218)

HELFORD RIVER

Follow in the wake of the smugglers and rivermen of old as you pilot a kayak down this beautiful, peaceful waterway. (p164)

Lundy Island

HARTLAND POINT

Bude
Widemouth Bay

BOSSINEY HAVEN   ST NECTAN'S GLEN

Launceston

DOZMARY POOL

Wadebridge
GOLITHA FALLS

Bodmin

Newquay

CLAY TRAILS

Liskeard

Perranporth

LANTIC & LANSALLOS

St Austell

Redruth   Truro

ZENNOR HILL   St Ives

St Just-in-Penwith   Hayle
Penzance   Falmouth

Land's End   Helston   HELFORD RIVER

Mousehole   The Lizard

MORTEHOE

If you've always had a soft spot for One Man & His Dog, head for the Exmoor village of Mortehoe, where you can learn to round up sheep under the guidance of a working shepherd. (p130)

NORTHAM BURROWS

Spot butterflies and birdlife in this wildlife reserve of sand dunes and salt-marshes hidden behind Westward Ho! beach. (p137)

GRAND WESTERN CANAL

Cycle along the towpaths or catch a horse-drawn barge along this 11.5-mile canal that winds through classic Devon countryside. (p65)

WISTMAN'S WOOD

Wander amongst the moss-covered trunks of this mysterious oak woodland, the last remainder of the great forest that once covered Dartmoor. (p116)

START POINT

Admire the wraparound view from this dramatic 19th-century lighthouse on the south Devon coast. (p88)

Map labels:

0 — 50 km
0 — 25 miles

Bristol Channel

Minehead
Watchet
Bridgwater
MORTEHOE
Exmoor National Park
NORTHAM BURROWS
Barnstaple
Taunton
Bideford
GRAND WESTERN CANAL
Tiverton
Chard
Cullompton
Honiton
Axminster
Okehampton
Exeter
Seaton
Lyme Regis
Range Danger Area
Dartmoor National Park
Sidmouth
WISTMAN'S WOOD
Bovey Tracey
Exmouth
Tavistock
Ashburton
Newton Abbot
Buckfastleigh
Torquay
Saltash
Paignton
Tor Bay
Plymouth
Brixham
Plympton
Dittisham
Devonport
Dartmouth
Start Bay
START POINT
English Channel

Accommodation

Accommodation Types

Devon and Cornwall's accommodation ranges from sleek and boutique to budget, basic and even wilderness.

B&Bs These small guesthouses are still common across the southwest. Standards vary: some are simple and no-frills, others surprisingly luxurious.

Hotels There's a hotel for all-comers: from simple seaside hotels to boutique pamper-pads and luxury country houses.

Hostels Some independent, but largely YHA hostels, many housed in rustic, coastal and/or historic buildings.

Camping Options span everything from facilities-laden, family-friendly seaside sites to 'wild' camping on Dartmoor.

See p266 for more information on different types of accommodation.

Booking Accommodation

If you're travelling within peak times, especially during holiday periods (Easter, mid-July to early September, and Christmas), booking ahead is essential. Top places are booked months in advance, although last-minute cancellations are sometimes available, so it's always worth emailing or phoning just in case.

You'll nearly always get the best deal by booking direct online with the hotel or B&B, as accommodation providers often charge more on booking websites to cover the fee.

Many people rent cottages or holiday houses for their stay, either through local booking agencies or home rental sites such as Airbnb.

Top Choices

Best Luxury Hotels

Gidleigh Park (www.gidleigh.co.uk; r £365-545 ste £750-1050) Dartmoor's grandest and fanciest hotel.

The Scarlet (www.scarlethotel.co.uk; r from £250) The last word in coastal luxury.

The Pig at Combe (www.thepighotel.com/at-combe; r £145-335) Country house hotel near Exeter with a sexy modern spin.

Fowey Hall (www.foweyhallhotel.co.uk; r £150-380) Sleep in the mansion that inspired Toad Hall in *Wind in the Willows*.

Hotel du Vin Exeter (www.hotelduvin.com/locations/exeter; r £135-190) Eye hospital turned swish city hotel.

Burgh Island (www.burghisland.com; d £400-680) Art Deco grandeur on Bantham Beach.

Horn of Plenty (www.thehornofplenty.co.uk) Heritage galore on the edge of Dartmoor.

Best B&Bs

Chapel House Penzance (https://chapel housepz.co.uk; r from £190) Minimalism meets history in Penzance.

The 25 (www.the25.uk; r £99-159) Pop art playfulness in seaside Torquay.

Trevose Harbour House (www.trevosehouse. co.uk; d £195-275) Nautical elegance in chi-chi St Ives.

Highcliffe Contemporary B&B (www.high cliffefalmouth.co.uk; d £99-150) Quirky, design-focused B&B in Falmouth.

Lower Barns (www.lowerbarns.co.uk; r from £115) Couples' getaway par excellence on the rural Roseland.

Reka Dom (www.rekadom.net; r £85-115) Watery views in Topsham.

Padstow Townhouse (www.paul-ainsworth.co.uk; r £280-350) Six luxury suites in foodie central.

Dartington Hall (www.dartington.org; d from £80) Sleep in stately surroundings on the Dartington Estate.

Minadab (www.minadab.co.uk; d £70-90) 1820s Teignmouth cottage offering nautical luxury.

Best Pubs & Inns

Gurnard's Head (www.gurnardshead.co.uk; r £115-180) Escape to Zennor for great food and wild views.

St Tudy Inn (www.sttudyinn.com; r from £160) Emily Scott's Bodmin Moor pub now has elegant rooms.

Old Coastguard Hotel (www.oldcoastguard hotel.co.uk; d £140-225) Smart inn near pretty Mousehole.

Mason's Arms (www.masonsarms.co.uk; d £100-175) Overnight in sleepy Branscombe in south Devon.

Dartmoor Inn (www.dartmoorinn.com; d £115) The classic Moorland bolthole.

Lugger Hotel (www.luggerhotel.co.uk; d £128-180) Sleep by the sea on the Roseland Peninsula.

Cott Inn (http://cottinn.co.uk; d £125) A beautiful old inn on the Dartington Estate.

Best for Families

Watergate Bay Hotel (www.watergatebay.co.uk; r £260-490) Sleep in style, then try surfing, SUP and hand-planing *en famille*.

Bedruthan Hotel (www.bedruthan.com; d from £156) Adults indulge, while kids are well looked after at this near-Newquay pad.

The Rosevine (www.rosevine.co.uk; r £150-220) A Roseland country house reconfigured as self-contained apartments.

Polurrian (www.polurrianhotel.com; r £200-270) This clifftop Lizard hotel is a haven for family travellers.

Soar Mill Cove (www.soarmillcove.co.uk; r from £185) This south Devon stalwart is both luxury and family-friendly.

Bayard's Cove (www.bayardscoveinn.co.uk, r from £137) Fun Dartmouth B&B with family suites and kids' cabins.

Saunton Sands (https://sauntonsands.co.uk; r from £260) Art deco style and comprehensive family facilities.

Best on a Budget

Baggy (www.baggys.co.uk; dm from £35) Sleek surf-styled lodge in Croyde.

YHA Eden Project (www.yha.org.uk; s £30-60) A new container-style hostel overlooked by the biomes.

Treyarnon Bay YHA (www.yha.org.uk; dm £15-29) Glorious cliffside hostel on the north Cornish coast.

Lizard YHA (www.yha.org.uk; dm £16-25) Possibly the best-sited hostel in Cornwall.

Dartmoor YHA (www.yha.org.uk; dm from £25) The perfect Dartmoor place to kip on the cheap.

Okehampton Bracken Tor YHA (www.yha.org. uk; dm £27) A 100-year-old house in 1.6 hectares of grounds.

Glamping & Camping

Loveland Farm (https://lovelandfarm camping.co.uk; pods from £150 per night) Geopod glamping on the Hartland Peninsula.

Berridon Farm (www.berridonfarm.co.uk; 6-person tents from £616 per week) Kip in safari tents near Clovelly.

Treloan (www.coastalfarmholidays.co.uk; campsites £15.50-27) Sleep under the stars on the Roseland.

Henry's Campsite (www.henryscampsite.co.uk; per adult/child £10/5) This Lizard campsite's as friendly as they get.

Cornish Tipi Holidays (www.cornish tipiholidays.co.uk; tipis from £725, camping from £10) Go native in a tipi near Padstow.

Vintage Vardos (www.fishertonfarm.com; 6-person site £290-330) Sleep in restored Romany caravans.

Salcombe Farm (facebook.com/salcombe farm; d £115-150) Sleep in a treehouse complete with creek-view deck.

Troytown Farm (https://troytown.co.uk; sites £20-30) Possibly the loveliest campsite on Scilly.

Getting Around

For more information, see Transport (p272)

Travelling by Car

Most people still travel to the southwest by car, which gives you maximum freedom and allows you to explore more remote areas that are inaccessible by public transport.

Car Hire

Cars can be hired in most major towns, as well as at mainline railway stations and major airports, including Newquay and Exeter. Standard rates are around £130 per week.

Driving Conditions

Road conditions throughout the southwest are generally good, especially along main A-roads. In rural areas, expect narrow, single-lane roads, and be prepared to reverse if you meet oncoming traffic.

Traffic

Traffic can be a big problem during busy holiday periods, especially around summer, Easter and bank holidays. Traffic jams along the main A30 between Devon and Cornwall can be especially heavy in July and August.

Parking

Parking isn't always easy in some of the southwest's coastal towns and villages, and it can work out expensive. Often, such as in places like Padstow, Port Isaac and St Ives, it's better to park in one of the large car parks on the edge of town and walk.

Park-and-ride schemes are a good option in bigger cities like Exeter and Plymouth.

DRIVING FAST FACTS

Road Rules
➡ Drive on the left.
➡ Manual gears are the norm.
➡ Legal driving age: 17.
➡ Speed limit: 70mph on dual carriageways, 50 or 60mph on single roads, 30mph on built-up areas.
➡ Seatbelts are compulsory.
➡ Give way to your right at junctions and roundabouts.
➡ Use the left-hand lane, and overtake on the right.
➡ Blood-alcohol limit 80mg/100mL (0.08%).

Motoring Organisations

The **Automobile Association** (AA; www.theaa.com; ☏0800 88 77 66) and the **RAC** (www.rac.co.uk; ☏0333 2000 999) provide 24-hour breakdown assistance.

Main Roads

The main route into Cornwall is the A30, which runs down the middle of Devon and Cornwall. It's mostly dual carriageway, but has some single-carriageway sections. The A38 is a slightly slower alternative, running along the south coasts of Devon and Cornwall.

Ferries & Bridges

The A38 is linked to Devon and Cornwall via the Tamar Bridge (www.tamarcrossings.org.uk). There's no toll travelling into Cornwall, but it costs £1.50 to leave.

Several other rivers are crossed by car ferry, including the River Dart (Dartmouth-Kingswear ferry), the River Fal (King Harry Ferry) and the River Fowey (Bodinnick Ferry).

No Car?

Bus

Most towns and villages are served by at least one bus service, although services can be frustratingly infrequent in rural areas, especially outside summer. If you're taking more than two journeys a day, a day pass such as the DevonDay (adult/child £8.50/5.70) or FirstDay (adult/child £12/6) often works out cheaper than standard fares.

Train

The main train line serves all the region's main towns, including Exeter, Plymouth, Bodmin, Truro and Penzance. Regional branch lines connect to coastal destinations including Barnstaple, Exmouth, Torquay and Paignton, Looe, Newquay, St Ives and Falmouth.

Day rail passes like the Devon Day Ranger (adult/child £10/5) and Ride Cornwall Ranger (adult/child £13/10) are good value, especially for longer journeys.

Bicycle

Cycling is a great way of exploring rural areas, as long as you avoid busy A-roads. There's a network of cycle paths and bridleways that criss-cross the region: consult Sustrans (sustrans.org.uk) for details. Bikes can be taken on most trains and ferries, but you might need to book a place.

PLAN YOUR TRIP GETTING AROUND

Resources

TravelineSW (www.travelinesw.com) Plan journeys by car, train, bus and boat.

National Rail (www.nationalrail.co.uk) Buy train tickets and consult timetables.

Great Scenic Railways of Devon and Cornwall (www.greatscenicrailways.co.uk) The southwest's prettiest train trips.

Road Distances (miles)

	Exeter	Penzance	Plymouth	St Ives
Penzance	110			
Plymouth	45	80		
St Ives	110	10	75	
Truro	85	25	55	25

Don't-Miss Drives

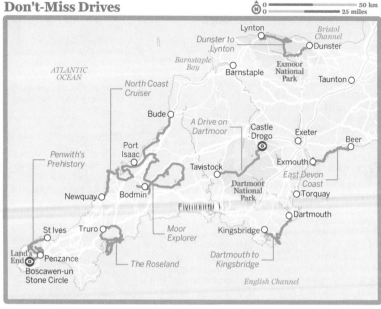

East Devon Coast Explore hedge-lined lanes, hidden villages and sea views.

Dartmouth to Kingsbridge Head out along south Devon's postcard-worthy coastline.

A Drive on Dartmoor Enjoy compelling 360-degree views of the southwest's wildest landscape.

Dunster to Lynton Take a backcountry drive across Exmoor National Park.

Moor Explorer Wild and windswept, this drive takes in the stirring sights of Bodmin Moor.

The Roseland Explore the Roseland's fields, beaches and out-of-the-way villages.

North Coast Cruiser Wind down your windows for this trip along north Cornish coast.

Penwith's Prehistory Discover Penwith's mysterious prehistoric monuments.

Plan Your Trip
Activities

Devon and Cornwall were made for adventure. Their national parks and stunning shores see you hiking iconic coastal paths, surfing England's best waves and cycling desolate moors. Trot on a horse, escape on a yacht, clamber over rocky tors – your break could spark a new passion or the rediscovery of an old one.

Walking

The South West Coast Path

It's billed as a 630-mile adventure – and it is. The South West Coast Path (SWCP) takes in the entire shore of Devon and Cornwall on its journey from Poole in Dorset to Minehead in Somerset. En route are cliffs crowned by tin mines, sparkling bays, pretty fishing villages and swaths of rural idyll. It's so gorgeous you'll forgive it the painful combined gradient of three Everests. In metric it's even more impressive: 1014km.

The path can be walked all year but it's at its best from April to September.

Few people tackle the whole trail in one go; if you do, you'll need around eight weeks (56 consecutive walking days). The trail's official website (www.southwest coastpath.org.uk) has an excellent overview, and a handy distance calculator. It also profiles day walks. The South West Coast Path Guide (£14) details the route, transport and on-trail accommodation.

Way marking is in the form of acorn symbols. Carrying Ordnance Survey maps is a good idea.

Day Walks

If you don't feel up to tackling the entire coast path, there are plenty of sections which make perfect day hikes.

Best Outdoor Experiences

Best Long-Distance Hikes

The epic 630-mile South West Coast Path; Devon's Two Moors Way; Cornwall's Saints' Way; Exmoor's Coleridge Way.

Best Places for Short Walks

Dartmoor and Exmoor National Parks; Bodmin Moor; countless coast path hikes.

Best Surfing Beaches

Surf-central Newquay draws the crowds. For less-frenetic wave-riding try Polzeath, Bude and Sennen Cove in Cornwall, plus Croyde and Bantham in Devon.

Best Cycle Trails

The West Country Way links Exmoor to north Cornwall. Plus Devon and Cornwall's Coast to Coast routes, Devon's Granite Way and Tarka Trail, and Cornwall's Camel Trail.

Best Horse-Riding Spots

Dartmoor and Exmoor National Parks offer wilderness trotting; Exmoor also has the equine-friendly Coleridge Way.

Lynmouth–Combe Martin (13 miles) The realm of the red deer, where vertiginous cliffs meet open moor.

Pendeen Watch–Sennen Cove (9 miles) Cracking views and the working Levant Mine.

Sennen Cove–Porthcurno (6 miles) From surfing beaches to a cliffside theatre, via Land's End.

Salcombe–Hope Cove (8 miles) Happy wanderings from a chic sailing port to an enchanting Devon fishing village.

Portreath–Trevaunance Cove (9 miles) Mining heritage, a surfing beach, sandy cove and 192m-high headland.

Branscombe–Beer (2 miles) From fishing village, via remarkable geology, to shipwreck beach. Bring a swimsuit.

Dartmoor

The 368 sq miles of Dartmoor are the emptiest, highest and wildest in southern England. Rounded hills, or tors, pepper a rolling, primitive landscape. Hiking here takes in stone circles and rows, burial mounds and massive Bronze Age settlements; you'll also encounter free-roaming Dartmoor ponies, sheep and cows.

The DNPA can advise on day hikes. The website www.moorlandguides.co.uk details a program of guided walks themed around history, legends and geology; they cost around £5 to £10.

LONG-DISTANCE HIKING ROUTES

Two Moors Way (www.twomoorsway.org) A coast-to-coast epic (117 miles, eight days) from Lynmouth on Exmoor, across Devon and Dartmoor to Wembury, on the south coast.

Coleridge Way (www.coleridgeway.co.uk) This 36-mile, three- to four-day jaunt runs from Exmoor to the Quantocks, in the footsteps of the poet Samuel Taylor Coleridge.

Saints' Way A 27-mile, three- to four-day cross-Cornwall, former pilgrims' route, from Padstow in the north to Fowey in the south.

Templar Way A leisurely stroll (18 miles, two days) from Haytor to seaside Teignmouth.

Longer self-guided hikes that encompass Dartmoor include the 117-mile Two Moors Way and the 18-mile Templar Way.

Good bases for hikers are Princetown (with its key visitor centre), Okehampton and Widecombe-in-the-Moor.

Exmoor

While Dartmoor is bigger, 267-sq-mile Exmoor National Park has a different asset – the sea. A compelling 34 miles of jaw-dropping, leg-testing coastline. Add ancient woods, time-warp villages, red deer and Exmoor ponies and you have a winner for walkers.

The Exmoor National Park Authority (ENPA) runs a superbly varied program of guided walks (free to £6). These include deer-watching at dawn, fungi foraging and wildlife- and heritage-themed strolls. The ENPA also produces a series of walking cards outlining day hikes; staff can also advise.

Long-distance, self-guided hikes linked to Exmoor include the 117-mile Two Moors Way, and the 36-mile Coleridge Way.

Cycling

Traffic-free routes and varied landscapes make the southwest one of the best cycling regions in the country. Many of the paths are on former rail or tram lines and snake around extinct mines or quarries. Sustrans (www.sustrans.org.uk) has further information and maps.

Dartmoor has good routes; the DNPA sells a map (£13). Exmoor's mountain-bike trails are graded, ski-run style, in the map, *Exmoor for Off-Road Cyclists* (£10).

West Country Way Part of this trail stretches from Exmoor, via Bodmin, to Padstow in north Cornwall.

Devon Coast To Coast Ilfracombe to Plymouth, 103 glorious miles – 70 of them traffic-free.

Camel Trail An 18-mile, car-free trip from Bodmin Moor to the north Cornwall coast.

Granite Way Eleven spectacular miles on a former Dartmoor railway line.

Cornwall Coast to Coast An 11-mile jaunt along the route of an old mineral tramway.

Tarka Trail A delightful, 30-mile loop through north Devon's lowlands.

Water Sports

Few regions are so rich in idyllic places to get on, and in, the water. Here you'll find hundreds of miles of beautiful beaches, scores of historic sailing ports and an array of sheltered estuaries. Add the most consistent quality surf in England and you have endless opportunities to surf, bodyboard, sail, kayak and dive.

Newquay (p196) Learn to surf at buzzing Fistral Beach or nearby Watergate Bay.

Croyde (p136) North Devon's chilled-out surfing hub, fringed by quaint thatched cottages.

Widemouth Bay (p186) Another beautiful Cornish surfing hot spot, 3 miles south of Bude.

Bantham (p95) Learn to surf, try stand-up paddleboarding or hire a sit-on-top kayak.

Exmouth (p62) Fancy harnessing wind and waves? Try kiteboarding here.

Salcombe (p92) South Devon yachting haven; learn to sail or head out on a sea-kayak expedition.

Surfing

The roots of the southwest's surf culture reach back more than a century – sepia archive images show people surfing in the region in 1904. The sport really took off in the 1950s, and now racks of wetsuits and boards tempt thousands into the waves.

The self-styled surfing (and party) capital is Newquay. More relaxed surf hubs include Polzeath, Perranporth, Bude and Sennen Cove in Cornwall, and Croyde, Woolacombe and tiny Bantham in Devon.

Braunton, near Croyde, also has a UK first – the ultra-cool Museum of British Surfing (p135) is the country's only permanent, wave-riding-related heritage display.

Kitesurfing & Windsurfing

Kitesurfing's growing popularity sees fleets of brightly coloured canopies sweeping the southwest's skies on windy days.

WATCHING WILDLIFE

Exmoor (p126) Head out on a dawn stag-watching walk.

Penwith (p214) Cornwall's westerly tip is prime territory for spotting basking sharks.

Dartmoor (p109) Herds of sturdy Dartmoor ponies roam this windswept wilderness.

Isles of Scilly (p238) Head out on a 'snorkelling with seals' safari.

Topsham (p59) One of the best places to watch birds in Devon and Cornwall.

British Kitesports (www.britishkitesports.org) lists approved schools; prices start from around £100 for a half-day. Exmouth, in Devon, is a particularly good place to learn.

Windsurfing also remains popular; the Royal Yachting Association (RYA; www.rya.org.uk) details courses. Taster sessions start from around £45. Places with approved centres include Bude and Falmouth in Cornwall, and Plymouth and Exmouth in Devon.

Whitewater Rafting

Dartmoor's deep, steep gorges ensure heavy winter rains turn stretches of the River Dart into foaming, fast-flowing water – riding them is a truly thrilling experience. The rapids are only open between October and March. Winter kayaking also takes place on the Rivers Barle and East Lyn on Exmoor. Both national park authorities can advise on these activities.

The British Canoe Union (BCU; www.bcu.org.uk) approves training centres; many require you to be BCU two-star standard before you can head onto 'moving water'. Prices start at around £45 for a half-day.

Kayaking & Stand-Up Paddleboarding

At many popular beaches you can hire sit-on-top kayaks; prices start at around £15 per hour (per day from £40).

MULTI-ACTIVITY CENTRES

These providers offer a range of adventure sports, ranging from abseiling and mountain biking, to archery and coasteering:

Adventure Okehampton (p119) Based in Dartmoor National Park

BF Adventure (p157) Set in 24 hectares near Falmouth.

Exmoor Adventures (☑07976-208279; www.exmooradventures.co.uk; Porlock Weir; per half-/full-day from £20/40) Wide range of activities in the national park.

Outdoor Adventure (☑01288 362900; www.outdooradventure.co.uk; Widemouth Bay, Bude; courses from £35) Based in Bude.

More and more centres are also renting out stand-up paddleboards (SUPs), which are broader and more stable than surfboards and can be a chilled-out way to explore coves and rivers. Prices are similar to those of rental kayaks.

For longer-distance paddling, Sea Kayak Salcombe (p93) runs courses (one/two days £150/300); the price falls to £80/160 if two people book. It also does tours (half-/full day £40/85) and mini-expeditions, with wild camping thrown in (three nights £250).

Operating from central Cornwall, **Evoke Adventures** (☑0797-225 0753; www.evoke adventure.com) runs adventurous trips with only a few paddlers. You can either spend a day exploring bays and sea caves (per person £85), or camp wild overnight, cooking freshly caught fish over a fire.

Falmouth-based **Sea Kayaking Cornwall** (☑01326-378826; www.seakayaking cornwall.com) stages one-day introductory sessions (£95) and five-day expeditions (from £475).

Wild Swimming

Wild swimming has seen a huge surge in popularity – all over the region beaming bands of hardy bathers gather to plunge into waves, rivers and moorland pools.

Devon and Cornwall Wild Swimming (www.devonandcornwallwildswimming. co.uk) is a good one-stop advice shop, featuring a map of suitable Devon spots and essential safety guidance. The Outdoors Swimming Society (www.outdoorswim mingsociety.com) is another useful resource.

Diving

The big dive attraction is the *Scylla* (www.divescylla.com), a gutted former Royal Navy warship that was sunk near Plymouth by the National Marine Aquarium in 2004 in order to study how reefs form. Note the vessel is not now considered safe to dive. Devon and Cornwall's coasts have more than 4600 wrecks; the Isles of Scilly alone has a remarkable 150 recognised dive sites.

The British Sub Aqua Club (www.bsac. com) approves training centres. Popular dive bases include Exeter and Falmouth. A half-day taster is around £50; four-day training courses start at around £395.

Sailing

The Royal Yachting Association (RYA; www.rya.org.uk) lists approved schools. Many are in the region's traditional maritime centres, including Falmouth, Mylor, St Mawes, Fowey and the Isles of Scilly in Cornwall; and Salcombe, Dartmouth, Torquay and Plymouth in Devon.

Half-day sessions in smaller craft (eg a topper) cost about £45. A weekend, live-aboard course for a RYA qualification costs from around £220 per person.

Horse Riding

Many stables on Dartmoor and Exmoor are either on, or within very easy reach of, the open moors. They cater to novices and experienced riders alike – expect to pay around £40 for a two-hour hack. The British Horse Society (www.bhs.org.uk) lists approved stables.

Many riding centres offer accommodation. This can range from luxurious farmhouses to basic camping; some will even put your horse up for the night, too.

Alternative Activities

True to their often counter-culture vibe, Devon and Cornwall do a good line in less obvious activities. Ranging from wild swimming to photography courses some, such as stand-up paddleboarding, have proved so popular they've entered the mainstream.

More active options include: trail running, Nordic walking, ballooning, off-road driving, hawking and tree surfing (think an arboreal assault course of rope bridges and zip wires).

There's also a good range of courses in photography, pottery and cooking (p254).

You can even learn survival skills on a bushcraft course with Dartmoor-based **Adventure 360 UK** (☑07957-762736; www. adventure360uk.com; per 8/24hrs £55/125) or **Bear Grylls Survival Academy** (www. beargryllssurvivalacademy.com; adult/family £350/400).

Useful Resources

Active Dartmoor (www.dartmoor.co.uk/active-dartmoor) Official guide to adventure activities on the moor.

Adventure Activities Cornwall (www.adventure-cornwall.co.uk) Collation of outdoors information.

Cornwall Area of Outstanding Natural Beauty (www.cornwall-aonb.gov.uk) Profiles Cornwall's 12 AONB locations.

Dartmoor National Park Authority (DNPA; www.dartmoor.gov.uk) The official website for Dartmoor National Park.

Exmoor National Park Authority (ENPA; www.exmoor-nationalpark.gov.uk) The official website for Exmoor National Park.

South Devon Area of Outstanding Natural Beauty (www.southdevonaonb.org.uk) Profiles the south Devon AONB.

Torbay Coast and Countryside Trust (www.countryside-trust.org.uk) Profiles Torbay's wild spaces.

Travel with Children

It's good to know in our digital, virtual world that channelling incoming tides around sandcastles still provides great joy. And wrap-around beaches aren't Devon and Cornwall's only child-friendly assets. Rafts of activities and bucketloads of attractions ensure the two counties are an absolute delight for kids, and adults reconnecting with childlike joys.

Best Regions for Kids

Newquay & the North Coast

This water-sports magnet has beaches galore, an aquarium, farm attraction and puffing steam trains. Investigate Bude, Perranporth and St Agnes, too.

Torquay & South Devon

Torquay offers oodles of beaches plus an eco-zoo, giant cliffside aviary, prehistoric caves and a model village. South Devon serves up surfing beaches and river trips.

South Cornwall

Head here for the Eden Project, a shipwreck museum, child-friendly maritime museum, and incredibly cute seal and monkey sanctuaries.

Exmoor & North Devon

North Devon dishes up superb surfing, huge dune-backed beaches, and the mega-attraction, the Big Sheep. Exmoor offers deer-watching and wildlife discovery days.

Devon & Cornwall for Kids

A plethora of child-focused attractions and activities ensures the southwest delivers fantastic family holidays. Many hotels, pubs and restaurants cater well for kids, but it pays to check. As elsewhere, some people will frown on breast-feeding, while others will barely notice.

Safety

The beaches of Cornwall and Devon are glorious, but do present safety issues; sadly fatalities are not unknown. Most of the key tourist beaches have lifeguards; head for one that does, then follow the lifeguards' advice. Be especially wary of rip currents and fast-rising tides. Lifeguard cover is seasonal (often Easter to September) and tends to finish at 5pm or 6pm. The RNLI Lifeboats website (www.rnli.org) lists which beaches it covers and when.

Some sections of the Devon and Cornwall coast are prone to cliff-falls; keep an eye out for warning signs.

Children's Highlights

Family-Friendly Attractions

Paignton Zoo, Torquay (p70) Innovative 32-hectare, multi-habitat eco-zoo.

Flambards, Helston (✆01326-573404; www.flambards.co.uk; adult/child incl rides £19.95/14.95; ⊙opens 10am, last entry 3pm) Theme park with heritage-themed features plus rollercoaster and log flume.

Camel Creek, Padstow (✆01841-540726; www.camelcreek.co.uk; adult/child/child under 92cm £19.95/9.95/free; ⊙10.30am-5.30pm) Some 60 rides and attractions set in 40 hectares.

The Big Sheep (www.thebigsheep.co.uk) All-weather theme park near Bideford, with an agricultural feel.

Rainy Days

Eden Project, South East Cornwall (p171) A heated eco-attraction with a playful feel.

National Marine Aquarium, Plymouth (p104) Underwater walkways reveal sharks, octopuses and huge rays.

Kents Cavern, Torquay (p70) Cavemen, a devil's toenail and Stone Age handprints.

National Maritime Museum, Falmouth (p156) Superb displays; crammed with hands-on activities.

Underground Passages, Exeter (p52) Ancient tunnels and stories of ghosts and cholera.

Kid-Friendly Heritage Sites

Arlington Court, North Devon (p137) Country estate with horse carriages, peacocks and bats.

Pendennis Castle, Falmouth (p156) An atmospheric Tudor Gun Room, and hands-on exhibits.

RAMM, Exeter (p52) Fun, child-friendly museum displays in a slick, modern setting.

Geevor Tin Mine, Pendeen (p217) Underground tour and an opportunity to pan for minerals at this iconic Cornish mine.

Castle Drogo, Dartmoor (p117) Crenellations and playhouses at the last castle to be built in England.

Porthcurno Telegraph Museum, Porthcurno (p216) Secret war-time tunnels and a whirring telegraphy kit.

Planning

When to Go

School holidays see accommodation demand, and prices, spike. But summer, Easter and half-term also see attractions extend their opening hours, often putting on special family-friendly events.

Accommodation

Families fare well for sleep spots in Devon and Cornwall. Self-catering and camping offer great flexibility. Look out for the new breed of 'comfy camping' options, where Romany caravans and safari-style tents come with their own fire pits.

Useful Organisations

All over Cornwall and Devon, organisations run superb child-focused events. Pirate parades, rock-pool rambles, night-time hikes and archery days – these family experiences can define your trip.

Cornwall Wildlife Trust (www.cornwallwildlifetrust.org.uk)

Dartmoor National Park Authority (DNPA; www.dartmoor.gov.uk)

National Trust (NT; www.nationaltrust.org.uk)

English Heritage (EH; www.english-heritage.org.uk)

Exmoor National Park Authority (ENPA; www.exmoor-nationalpark.gov.uk)

South Devon Area of Outstanding Natural Beauty (AONB; www.southdevonaonb.org.uk)

Torbay Coast & Countryside (www.countryside-trust.org.uk)

Information Sources

For all-round information and advice, check out Lonely Planet's *Travel with Children*.

Cornwall Beach Guide (www.cornwallbeachguide.co.uk) Detailed guide to Cornwall's beaches.

Day out with the Kids (www.dayoutwiththekids.co.uk) Activity directory, searchable by region.

Visit Cornwall (www.visitcornwall.com) Filters attractions by age-range.

Visit Devon (www.visitdevon.co.uk) Has subsections on family-friendly attractions and free days out.

Regions at a Glance

Coast and countryside, cities and villages, bluffs and bays – there's a reason to visit every corner of Devon and Cornwall. In general the north coast tends to be wilder and craggier, characterised by high cliffs, big beaches and wild waves – perfect for surfing and other watery activities. The south coast feels gentler and greener: it's home to country estates, a wealth of fabulous gardens and a web of quiet creeks and estuaries. And down the spine of both counties runs a streak of ancient granite that's exposed on the high moors – principally around Dartmoor, Bodmin Moor and Penwith. Best of all, the region's compact dimensions mean it's easy to explore – you can travel from city to village, moorland to coast, all in a single day.

Exeter & East Devon

History
Coastline
Countryside

Exeter Cathedral

Centring around its majestic Gothic cathedral, the elegant city of Exeter has a history stretching back to Roman times. Don't miss the beautiful cathedral close and the city's spooky underground passages.

Jurassic Coast

The rust-red cliffs of east Devon form part of the Jurassic Coast World Heritage Site, a majestic landscape famous for its fragile cliffs and fossils. Hike the coast path, then head for some fresh crab and local beer in Beer.

Classic Countryside

East Devon's landscape is wonderfully varied, ranging from the marshy banks of the Exe Estuary to the salty old harbours of Sidmouth, Beer and Branscombe. It's many people's idea of what Devon should be like.

p46

Torquay & South Devon

Beaches
Countryside
Food

Sand Galore

There's a beach to suit all tastes in south Devon, from the bucket-and-spade sands of Torbay and Bigbury-on-Sea to quieter coves only reachable from the coast path. Don't miss the stunning lighthouse at Start Point, and the nearby tidal lagoon at Slapton Sands.

The South Hams

The rolling hills and sleepy waterside towns of the South Hams are picture-postcard Devon. They're made for leisurely exploring, whether you choose to do it on foot, by bike or in a kayak.

Fine Food

South Devon has a fast-growing food scene. Taste seafood, oysters and crab in Salcombe, sample world-class wines at Sharpham, and finish up with 100% organic meat and veg at the renowned Riverford Field Kitchen.

p66

Plymouth & Dartmoor

Activities
History
Views

A Storied Past

Francis Drake began his circumnavigation in Plymouth, and the Pilgrim Fathers embarked for the New World. Beyond the city, Dartmoor is home to some fascinating ancient sites: hut circles, burial barrows and stone alignments.

Moors & Tors

Dartmoor's stark and stunning landscape is as close as England gets to wilderness: a world of weird rock stacks, ancient woodlands and wild heaths, where many rare plant, insect and animal species survive.

Great Outdoors

Plymouth's full of watery possibilities, from stand-up paddleboarding around Plymouth Sound, to relaxing in the Tinside Lido. In Dartmoor you can hike in the hills, cycle the trails and wild camp under pitch-black skies.

p98

Exmoor & North Devon

Villages
Activities
Scenery

Traditional Villages

From farming hamlets to seaside harbours, north Devon has scores of villages crammed with history. Lynton, Ilfracombe, Porlock and Clovelly are classic seaside destinations, while Dulverton, Challacombe and Exford have a more rural vibe.

Exploring the Moor

There's no end of ways you can explore Exmoor: saddle up for a horse-ride, strap on your hiking boots, hire a mountain bike or book a wildlife safari. Autumn's the time to see red deer.

Sea & Country

Exmoor is half coast, half countryside. Spend the morning swimming, go hiking in the afternoon, then head out for some late-night stargazing – this is the southwest's only official Dark Sky Reserve.

p120

Bodmin & East Cornwall

Scenery
Wildlife
Hiking

Cornwall's Roof

A slash of wildness sandwiched between Cornwall's north and south coasts, Bodmin Moor has a stark beauty all its own. Similar in feel to Dartmoor, it has surprises in store too – such as tranquil Golitha Falls and the underground chambers of Carnglaze Caverns.

Flora & Fauna

The moor is a haven for rare wildlife, from adders and lizards to stonechats and skylarks. It's also home to its own breed of pony, and is supposedly stalked by the Beast of Bodmin Moor.

Hit the Trail

Hikers make a beeline for the high points of Brown Willy and Rough Tor, which are relatively small in mountain terms, but still pack a mighty scenic punch. It's also a great area for horse-riding.

p140

South Cornwall

Villages
Gardens
Countryside

Seaside Towns

Cornwall's south-coast harbours were once the heart of the county's fishing industry. While only a handful of boats remain, they're still full of maritime atmosphere: Falmouth, Mevagissey, Polperro and Looe are must-sees.

Garden Greenery

Etched with sheltered valleys and nurtured by the temperate air of the Gulf Stream, Cornwall's south coast is home to some wonderful garden estates including the Lost Gardens of Heligan and Glendurgan.

Peninsular Splendour

Two of Cornwall's prettiest peninsulas jut out from the southern coastline: the rural Roseland, spotted with pretty hamlets and farms; and the remote Rame Peninsula, with a collection of aristocratic estates.

p150

Newquay & North Cornwall

Beaches
Surfing
Food

Classic Coastline

The north coast is home to Cornwall's quintessential beaches: golden sweeps of sand, backed by dunes and rocky cliffs. Fistral, Perranporth, Padstow and Bude have glorious beaches, but there's more besides – like Tintagel's clifftop castle, and the rock towers of Bedruthan Steps.

Surf's Up

The Atlantic coastline is blessed with Cornwall's biggest waves, so it's the top spot for the county's surf culture. Try Newquay, Bude, Perranporth or Polzeath.

Starry Cuisine

Rick Stein's restaurant in Padstow turned him into Cornwall's first celebrity chef, but he's far from alone these days, with competition from Nathan Outlaw, Paul Ainsworth and others.

p180

West Cornwall & the Isles of Scilly

Coastline
Islands
History

Cliffs & Beaches

The sea-smacked coast here has an extra-special grandeur: it's craggy, wild and dramatic. The far west of Penwith and the Lizard Peninsula's remote cliffs and beaches are especially exploration-worthy.

Island Escapes

The Isles of Scilly are a low-lying archipelago of islands that sit 28 miles west of Land's End. With a laid-back lifestyle, fabulous beaches and precious few people, they're perfect when you want to escape the modern world.

Prehistoric Sites

The Penwith moors have more prehistoric sites than almost anywhere else in Britain. You'll find numerous stone circles here, as well as many quoits, dolmens, menhirs and hillforts.

p204

On the Road

Exeter & East Devon

Best Places to Eat

➡ River Cottage HQ (p60)

➡ Rusty Bike (p54)

➡ River Exe Cafe (p62)

➡ Salutation (p61)

➡ Pebblebed Wine Cellar (p60)

➡ Exploding Bakery (p54)

Best Places for History

➡ Exeter Cathedral (p52)

➡ Exeter's Underground Passages (p52)

➡ Powderham Castle (p54)

➡ Knightshayes Court (p61)

➡ A La Ronde (p61)

➡ Grand Western Canal (p65)

Why Go?

From the heritage city of Exeter to rural idylls and spectac-ular shores, Devon's eastern corner delivers it all. On the Jurassic Coast, wave-carved cliffs range from russet-red to creamy-white. In between sit long pebble beaches, genteel resorts and quaint fishing villages, perfect for hiking, kite-surfing, fishing or strolling along the prom. In history-rich Exeter, discover Roman walls, a fine cathedral and a lively arts scene. The snaking River Exe estuary is ripe for explo-ration by boat, bike or on foot. Behind the shore, rolling red-soil hills shelter tucked-away villages and stately homes, while the village of Topsham offers birdwatching, boat trips and foodie stops galore. It's also a place to really experience local ways of life in action, whether at a livestock market, a village beach party or a rural pub.

When to Go

➡ **Easter** Sights, campsites and boat trips swing into action.

➡ **Apr** Foodies flock to Exeter's South West Food & Drink (www.exeterfoodanddrinkfestival.co.uk) festival.

➡ **Jun & Sep** Prime visiting times – fewer crowds and less traffic.

➡ **Jul & Aug** Warmer, dryer weather, but school holidays bring higher accommodation costs and busier beaches and roads.

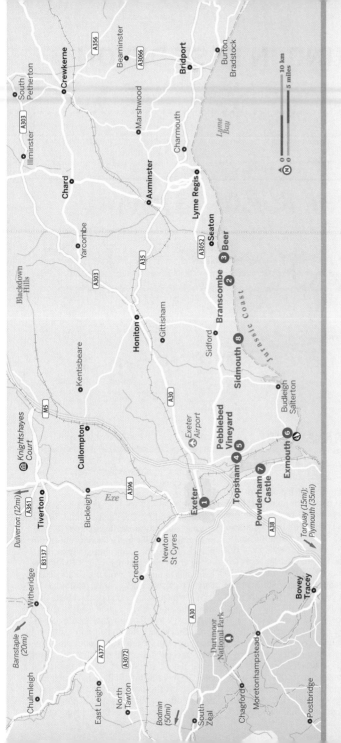

Exeter & East Devon Highlights

1 Exeter Cathedral (p52) Taking in sweeping rooftop views on a tour amid gloriously Gothic architecture.

2 Branscombe (p64) Exploring the millennia-old Jurassic Coast from this postcard-pretty village.

3 Beer (p64) Catching your own supper on a fishing trip.

4 Topsham (p60) Hopping on the *Sea Dream* ferry to head out into the marsh-fringed Exe estuary.

5 Pebblebed Vineyard (p60) Touring the vines then enjoying a tutored tasting.

6 Exmouth (p62) Getting a totally natural high kitesurfing.

7 Powderham Castle (p54) Glimpsing life as it was 'below stairs' at this endearing stately home.

8 Sidmouth Folk Week (p63) Joining an impromptu jam session beside the beach during this vibrant annual music festival.

WALKING IN EAST DEVON

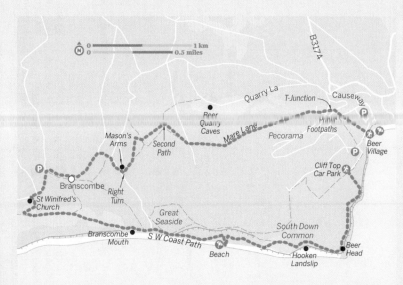

Lyme Bay

BEER TO BRANSCOMBE

START/END BEER
DURATION/DISTANCE 4 HOURS/6 MILES
DIFFICULTY MODERATE

From Beer's southerly **Cliff Top car park**, the flint-studded coast path leads up to **Beer Head** and extraordinary views. Behind you are Beer's trademark creamy-white cliffs; ahead of you, the Jurassic Coast's russet-red shoreline undulates to Exmouth. Next follow the path west until the **Hooken Landslip**, a sunken swathe of coast from where 150 million tonnes of cliff slid away one night in 1790. Take the path forking left here, down the cliff edge (signed Branscombe Mouth). This insanely steep, improbable-looking track of steps and switchbacks descends into the landslip itself – a tree-shaded landscape where birdsong replaces the sounds of the sea. Soon, a path cuts left to the pebble **beach**, a tempting spot for a dip. Half a mile later you'll arrive at the huge anchor beside the beach at **Branscombe Mouth**. It belonged to the MSC *Napoli*; a 62,000-tonne cargo ship that beached off-shore in January 2007. Nearly 60 containers, carrying everything from BMW motorbikes to cat food, washed ashore in Branscombe Bay; the ensuing mad scramble to raid their contents became international news. It took 18 months to clean up the wreckage.

From there a path heads up grassy **West Cliff Hill**, heading diagonally inland, before cutting right towards Branscombe village, emerging at **St Winifred's Church**, a beautiful barrel-vaulted Norman church. Turn right, down past the National Trust's **Old Bakery** tearooms and the working **Blacksmith's Forge**. The lane winds past the **Mason's Arms** (p64), which is a good spot to refuel. Take the next right turn, signed Beach, then a switchback left, then a right, heading steeply up **Stockham's Hill**. When two paths appear, take the second path, leading to a lane that sweeps downhill, revealing gorgeous Lyme Bay views. Where Mare Lane reaches a T-junction, turn left, then immediately after, on the bend, turn right onto two, easy-to-miss public footpaths, leading down between houses, back to Beer village (p64).

This breathtaking hike will have you climbing cliff paths and crossing beaches. Wear good boots and take your swimsuit.

Branscombe Mouth

ROAD TRIP >
EAST DEVON COAST

Many bypass East Devon's rural roads in favour of speedier A routes, but the region's steep, hedge-backed lanes lead to hidden villages and views of the sea.

❶ A La Ronde

To begin explorations, head for the unique National Trust property, **A La Ronde** (p61). This dainty 16-sided house was built for two unwed sisters as a repository for the treasures they gathered on their 18th-century European Grand Tour. Hence the intriguing assemblage of mosaic work, papercuts, shells and feather friezes on display.

❷ Orcombe Point

From A La Ronde take the road into the resort town of Exmouth itself, following signs to **Orcombe Point**. This marks the western tip of the Jurassic Coast – a 95-mile stretch of shore that undulates east to Dorset. England's first natural World Heritage Site, it has layers of geology along its length that represent eras spanning 185 million years. The vivid red rocks you see at Exmouth date

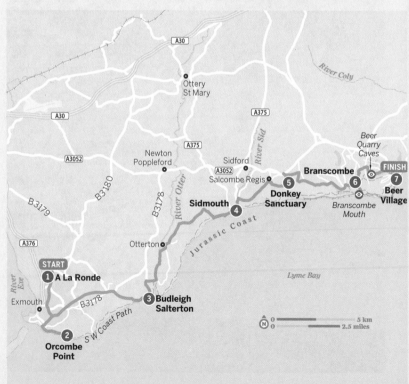

from the Triassic era – some 200 to 250 million years old. At Orcombe Point also hunt out the Geoneedle, which contains rocks from the coast's other eras.

❸ Budleigh Salterton

Next, it's back to the car to pick up the B3178. It meanders east to **Budleigh Salterton**, an unhurried seaside town where the main street features an array of architectural styles and the beach boasts impressive cliffs. The pebbles on the shoreline here are 250 million years old and date from the Triassic era. Taking the B3178 towards Sidmouth heading north out of Budleigh, divert right and onto a rural route that snakes to **Otterton**, where well-kept thatches and tearooms line roadside watercourses.

❹ Sidmouth

From here, back roads wind to Regency **Sidmouth** (p63). In this select resort, strolling along the Esplanade reveals red cliffs and ornate architecture – the town has some 30 blue plaques. Highlights include the cottages at the far west end on Clifton Pl – look out for the Swiss-chalet-style Beacon Cottage. Towards the centre of town you'll encounter the crenellated Belmont Hotel, the late-Georgian Riviera Hotel and, finally, the huge Kingswood Hotel, formerly the home of the town's hot and cold saltwater baths. For more on Sidmouth's past, drop by the town's museum, which has a particularly fine collection of fossils that have been found on these shores.

Back in the car, avoid the main route to Sidford and instead hug the shore up steep Salcombe Hill Rd, passing the Norman Lockyer Observatory. After the sharp descent to sleepy **Salcombe Regis**, the lane doglegs through the village, past ancient cottages and a picturesque church.

❺ Donkey Sanctuary

Soon, the irresistible **Donkey Sanctuary** (p63) demands a detour, where you'll encounter fields and paddocks full of happily retired equines. At the mini-roundabout, pick up signs to Branscombe, a flatter, straighter route. Then the hills return in an idyllic drive along steep, single-track lanes lined with high hedges, interspersed with passing places and first-gear bends.

❻ Branscombe

At **Branscombe**, a string of thatches winds to a central triangle; pause at the **Mason's Arms** (p64) for lunch. Then fork right (signed simply Beach) to picturesque **Branscombe Mouth,** the perfect spot for a dip or a paddle in the sea. As the signs suggest, the climb east out of Branscombe is narrow and steep.

❼ Beer

Once you've crested the rise, next comes the descent to **Beer Quarry Caves** (p64). Here you're guided around a network of passages chiselled out by quarriers over thousands of years. They were after Beer stone – a prime material that features in some of Britain's most prestigious buildings. From the caves, drive down into **Beer** (p64) itself. Explore this picturesque village, taking in a main street lined by water-filled leats and flint-flecked houses.

Peckish? Head to Steamers for classy dishes (the fish is particularly fine) or to the Anchor Inn, a characterful old pub that has a beer garden clinging to the cliff edge. Stroll two minutes down to the beautiful pebbled semicircle that is Beer beach. Here you'll find fishing boats that have been hauled up away from the reach of the waves, a fish stand and striking creamy-white cliffs. These are comprised of chalk from the Cretaceous period – a mere 65 million years old. That means in your 20-mile journey from Triassic-era Orcombe Point, you've travelled through 185 million years of geological time.

To explore this stunning coast and its geology further, consider the 6-mile circular coast walk between Beer and your earlier stop of Branscombe.

EXETER

☑ 01392 / POP 117,800

Well-heeled and comfortable, Exeter exudes evidence of its centuries-old role as the spiritual and administrative heart of Devon. The city's Gothic cathedral presides over pockets of cobbled streets; medieval and Georgian buildings and fragments of the Roman city stretch out all around. A snazzy contemporary shopping centre brings bursts of the modern; thousands of university students ensure a buzzing nightlife; and the vibrant quayside acts as a launch pad for cycling or kayaking trips. Throw in some stylish places to stay and eat, and you have a relaxed but lively base for explorations.

◎ Sights

★ **Exeter Cathedral**   CATHEDRAL

(Cathedral Church of St Peter; ☑ 01392- 285983; www.exeter-cathedral.org.uk; The Close; adult/child £7.50/free; ⊘ 9am-5pm Mon-Sat, 11.30am-5pm Sun) Magnificent in warm, honey-coloured stone, Exeter's cathedral is one of Devon's most impressive ecclesiastical sights. Dating largely from the 12th and 13th centuries, the **west front** is framed by extraordinary medieval statuary, while inside the ceiling soars upwards to the longest span of un-broken Gothic vaulting in the world, dotted with ornate ceiling bosses in gilt and vibrant colours. Look out for the scale Lego model that's being built beside the main entrance; for £1 you can add a brick.

★ **RAMM**   MUSEUM

(Royal Albert Memorial Museum & Art Gallery; ☑ 01392-265858; www.rammuseum.org.uk; Queen St; ⊘ 10am-5pm Tue-Sun) **FREE** The imposing red-brick exterior looks every inch the Victorian museum, but a £24-million revamp has brought the exhibits bang up to date. Interactive displays focus on Exeter's heritage from prehistory to the present, as well as global exploration and the concept of collecting. Look out for Exeter's Roman-era artefacts, local Tudor carvings and the striking ethnographic displays, which include African masks, samurai armour and the mummy of Shep en-Mut.

★ **Underground Passages**   TUNNEL

(☑ 01392-665887; www.exeter.gov.uk/passages; 2 Paris St; adult/child £6/4; ⊘ 9.30am-5.30pm Mon-Sat, 10.30am-4pm Sun Jun-Sep, 10.30am-4.30pm Tue-Fri, 9.30am-5.30pm Sat, 11.30am-4pm Sun Oct-May) Prepare to crouch down, don a hard hat and possibly get slightly wet in what is the only publicly accessible system of its kind in England. These medieval vaulted passages were built to house pipes bringing fresh water to the city. Guides lead you on a scramble through the network, relating tales of ghosts, escape routes and cholera. The last tour is an hour before closing; they're popular – book ahead.

Exeter Quay   WATERFRONT

(The Quay; ℗) On fine sunny days the people of Exeter head to the quay. Cobbled paths lead between former warehouses that have been converted into antique shops, quirky stores, craft workshops, restaurants and pubs (popular spots for alfresco drinks and people-watching).

Bill Douglas
Cinema Museum   MUSEUM

(☑ 01392-724321; www.bdcmuseum.org.uk; Old Library, Prince of Wales Rd; ⊘ 10am-5pm; ℗) **FREE** This eccentric museum is a must for cinephiles. It contains a vast hoard of film-themed memorabilia amassed by Scottish film-maker Bill Douglas, best known for his semi-autobiographical trilogy about his childhood. Douglas was also an avid collector, amassing more than 50,000 cinematic collectibles that encompass magic lanterns, peep shows, original celluloid from Disney films, Charlie Chaplin bottle stoppers, James Bond board games, vintage film posters, *Star Wars* toys and more. It's on the Exeter University campus, a mile northwest of the city centre.

Exeter Livestock Market   MARKET

(☑ 01392-251261; www.kivells.com; Matford Park Rd; ⊘ sales usually 9.30am Mon & Fri) For a sense of what life's like on the farms tucked into East Devon's red-soil hills, head to one of the

---

DON'T MISS

ROOFTOP VIEWS

For a sensational view of Exeter Cathedral (p52), book one of the high-rise guided **walks** (☑ 01392-285983; www.exeter-cathedral.org.uk; incl Exeter Cathedral admission adult/child £13/5; ⊘ 2pm Tue, 10.30am Sat Apr-Sep). Climb 251 steps up spiral staircases, head out onto the sweeping roof, then gaze down on the city from the edge of the North Tower. Tours are popular, so book at least two weeks ahead.

Exeter

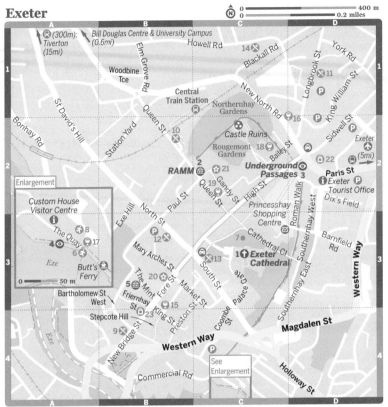

Exeter

POWDERHAM CASTLE

The historic home of the Earl of Devon, Powderham (☑ 01626-890243; www. powderham.co.uk; adult/child £11.50/9.50; ☺ 11am-4.30pm Sun-Fri Apr-Jun, Sep & Oct, to 5.30pm Jul & Aug; ℗) is a stately but still friendly place built in 1391 and remodelled in the Victorian era. A visit takes in a fine wood-panelled Great Hall, parkland with 650 deer and glimpses of life 'below stairs' in the kitchen. Powderham is on the River Exe near Kenton, 8 miles south of Exeter.

auctions at Exeter Livestock Market. Join farmers leaning on the showing rings' circular rails, while the auctioneer's sing-song chant raises the price. Then have lunch with the buyers and sellers in the on-site eatery. Full of ripe smells and specialised language (prime stock and store stock, suckler cows and breeding bulls), it's an authentic insight into rural Devon life.

🏃 Activities

Saddles & Paddles OUTDOORS
(☑ 01392-424241; www.sadpad.com; Exeter Quay; ☺ 9am-6pm) Rents out bikes (adult per hour/day £6/15), kayaks (£10/35) and Canadian canoes (£15/50); the tourist office stocks maps.

Exeter Cruises CRUISE
(☑ 07984 368442; Exeter Quay; adult/child/family return £6/3/15; ☺ daily Jun-Aug, Sat & Sun only Apr, May & Sep) The *Southern Comfort* makes the 45-minute trip down the Exeter Ship Canal from Exeter Quay to the Double Locks pub.

☞ Tours

★ Redcoat Tours WALKING
(☑ 01392-265203; www.exeter.gov.uk/leisure-and -culture; ☺ 3-6pm daily Apr-Oct, twice-daily Nov-Mar) FREE For an informed and entertaining introduction to Exeter's history, tag along on one of these 1½-hour tours. Themes range from murder and trade to the Tudors and religion – there are even torchlight prowls through the catacombs and evening ghost walks. Most tours leave from Cathedral Green; a few in summer depart from Exeter Quay. There's no need to book.

Exeter Cathedral Guided Tours ARCHITECTURE
(www.exeter-cathedral.org.uk/visiting) Free guided tours of the cathedral are included in the Exeter Cathedral (p52) admission price, and explore the building's history and architecture.

✖ Eating

★ Exploding Bakery CAFE £
(☑ 01392-427900; www.explodingbakery.com; 1b Central Cres, Queen St; snacks £2.50; ☺ 8am-4pm Mon-Fri, 9am-4pm Sat) Excellent news: one of Exeter's hippest little bakeries has now added half-a-dozen tables, meaning there's even more room to sample superb flat whites, macchiato and inventive cakes – the lemon, polenta and pistachio is a hit.

It also has regular guest coffees from some of the UK's top roasters.

Plant Cafe VEGETARIAN £
(1 Cathedral Yard; mains £6-9; ☺ 8.30am-5pm Mon-Sat; ☑) Seats are at a premium at this casually cool wholefood cafe. That'll be down to its prime spot overlooking Cathedral Green and its imaginative frittata, pies and salads. When it's sunny you can sit outside.

Museum Cafe CAFE £
(☑ 01392-265858; www.rammuseum.org.uk; Queen St; snacks from £3; ☺ 10am-4.30pm Tue-Sun; ☎) This is the kind of museum cafe that England does so well. Set inside the Royal Albert Memorial Museum, its bright, galleried space opens out into exhibition halls. The cakes and light meals are tasty and homemade.

★ Rusty Bike MODERN BRITISH ££
(☑ 01392-214440; www.rustybike-exeter.co.uk; 67 Howell Rd; mains £15-21; ☺ 5-10pm Mon-Sat, noon-10.30pm Sun) It may be in the city, but Rusty's has a soul rooted deep in the countryside. The farm-to-plate dining (or 'welly to belly', as they put it) showcases produce from Devon suppliers, such as game from local estates, wild veg foraged by hand and Aberdeen Angus beef reared at nearby farms. The quality produce and careful preparation comes through in the taste.

Rodean MODERN BRITISH ££
(☑ 01626-890195; www.rodeanrestaurant.co.uk; The Triangle, Kenton; 2-/3-course menu £20/24; ☺ 6-9pm Tue-Sat, noon-2pm Sun) Run by the same family for 15 years, the Rodean serves inventive cuisine that has built a loyal following and notched up a string of awards.

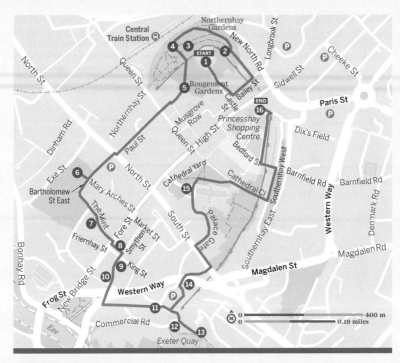

City Walk
Exeter's City Walls

START CASTLE RUINS
END ROMAN WALK
LENGTH 2 MILES, 2.5 HOURS

Start at the gatehouse to Exeter's **1 Castle Ruins**, the remains of a fortification built by the Normans after an 18-day siege. A plaque commemorates three Devon women, hanged after being tried here for witchcraft in 1685. In Northernhay Gardens, take the path along the wall that is crowned by **2 Civil War–era parapets**; in an era of shifting loyalties, Exeter had to defend itself against both Royalists and Parliamentarians.

Pass the arch of 12th-century **3 Athelstan's Tower**. Head through the **4 archway** in the wall and follow the path through the park, cutting right at the **5 rainbow sun sculpture** to emerge beside the Exeter Phoenix.

Paul St leads to **6 Bartholomew Cemetery**. Stepping through its gate sees you standing on top of 19th-century catacombs. At Bartholomew St East's right-hand bend, turn off into The Mint, passing the crumbly walls of the 11th-century **7 St Nicholas Priory**.

Turn right down Fore St, before cutting left down John St, where the **8 Fat Pig** (p56) microbrewery is a friendly place to pause for a drink. Next stroll on towards cobbled **9 Stepcote Hill**, where half-timbered houses lead to the russet-red **10 St Mary's Steps Church**, complete with ornate figure-flanked clock.

Cross busy Western Way, then pass some of the **11 city wall** on the left, making your way along to historic **12 Exeter Quay** (p52). Here, **13 On the Waterfront** (p56) is another enjoyable refreshment stop. After a break, climb the hill, cutting left up steps to the car park; the footpath on its eastern edge runs along the top of the historic wall itself. Climb steps to the footbridge, looking down to see **14 Roman facework** and volcanic blocks.

From South St, branch off into the Palace Gate to admire the architecture of **15 Cathedral Close**, before cutting north along Southernhay West, then up Bedford St and into the walkways of the Princesshay Shopping Centre. You'll finish your tour alongside a well-preserved Roman section of wall on aptly named **16 Roman Walk**.

Classic, often local, ingredients are given a contemporary twist: seared hake with tempura cauliflower; pork cheeks with black pudding and pear. It's 7 miles southwest of Exeter.

Harry's BISTRO ££

(☑ 01392-202234; www.harrysrestaurants.co.uk; 86 Longbrook St; mains £12-25; ⊙9am-2.30pm & 6-11pm) An old staple in central Exeter, Harry's is a good bet for solid, no-fuss dining. The decor is all wooden chairs, blackboard menus and gilt mirrors; comfort food includes sizzling fajitas, Creedy Carver chicken, leek and taleggio risotto, and hog 'n' mac (a pulled-pork roll with macaroni cheese).

Herbies VEGETARIAN ££

(☑ 01392-258473; 15 North St; mains £7-12; ⊙11am-2.30pm Mon-Sat, 6.30-9.30pm Tue-Sat; 🖉) Herbies has been cheerfully feeding Exeter's vegetarians and vegans for more than 20 years. It's a cosy spot to tuck into Greek vegetable pie, mushroom and butternut-squash risotto or Moroccan tagine.

@Angela's MODERN BRITISH £££

(☑ 01392-499038; www.angelasrestaurant.co.uk; 38 New Bridge St; mains £21-30; ⊙6-9pm Wed-Sat) Rich, filling dishes feature strongly at this formal, fine-dining restaurant, as do local ingredients – the mussels and day-boat fish are from South Devon ports and the meat is from pedigree herds around 20 miles away. These are transformed into treats such as rosemary and garlic lamb loin and roast monkfish in creamy sauce.

🍷 Drinking & Nightlife

⭐ **Fat Pig** MICROBREWERY

(☑ 01392-437217; www.fatpig-exeter.co.uk; 2 John St; ⊙5-11pm Mon-Fri, noon-11pm Sat, noon-5pm Sun) It really doesn't get much better: a microbrewery downstairs, a distillery upstairs and a bright, convivial pub in between. Sample home-crafted ales, gin, vodka and moonshine (yes, really; it's a corn-based spirit) in friendly surrounds.

The food too is innovative, locally sourced, and often home-smoked and homemade; try the treacle-cured salmon, or smoked cauliflower and pea fritters with curried mayonnaise. Mains £13 to £18; from 6pm to 10pm Monday to Saturday, plus noon to 3pm weekends.

Old Firehouse PUB

(☑ 01392-277279; www.oldfirehouseexeter.co.uk; 50 New North Rd; ⊙noon-2am Mon-Wed, to 3am Thu-Sat, to 1am Sun) Step into the snug, candlelit interior of this Exeter institution and instantly feel at home. Dried hops hang from rafters above flagstone floors and walls of exposed stone. The range of draught ciders and cask ales is truly impressive, while the pizzas, served after 9pm, have kept countless students fed.

On the Waterfront BAR

(☑ 01392-210590; www.waterfrontexeter.co.uk; The Quay; ⊙10am-11.30pm) In 1835 this was a warehouse; now its red-brick, barrel-vaulted ceilings stretch back from a thoroughly modern bar. The tables outside are a popular spot for a riverside pint.

Timepiece CLUB

(☑ 01392-493096; www.timepiecenightclub.co.uk; Little Castle St; ⊙9.30pm-1.30am Mon-Wed, 10pm-2am Fri & Sat) A students' late-night favourite, with nights devoted to indie, electro, house and cheesy club classics.

Vaults GAY & LESBIAN

(www.vaultsexeter.co.uk; Gandy St; ⊙10pm-2.30am Mon, Wed & Thu, to 3am Fri-Sun & Tue) At Exeter's main LGBT venue you'll find two bars, club nights, classy cocktails, funky lights, glittery features and crowds of people having a good time.

WORTH A TRIP

YEARLSTONE VINEYARD

Having been closed for building works in 2017, Yearlstone is due to reopen in spring 2018. It's a picturesque place, set amid an amphitheatre of deeply wooded, sharply sloping hills above the rushing River Exe. Tours range from guide-yourself affairs to detailed explorations of the winemaking process. Call ahead to check opening times.

Yearlstone's range of award-winning white, red, rosé and sparkling wines includes the pale gold Vintage Brut (£18), the light and fruity red Yearlstone No 4 (£10) and the tangy, dry white Yearlstone No 1 (£9). There's also a lovely cafe, the **Deli Shack** (☑ 01884-855700; www.delishackcafe.co.uk; 🖉).

Yearlstone is on the outskirts of Bickleigh, 10 miles north of Exeter on the A396.

BEN IVORY / GETTY IMAGES ©

Exeter Cathedral (p52)

Beer Engine   MICROBREWERY
(☑ 01392-851282; www.thebeerengine.co.uk; Newton St Cyres; ⊙11am-11pm) The decor in this former railway hotel is varnished floorboards, leather settles and exposed red brick, but the best bit is downstairs: the brewery's gleaming stainless-steel tubs and tubes. The building's past is the inspiration for the brews' names: fruity Rail Ale (3.8% abv), sharp and sweet Piston Bitter (4.3% abv) and well-rounded Sleeper Heavy (5.4% abv).

Flavoursome food includes slow-cooked shoulder of West Country lamb, a range of ploughman's platters made with local Quickes cheddar, and steak and Sleeper Ale pie (mains £12; noon to 3pm and 6pm to 9.30pm Monday to Saturday, noon to 6.30pm Sunday). Newton St Cyres is on the A377, 5 miles north of Exeter. Train services from Exeter (return £7) chug into the village in time for supper; the return trip just after 11pm (10.30pm on Sunday) is very handy indeed.

☆ Entertainment

Bike Shed   THEATRE
(☑ 01392-434169; www.bikeshedtheatre.co.uk; 162 Fore St; ⊙5pm-midnight Mon-Thu, to 2am Fri & Sat, to 11pm Sun) Emerging writers are profiled in the Bike Shed's rough 'n' ready subterranean, brick-lined performance space. Its vintage cocktail bar makes a hip setting for live music and DJ sets on Friday and Saturday nights.

Exeter Phoenix   ARTS CENTRE
(☑ 01392-667080; www.exeterphoenix.org.uk; cnr Bradninch Pl & Gandy St; ⊙10am-11pm Mon-Sat; ☎) Exeter's art and soul, the Phoenix is a buzzing blend of indie cinema, a performance space, galleries and a cool cafe-bar (snacks to 7pm).

🛍 Shopping

Real Food Store   FOOD
(www.realfoodexeter.co.uk; 11 Paris St; ⊙9am-6pm Mon-Fri, to 5pm Sat) Boxes and bags full of field-fresh veg, racks of fragrant bread, ranks of local cheeses and piles of cured meat and fish. Some 70% of the goods in this community-run cafe-cum-store are from Devon, and the other 30% is from the wider southwest.

Real McCoy   VINTAGE
(☑ 01392-410481; www.therealmccoy.co.uk; 21A McCoy's Arcade, Fore St; ⊙10am-5.30pm Mon-Sat, 11am-4pm Sun) This Aladdin's cave of retro

threads has long been a magnet for Exeter's fashionistas. It proudly proclaims stock spanning 100 years (1880s to 1980s): downstairs has everything from cricket blazers and cravats to beaded evening gowns, while upstairs is the domain of 1950s leather jackets, '70s jeans and checked shirts galore.

ⓘ Information

Custom House Visitor Centre (☑ 01392-271611; customhouse@exeter.gov.uk; 46 The Quay; ⊘10am-5pm Apr-Oct, 11am-4pm Nov-Mar) Visitor centre near the quay, which features heritage displays.

Exeter Tourist Office (☑ 01392-665700; www.visitexeter.com; Dix's Field; ⊘9am-5pm Mon-Sat Apr-Sep, 9.30am-4.30pm Mon-Sat Oct-Mar) Efficient and well run, with plenty of info on Exeter and the rest of Devon.

ⓘ Getting There & Away

AIR

Exeter International Airport (p272) is 6 miles east of the city. Flights connect with several UK cities, including Manchester, Newcastle, Edinburgh and Glasgow, and with the Isles of Scilly and the Channel Islands. Flights also travel to European cities, including Paris, Amsterdam and Dublin.

BUS

Exeter's bus station (Paris St) is due a multi-million-pound revamp, during which time some services may depart from other locations. There's no set date. Check with the tourist office for the latest.

Services include the following:

Exmouth Bus 57 (£4.20, 35 minutes, two to four per hour)

Lyme Regis Bus X52 (£8, six daily Monday to Friday, four Saturday and Sunday), via Beer. No Sunday service in winter.

Plymouth Bus X38 (£7.30, 1¼ hours, six daily Monday to Friday, four Saturday, two Sunday)

Sidmouth Bus 9/9A (£6.70, 35 minutes, two per hour Monday to Saturday)

Topsham Bus 57 (£3.10, 10 minutes, two to four per hour)

Totnes Bus X64 (£7.70, 50 minutes, seven daily Monday to Friday, six Saturday, two Sunday)

CAR

Exeter is at the southern end of the M5 motorway; junctions 29 and 30 provide useful, if congested, routes into the city. Most major car-hire firms have branches in the city or at the airport. The very centre of Exeter is off-limits to cars.

TRAIN

Main-line trains stopping at St David's train station include the following:

EDUCATION IMAGES / CONTRIBUTOR / GETTY IMAGES ©

Pebblebed Vineyard (p60)

EXPLORING AROUND EXETER

Foot and cycle paths head southeast from Exeter Quay to join the Exe Valley Way, a trail shadowing both the Exeter Canal and the wide River Exe, and meeting the sea around 10 miles away. The paths make for good biking, hiking and kayaking trips: the first 3 miles are a blend of heritage city, countryside and light industrial landscape; the later sections are more rural. The Custom House Visitor Centre (p58) stocks *Exe Valley Way* leaflets.

About 1.5 miles downstream from Exeter Quay the route reaches the laid-back Double Locks (www.doublelocks.com) pub, which features real ale and a waterside terrace. The RSPB (Royal Society for the Protection of Birds) Exminster Marshes Nature Reserve starts about 2 miles further on. Around 2 miles inside the reserve, the waterside Turf pub (p61) clings to a slither of land, and is an idyllic setting to enjoy good grub and summer barbecues. From there a rougher trail connects with a path to the appealing Powderham Castle (p54). You can also navigate much of the above route by kayak, making an enjoyable, non-tidal paddle past pubs.

Hire bikes, kayaks and canoes from Exeter's Saddles & Paddles (p54).

Bristol £22, 1¼ hours, half-hourly

London Paddington £45, 2½ hours, half-hourly

Paignton £6.60, 50 minutes, half-hourly

Penzance £22, three hours, half-hourly to hourly

Plymouth £9.40, one hour, half-hourly

Torquay £6.80, 45 minutes, half-hourly to hourly

Totnes £6.80, 35 minutes, half-hourly

Some branch-line services also go through Exeter Central train station.

ⓘ Getting Around

BOAT

Butt's Ferry (The Quay; adult/child 50/30p; ☺11.30am-4.30pm daily Jun-Aug, Sat & Sun Easter-May & Sep) This tiny boat shuttles across the River Exe from the quayside.

BUS

Bus H (two to four per hour) links St David's train station with Central train station (£1) and the High St, passing near the bus station.

CAR

Major car-hire firms have desks at the airport. Some have concessions at St David's train station, too.

TAXI

There are taxi ranks at St David's train station and on High and Sidwell Sts.

Taxi firms include the following:

Apple Central Taxis (☏01392-666666; www.appletaxisexeter.co.uk)

Exeter City Cars (☏01392-975808; www.exetercitycars.com; ☺24hr)

Z Cars (☏01392-595959)

EAST DEVON

East of Exeter, Devon's red-soil fields and red-rock cliffs undulate towards Dorset. A few miles south of the city lies Topsham, a charming, ancient port overflowing with fine places to eat and stay. Next comes the faded resort of Exmouth, launch pad for Jurassic Coast cruises and adrenaline sports. Regency Sidmouth delivers old-world seaside charm, stargazing and an irresistible equine sanctuary. Captivating Beer offers the chance to land your own lunch and explore an ancient network of caves. Meanwhile, the River Cottage eateries of TV chef Hugh Fearnley-Whittingstall lie inland, rustling up truly memorable meals.

Topsham

☏01392 / POP 5160

Topsham stretches languidly down the banks of the River Exe, its atmospheric Fore St flanked by heritage buildings, and its long waterfront providing picturesque views of an estuary widening into the sea. Despite being just 4 miles south of busy Exeter, this appealing settlement has retained a market-town feel. Add an exceptional selection of places to dine and sleep, an irresistible vineyard and some compelling boat trips, and you have a very attractive edge-of-Exeter base.

⊙ Sights

Topsham has been an important port since the medieval era, and its wealth is evident in the Dutch-gable merchants houses that

EXETER & EAST DEVON TOPSHAM

RIVER COTTAGE

Known for his media campaigns on sustainability and organic food, TV chef Hugh Fearnley-Whittingstall has broadcast most of his TV shows from his home base at **River Cottage HQ** (01297-630300; www.rivercottage. net; Trinity Hill Rd, Axminster; 2-course lunch £50, 4-course dinner £70-90), near Axminster, 30 miles from Exeter. If you fancy seeing where the magic happens, you can book in for a sumptuous four-course meal, made with produce from Hugh's own garden, or attend one of the regular cooking courses. A cheaper option is to dine at his canteen (01297-631715; Trinity Sq, Axminster; mains £7-18; ⊙9am-5pm Sun-Tue, to 11pm Wed-Sat; ✎) in Axminster village nearby.

march through the middle of town. Explore by heading down the doglegged Fore St into the Strand, before heading back alongside the water. You'll encounter independent shops, eateries, the town museum and ferry trips along the way.

Pebblebed Vineyard   WINERY
(☎07814 788348; www.pebblebed.co.uk; Marianne Pool Farm, Clyst St George; per person £20; ⊙tours 4pm Thu, 11am & 3pm Sat May–mid-Oct) You get more than a whiff of southern Europe on these winery tours that take in south-facing slopes, neatly staked vines and the heady aroma of fermenting grapes. The hour-long strolls end with a tutored tasting of four wines, including a fruity red, a fresh rosé, a dry white and a Devon sparkling. Book ahead. Pebblebed is 1.5 miles east of Topsham.

If you miss a tour, head for the Topsham wine cellar and sample the vintages there.

Topsham Museum   MUSEUM
(☎01392-873244; 25 The Strand; ⊙2-5pm Sat-Mon, Wed & Thu Apr-Oct) **FREE** Artefacts from Topsham's salty past fill this 17th-century waterfront building, including model sailing ships, shipwrights' tools and tublike historic boats. There's also a surprising Vivien Leigh room (she was the sister-in-law of the museum's founder), where memorabilia includes the nightdress the film star wore in *Gone with the Wind*.

🏃 Activities

Sea Dream   CRUISE
(www.topshamtoturfferry.co.uk; The Quay; adult/child return £5/3; ⊙4-6 daily Apr-Sep) For a true taste of Topsham's maritime links, board the *Sea Dream* and glide past mudflats and marsh land, passing a panorama of the town. The 15-minute trip leads to a tiny slither of land jutting out from the River Exe's south bank, on which sits the Turf (p61) pub.

From there you can stroll a mile further downstream to visit stately Powderham Castle (p54). Or walk upstream, beside the canal, to the Topsham Ferry, which shuttles back to Topsham.

Bowling Green Marsh   BIRDWATCHING
(RSPB; ☎01392-833311; www.rspb.org.uk; Bowling Green Rd) **FREE** As the main high-tide roost on the River Exe, this is one of the best places to spot birds in Devon and Cornwall. At the hide (which is signed) in summer look out for greenshank, ringed plover and little egret; winter brings masses of wigeon, pintail and teal, as well as black-and-white avocet.

Topsham Ferry   BOATING
(☎07801 203338; one way £1.20; ⊙9.30am-5.30pm Wed-Mon Easter-Sep, 10am-5pm Sat & Sun Oct-Easter) A blink-and-you'll miss it trip from Topsham to the south bank of the Exe, crossing the river at its narrowest point. Tranquil waterside paths lead 2 miles downriver to the Turf pub (p61), where the *Sea Dream* ferry (p60) sails back to Topsham.

Note: it doesn't run on very low tides.

🍴 Eating

⭐**Pebblebed Wine Cellar**   BISTRO £
(☎01392-661810; www.pebblebed.co.uk; Ferry Rd; mains £8; ⊙5-9.30pm Mon-Sat) Add this to your must-visit list. Trestle tables, whitewashed walls and ranks of balanced bottles lend this vaulted wine cellar an air of rustic charm. Food comes in the form of thin-crust pizzas, and local cheese and meat platters, but the stars of the show are the vintages from Pebblebed's own local vineyard.

⭐**GlassHouse**   BISTRO, CAFE ££
(☎01392-873060; www.salutationtopsham.co.uk; 68 Fore St; mains £7-20; ⊙8.30am-5pm; ✎) The

setting is sleek and so is the food: an atrium encloses a historic courtyard, creating a stylish space where Paris-quality patisserie comes at Devon prices (£3). The light lunches range from sandwiches, omelettes, and fish and duck platters to lobster and fragrant gnocchi. The *prix fixe* menus (two/three courses £20/25) are a steal.

Pig & Pallet BISTRO, DELI ££

(☑ 01392-668129; www.facebook.com/pigand pallet; Topsham Quay; mains £8-13; ☺ 10am-10pm) This friendly, shedlike bistro-cum-deli smokes and roasts the meats in-house, producing intensely flavoured charcuterie, ribs, BBQ, burgers and pulled pork. The extras are excellent (try the bacon jam), while the drinks list takes in local beer, cider and gin. Hog heaven for carnivores.

Turf PUB FOOD ££

(☑ 01392-833128; www.turfpub.net; near Exminister; mains £7-12; ☺ noon-2.30pm Mon-Fri, to 3pm Sat & Sun Easter-Oct, hours vary Nov-Easter) The location of this former lock-keeper's house is simply superb: bookending a slither of land snaking between mud-flats and a canal. The views are expansive; the welcome is warm; and the bar food is a cut above the norm. Get here either on the Sea Dream ferry (p60), or by footpath from the Exminster Marshes Nature Reserve (1 mile).

There's a hideaway feel to the two beach hut-chic B&B rooms (single/double £50/100); camping is either in your own tents (per two people £10) or in a yurt.

★**Salutation** MODERN EUROPEAN £££

(☑ 01392-873060; www.salutationtopsham.co.uk; 68 Fore St; 4/6/8 courses £40/60/80; ☺ 6.30-9pm Mon-Sat; ℙ ☑) You can almost taste ambition at this exquisite restaurant-with-rooms: chef Tom Williams-Hawkes has worked with international financiers the Roths-childs, chef Gordon Ramsay and at Devon's double-Michelin-starred Gidleigh Park. The French-themed cuisine incorporates highly technical tasting menus, which see Devon mussels, pork, lamb and scallops transformed by the use of consommé, confit and jus.

The bedrooms (doubles £135, suites £185 to £225) are as delicious as the food: contemporary-chic checks and stripes, and crisply designed lines.

DON'T MISS

DEVON'S DOWNTON ABBEY

For full-blown Victorian architectural excess, **Knightshayes Court** (NT; ☑ 01884-254665; www.nationaltrust.org. uk; Bolham; adult/child £11/5.51; ☺ 10am-5pm Mar-Oct, to 4pm Nov-Feb; ℙ) delivers in spades. It was designed by the ec-centric architect William Burges for the Tiverton MP John Heathcoat Mallory in 1869. Burges' obsession with the Middle Ages resulted in a plethora of stone curlicues, ornate mantles and carved figurines, plus lavish Victorian decora-tion (the smoking and billiard rooms feel just like a gentlemen's club). Outside is a water-lily pool, topiary, formal terraces and a kitchen garden. It's 1 mile east of Tiverton at Bolham.

🍸 Drinking & Nightlife

Lighter PUB

(☑ 01392-875439; www.lighterinn.co.uk; ☺ 11am-11pm Mon-Sat, to 10.30pm Sun) The Lighter is one of those age-old inns where tankards hang from the rafters, the alcoves are snug and the water-view terrace is the place for a pint on sunny days.

ℹ Getting There & Away

Bus 57 links Topsham with Exeter (£2.40, 15 minutes, two to four per hour) and Exmouth (£3.10, 10 minutes). Trains also run to Exeter and Exmouth.

Exmouth

☑ 01395 / POP 7020

Exmouth is a curious combination of well-worn Georgian resort and adrenaline frenzy. The town's exposed position at the mouth of the River Exe draws wind and fleets of kitesurfers who whip across the water on gusty days. The area also has a unique pint-sized National Trust (NT) property and is the beginning, or the end, of the Jurassic Coast.

👁 Sights

A La Ronde HISTORIC BUILDING

(NT; ☑ 01395-265514; www.nationaltrust.org.uk; Summer Lane; adult/child £8.90/4.40; ☺ 11am-5pm early Feb-Oct; ℙ) This quirky 16-sided cottage was built in 1796 so two spinster

SALTY MONK

An irresistible air of indulgence infuses the sublime Salty Monk (☑ 01395-513174; www.saltymonk.co.uk; Church St, Sidford; s £85, d £130-180; [P] [🛜]): beautifully lit, super-stylish baths, sumptuous fabrics, antiques and ancient beams. De-stress in the hot tub, sauna and massage room, then opt for fine-dining dishes crafted from local, largely organic ingredients; perhaps chicken terrine dotted with pistachios or twice-baked goats-cheese soufflé. Served 6.30pm to 9pm Tuesday to Saturday.

It's in the village of Sidford, 2 miles north of Sidmouth.

cousins could display a mass of curiosities acquired on their 10-year European grand tour. Its glass alcoves, low lintels and tiny doorways mean it's like clambering through a doll's house. Highlights are a delicate feather frieze in the drawing room and a gallery smothered with a thousand seashells. The house is 2 miles north of Exmouth; bus 57 (£2.20, five minutes, every 15 minutes) runs close by.

🏃 Activities

ExePlorer Water Taxi
BOATING

(☑ 07970 918418; www.exeplorerwatertaxis.co.uk; Exmouth Marina; adult/child return £4/3; ◷ 8am-5pm Apr, May & Sep, to 7pm Jun-Aug) To get a feel for the sheer width of the River Exe at its mouth, take this tublike red-and-blue water taxi for the 15-minute cross-estuary trip to the Dawlish Warren Nature Reserve (p78), a wind-whipped slither of sand that juts out into the river. The taxi is normally at Exmouth Marina on the hour and half past.

Edge Kitesurfing
WATER SPORTS

(☑ 01395-222551; www.edgewatersports.com; Pier Head, Exmouth Marina) The wind whips across the mouth of the River Exe's wide estuary at Exmouth, creating prime kite- and windsurfing conditions. A series of sandbanks also ensures plenty of shallow, flat-water areas ideal for learners. Lessons include kitesurfing for beginners (£110 per three hours) and intermediates 1-2-1 sessions (£175 per hour); and stand-up paddleboarding (SUP; £35 per two hours for two people).

SUP hire costs £25 for three hours, including wetsuit.

👉 Tours

Stuart Line
CRUISE

(☑ 01395-222144; www.stuartlinecruises.co.uk; from £7.50) Stuart Line runs a string of trips from Exmouth Marina. The pick are the sailings along Devon's Jurassic Coast (£10) past the rust-red cliffs and the impressive sea stacks that emerge at Ladram Bay. The chance of dolphin sightings adds to the appeal.

Winter birdwatching cruises (£12.50) are hugely popular. Other options include a voyage up the River Exe (£7.50), and day trips to Sidmouth (£7.50), and Torquay and Brixham (£12.50).

🍴 Eating

⭐ Ruby at the Grapevine
BURGERS ££

(☑ 01395-222208; www.rubyburgers.com; 2 Victoria Rd; mains £9-13; ◷ 5-9pm Mon-Fri, noon-9pm Sat & Sun) Juicy patties laced with blue cheese, panko-crusted chicken fillets, five-dollar shakes and chilli-cheese fries: the best Devon ingredients meet the American burger dream. It's all set in a beatnik brewhouse (open until 11pm), where battered leather bar stools sit in front of an impressive array of Belgian, German and homemade craft ales.

⭐ River Exe Cafe
MODERN BRITISH ££

(☑ 07761 116103; www.riverexecafe.com; Exmouth; mains £12-22; ◷ noon-10.30pm Mon-Sat, to 8.30pm Sun Apr-Oct) An idyllic, chilled-out, chalet-style restaurant on a barge floating in the wide waters of the River Exe. The super fresh food lives up to the setting: scallops baked with white port, clams steamed with smoked pancetta, Exmouth mussels with fennel and Pernod. Book the water taxi from Exmouth (per person return £5) with your table; it runs until 11pm.

Rockfish
SEAFOOD ££

(☑ 01395-272100; www.therockfish.co.uk; Pier Head; mains £12-20; ◷ noon-9.30pm) This Exmouth outpost of Mitch Tonks' Devon empire excels at the award-winning chef's signature superfresh seafood. Expect salt-and-pepper prawns, crispy fritto misto and superlative (sustainable) fish and chips. It's all served up in a bustling bistro beside the town's slipway so – especially on the waterside deck – you also get fine estuary views.

ℹ️ Information

Exmouth Tourist Office (☑ 01395-830550; www.exmouth-guide.co.uk; 42 The Strand; ◷ 10am-4pm Mon-Sat Apr-Sep, to 2pm Mon-Sat Oct-Mar)

ℹ️ Getting There & Away

BUS
Bus 57 runs between Exmouth and Exeter (£4.20, 35 minutes, two to four per hour), stopping at Topsham (£3.10, 10 minutes) en route.

TRAIN
Two trains per hour shuttle between Exeter St David's and Exmouth (£4.30, 30 minutes).

Sidmouth
🌀 01395 / POP 5170

The select resort of Sidmouth is the English seaside at its most stately, serene and salubrious. Hundreds of listed buildings line up elegantly behind the Esplanade; freshly painted pillars support bright-white balconies; and well-tended flowers tumble from window boxes. But this slice of old England also offers a frenetic summer folk festival, an incredibly cute donkey sanctuary and a renowned observatory.

The village of Sidford, with eateries and B&Bs, sits on the busy A3052, 2 miles to the north.

◉ Sights

Donkey Sanctuary   ANIMAL SANCTUARY
(🌀 01395-578222; www.thedonkeysanctuary.org.uk; Slade House Farm; ⊙ 9am-dusk; 🅿) **FREE** This irresistible attraction is home to around 400 donkeys, some rescued from mistreatment or neglect, others retired from working the beaches. Walkways pass fields full of the creatures happily grazing, trotting and rolling in the grass. In the main yard you can mingle freely with animals specially chosen for their fondness of people. It's 3 miles east of Sidmouth. Donations welcome.

**Norman
Lockyer Observatory**   OBSERVATORY
(🌀 01395-579941; www.normanlockyer.com; Salcombe Hill Rd; adult/child £8/4; ⊙ hours vary; 🅿) Because of relatively low light pollution, high cliffs and an expanse of sea, East Devon is prime stargazing territory. At this observatory, high-powered telescopes reveal astonishing clusters of constellations. Book your place (two to four per month) and hope for clear skies. The observatory is around a mile east of Sidmouth.

Sidmouth Museum   MUSEUM
(🌀 01395-516139; Church St; ⊙ 10am-4pm Tue-Sat, 1-4pm Mon Apr-Oct) **FREE** East Devon's history emerges here, from the town's connections to crime novelist Sir Arthur Conan Doyle to the incisive Victorian diarist Peter Orlando Hutchinson. There are also impressive displays of Triassic-era fossils (including a tooth-studded jaw of a reptile that predated the dinosaur), and of local, handmade lace (known as Honiton lace) – look out for the intricate collar worn by Queen Victoria.

🎭 Festivals & Events

**Sidmouth
Folk Week**   MUSIC
(www.sidmouthfolkweek.co.uk; ⊙ early Aug) Sidmouth is transformed by this vibrant annual festival of world and traditional music. Around 700 sessions are staged in scores of venues around town – including pubs and beer gardens – with impromptu performances often spilling over into the streets.

HISTORIC SIDMOUTH

The town's tourist office sells *Historic Sidmouth* (£2), a guide to the 30 significant heritage buildings that are marked with distinctive blue plaques. Follow the trail or just investigate ones that catch your eye; the Esplanade is a good hunting ground.

At the Esplanade's far west end, Clifton Pl is a strip of pretty, largely Georgian cottages set right beside the sea; look out for the Swiss-chalet-style Beacon Cottage (1840), with pointed black-framed windows, long verandas and a crowning of thatch.

Heading east, a crenellated red-stone gateway signals the Belmont Hotel; further down, the all-cream Riviera Hotel (1820) has a grand bowed entrance, while the vast lemon-yellow Kingswood Hotel (c 1890s) was formerly the location of the hot and cold brine baths. The white-and-black Beach House was built in 1790 and revamped in Gothic style in 1826; it was a fashionable meeting spot for the gentry.

Towards the Esplanade's east end is the Royal York & Faulkner (🌀 0800 220714; www.royalyorkhotel.co.uk; The Esplanade; d £93-114; 🅿 📶), Sidmouth's first purpose-built hotel (1810), with blue-and-white pillars and a long veranda. Notable guests have included Edward VII when he was Prince of Wales.

DON'T MISS

MASON'S ARMS

Bedrooms at the **Mason's Arms** (☑ 01297-680300; www.masonsarms.co.uk; Branscombe; d £100-175; P 🛜) are deeply tasteful, with patches of exposed stone, oak beams and neutral tones. Styles range from contemporary to restrained rustic; gleaming bathrooms sport posh toiletries; and the best bedrooms have expansive rural views.

The horse-brass and tankard-framed bar (mains £12 to £18) dishes up locally sourced delights such as chargrilled Devonshire steak, steamed River Exe mussels and Branscombe crab sandwiches from noon to 2.15pm and 6.30pm to 9pm.

It's in the picturesque village of Branscombe, 2.5 miles west of Beer. The beach is a 20-minute walk away.

Drinking & Nightlife

Anchor   PUB
(☑ 01395-514129; www.theanchorinnsidmouth.co.uk; Old Ford St; ⊙11am-11pm) During Sidmouth's Folk Week festival in August, music overflows from the Anchor, with fiddlers, singers and accordion players creating a festival atmosphere, both inside and out. It's a great spot year-round, and a convivial place for a pint with the locals.

Hearty bar food is also served (mains £13, from 10am to 9pm).

ℹ Information

Sidmouth Tourist Office (☑ 01395-516441; www.visitsidmouth.co.uk; Ham Lane; ⊙10am-5pm Mon-Sat, to 4pm Sun May-Sep, 10am-1.30pm Mon-Sat Oct-Apr)

ℹ Getting There & Away

Beer Bus 899 (£5, 35 minutes, three daily Monday to Saturday)

Exeter Bus 9/9A (£6.70, 35 minutes, two per hour Monday to Saturday)

Beer

☑ 01297 / POP 1320

Set in a deep fissure in creamy-white cliffs, Beer manages to be both a proper working fishing village and thoroughly picturesque at the same time. Multicoloured, snub-nosed boats line its steeply sloping beach beside the winches and wires used to haul them ashore; deckchairs and crab pots lie scattered around. Water-filled leats and chalk- and flint-faced buildings frame the main street (Fore St). With its unusual cave networks, superb coast path and appealing places to stay and eat, the village is a charismatic base for East Devon explorations.

The picture-postcard-pretty village of Branscombe sits just 3 miles west, a ribbon of thatches, tearooms and pubs that meanders behind a cliff-backed beach called Branscombe Mouth.

⊙ Sights

★ **Beer Quarry Caves**   CAVE
(☑ 01297-680282; www.beerquarrycaves.co.uk; Quarry Lane, Beer; adult/child/family £8/6/25; ⊙10am-4.30pm Apr-Sep, to 3.30pm early-late Oct; P) Beer's creamy chalk cliffs hint at the presence of a seam of high-quality masonry material called Beer stone. It's been used in countless famous buildings, including 24 cathedrals, the Tower of London and Windsor Castle. The quarry has been worked since Roman times; tours see you donning a hard hat before being led into an evocative maze of quarry tunnels, some with 2000-year-old tool marks on the walls.

You'll also hear tales of smuggling, including those of 18th-century excise-dodger Jack Rattenbury, who snuck barrels of French brandy ashore and secreted them in the caves. The quarry was worked until the 1920s and evokes harsh working conditions: the incessant ringing of hammer and chisel gave rise to the phrase 'stone deaf'.

🏃 Activities

For the ultimate find-your-own-food experience, sign up for a mackerel fishing trip (adult/child £9/6 per hour) from Beer beach. A wheeled jetty is rolled partway into the sea, allowing you to hop aboard.

Paul   FISHING
(☑ 07779 040491; Beer beach; adult/child £9/6) Paul's hour-long trips out to sea will see you fishing for mackerel beside Beer's creamy-white cliffs.

Kim   FISHING
(☑ 07989 631321; Beer beach; adult/child £9/6) One of several fishers running angling trips out of Beer beach. The most likely catch? Silver- and blue-scaled mackerel.

THE GRAND WESTERN CANAL

Built in 1814, the stately 19th-century canal (☑01884-254072; www.devon.gov.uk/grandwesterncanal; Canal Hill, Tiverton; ℗) that meanders around the hills above Tiverton provides an intriguing insight into life on constructed inland waterways. Tub-boats carrying limestone from local quarries worked this waterway for 130 years before the network declined. This 11-mile stretch is all that's left. At the canal basin, a visitor centre (open daily from 9.30am to 4.30pm) charts its history.

The best way to explore is, of course, by boat. The boat hire centre (☑01884-253345; www.tivertoncanal.co.uk; The Wharf, Canal Hill; ⊙noon-3pm Tue-Sun May, Jun & Sep, 10.30am-3pm Sun-Fri Jul & Aug) rents out motor boats (two/four hours £65/85), row boats (one/four hours £15/30) and Canadian canoes (one/four hours £15/30).

Alternatively, Tiverton Canal Company (☑01884-253345; www.tivertoncanal.co.uk; The Wharf, Canal Hill; adult/child from £10.25/7.75; ⊙1-2 trips daily Tue-Sun May-Sep) runs endearingly old-fashioned trips in brightly painted, horse-drawn barges. Look out for moorhens, kingfishers, little grebes and roe deer, and take time to enjoy the sound of gurgling water and the clip-clopping of hooves along the bank as horses pull the boat along.

Afterwards, you can have lunch or afternoon tea in Ducks Ditty (☑01884-253345; www.tivertoncanal.co.uk; The Wharf, Canal Hill; snacks £3; ⊙noon-4pm Tue-Sun Apr-Oct), a sweet cafe in a converted canal boat by the wharf.

✗ Eating

Chapels   CAFE £
(snacks from £3; ⊙9am-5pm May-Oct) Set right on Beer's pebble beach and sandwiched between brightly coloured beach huts and picnic tables, Chapels rustles up all-day breakfasts, local crab sarnies, cakes and teas.

Seafood Platter   SEAFOOD ££
(☑01297-20099; www.theseafoodplatter.co.uk; Fore St; mains £13; ⊙noon-2pm & 6-9pm) A clue is in the name: net-fresh fish is the speciality at this appealing gastropub. The eponymous seafood platter (£70) to share between two comes crammed with local lobster and crab. Other dishes include herby roasted Lyme Bay sole and 28-day hung local steak.

Steamers   MODERN BRITISH ££
(☑01297-22922; www.steamersrestaurant.co.uk; New Cut; mains £12-20; ⊙noon-1.45pm & 7-9pm Tue-Sat) Produce from local hills and bays makes its way onto the innovative menu here. Classy creations include sautéed, curried crab and prawn cake; grilled brill with onion marmalade; and venison with a berry and sherry sauce. Plus some seriously sticky puddings.

☕ Drinking & Nightlife

Anchor Inn   PUB
(Fore St; ⊙11am-11pm) Surely one of the best sea-view beer gardens in Devon. The Anchor's grassy terrace stretches to the very cliff edge, providing views of the wide bay and fishing boats on the pebbly beach below.

🛍 Shopping

Beer Fish   FOOD
(☑01297-0297; Sea Hill; ⊙10am-3pm) In this tiny hut on the slipway to Beer beach, you'll find glistening, just-caught fish that's been landed only yards away. You can also opt for succulent cooked crab (£4 to £8) and lobster (£10 to £22), or prawns, cockles and welks at £3 per tub.

Woozie's   FOOD
(☑01297-20707; Fore St; ⊙9am-5pm) It's the perfect beach-picnic stop: counters are crammed full of flans, local cheeses, olives, fresh-baked bread, and tasty home-baked pasties and pies.

ℹ Getting There & Away

Bus 899 runs from Seaton to Beer (£2, seven minutes, nine services Monday to Friday, four Saturday); three services daily go on to Branscombe and Sidmouth.

Torquay & South Devon

Best Places to Eat

➡ Britannia @ the Beach (p88)

➡ Seahorse (p86)

➡ Elephant (p74)

➡ Riverford Field Kitchen (p81)

➡ Millbrook Inn (p89)

Best Beauty Spots

➡ Dartington Estate (p79)

➡ Dittisham (p97)

➡ Dawlish Warren (p78)

➡ Start Point (p88)

➡ The River Dart (p80)

Why Go?

South Devon is holiday heaven. At its core sits Torquay, a breezy, family-friendly resort with bundles of museums, unique attractions, stylish sleep spots and top-notch eateries. It's the place for boat trips and zoos, saucy postcards and fishing ports, palm trees and proms.

Outside the resort, the character changes. Paved esplanades give way to soaring cliffs, and amusement-backed beaches become untamed stretches of sand. In the neighbouring scenic South Hams, you'll discover chic yachting havens, prime surf breaks, hip eco-hang-outs, and villages and historic homes straight out of an Agatha Christie murder mystery. There are also some absolutely superb places to eat and stay, and plenty of activities: kayak up a tranquil creek; catch crabs on a harbour wall; or go barefoot beachcombing on a huge sweep of sand. No matter if you go resort or rural, you'll experience a cracking bit of coast either way.

When to Go

➡ **Easter, Jul & Aug** Accommodation is in especially high demand, beaches get busier. Book ahead for a restaurant table.

➡ **Jun–Aug** Regatta season brings a party atmosphere to Torquay and Dartmouth, and major music and literature festivals to Dartington, near Totnes.

➡ **Sep** Summer crowds melt away; accommodation bills edge down. Attractions remain open and the seas are at their warmest.

➡ **Oct** Dartmouth's food festival draws top-name chefs to the town.

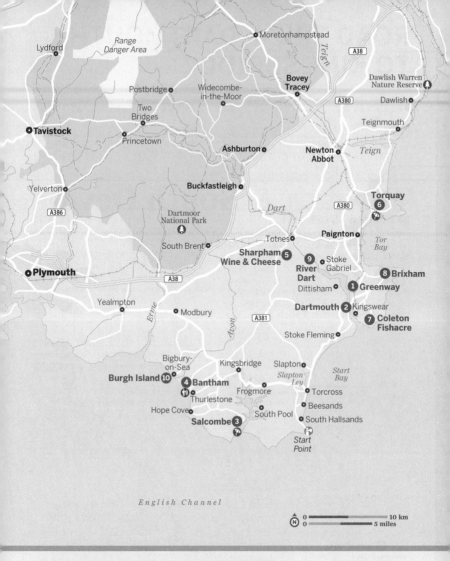

Torquay & South Devon Highlights

1 **Greenway** (p82) Cracking the clues at Agatha Christie's bewitching holiday home.

2 **Dartmouth** (p82) Gazing at gorgeous architecture in a picture-postcard-pretty port.

3 **Salcombe** (p92) Hopping on a ferry to a sandy cove from a yachting haven.

4 **Bantham** (p95) Learning to surf at a chilled-out bay.

5 **Sharpham Wine & Cheese** (p81) Drinking in lush views and sampling fine wines.

6 **Torquay** (p70) Revelling in seaside fun at an eco-zoo, model village and cave.

7 **Coleton Fishacre** (p86) Experiencing jazz-age glamour and luxuriant gardens.

8 **Brixham Fish Market** (p76) Enjoy a behind-the-scenes tour.

9 **River Dart** (p80) Escaping the crowds as you paddle to your own secret spot.

10 **Burgh Island** (p96) Riding the world's only sea tractor.

ROAD TRIP > DARTMOUTH TO KINGSBRIDGE

Head out along south Devon's postcard-worthy coastline, from historic Dartmouth via the sands of Slapton and Start Point's lighthouse to Kingsbridge.

❶ South Embankment

From Dartmouth's pretty **South Embankment**, turn right to head along a steep route revealing the gorgeous River Dart. You're headed to **Dartmouth Castle** (p83), a sturdy 14th-century fortification with displays revealing the port's connections to Chaucer's *Canterbury Tales*, and a high-tech evocation of an 18th-century gun drill. There's also a cafe

with grandstand views and, tucked into the cliffs just below, the diminutive Castle Cove, accessed by 100 steps.

Double-back on your drive slightly to Warfleet Pottery, where you'll fork left, onto the B3205 and then the A379 towards Torcross. Dogleg through quaint **Stoke Fleming**, emerging for buzzard's-eye views of Start Bay's scalloped coves. At **Blackpool Sands** (p84), perhaps pause for a swim; the cafe here is

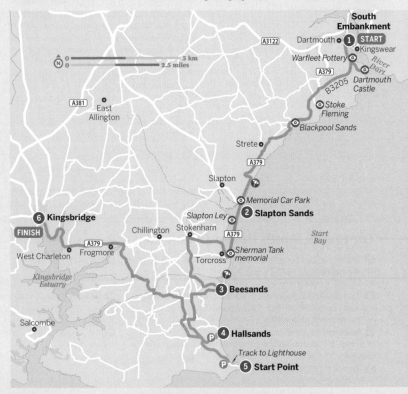

excellent and packed with local produce; it rents out SUPs and kayaks, too.

❷ Slapton Sands

Next drive up 16% gradients, around switchbacks, and along view-framed bends. After Strete's pastel-painted cottages, the 3-mile pebble ridge of Slapton Sands suddenly fills the windscreen; watery Slapton Ley is just behind. U-bends and a brake-burning descent lead to a glorious, flat, straight strip of land between sea and ley called the Slapton Line; persistent erosion could see it washed away within decades. Pull into the Memorial Car Park, then clatter down the pebbles to drink in long views at **Slapton Sands Beach**.

Next, stroll inland around reed-filled **Slapton Ley** (p87). Even just a short stroll from the entrance reveals a broad expanse of water, snaking trails and the first signs of birdlife. A better option is to take the circular 1¾-mile trail that edges the ley, heading past reed beds and twisted trees, where more wildlife is revealed as the road recedes behind; great crested grebes and otters are the highlights here. The trail leads to quaint Slapton village; walk along the lane into the village to emerge back at the car park.

Carry on along the A379 before pausing at the poignant WWII **Sherman Tank Memorial** (p87). This commemorates the 639 American servicemen who died on Slapton Sands in 1944, during training exercises for the D-Day invasions. Their boats were torpedoed by a German vessel.

❸ Beesands

Curl around the head of the ley, passing cottages and fields, before turning off towards **Beesands**. An ever-narrowing route through steep, twisting lanes spills you out at this ancient fishing village, which is strung out on a lobster- and crab-pot-lined shore. For lunch, **Britannia @ the Beach** (p88) offers excellent net-fresh seafood, while the Cricket Inn has more restaurant-style surroundings.

❹ South Hallsands

Once sated, it's back in the car and out of Beesands, heading to **South Hallsands**. Park, then stroll to the viewing platform to discover more startling evidence of this deeply eroded shore. To your right sits the huddled remains of an entire village, much of which was swept out to sea en mass one night in 1917 during a fierce storm. The waves claimed more than 23 properties but – miraculously – no lives. Although you can't walk among the ruins, the sepia images displayed tell the story well.

❺ Start Point

Then it's time to drive south to Start Point's windswept **lighthouse** (p88). Here you can join a tour that leads up hundreds of steps to the top – the final section is a clamber up a ladder into the optic chamber, a circular, glass-fronted bubble that houses the 815,000 candela bulbs. Looking north brings views down over the wide sweep of Start Bay, and across your route so far. You'll also look down on a sand and shell reef known as the Skerries – your guide may regale you with tales of Victorian boat trips onto these sometimes-tidal banks, where games of cricket are said to have been played.

❻ Kingsbridge

Leaving Start Point behind, navigate narrow lanes through a string of villages: Frogmore, East Charleton and West Charleton included, and past chequerboard fields and stretches of creek to **Kingsbridge**, an appealing market town that's a delight to explore. Heading up Fore St leads to independent bookshops, galleries and clothes shops, plus the **Cookworthy Museum** (p88), which is strong on agricultural artefacts and has an extensive photographic archive. Nearby you'll find the locals' favourite, the **Mangetout** (p89) cafe-deli, its counters piled high with salads, meats and more than 50 cheeses. Otherwise, head back towards the quayside for cheerful, quality eats at the Old Bakery or riverside pub food at the Crabshell.

TORQUAY & AROUND

It may face the English Channel rather than the Mediterranean but the coast around Torquay has long been dubbed the English Riviera, famous for its palm trees, piers and russet-red cliffs. At first glance Torquay itself is the quintessential English seaside resort in flux, beloved by both the coach-tour crowd and stag- and hen-party animals. But a mild microclimate and an azure circle of bay also draws a smarter set, and Torquay now competes with foodie-hub Dartmouth for fine eateries. The area boasts unique attractions that range from an immense aviary to a surreal model village. Add an Agatha Christie connection, fishing boats and steam trains, and it all adds up to some grand days out beside the sea.

Torquay's neighbouring resort **Paignton** sits 3 miles south. The fishing port of Brixham (p76) is 5 miles further south again.

Torquay

☑ 01803 / POP 114,270

Torquay has been a holiday hot spot since the French wars of the 18th century fired its development as a watering place; touring Europe at the time was suddenly not such a good idea. In the Victorian era, rows of sea-view villas popped up (look out for them still stacked up like dominoes on the steeply sloping hills), and the Prince of Wales bagged a few sailing victories in the regattas. The modern sailing incarnation, August's Torbay Regatta, still sees hundreds of vessels competing in races.

◉ Sights

★ Living Coasts   ZOO
(☑ 01803-202470; www.livingcoasts.org.uk; Beacon Quay; adult/child £12.20/9.15; ☺ 10am-5pm Apr-early Jul, Sep & Oct, to 6pm early Jul-Aug, to 4pm Nov-Mar; ℗) Clinging to the cliffs beside Torquay Harbour, the open-plan Living Coasts aviary brings you close to exotic birds. The immense enclosure features a series of underwater viewing tunnels and mocked-up microhabitats that include Penguin Beach, Auk Cliff and Fur Seal Cove.

The result is an up-close view of free-roaming penguins, punk-rocker-style tufted puffins and disarmingly cute bank cormorants. The Local Coasts feature reveals the starfish, bizarre-looking cuttlefish and appealing seahorses that inhabit the water just offshore.

For optimum squawking and waddling, time your visit to coincide with penguin breakfast (10.30am) or lunch (2.30pm).

★ Kents Cavern   TUNNEL
(☑ 01803-215136; www.kents-cavern.co.uk; 89 Ilsham Rd; adult/child £10/9; ☺ tours 10.30am-4pm; ℗) Expect stalactites to drip water on your head and temperatures to dip to 14°C in these atmospheric caves. Hour-long guided tours lead through a maze of uneven rusty-red tunnels linking rock galleries, arcades and chambers, some of which soar to impressive heights.

Bones found here revealed evidence of Torbay's prehistoric animals – cave lions, giant mammoths and sabre-tooth cats. There are also hyena lairs and cave-bear dens; look out for the skull of *Ursus deningeri* (Deninger's bear) embedded in the rock in the Water Gallery.

Kents Cavern is also the oldest recognisable human dwelling in Britain. Flint hand axes unearthed here have been dated to 450,000 years old, while a 35,000-year-old jawbone uncovered here is the oldest directly dated human bone in Britain.

★ Paignton Zoo   ZOO
(☑ 01803-697500;   www.paigntonzoo.org.uk; Totnes Rd, Paignton; adult/child £15.40/11.55; ☺ 10am-4pm Apr-Oct, to 3.30pm Nov-Mar; ℗) A conservation charity runs this innovative, 32-hectare zoo, where spacious enclosures recreate habitats as varied as savannah, wetland, tropical forest and desert. Highlights include the orangutan island, a vast glass-walled lion enclosure and a lemur wood, where you walk over a plank suspension bridge as the primates leap around in the surrounding trees. Then there's the steamy crocodile swamp with pathways winding over and beside Nile, Cuban and saltwater crocs, some up to 6m long.

★ Babbacombe Model Village   MUSEUM
(☑ 01803-315315; www.model-village.co.uk; Hampton Ave; adult/child £11/9; ℗) Thousands of tiny buildings and even tinier people pack an absorbing attraction chock-full of English eccentricity. The imagination and attention to detail is remarkable, with Lilliputian tableaux that are in turns witty, bizarre and unnerving. Open until 9pm some summer evenings.

Settings include a small-scale Stonehenge, a football stadium, a beach (complete with nude sunbathers), an animated circus,

TORQUAY & AGATHA CHRISTIE

Torquay is the birthplace of one-woman publishing phenomenon Dame Agatha Mary Clarissa Christie (1890–1976), a writer of murder mysteries who is beaten only by the Bible and William Shakespeare in terms of sales. Her characters are world famous: Hercule Poirot, the moustachioed, immodest Belgian detective; and Miss Marple, the surprisingly perceptive busybody spinster.

Born Agatha Miller in Torquay's Barton Rd, the young writer had her first piece published by the age of 11. By WWI she'd married Lieutenant Archie Christie and was working at the Red Cross Hospital in Torquay Town Hall, acquiring a knowledge of poisons that would lace countless plot lines, including that of her first novel, *The Mysterious Affair at Styles* (1920). Christie made her name with *The Murder of Roger Ackroyd* six years later with the use of what was then an innovative and cunning plot twist.

Then came 1926: in one year her mother died, Archie asked for a divorce and the writer mysteriously disappeared for 10 days, her abandoned car prompting a massive search. She was eventually discovered in a hotel in Harrogate, where she'd checked in under the name of the woman her husband wanted to marry. Christie always maintained she'd suffered amnesia; some critics saw it as a publicity stunt.

Christie later married archaeologist Sir Max Mallowan, and their trips to the Middle East provided masses of material for her work. By the time she died in 1976, Christie had written 75 novels and 33 plays.

Torquay's tourist office (p76) stocks the free *Agatha Christie Literary Trail* leaflet (also available to download from the website), which guides you around significant local sites. Torquay Museum has a fine collection of photos, handwritten notes and displays devoted to Christie's famous detectives. The highlight, though, is Greenway (p82), the author's summer home near Dartmouth. Get there via the ferry from Dartmouth (p86) or take the steam train from Paignton (p73) to Greenway Halt, from where it's a half-mile walk through the woods to the house itself.

TORQUAY & SOUTH DEVON TORQUAY

a castle (under attack from a fire-breathing dragon) and a thatched village where firefighters are tackling a blaze. Visit in the evening for illuminations; think Piccadilly Circus, complete with flashing banner ads.

Torquay Museum MUSEUM
(📞 01803-293975; www.torquaymuseum.org; 529 Babbacombe Rd; adult/child £6.45/4; ⏰ 10am-4pm Mon-Sat) The collection at Torquay's town museum is eclectic, taking in everything from samurai suits of armour to Egyptian mummies and taxidermied butterflies. The highlight is the intriguing collection of Agatha Christie ephemera, including handwritten notes, photos and display cases devoted to the murder-mystery author's famous detectives, as well as a recreation of Hercule Poirot's art deco study.

Cockington Country Park PARK
(📞 01803-520022; www.countryside-trust.org.uk; Cockington, Torquay; 🅿) **FREE** At 182 hectares, Cockington provides a welcome oasis of calm, green space, just a mile from Torquay's seafront bustle. Walking trails wind through fields, woods and parkland surrounding a

17th-century manor house, a walled garden and craft studios.

A heavily thatched village comes complete with forge, mill, gamekeeper's cottage, 14th-century church and an architectural rarity: a thatched pub designed by Sir Edwin Lutyens, the 1936 Drum Inn (p74).

Check to see if there's a match taking place on Cockington's cricket pitch (summer weekends offer the best chance).

Torre Abbey Gardens GARDENS
(📞 01803-293593; www.torre-abbey.org.uk; King's Dr; adult/child £4/3; ⏰ 10am-5pm Easter-Sep) The gardens here feature the Potent Plant plot, a collection of species which can be used to make the poisons that feature in local crime writer Agatha Christie's novels. Particularly deadly are the prunus family (its fruit stones can be used to make one of Christie's favourites: cyanide), foxglove and monkshood.

Paignton Pier AMUSEMENT PARK
(📞 01803-522139; www.paigntonpier.co.uk; Paignton Sands, Paignton; ⏰ 24hr) **FREE** To indulge in pure holiday nostalgia, head to this grand old Victorian pier where you can

Torquay

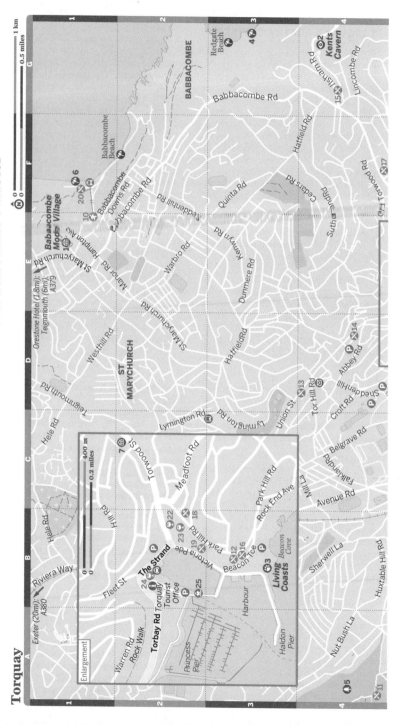

0   0.5 miles
0   1 km

BABBACOMBE

Redgate Beach

4 🏊

2 ◎ **Kents Cavern**

15 🛏

Lincombe Rd

Babbacombe Rd

Babbacombe Beach

6 🏊 ✕ 20 🍴 11

Babbacombe Model Village

19 🏬 10

Hatfield Rd

Cedars Rd

Sutherland Rd

Lwr Forwood Rd

17 ✕

Quinta Rd

Kenwyn Rd

Dunmere Rd

Fernham Ave

Babbacombe Downs Rd

Babbacombe Rd

Manor Rd

Reddenhill Rd

St Marychurch Rd

Warbro Rd

Orestone Hotel (1.8mi); Teignmouth (6mi); A379

St Marychurch Rd

ST MARYCHURCH

Westhill Rd

Hele Rd

Teignmouth Rd

Hatfield Rd

Hatfield Rd

Lymington Rd

Lymington Rd

13 ✕

Union St

Tor Hill Rd

14 ✕

Abbey Rd

P

P

Sheddenhill

Croft Rd

P

Belgrave Rd

Falkland Rd

Avenue Rd

Mill La

Sherwell La

Huxtable Hill Rd

Nut Bush La

Enlargement

0   0.2 miles
0   400 m

Torwood St

7 🏬

Meadfoot Rd

H Ill Rd

Park Hill Rd

Rock End Ave

22 ✕

18 ✕

23 🍴 19 ✕

Beacon Tce

12 ✕ 16 ✕

3 ◎ **Living Coasts**

Beacon Cove

The Strand

24

P

Victoria Pde

Park Hill Rd

Fleet St

25 ✕

Torquay Tourist Office 🛈

P

Torbay Rd

Warren Rd

Rock Walk

Riviera Way

Exeter (20mi); A380

Harbour

Princess Pier

Haldon Pier

5 ★

1 ✕

N

Torquay

◎ Top Sights
1 Babbacombe Model Village	E1
2 Kents Cavern	G4
3 Living Coasts	B3

◎ Sights
4 Anstey's Cove	G3
5 Cockington Country Park	A4
6 Oddicombe Beach	F1
7 Torquay Museum	C2
8 Torre Abbey Gardens	C5
9 Torre Abbey Sands	C5

⊕ Activities, Courses & Tours
10 Babbacombe Cliff Railway	E1

⊗ Eating
11 Drum Inn	A4
12 Elephant	B3
13 Gemelli	D4
14 Green Leaf Café	D4
15 Me & Mrs Jones	G4
16 Number 7	B3
17 Old Vienna	F4
18 Orange Tree	B2
19 Rockfish	B2
20 Three Degrees West	F1

◯ Drinking & Nightlife
21 CoCo	D5
22 Foundry	B2
23 Hole in the Wall	B2
24 Soho	B2

ⓘ Transport
25 Western Lady Departure Point	B2

parade along the long wooden deck, jump in a dodgem, bounce around on a trampoline and have a game of crazy golf.

🏃 Activities

Torquay boasts no fewer than 20 beaches and an impressive 22 miles of coast. Tidal **Torre Abbey Sands** (Torbay Rd) is central; locals head for the sand-and-shingle beaches beside the 73m red-clay cliffs at **Oddicombe Beach**; and sea swimmers love picturesque **Anstey's Cove**.

★**Dartmouth Steam Railway**　RAIL
(☏ 01803-555872; www.dartmouthrailriver.co.uk; Torbay Rd, Paignton; adult/child/family return £17/10/46; ☉ 4-9 trains daily mid-Feb–Oct) Chugging from seaside Paignton to the beautiful banks of the River Dart, these vintage trains roll back the years to the age of steam. The 7-mile, 30-minute journey puffs past Goodrington Sands, stopping at Greenway Halt

(near Agatha Christie's former home), then the village of Kingswear, where ferries shuttle across to picturesque Dartmouth.

The service is run by the Dartmouth Steam Railway & Riverboat Company (p84). It operates a wealth of other trips, including coastal cruises and excursions on a paddle steamer; see website for full round-up.

Babbacombe Cliff Railway RAIL
(☑ 01803-328750; www.babbacombecliffrailway. co.uk; Babbacombe Downs Rd; adult/child return £2.50/2; ☺ 9.30am-4.30pm Feb-Oct) Babbacombe's glorious 1920s funicular railway sees you climbing into a tiny carriage and rattling up and down rails set into the cliff.

✯✯ Festivals & Events

Torbay Royal Regatta SAILING
(www.torbayroyalregatta.co.uk; ☺ Aug) One of the most popular sailing regattas on the south coast, Torbay's regatta attracts hundreds of competitors. Racing vessels range from yachts and keel boats to rowing. The horseshoe-shaped bay delivers plenty of vantage points, while funfairs and fireworks ensure amusements ashore, too.

✗ Eating

Me & Mrs Jones CAFE £
(☑ 01803-298745; www.meandmrsjonesdeli.com; 11 Ilsham Rd; dishes from £6; ☺ 8am-5.30pm Mon-Fri, 9am-4pm Sat) In this chilled-out cafe-deli, twinkling fairy lights are strung above a scattering of upcycled tables surrounded by gourmet goodies: organic sourdough, 'squealer' (pork) pies, flavoursome salads, quality charcuterie and oozing cheeses.

The punchy coffee, flaky croissants, French toast and granola may mean that even if you've had breakfast, you'll still want brunch.

Three Degrees West BISTRO £
(☑ 01803-311202; www.oddicombebeach.co.uk; Beach Rd, Oddicombe Beach; snacks & light meals £3-9; ☺ 9am-5pm) Sandwiched between the seafront and crumbling russet-red cliffs, the terrace of this bar-bistro has uninterrupted views of the waves. The menu spans everything from chips, burgers and cakes to tapas and griddled sardines.

Green Leaf Café CAFE £
(☑ 01803-293207; www.greenleafcafe.co.uk; 22 Lower Union Lane; mains £4-10; ☺ 10am-2.30pm Mon-Sat; ☑) This humble wholefood cafe is a local's favourite for brunch or lunch, offering

tempting treats such as jerk chicken wraps, yummy burgers and copious jacket spuds. There are lots of options for vegetarians, too. It's as cheap as chips, and the vibe is cheery.

★ Elephant MODERN BRITISH ££
(☑ 01803-200044; www.elephantrestaurant.co.uk; 3 Beacon Tce; lunch 2/3 courses £17/20, dinner mains £16-25; ☺ noon-2pm & 6.30-9pm Tue-Sat) This fine-dining beauty remains Torquay's premier foodie destination – and the proud possessor of a Michelin star. Chef Simon Hulstone's taste for seasonal food, prime Devon ingredients and elaborate presentation is firmly in evidence, with dishes such as smoked vodka sea trout gravlax, hake with eel butter and rhubarb with champagne jelly.

The eight-course tasting menu (£68) is a treat; match it with wine for an extra £29.

Rockfish SEAFOOD ££
(☑ 01803-212175; www.therockfish.co.uk; 20 Victoria Pde; mains £12-20; ☺ noon-9.30pm) The Torquay branch of award-winning chef Mitch Tonks' minichain of seafood restaurants showcases his taste for relaxed catch-of-the-day dining. Whitewashed wood and nautical knick-knacks give a shipshape ambience, while the food takes in everything from classic fish and chips and monkfish scampi to chargrilled seafood platters and seaweedy tartare sauce. For Devon lobster, preorder.

Old Vienna EUROPEAN ££
(☑ 01803-380180; www.oldvienna.co.uk; 7 Lisburne Sq; mains £15-20; ☺ 7-9pm Tue-Sun) It may be run by an engaging Austrian, but plenty of local produce finds its way onto the tables at this acclaimed, intimate eatery. The result is an unusual menu where Brixham crab, confit duck and scallops sit alongside sauerkraut, wild boar and Linzertorte.

Drum Inn PUB FOOD ££
(☑ 01803-690264; www.vintageinn.co.uk/thedrum inncockington; Cockington Village, Torquay; mains £7-20; ☺ noon-8.30pm) This thatched pub, designed by architect Sir Edwin Lutyens, is an atmospheric spot in which to tuck into classy pub grub – think seared sea bass and slow-cooked ham hock – or crispy pizzas and fries.

Gemelli ITALIAN ££
(☑ 01803-294183; www.gemellirestaurant.co.uk; 172 Union St; pizzas £7-9, mains £12-16; ☺ 6.30-9pm Wed-Mon, plus noon-2pm Mon & Wed-Fri; ☑) At this snug family-run restaurant, goodies

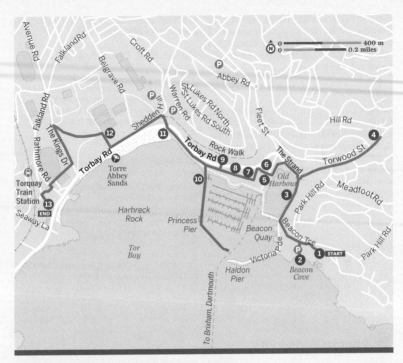

Walking Tour
Agatha Christie's Torquay

START IMPERIAL HOTEL
END GRAND HOTEL
DISTANCE 2 MILES
DURATION THREE HOURS
DIFFICULTY EASY

Torquay is dotted with locations linked to the life and works of famous crime writer Agatha Christie. Crack the clues on this tour.

Begin your deductions with a drink on the terrace of the **1 Imperial Hotel** – Christie's fictional detective Miss Marple would choose tea and Poirot a tisane. This fine establishment appears in three Christie novels. Next take a peep at the waters of **2 Beacon Cove**, where Agatha had to be rescued from drowning as a girl. Stroll beside the **3 Old Harbour**, past souvenir shops and boards promoting boat trips, before heading up Torwood St to **4 Torquay Museum** (p71). Here you can take in the evocative displays in the Agatha Christie Gallery. Look out for the story of how she worked in the resort first as a nurse during WWI, then as a pharmacy dispenser – which is where she acquired that

famous knowledge of poisons. Back at the harbour, cut in beside the **5 tourist office** (p76) – there's more Christie merchandise inside – and past the **6 Christie bust**, which was put up to commemorate her centenary year. Next comes the **7 Pavilion**; now a shadow of its former glory, it was here that Archie Christie proposed to Agatha at a classical-music concert in 1913. Neighbouring **8 Princess Gardens** crops up in *The ABC Murders*. As **9 Rock Walk** rears steeply on the right, divert left onto the late-Victorian **10 Princess Pier**, one of Agatha's favourite childhood roller-skating spots. At **11 Torre Abbey Sands**, turn inland, strolling past tennis courts and pitch 'n' putt greens to **12 Torre Abbey Gardens** (p71), where you'll discover plants that can be used to produce the poisons that feature in Christie's plots. Next cut down beside more playing fields, past the train station to end at the suitably named **13 Grand Hotel**. This is where Agatha honeymooned with first husband Archie after they married secretly on Christmas Eve in 1914. Time, perhaps, for another cup of tea.

range from authentic pizzas and golden pasta to dishes mixing local produce with a dash of the Med – look out for Devon fillet steak with prawn and mushroom sauce, and baked sea bass with pesto.

The extensive meat-free menu will make vegetarians smile.

Orange Tree MODERN BRITISH **££**
(📞 01803-213936; www.orangetreerestaurant. co.uk; 14 Park Hill Rd; mains £15-27; ⏰ 7-9pm Tue-Sat) English meets European cuisine here in dishes majoring on local fish, meat and game. Prepare to enjoy sweet-potato gnocchi with rich Devon Blue cheese, chicken with spicy chorizo, and South Devon beef steaks with a Madeira and mushroom sauce.

Number 7 SEAFOOD **££**
(📞 01803-295055; www.no7-fish.com; 7 Beacon Tce; mains £14; ⏰ noon-1.45pm Wed-Sat year-round, plus 7-9pm daily Jul-Sep, Tue-Sat Oct-Jun) No-fuss fish is the order of the day at this small family-run bistro. Superfresh crab, lobster, scallops and cod steaks can be seared, grilled or roasted, and laced with garlic butter or dusted with Moroccan spices.

🍸 Drinking & Nightlife

Soho COCKTAIL BAR
(www.sohotorquay.co.uk; 1 Palk St; ⏰ 5pm-2.30am) DJ sets, gloriously over-the-top decor, neon-lit bars, 80 cocktails and friendly staff keep the party crowd happy at this harbourside spot.

Foundry CLUB
(📞 01803-213903; www.thefoundrytorquay.com; Torwood St; ⏰ hours vary) Set in the historic Scala buildings, the Foundry sits in a cluster of clubs hosting top-flight DJs, acoustic acts and bands.

Hole in the Wall PUB
(📞 01803-200755; www.holeinthewalltorquay. co.uk; 6 Park Lane; ⏰ 11am-11pm) A heavily beamed Tardis-like boozer with a tiny terrace; an atmospheric spot for a pint.

CoCo COCKTAIL BAR
(www.cocotorquay.co.uk; 1 Abbey Cres; 5pm-midnight Mon-Fri, 11am-midnight Sat & Sun) Balearic beats, classy cocktails and a sea-view terrace.

ℹ Information

English Riviera (www.englishriviera.co.uk) Guide to Torquay, Paignton and Brixham.
Torquay Tourist Office (📞 01803-211211; www.theenglishriviera.co.uk; 5 Vaughan Pde;

⏰ 10am-5pm Mon-Sat, to 3pm Sun) Main branch by the central harbour.

ℹ Getting There & Away

BOAT
Between April and September the *Western Lady*, run by the Dartmouth Steam Railway (p84), shuttles between Torquay and Brixham (one way/return £2/3, 35 minutes, one to two per hour).

BUS
Services from Torquay bus station (Lymington Rd):
Brixham Bus 12 (£4.30, 45 minutes, half-hourly) runs via Paignton.
Totnes Stagecoach Gold (£3.70, 45 minutes) runs half-hourly to hourly. From Totnes bus X64 goes on to Dartmouth.

TAXI
Taxi ranks include those by the central harbour and outside Torquay train station.

TRAIN
Trains run from Exeter St David's to Torquay (£12, 45 minutes, half-hourly to hourly) and on to Paignton (£12.30, 52 minutes).

Brixham

📞 01803 / POPULATION 17,460
An appealing, pastel-painted tumbling of fisher cottages leads down to Brixham's horseshoe harbour, where arcades and gift shops coexist with winding streets, brightly coloured boats and one of England's busiest fishing ports. Although picturesque, Brixham is far from a neatly packaged resort, and its brand of gritty charm offers an insight into work-a-day life along Devon's coast.

◎ Sights

⭐ **Fish Market** FOOD & DRINK
(www.englishriviera.co.uk; The Quay; tours incl breakfast £15; ⏰ Apr-Oct) Life in Brixham revolves around the fish market. You get behind-the-scenes insights on these tours, which take in ice-lined fish trays, white-coated buyers and a bustling auction, before enjoying a fishy breakfast at nearby restaurant Rockfish. Tours start at 6am. They're hugely popular – book well in advance.

Golden Hind SHIP
(📞 01803-856223; www.goldenhind.co.uk; The Quay; adult/child/family £7/5/18; ⏰ 10.30am-4pm Mar-Oct) Devon explorer Sir Francis Drake

carried out a treasure-seeking circum-navigation of the globe aboard the *Golden Hind* in the late 1500s. This full-sized replica sees you crossing the gangplank, clambering below decks, peering into the captain's cabin and prowling around the poop deck.

Brixham Heritage
Museum MUSEUM
(☑ 01803-856267; www.brixhamheritage.org.uk; New Rd; ⊙ 10am-4pm Tue-Fri, to 1pm Sat Apr-Oct) ⬛FREE An eclectic collection of exhibits explores the town's salty history, majoring in sailboats, smuggling, shipbuilding and sea rescues. There are reconstructions of a fisher's cottage and a police cell, but it's the sepia-tinted photos of the town's past that steal the imagination.

 Activities

Funfish FISHING
(Sea Spray III; ☑ 07711 042229; www.funfishtrips. co.uk; The Quay; adult/child £15/10; ⊙ 9am-6pm Apr-Oct) These two-hour trips see you setting out from Brixham Harbour to a prime mackerel fishing ground to try your luck with a rod and line.

✖ Eating

Curious Kitchen CAFE **£**
(☑ 01803-854816; www.thecuriouskitchen.co.uk; 16 Middle St; mains £8-10; ⊙ 9am-4pm daily, 7-9pm Fri & Sat; ☑) There's a firm emphasis on homemade and healthy in this hip hangout, which means menus full of smashed avocado, baked eggs, rice-paper wraps, beef brisket and mezze are also graced by housemade peanut butter, ketchup and granola. The coffee, roasted in Cornwall, is cracking.

Booking is required for three-course evening meals (£15); they're worth it.

David Walker & Son SEAFOOD **£**
(☑ 01803-882097; www.davidwalkerandson.com; Unit B, Fish Market; ⊙ 9am-3pm Mon-Fri, 8am-1pm Sat) Fish doesn't get any fresher than at Mr Walker's fish stall, where all the catches of the day are piled high on beds of ice. Crab, lobster, skate, hake, sea bass... There's no telling which little fishy you'll find for your dishy.

Poop Deck SEAFOOD **££**
(☑ 01803-858681; www.poopdeckrestaurant.com; 14 The Quay; mains £15-19; ⊙ noon-2.30pm Fri-Sun, 6-9.30pm Tue-Sun) It can be hard to decide at Poop Deck: the catch of the day is landed just yards away, so it's tempting to have it simply grilled with garlic-butter or olive oil; or opt for the Dover sole with brandy sauce. But you don't want to miss the hot shellfish platter (£30), or a steaming pile of lobster, crevettes, scallops and crab...

Lunchtime specials are a bargain (£6 to £8); the Brixham fish soup is a creamy treat.

Beamers SEAFOOD **££**
(☑ 01803-854777; www.beamersrestaurant.co.uk; 19 The Quay; mains £18-25; ⊙ 6.30-9pm Wed-Mon; ☑) The fish you'll tuck into at this popular local bistro is selected by the chef-owner that morning from the nearby market. Supremely fresh offerings might include brill and monkfish dusted with pesto powder, or roasted wild sea bass with Pernod cream.

🍷 Drinking & Nightlife

Maritime PUB
(www.themaritime.co.uk; 79 King St; ⊙ 7-11pm) Eccentric old boozer decorated with thousands of key rings, stone jugs and chamber pots, presided over by a chatty parrot called Mr Tibbs.

ℹ Getting There & Away

BOAT
The **Dartmouth Steam Railway** (p84) ferry, the *Western Lady*, runs between Brixham Harbour and Torquay (one way/return £2/3, 35 minutes, one to two per hour, April to September).

BUS
Kingswear Bus 18 (£3.40, 15 minutes, half-hourly to hourly) connects from Brixham. **Higher Ferry** (p86) connections continue from Kingswear to Dartmouth.
Torquay Bus 12 (£4.30, 45 minutes, half-hourly), via Paignton.

Teignmouth
☑ 01626 / POP 124,200
Hugging the shore where the River Teign meets the sea, Teignmouth has all the trappings of a traditional resort. Georgian terraces back a seafront lined with rough red-gold sand, and a classic Victorian pier juts proudly out to sea. But the town has another side: home to a small port, its network of lanes, lined by candy-coloured fishers' sheds and seafarers' pubs, lends the place a bustling, nautical air.

TEIGNMOUTH TO DAWLISH WARREN

The 6-mile stretch of coast between Teignmouth and the nature reserve at Dawlish Warren is edged by red sandstone cliffs that have been eroded into a series of bizarre stacks, coves and undulating headlands. Here the coast path is sandwiched between the sea and a train line that is itself squeezed in alongside rocks. It makes for an atmospheric hike – taking the coast path north out of Teignmouth actually involves walking on the sea wall. About a mile along, the trail cuts sharply inland, skirting the striking Parson and Clerk rock formation, before descending steeply to the seafront at the resort of Dawlish, a mile further on. Look out for the weirdly shaped Horse, Old Maid and Cowhole rocks on the way. From Dawlish, a 2-mile stroll leads past deeply eroded russet cliffs, a wide beach and a cluster of fairground rides to the Dawlish Warren Nature Reserve.

If the walk back seems too much, you could ride the route instead: there are train stations at Dawlish Warren, Dawlish and Teignmouth. Trains tend to call roughly hourly (£3.50, 12 minutes), but times vary, so it's best to check ahead.

Sights & Activities

Dawlish Warren WILDLIFE RESERVE
(www.dawlishwarren.co.uk; The Warren; P) Clinging to the coast at the mouth of the River Exe, a curling sand spit reaches far out into the water, offering exhilarating views up the river and out to sea. The variety of habitats ranges from dunes and grasslands to salt marshes and mudflats, attracting flocks of wildfowl and wading birds.

You can walk to Dawlish Warren from Teignmouth along the coast path; trains shuttle between the two roughly hourly (£3.50, 12 minutes), but times vary so it's best to check. It's 5 miles north of Teignmouth.

Teignmouth & Shaldon Museum MUSEUM
(Teign Heritage Centre; 01626-777041; www.teignheritage.org.uk; 29 French St; adult/child £2.50/free; 10am-5pm Tue-Sat Apr-Sep, to 4.30pm Mar & Oct) It's as far from a fusty old museum as you can get, with engaging exhibits filling a stylish new building. Step into a Victorian bathing machine, heft a cannonball and try your hand at Punch 'n' Judy. Look out for cannons from a 16th-century Venetian shipwreck, and displays on Admiral Pellew, the inspiration for author CS Forester's *Hornblower* series of novels.

Teign Ferry FERRY
(07896-711822; www.teignmouthshaldonferry. co.uk; Back Beach; adult/child return £3/1.40; 8am-dusk mid-Jul–Aug, to 6pm Apr–mid-Jul, Sep & Oct, to 4.30pm Nov-Mar) The open-topped Teign Ferry shuttles from Teignmouth to the appealing village of **Shaldon** on the south bank of the Teign. The ferry service began life around the 10th century, but the distinctive black-and-white colour scheme of the current boat is Elizabethan. Departures from Teignmouth's River (or Back) Beach, just behind the Point (seafront) car park. The schedule can be weather-affected; times are posted on beachside boards.

It's an evocative crossing. You embark by walking up a gangplank, and the voyage brings a crumbling, red headland ever closer. Once in Shaldon, hunt out Ness Beach, accessed via a smugglers' tunnel that's been hacked out of the rock.

Eating

⭐**Blue Hut** SEAFOOD £
(07814-177307; www.theteigncanteen.com; Back Beach; snacks from £3; 9am-5pm May-Sep) This new arrival may look like the kind of shack that just sells cockles and mussels, but you'll get real street-food rarities here. To the crab and lobster landed just yards away add Teign Valley sand eels and wild venison; treatments range from burgers to Asian noodle soup.

Crab Shack SEAFOOD ££
(01626-777956; www.crabshackonthebeach. co.uk; Back Beach; mains £10-20; noon-3pm & 6-9pm Wed-Sun) The location couldn't be better for superfresh fish: Crab Shack overlooks the sheltered Teign estuary, and the fleet that brought your supper ashore. The restaurant even owns a couple of fishing boats. Grab a table on the lobster-pot-framed terrace, then feast on *moules* (mussels), whole grilled lobster or a bucket of garlic-roasted crab claws.

Owl & the Pussycat MODERN BRITISH ££

(01626-775321; www.theowlandpussycat.co.uk; 3 Teign St; mains £18-22; ⊗6-9pm Mon-Sat & noon-2pm Sat) A stylish, crisp restaurant that's brimming with West Country produce. South Devon beef is combined with truffle oil; Creedy Carver duck gets infused with garlic and honey; and smoked duck comes with pickled fennel and pear.

🍷 Drinking & Nightlife

Ship Inn PUB

(✔01626-772674; www.shipteignmouth.co.uk; 2 Queen St; ⊗11am-11pm) Rustic tables and beams help make the mellow Ship one of the most atmospheric pubs in town; its beers (including two local Otter Ales) are well kept, too. On a summer's evening the waterside terrace is perfect for enjoying tasty pub grub (mains from £9; noon to 2.30pm and 6pm to 9pm), a tangy pint and memorable sunset views.

ⓘ Information

Teignmouth Tourist Office (✔01626-215665; www.visitsouthdevon.co.uk; Den Cres; ⊗10am-3pm Mon-Sat) An information point, inside the Pavilions Theatre.

ⓘ Getting There & Away

BUS

Exeter Bus 2 (£2.10, one hour, one to two per hour daily).

Torquay Bus 22 (£4.90, 40 minutes, seven daily).

TRAIN

Exeter £4.30, 30 minutes, half-hourly.

Torquay £5.70, 20 minutes, half-hourly to hourly.

SOUTH DEVON

Totnes

✔01803 / POP 8040

Totnes has such a reputation for being alternative that local jokers wrote 'twinned with Narnia' under the town sign. For decades famous as Devon's hippie haven, ecoconscious Totnes also became Britain's first 'transition town' in 2005, when it began to wean itself off a dependence on oil. Sustainability aside, Totnes boasts a tempting vineyard, a sturdy Norman castle and a mass of fine Tudor buildings, and is the springboard for a range of outdoor activities.

History

The Normans built a castle here in the 11th century, realising that access to the River Dart lent Totnes a strategic importance. Tudor times brought wealth through the tin trade; one legacy of this is the 60 merchants' houses lining the main streets. Totnes' transition to an alternative hub began in 1925 when Dorothy and Leonard Elmhirst bought the nearby Dartington Estate, setting up an experiment in rural regeneration and a progressive school. Dartington College of Arts opened in 1961, reinforcing the town's New Age image. The college decamped to Falmouth in 2010, but the pioneering environmental movement, Transition Town Totnes, continues the sustainability theme.

◉ Sights

Dartington Estate HISTORIC SITE

(✔01803-847000; www.dartington.org; ⊗gardens dawn-dusk, visitor centre 9am-5pm; P) FREE Henry VIII gave this pastoral 324-hectare estate to two of his wives (Catherines Howard and Parr). For many years it was home to the town's art college; now the 14th-century manor house hosts events, including renowned classical-music and literature festivals. There's also an art-house cinema, shops, a decent pub and B&B accommodation. The grounds are also worth exploring. It's about 2 miles northwest of Totnes.

Dartington's 14th-century manor house edges a grassy space reminiscent of an Oxbridge quadrangle. In the landscaped gardens impressive terraced banks frame an area known as the Tiltyard, while flower-filled borders lead down to glades, meadows and thatched cottages. Amid the tiny paths and secret benches you can hunt out Henry Moore's carved stone sculpture *Memorial Figure*, the swirling bobbles of Peter Randall Page's *Jacob's Pillow* and the bronze *Donkey* by Willi Soukop. The Japanese Garden, complete with raked gravel and cedar-wood shelter, is beside the ruined church.

Totnes Castle CASTLE

(EH; ✔01803-864406; www.english-heritage.org. uk; Castle St; adult/child £4/2.40; ⊗10am-6pm Apr-Sep, to 5pm Oct, to 4pm Sat & Sun Nov-Mar)

The outer keep of Totnes' Norman motte-and-bailey fortress crowns a hill at the top of town, providing engrossing views over higgledy-piggledy rooftops and the river valley. Look out for the medieval toilet, too (but don't use it).

Elizabethan Garden   GARDENS

(Fore St; ☺9am-5pm) **FREE** Signs in this tiny walled garden cast light on 16th-century medical thinking, outlining which herbs were used to cure which ailment: soapwort for syphilis, woad to staunch bleeding and bay for bee stings. It's accessed via an easy-to-miss gate and cobbled alley at the side of the Totnes Elizabethan Museum.

🏃 Activities

★ Totnes Kayaks   KAYAKING

(☑07799 403788; www.totneskayaks.co.uk; The Quay, Stoke Gabriel; per half-/full day £30/40; ☺10am-5pm Fri-Sun Apr-Jun, Sep & Oct, daily Jul & Aug) The best way to explore the River Dart is to head to sleepy Stoke Gabriel, 5 miles southeast of Totnes, from where you can paddle out between unspoilt hills. Go with the tide (owner Tom will advise); it may take you upriver to Sharpham Vineyard and Totnes, or downriver to Dittisham. It's gorgeous either way.

★ Dynamic Adventures   ADVENTURE SPORTS

(Map p110; ☑01803-862725; www.dynamic adventurescic.co.uk; Park Rd, Dartington Hall) The superb activities on offer include canoeing and kayaking (per half-/full day £35/70) and sea kayaking (from £75), as well as caving (per half-day £35), rock climbing and archery (both per hour £15). Booking is required.

It's based 2 miles northwest of Totnes on the Dartington Estate.

South Devon Steam Railway   RAIL

(☑01364-644370; www.southdevonrailway.co.uk; adult/child return £15/9; ☺Apr-Oct) Train enthusiasts rejoice: this quaint steam railway chuffs along a superbly scenic stretch of track from Totnes to Buckfastleigh, on the edge of Dartmoor. There are nine trains a day in summer, dropping to three in spring and autumn, and only certain days in winter. Tickets stay valid all day.

Canoe Adventures   CANOEING

(☑07706 343744; www.canoeadventures.co.uk; adult/child £28/20; ☺Apr-Oct) 🛶 Voyages in 12-seater Canadian canoes. The monthly moonlit paddles are a treat.

★★ Festivals & Events

Ways with Words   LITERATURE

(☑01803-867373; www.wayswithwords.co.uk; Dartington Estate; ☺Jul) Key authors attend this classy lit fest, where venues include the Tudor Great Hall and the restored Barn. The central grassy courtyard is dotted with book signings, food stalls, and people reading and chatting in deckchairs.

**Dartington International
Summer School & Festival**   MUSIC

(☑01803-847070; www.dartington.org/summer-school; Dartington Estate; ☺from late Jul) Courses at this month-long festival include everything from composition and orchestral conducting to vocal techniques and piano skills. Around three public concerts a day are also held; expect early music and full-blown opera, as well as tango, junk music and tea dances.

HISTORIC TOTNES

Totnes has one of the best collections of Tudor architecture in Devon, with impressive buildings lining its steep, central High and Fore Sts. Towards the top, where Castle St meets High St, look out for Poultry Walk. This wonky row of Tudor jettied buildings, propped up by an array of columns, was where the town's poultry market was once held. Downhill, on the left, the 16th-century Butterwalk used to shelter dairy markets. Many of the houses have elaborate Tudor plasterwork ceilings; two of the best preserved are at Bogan House, in the **Totnes Fashion & Textile Museum** (☑01803-862857; info@totnesfashionandtextiles museum.org.uk; 43 High St; adult/child £2.50/1; ☺11am-5pm Tue-Fri mid-May–Sep).

Church Close cuts sharply left off the High St, leading beside the 15th-century red sandstone St Mary's Church. Hidden in behind is the ancient **Guildhall** (☑01803-862147; www.totnestowncouncil.gov.uk; Ramparts Walk; entry by donation; ☺11am-3pm Mon-Fri). Ramparts Walk curves around the church, tracing the line of the original Saxon town boundary. At the bottom of Fore St, Bank Lane features an ornate, lemon-yellow 18th-century house built in a style known as Strawberry Hill Gothic.

✖ Eating

It's all about local dining here: the town is passionate about the produce on its doorstep, and you'll find it championed on every menu.

Green Table BISTRO £
(www.dartington.org; Dartington Estate; dishes £5-9; ☺9am-5pm Sun-Thu, to 8pm Fri & Sat; 🛜🖉) 🖉 It's the ethos and ingredients that make this stylish, light-filled bistro stand out. Creations from local craftspeople line the shelves, while plates are filled with locally sourced, seasonal, often organic food.

Daily-changing menus might feature chard torte, pesto-drizzled lamb and spelt stew, or meat or vegetable tasting plates.

Willow VEGETARIAN £
(☑01803-862605; 87 High St; mains £6-10; ☺10am-5pm Mon-Sat, plus 6.30-9pm Wed, Fri & Sat; 🖉) 🖉 Firmly occupying a warm place in the heart of Totnes' alternative crowd, Willow is a long-established veggie, vegan and wholefood cafe. Quiches, hotpots, salads, moussaka, gluten-free cakes and an eco vibe: you'll find it all here.

Wednesday is curry night.

★**Riverford**
Field Kitchen MODERN BRITISH ££
(☑01803-762074; www.riverford.co.uk; Wash Farm; 3-course lunch/dinner £23.50/27.50; ☺sittings 12.30pm Mon-Sat, noon & 3.30pm Sun, 7pm most evenings; 🖉) 🖉 This ecofriendly, organic, plough-to-plate farm is where everyone wants to eat when they visit Totnes. It began as a food-box scheme, and has now branched out into a delightful barn bistro, where diners sit communally at long wooden tables and share dishes of the day. Rustic flavours rule: expect delicious salads, roast meats and imaginative veggie options. Bookings required.

Riverford also runs farm tours on Tuesdays, Wednesdays and Fridays (April to October), or you can pick up a map and an MP3 player and guide yourself. The Field Kitchen is 5 miles northwest of Totnes.

★**Vineyard Kitchen** BISTRO ££
(☑01803-732178; www.sharpham.com/cafe; Sharpham Wine & Cheese vineyard; mains £10-15; ☺noon-2.30pm Wed-Sun May-Sep; 🖉) After a tour of the vines, sit down for delicious food from a daily-changing blackboard menu at Sharpham Wine & Cheese's rustic bistro.

SHARPHAM WINE & CHEESE

This is one of Devon's most prestigious vineyards, particularly known for its crisp, sparkling whites. You can explore the steep vine-covered hills on your own (£2.50), and then head to the shop for a taster of four wines (£6) and three cheeses (£2.50). Or opt for a full guided tour of vineyard and winery, plus wine and cheese tasting (£20; 3pm Saturday and Sunday, May to September). The winery is also home to the excellent Vineyard Kitchen.

The vineyard is 3 miles south of Totnes, off the A381. An atmospheric way to get there is to hike from Totnes along the Dart Valley Trail.

The choices revolve around local treats, so expect smoked fish, crab salad and Lyme Bay scallops, as well as the estate's own wines and cheeses. It's all delicious. Book ahead. Opens longer hours in summer.

Rumour PUB FOOD ££
(☑01803-864682; www.rumourtotnes.com; 30 High St; mains £9-18; ☺noon-3pm Mon-Sat, 6-10pm daily; 🖉) 🖉 Rumour is a local institution – a narrow, cosy pub-restaurant with low lighting, funky local art and newspapers for reading. It's legendary for its pizzas (£9.50), but there's plenty to choose from, such as risottos, steaks, stews and fish of the day. The bar is open from 10am to 11pm.

White Hart PUB FOOD ££
(☑01803-847111; www.dartingtonhall.com; Dartington Estate, near Totnes; mains £15-23; ☺noon-3pm & 5.30-9pm; 🖉) 🖉 A refined gastropub that's beamed, whitewashed and surrounded by the green lawns of the Dartington Estate. The food is firmly sophisticated, and precisely and colourfully presented. Expect dishes such as crab and scallop remoulade, and cocoa-rolled Devon venison. Bar opens noon to 11pm.

☆ Entertainment

Barn CINEMA
(☑01803-847070; www.dartington.org/barn-cinema; Dartington Estate, near Totnes) An atmospheric independent cinema with a strong international program.

🛍 Shopping

Totnes Good Food
FOOD & DRINKS

(www.totnesgoodfood.co.uk; Civic Sq; ⊙10am-3pm 3rd Sun of month) Once a month, one of Devon's biggest food markets takes over Totnes' central square. Expect more than 60 traders, selling everything from local meats, cheeses and artisan breads to olives and chocolates. Hot-food stalls span global cuisines, including Thai, Indian and Caribbean.

Totnes Market
MARKET

(www.totnesmarket.co.uk; Civic Sq; ⊙9am-4pm Fri & Sat) Each Friday and Saturday scores of stalls, selling everything from vintage threads and furniture to fudge, fill Civic Sq.

Ben's Farm Shop
FHHHH

(☑01803-863959; www.bensfarmshop.co.uk; 38 High St; ⊙9am-5.30pm Mon-Sat) Plot your picnic at this acclaimed eco-deli, where you'll find piles of organic local veggies, pies, pasties, bread and cheese.

Shops at Dartington
SHOPPING CENTRE

(☑01803-847500; www.dartington.org/shops; Dartington Estate; ⊙10am-5pm) Jewellery, kitchenware, books, glassware, clothes, toys, fine foods and a cafe fill the attractive outbuildings of this former cider press.

ℹ Information

There's a tourist information point with leaflets and maps within the **Totnes Bookshop** (www. visittotnes.co.uk; 42 High St; ⊙9.30am-5.30pm Mon-Sat, 10am-4pm Sun).

ℹ Getting There & Away

BOAT
Boats shuttle downriver to Dartmouth with the Dartmouth Steam Railway & Riverboat Company (p84).

BUS
Totnes is well serviced by bus.

Exeter Stagecoach Bus X64 (£7.70, 50 minutes, seven daily Monday to Friday, six Saturday, two Sunday); continues to Dartmouth in the opposite direction.

Kingsbridge Bus 164 (£3.90, 50 minutes, seven daily Monday to Saturday).

Plymouth Stagecoach Gold (£3.40, one hour, half-hourly Monday to Saturday, hourly Sunday).

Torquay Stagecoach Gold (£3.70, 45 minutes, half-hourly Monday to Saturday, hourly Sunday).

TRAIN
Trains run at least hourly to Exeter (£13, 35 minutes) and Plymouth (£9, 30 minutes).

The quaint South Devon Steam Railway (p80) chuffs to Buckfastleigh, on the edge of Dartmoor.

Dartmouth

☑01803 / POP 10,720

Home to the nation's most prestigious naval college, the riverside town of Dartmouth is one of Devon's prettiest, awash with pastel-coloured, punch-drunk 17th- and 18th-century buildings leaning at angles, and a picturesque harbour stacked with yachts and clanking boat masts. It may no distinctly chic these days, but it's still a working port, and the triple draw of regular riverboat cruises, the art deco house of Coleton Fishacre and the former home of Agatha Christie make Dartmouth all but irresistible.

Dartmouth is on the west side of the Dart estuary. It's linked to the village of Kingswear on the east bank by fleets of car and foot ferries, also providing a key transport link to Torquay.

History

Dartmouth's history is salty and compelling: ships headed off on the Crusades from here in the 12th century, and the Pilgrim Fathers first left from here for America in 1620 – only to have to put in at Plymouth, where they would later depart from the famous Mayflower Steps, because one of the boats sprang a leak. In WWII thousands of American servicemen set off from Dartmouth for the carnage of the Normandy landings. Echoes of that martial past are still present; the hills above town are home to the Britannia Royal Naval College, the imposing 100-year-old mansion where the Royal Navy still trains all its officers.

👁 Sights

★ Greenway
HISTORIC BUILDING

(NT; ☑01803-842382; www.nationaltrust.org. uk; Greenway Rd, Galmpton; adult/child £11/5.50; ⊙10.30am-5pm daily mid-Feb-Oct, 11am-4pm Sat & Sun Nov & Dec) High on Devon's mustsee list, the captivating summer home of crime writer Agatha Christie sits beside the placid River Dart. Part-guided tours allow you to wander between rooms where the furnishings and knick-knacks are much as the author left them. The bewitching waterside gardens include features that pop up in Christie's mysteries, so you get to spot locations made notorious by fictional murders. Car parking must be prebooked; the better options are to arrive by Greenway Ferry (p86) or on foot.

Christie owned Greenway between 1938 and 1959, and the house feels frozen in time: check out the piles of hats in the lobby, the books in her library, the clothes in her wardrobe, and listen to her speak (via a replica radio) in the drawing room. The gardens feature woods speckled with magnolias, and daffodils and hydrangeas frame the water. The planting creates intimate, secret spaces – the boathouse and the views over the river are sublime. In Christie's book *Dead Man's Folly*, Greenway doubles as Nasse House, with the boathouse making an appearance as a murder scene.

The Greenway Ferry runs to the house when it's open, or you can take the Dartmouth Steam Railway (p73) from Paignton to Greenway Halt and walk half a mile through the woods. You can also arrive by hiking along the picturesque **Dart Valley Trail** from Kingswear (4 miles).

Britannia
Royal Naval College   HISTORIC BUILDING
(☑01803-677565; www.britanniaassociation.org.uk/tours; College Way; adult/child £12/5; ⊙tours Mon & Wed Apr-Oct) The imposing building crowning the hills above Dartmouth was built in 1905 and is where the Royal Navy still trains all its officers. Guides lead you around the stately rooms and grounds, recounting the building's history and tales of its students. Alumni include Princes Charles and Andrew, and it's also where the Queen first met the Duke of Edinburgh in 1939. Visits are by prebooked guided tour only; the pick-up point is in central Dartmouth. Bring photo ID.

Dartmouth Castle   CASTLE
(EH; ☑01803-833588; www.english-heritage.org.uk; Castle Rd; adult/child £6.10/3.70; ⊙10am-6pm Apr-Sep, to 5pm Oct, to 4pm Sat & Sun Nov-Mar; ℗) Discover maze-like passages, atmospheric guardrooms and great views from the battlements of this picturesque castle. The best way to arrive is via the tiny, open-top Castle Ferry (p86), or walk or drive along the coast road from Dartmouth (1.5 miles).

The castle started life in the 14th century to protect the harbour from seaborne raids.

BERRY POMEROY CASTLE

Even the most level-headed person is set to get spooked at 17th-century Berry Pomeroy (☑01803-866618; www.english-heritage.org.uk; Berry Pomeroy; adult/child £5.60/3.30; ⊙10am-6pm Apr-Sep, to 5pm Oct, to 4pm Sat & Sun Nov-Mar; ℗). Unusually for ruins, the crumbling walls soar up to three floors high; that these fragments are so recognisably part of a former structure underlines the sense of desolation and destruction. The feeling of menace increases at St Margaret's Tower, where Lady Margaret Pomeroy is said to have been imprisoned and starved to death by her jealous sister. Her ghost (apparently) roams the battlements today.

It's 2 miles east of Totnes.

It was commissioned by Dartmouth's privateering mayor, John Hawley – said to be the inspiration for the 'Shipman' in Chaucer's *Canterbury Tales*. The fortification saw additions in the 15th century, the Victorian era and WWII. Today its passages, guardrooms and battlements provide an evocative insight into life inside; there's also an audiovisual recreation of a Victorian gun drill.

Butterwalk   HISTORIC BUILDINGS
(Duke St) Dartmouth's Butterwalk is a row of ancient timber-framed buildings that lean at an improbable angle. Despite looking as though they could collapse at any moment, they've managed to remain standing since the late 17th century.

Dartmouth Museum   MUSEUM
(☑01803-832923; www.dartmouthmuseum.org; Duke St; adult/child £2/50p; ⊙1-4pm Sun & Mon, 10am-4pm Tue-Sat Apr-Oct, noon-3pm daily Nov-Mar) An eclectic collection of costumes, swords, ships in bottles and vintage toys, plus evocative WWII exhibits explaining how the area was a mustering point for 485 vessels that embarked overnight on 5 June 1944 for the D-Day landings.

Bayard's Cove   WATERFRONT
(Bayard's Cove) It's worth tracking down Dartmouth's quaintly cobbled Bayard's Cove, the quay from which the Pilgrim Fathers set sail to America, having put into Dartmouth for repairs.

Dartmouth

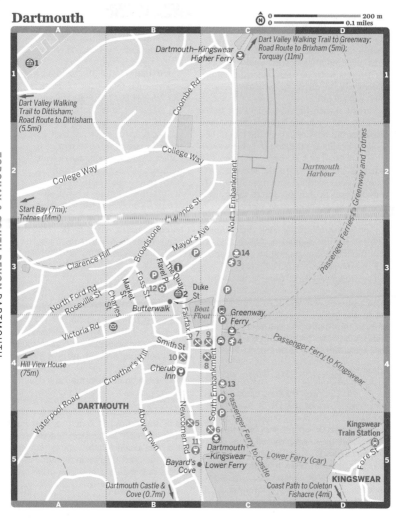

Activities

Dartmouth Steam Railway & Riverboat Company   CRUISE, RAIL
(☑ 01803-555872; www.dartmouthrailriver.co.uk; North Embankment) Boats leave frequently on a number of cruises available from Dartmouth's quay, including trips along the River Dart (adult/child return £8.50/3) and to Totnes (return £14/8.50).

You can also combine a cruise with a ride on the old-fashioned Dartmouth Steam Railway (p73) between Paignton and Kingswear via Greenway Halt (near Agatha Christie's house). Ferries shuttle from Kingswear back to Dartmouth.

Blackpool Sands   BEACH
(☑ 01803-771800; www.blackpoolsands.co.uk) Sun-loving locals head 3 miles south of Dartmouth to this curl of coarse sand, lured by beautiful views, kayak and SUP hire (per hour/day £15/40), and a licensed cafe (open daily from 8.30am to 5pm) stacked with organic, local produce.

Take bus 3 from Dartmouth (20 minutes, hourly Monday to Saturday, two on Sunday).

Dartmouth

Castle Cove　　　　　　　　　　SWIMMING
For a close-to-Dartmouth swim, clamber down the 100 steps and join the bathers at tiny Castle Cove; it's tucked in just west of Dartmouth Castle.

Keep an eye on the tide, as sections become cut off at high water.

Dartmouth Boat Hire　　　　　　BOATING
(☏07850-118920; www.dartmouth-boat-hire.co.uk; North Embankment; per hr/day £50/150; ⊙Apr-Oct) Chug about the Dart on a hired motor-boat.

⚘ Festivals & Events

★ **Royal Regatta**　　　　　　　　SAILING
(www.dartmouthregatta.co.uk; ⊙Aug) Dartmouth's big annual party falls on August Bank Holiday weekend. Expect plenty of contests, ranging from sailing and rowing to swimming, comedy races and tennis, plus plenty of late-night revelry. It packs out the town; book ahead for accommodation.

Dartmouth
Food Festival　　　　　　　FOOD & DRINK
(www.dartmouthfoodfestival.com; ⊙late Oct) One of Devon's biggest food festivals.

Dart Music　　　　　　　　　　　MUSIC
(www.dartmusicfestival.co.uk; ⊙mid-May) Three days of music-making encompasses folk, classical and jazz.

✕ Eating

★ **Alf Resco**　　　　　　　　　　CAFE £
(☏01803-835880; www.cafealfresco.co.uk; Lower St; mains from £6; ⊙7am-2pm; ☏) An eclectic crowd hangs out at Alf's – you'll be eating among hipsters, families, tourists and riverboat crews. The same menu spans breakfast through to lunch: expect piled-high fry-ups, irresistible pastries and eye-opening espressos.

Smith St Deli　　　　　　　　　DELI £
(☏01803-833616; www.facebook.com/Smith StreetDeli; Smith St; mains £6-11; ⊙9am-5pm Mon-Sat; ☏) Big bowls of olives, large jars of coffee beans, jazz on the soundtrack and a counter crammed with local cheeses, including Ticklemore, Sharpham brie and Devon Blue. Choose picnic supplies or sit at the clutch of tables and tuck into quiche, bruschetta, and cheese or charcuterie platters.

Crab Shell　　　　　　　　SANDWICHES £
(1 Raleigh St; sandwiches £5; ⊙10.30am-2.30pm Apr-Dec) Sometimes all you want is a classic crab sarnie, and this little establishment will happily oblige: the shellfish is landed on the quay a few steps away. Salmon, lobster and mackerel butties also available.

Rockfish　　　　　　　　　　SEAFOOD ££
(☏01803-832800; www.rockfishdevon.co.uk; 8 South Embankment; mains £10-18; ⊙noon-9.30pm) At the Dartmouth outpost of award-winning chef Mitch Tonks' five-strong bistro chain, seafood is firmly the speciality, and the weathered boarding and maritime decor fit right in along Dartmouth's streets. The fish and chips are delicious.

Venus Cafe, Blackpool Sands　　CAFE ££
(☏01803-770209; www.lovingthebeach.co.uk; Blackpool Sands; mains £10-20; ⊙8.30am-5pm Sep-Jun, to 8pm Jul & Aug; ☏) In summer the huge doors open directly onto the beach; in winter there's a warming log fire. All year round, organic Devon goodies stack the menu: try the garlicky crab bisque, tender Start Bay lobster or succulent Devon beef burgers, washed down with Totnes-brewed Venus Ale.

TORQUAY & SOUTH DEVON DARTMOUTH

DON'T MISS

COLETON FISHACRE

For an evocative glimpse of jazz-age glamour, swing by **Coleton Fishacre** (NT; ☑ 01803-842382; www.nationaltrust. org.uk; Brownstone Rd, near Kingswear; adult/child £11/5.50; ⊙ 10.30am-5pm mid-Feb–Oct, 11am-4pm Sat & Sun Nov & Dec; P), the former home of the D'Oyly Carte family of theatre impresarios. Built in the 1920s, its faultless art deco embellishments include original Lalique tulip uplighters, comic bathroom tiles and a stunning saloon – complete with tinkling piano. The croquet terrace leads to deeply shelved subtropical gardens and suddenly revealed vistas of the sea. Hike the 4 miles along the cliffs from Kingswear, or drive.

Bushell's Riverside MODERN BRITISH ££
(☑ 01803-833540; www.bushells.org.uk; 24 South Embankment; mains £15-25; ⊙ 6-9pm Wed-Sat) The picture windows at this intimate eatery look straight out onto the boat-dotted estuary. Fittingly, seafood features strongly on the menu: potted crab, scallops and grilled lemon sole are likely to appear alongside Devon beef, lamb and cheese. It's artfully presented, flavourful food.

★**Seahorse** SEAFOOD £££
(☑ 01803-835147; www.seahorserestaurant.co.uk; 5 South Embankment; mains £20-31; ⊙ noon-2.30pm & 6-9.30 Tue-Sat) What celebrity chef Rick Stein is to neighbouring Cornwall, Mitch Tonks is to Devon – a seafood supremo, with a clutch of restaurants across the county. The Seahorse is the original, and still the best: a classic fish restaurant where the just-landed produce is roasted over open charcoals. Leather banquettes, wood floors and a wine wall give it a French bistro feel. Book ahead.

🍷 Drinking & Nightlife

Dartmouth Arms PUB
(☑ 01803-832903; www.facebook.com/the dartmoutharmsdartmouth; 26 Lower St; ⊙ 11am-11pm) As an antidote to Dartmouth's sailing chic, join the locals for an unpretentious pint in an ancient bar smothered in polished wood. Navigational lights and cross-sections of ships dot the walls. Summertime drinking spills over onto Bayard's Cove outside.

Cherub Inn PUB
(☑ 01803-832571; www.the-cherub.co.uk; 13 Higher St; ⊙ 11am-11pm) The cosy Cherub lays claim to being Dartmouth's oldest building, dating from around 1370. Original interior features include old ships' timber. Cask ales from local breweries are a speciality – look out for Proper Job and Cherub (St Austell), Ferryman (Exeter) and Dartmouth Pride (South Hams).

☆ Entertainment

Flavel ARTS CENTRE
(☑ 01803-839530; www.theflavel.org.uk; Flavel Pl) Hosts small-scale theatre and dance, plus live music and films.

ℹ️ Information

Tourist Office (☑ 01803-834224; www. discoverdartmouth.com; Mayor's Ave; ⊙ 10.30am-2.30pm Mon, Tue & Thu-Sat)

ℹ️ Getting There & Away

BOAT
Several ferries run from Dartmouth's waterfront:
Castle Ferry (www.dartmouthcastleferry. co.uk; adult/child return £5/3; ⊙ 10am-4.45pm Easter-Oct) Runs to Dartmouth Castle.
Dartmouth–Dittisham Ferry (☑ 01803-882811; www.greenwayferry.co.uk; adult/child return £8.50/6.50; ⊙ Easter-Oct) Shuttles upriver to the quaint village of Dittisham.
Dartsmouth–Kingswear Higher Ferry (☑ 07866 531687; www.dartmouthhigherferry. com; car/pedestrian one way £5.60/60p; ⊙ 6.30am-10.50pm Mon-Sat, from 8am Sun) Carries cars and pedestrians across the estuary every six minutes, enabling you to avoid the town's narrow streets.
Dartmouth–Kingswear Lower Ferry (www. southhams.gov.uk/DartmouthLowerFerry; per car/pedestrian £5/1.50; ⊙ 7.10am-10.45pm) The town's oldest ferry service, in business since the 1300s. It's a floating platform that's pulled by a tug moored alongside.
Greenway Ferry (☑ 01803-882811; www. greenwayferry.co.uk; adult/child return £8.50/6.50; ⊙ 5-8 daily mid–Mar-Oct) Boats to Greenway and onto Dittisham, plus scenic river cruises.

BUS
Plymouth Stagecoach bus 3 (£7.20, 2½ hours, hourly Monday to Saturday) travels via Kingsbridge. On Sunday two **buses** travel as far as Kingsbridge (£6.40, one hour).
Totnes Stagecoach bus X64 (£3.70, 50 minutes, every two hours Monday to Saturday, two

Sunday) heads to Totnes and then continues to Exeter (£6.60, two hours).

TAXI
There's a taxi rank on South Embankment.

TRAIN
The Dartmouth Steam Railway (p73) links Kingswear and Paignton.

Start Bay

Start Bay curves out in an elongated crescent towards Devon's most southerly tip. This is one of the county's most spectacular sections of coast: the road climbs steeply in a series of hairpin bends; fields roll up to precipitous cliffs; and villages cluster beside the sea.

It's a landscape most people bypass, but it offers unforgettable places to stay and unusual sights ranging from a ruined village and a lighthouse to a massive freshwater lake.

◉ Sights

Slapton Ley   NATURE RESERVE
(☑01548-580466; www.slnnr.org.uk; Slapton Sands; P) FREE Slapton Ley's broad sweep of water is ringed by a nature reserve and fringed by reed beds and woods. A 1.75-mile trail skirts the ley, crossing the reed beds via a series of boardwalks. While walking, look out for yellow iris, tufted ducks, great crested grebes and – if you're lucky – otters.

To explore, park at the Memorial Car Park halfway along Slapton Sands and walk across the road (signed Slapton village). The reserve entrance is on the left, immediately after the bridge. Soon the path heads up to Slapton itself, a quintessential Devon village where houses huddle around mazelike lanes. It has a time-warp village shop, robust church and 14th-century ruined tower. From the village, a path beside the road takes you back to the coast and your car.

Slapton Sands   BEACH
(P) The name is misleading: Slapton Sands is actually a spectacular pebble ridge that's 3 miles long. You can find solitude here on even the busiest days. It's backed by the southwest's largest freshwater lake, Slapton Ley, with just enough room for a narrow strip of road between the ley and the sea.

At the southern, Torcross end, you'll quite often come across fishers casting their lines from the shore.

Sherman Tank   MEMORIAL
(www.exercisetigermemorial.co.uk; Torcross; P) FREE Wave-dashed as they are today, Slapton Sands have an even more dramatic past. During WWII, thousands of American servicemen trained here for D-Day using live ammunition. On one rehearsal in 1944, *Exercise Tiger*, a German torpedo boat, sank several landing craft; 639 American servicemen died. One of the tanks that sank during the exercise has been winched from 20m of water just offshore. Painted black, it now sits beside the car park at Torcross as a memorial.

Signs alongside outline the remarkable role this area played in WWII; from 1943 the residents of seven local villages, including Slapton, were evacuated from their homes for a year while the D-Day rehearsals took place.

South Hallsands   HISTORIC SITE
(South Hallsands; P) The shells of a handful of houses clinging to the cliff at South Hallsands are the remains of a thriving fishing village. In 1917 a severe storm literally swept this community out to sea. More than 20 cottages, a pub and a post office were lost overnight; remarkably, none of the 128 residents were killed. You can't wander amid the ruins, but you can see them clearly from a cliff-side viewing platform that features evocative images of the village and its indomitable inhabitants.

A DAY AT THE RACES

In a glorious collision of smartly dressed county set and hard-bitten gambling fraternity, the 19-fixture jumps season at **Newton Abbot Races** (☑01626-353235; www.newtonabbotracing.com; Newton Rd, Newton Abbot; £12-19; ⊗Apr-Sep) lasts all summer. The course is a flat, mile-long, oval, left-hand circuit, with seven fences. Opt for the pricier Paddock Enclosure ticket (£19) for close-up views of the Parade Ring and winning post, or head for the Course Enclosure (£12) for more-distant views of the whole track. Either way there'll be posh frocks, tweeds, silks, thundering horses and, of course, champagne.

The racecourse is just a short drive from Exeter and the M5, and Newton Abbot is a 10-minute train ride from Torquay.

OFF THE BEATEN TRACK

START POINT LIGHTHOUSE

Sitting on one of England's most exposed peninsulas, the 815,000 candela beam of this bright-white lighthouse (☑ 01803-771802; www.trinityhouse.co.uk; Start Point; adult/child £5/3; ☺ tours Sun-Thu mid-Jul–Aug, Sun & Wed Apr, Jun–mid-Jul & Sep, Sun May & Oct; ☑) can be seen for 25 nautical miles. Tours (on the hour, from 11am to 4pm) last 45 minutes and wind up hundreds of steps, through tiny circular rooms. The highlight is the final climb, by ladder, to the top platform, where you stand alongside the massive optics and look out with 360-degree views and down onto a chilling sea.

The lighthouse was built in 1836, went electric in 1959, and was staffed right up until 1993; it's now controlled automatically from Trinity House's HQ in Essex. The lighthouse is sometimes open on additional days – check the website for details.

✕ Eating

Seafood and sea views rule here, and there are some superb local eateries.

★ Britannia @ the Beach   BISTRO ££
(☑ 01548-581168; www.britanniaatthebeach.co.uk; Seafront, Beesands; mains £9-27; ☺ 10am-8.45pm) They've tacked a smashing, pocket-sized eating terrace onto this old beachside fishmonger's shack, so now you can tuck into perfectly cooked shellfish, bass, bream and monkfish just yards from where it was hauled ashore. On fine summer evenings, diners spill out onto tables lining the sea wall; there are blankets provided to keep your legs warm.

Also sells takeaway fish and chips (£4.50 to £7.20). Bring-your-own wine (free corkage) keeps the price down.

Start Bay Inn   FISH & CHIPS ££
(☑ 01548-580553; www.startbayinn.co.uk; Torcross, Slapton Sands; mains £7-14; ☺ 11.30am-2.15pm & 6-9.30pm) A legendary south-coast fish-and-chip stop, the thatched Start Bay Inn has been feeding folk since the 14th century. Today a steady stream of beach walkers, birdwatchers and shore anglers continue to drop by its door. In fine weather, grab a shoreside table; if wet, soak up the atmosphere indoors.

Laughing Monk   BISTRO ££
(☑ 01803-770639; www.thelaughingmonkdevon. co.uk; Totnes Rd, Strete; mains £17-25; ☺ 6.30-9pm Tue-Sat) Although the produce is overwhelmingly local, the flavours are from much further afield: delight in piri-piri mackerel, seafood tapas or home-cured black treacle salt beef. The cheeseboard features four classic West Country varieties served with quince and walnut jelly. Book ahead.

Tower Inn   PUB FOOD ££
(☑ 01548-580216; www.thetowerinn.com; Church Rd, Slapton; lunch £7-15, dinner £14-21; ☺ noon-2.30pm & 6.30-9.30pm, closed Mon & Sun dinner Oct-Mar) It's a bit of a winner: rich flavours (think squid, chorizo, octopus, crab) combine with innovative treatments ('Bloody Mary' salad; lime and tequila posset) at an atmospheric inn, where the beer garden overlooks a 14th-century tower.

❶ Getting There & Away

Bus 3 runs from Dartmouth to Strete (£3.90, 20 minutes, hourly Monday to Saturday, two Sunday) and on to Torcross (£6.40, 30 minutes) and Kingsbridge (£6.40, 50 minutes).

Kingsbridge

☑ 01548 / POP 6110

Despite being on the same estuary as nearby chi-chi Salcombe, Kingsbridge has preserved the feel of a sleepy, waterside market town. It offers a genuine glimpse of rural Devon life, and browsing its independent shops or lingering by its quay is a pleasant way to spend an afternoon.

◉ Sights & Activities

Cookworthy
Museum of Rural Life   MUSEUM
(☑ 01548-853235; www.kingsbridgemuseum.org. uk; 108 Fore St; adult/child £3/2.50; ☺ 10.30am-4pm Mon-Sat May-Oct) An engaging collection of school desks, cooking ranges, wagons and ploughs, plus a particularly fine photographic archive.

Singing Paddles   CANOEING
(☑ 07754 426633; www.singingpaddles.co.uk; adult/child £25/10) ✐ These memorable, chilled-out kayak and canoe tours range from family safaris to overnight camps (adult/child £60/30), and often involve wildlife-watching, beachside brews, hot sausages and cakes. They run from Bowcombe Creek (near Kingsbridge) and Aveton Gifford (near Bantham).

✗ Eating

Mangetout   CAFE, DELI **£**
(📞 01548-856620; www.mangetoutdeli.com; 84 Fore St; mains £5-8; ⊙8am-5.30pm Mon-Sat; 🅿) Hike to the top of town to visit this diet-defying deli-cum-cafe with a smorgasbord of goodies. Choose from Devon hams, chorizo, zesty salads, olives, fresh breads, cakes and croissants.

The cheese selection is a who's who of local producers: Devon Oke, Ticklemore, Sharpham brie, Quickes cheddar and the pungent Devon, Beenleigh and Exmoor Blues.

Scoops   ICE CREAM **£**
(📞 01548-288188; www.facebook.com/scoops kingsbridge; 4 Fore St; ice creams from £2.50; ⊙10am-5pm) Some 18 flavours made by the Dartmouth Ice Cream Company (fancy bubblegum, or Devon cream tea?) are available inside this bright pink shop, alongside handmade chocolates, fudge and jars of sweets.

★ Millbrook Inn   PUB FOOD **££**
(📞 01548-531581; www.millbrookinnsouthpool. co.uk; South Pool; mains £11-20; ⊙noon-5pm & 7-9pm, bar noon-11pm) Mix together one French chef, an ancient British inn and piles of choice Devon produce and what do you get? Gutsy, classically influenced food in charming surrounds. The nose-to-tail ethos produces flavour-packed dishes, such as *pot-au-feu* (stew) and guinea fowl, bouillabaisse, and plum and apple crumble with clotted cream. The *menu du jour* (two/three courses £12/15) is a bargain.

There's also a beautifully converted loft apartment (single/double £135/150), where high ceilings meet beams and an upcycled vibe. The Millbrook is in the village of South Pool, 6 miles south east of Kingsbridge

Crabshell   PUB FOOD **££**
(📞 01548-852345; www.thecrabshellinn.com; The Quay, Embankment Rd; mains £9-15; ⊙noon-3pm & 6-9pm) On a sunny day, in-the-know locals make a beeline for the waterside beer terrace of the Crabshell, where you can watch boats and stand-up paddleboarders glide by. Lunch might be a spicy sea bass and Salcombe crab tagliatelle, wild boar and apple sausages, pizzas (served from noon to 9.30pm) or a Moroccan tagine, washed down with some carefully chosen wines.

Old Bakery   BISTRO **££**
(📞 01548-855777; www.theoldbakerykingsbridge. co.uk; The Promenade; tapas £4-8.50, mains £13-18; ⊙9am-3.30pm & 6.30-9.30pm Tue-Sat; 🅿) The kind of hip, happy eatery every town should have, where huge bowls of olives sit alongside piles of home-baked bread. Brunch features chorizo and Serrano ham, while tapas-style grazing dishes include smoky baba ganoush, mounds of charcuterie and garlic-laced seafood. The lunchtime Spuntino five-dish platters (£10) are a treat, and can also be vegetarian or fish-themed.

☆ Entertainment

Kings Cinema   CINEMA
(📞 01548-856636; www.kingsbridge.merlin cinemas.co.uk; Fore St) A sweet, three-screen movie house, towards the top of Fore St.

🔒 Shopping

Catch of the Day   FOOD
(📞 01548-852006; 54 Fore St; ⊙9am-4pm Mon-Wed & Fri, to 1pm Thu & Sat) Staff smoke the famous Salcombe Smokies (mackerel) at this fishmongers; try the flavoursome smoked salmon and prawns, too.

@Bakery   FOOD
(📞 01548-854073; www.dartfinefood.co.uk; 11 Fore St; ⊙9am-3.30pm Mon, Tue & Thu-Sat, to 2pm Wed) Bakery specialising in award-winning pastries, cakes and specialist breads; the home-cooked ham and coleslaw baguette is a winner.

Harbour Bookshop   BOOKS
(📞 01548-857233; www.harbourbookshop.co.uk; 2 Mill St; ⊙9am-5pm Mon-Fri to 4pm Sat) Well-stocked, independent bookseller, with a good range of literary fiction, crime and children's titles.

❶ Information

Kingsbridge Tourist Office (📞 01548-853195; www.welcomesouthdevon.co.uk; The Quay; ⊙9am-5pm Mon-Sat) Volunteer run, so times can vary.

❶ Getting There & Away

Dartmouth Bus 3 (£6.40, one hour, hourly Monday to Saturday, two Sunday), via Start Bay (30 minutes).

Hope Cove Bus 162 (£3.40, 40 minutes, three daily Monday to Saturday). Two daily stop at Thurleston (£3.15, 15 minutes).

Plymouth Bus 3 (£7.20, 1¼ hours, hourly Monday to Saturday).

Salcombe Bus 606 (£3.15, 20 minutes, hourly Monday to Saturday).

Totnes Bus 164 (£3.90, 50 minutes, seven daily Monday to Saturday).

LAZY DAYS

Devon's outdoor spaces offer activities galore but they're also places to switch off and chill out. Try heading to the county's beaches and gardens to kick back and relax.

DAY AT THE BEACH

Devon's beaches are fabulous places to laze about and enjoy getting sand between your toes. In North Devon, **Braunton Burrows** (p137) and **Northam Burrows** (p137) offer vast stretches of sand backed by dunes. In South Devon, the gorgeous sandy shorelines at **Bantham Beach** (p95), **Blackpool Sands** (p84), **Mill Bay** (p92) and **South Sands** (p92) are relatively undeveloped.

For solitude, head for 3-mile **Slapton Sands** (p87), backed by a giant lagoon. Torquay's 20 beaches include tidal **Torre Abbey Sands** (p73), and **Oddicombe Beach** (p73), while yachting haven Dartmouth offers tiny **Castle Cove** (p85). Or laze on the sun terraces at Plymouth's beautiful art deco lido, **Tinside Pool** (www.everyone active.com).

LAZING IN GARDENS

Devon's gardens are one of the county's true delights. Take a book, find a bench and feel stresses ease away.

The county's most prestigious gardens are **Rosemoor** (p134) in North Devon. On the southern fringes of Dartmoor, the **Garden House** (p112) is a masterpiece of imaginative planting, while **Broomhill Sculpture Gardens** (p137), near Barnstaple, blends wit, plants and art.

In South Devon, the riverside gardens of Agatha Christie's holiday home at **Greenway** (p82) are enchanting, or head for the glorious grounds of **Dartington Estate** (p79), near Totnes, set around a 14th-century manor house.

1. Bantham Beach (p95)
2. Blackpool Sands (p84)
3. Rosemoor (p134)

M J HERITAGE / SHUTTERSTOCK ©

Salcombe

☑ 01548 / POP 3350

Oh-so-chic Salcombe sits charmingly at the mouth of the Kingsbridge estuary, its network of ancient, winding streets bordered by sparkling waters and sandy coves. Its beauty has pushed many properties here above the £1 million mark, and a significant number of houses are second homes. Out of season, Salcombe can have a ghost-town feel, but the pretty port's undoubted appeal remains, offering tempting opportunities to catch a ferry to a beach, head out kayaking or soak up some nautical history.

◎ Sights

Today Salcombe is a smart holiday hot spot, but in the 17th century the town had a very different trade. Salcombe's fishers worked the Newfoundland Banks. By the 1800s scores of shipyards built fast fruit schooners bound for the Azores. In those days the area immediately around the central Whitestrand Quay contained four boatyards and streets full of sail lofts, landing quays and warehouses. All competed for a precious section of shore, resulting in long, thin buildings, set side-on to the harbour. Many of these remain, framed by incredibly narrow lanes; it's worth heading down a few to see where they lead. The Maritime Museum sells a map of the town as it was in 1842. Or just explore the area between Fore St and the water, especially near Clifton Pl and the Ferry Inn.

★ **Overbeck's**   HISTORIC BUILDING

(NT; ☑ 01548-842893; www.nationaltrust.org.uk; Sharpitor; adult/child £8.80/4.40; ⊙ 11am-5pm mid-Feb–Oct; ℗) An Aladdin's cave of curios, Edwardian country house Overbeck's crowns the cliffs at Salcombe's estuary mouth. It's set in 3 hectares of lush, subtropical gardens, with exotic plants framing wide views. It's named after former owner Otto Overbeck, an inventor who pioneered a machine called the Rejuvenator, which claimed to cure disease using electric currents – one of these devices is on display.

Rooms are packed with Otto's quirky collections of stuffed animals, snuffboxes, and nautical bits and pieces. Look out for displays about the *Herzogin Cecilie*, a beautiful four-masted barque that sank in 1936 at Starehole Bay, just a mile to the south; a dramatic coast path leads to the spot.

You can drive to Overbeck's or walk the steep 2¼ miles from Salcombe; keep heading south on Cliff Rd until you see the sign.

★ **Maritime Museum**   MUSEUM

(www.salcombemuseum.org.uk; Market St; adult/child £2/50p; ⊙ 10.30am-12.30pm & 2.30-4.30pm Apr-Oct) Here be treasure: the highlight of the hauls from local shipwrecks are the 500 glittering Moroccan gold dinars from the Salcombe Cannon wreck site, dating from the 13th to the 17th centuries. Evocative tools of the shipbuilding trade are also displayed – stretching hooks, caulking irons and drawing knives – alongside models of the boats they helped build.

★ **Mill Bay**   BEACH

(℗) Salcombe's best high-tide beach, sand-filled Mill Bay sits across the water on the east side of the estuary. It's reached by either walking the lane south from East Portlemouth's ferry dock, or – at low tide – strolling along the sandy shore.

★ **South Sands**   BEACH

(℗) Although it gets busy in the summer holidays, South Sands has immense charm. It's something to do with the broad beach (at low tide), the mini watersports centre, cool cafe, chic hotel and the impossibly

Salcombe

cute South Sands Ferry, which delivers you onto an improbable motorised platform. It's 2 miles south of Salcombe, on the estuary road.

Activities

★Sea Kayak Salcombe   KAYAKING, SAILING
(☑01548-843451; www.southsandssailing.co.uk; South Sands) Rents out sit-on-top kayaks and stand-up paddleboards (per one/three hours £18/37); prices include wetsuits and all kit. Also runs sea-kayaking tours (half-/full day £40/85) and courses (one/two days £150/300). The mini expeditions (three nights £250) feature wild camping and are excellent.

South Sands Ferry   BOATING
(☑01548-561035; www.southsandsferry.co.uk; Whitestrand Quay; adult/child one way £3.60/2.60; ☺9.45am-5.15pm Easter-Oct) This yellow-and-

blue passenger boat shuttles from Whitestrand Quay to South Sands, where an ingenious motor-powered landing platform trundles into the water to help you ashore. The ferry runs every half hour; the trip takes 20 minutes.

East Portlemouth Ferry   BOATING
(☑01548-842061; return adult/child £3/2; ☺8am-6.30pm) The half-hourly East Portlemouth Ferry (passenger only) chugs to the sandy shores opposite Salcombe. Between April and October it departs from Jubilee Pier (off Fore St); from November to March it leaves from Whitestrand Quay.

Whitestrand   BOATING
(☑01548-843818; www.whitestrandboathire.co.uk; Whitestrand Quay; per hr/day/week from £30/95/£340; ☺9am-5pm) Rents out motorboats, so you can explore the Salcombe estuary at your own pace.

WORTH A TRIP

THURLESTONE
··

Thurlestone is marked by a bijou rock arch rising from the sea in a bay edged by the dune-backed beach of South Milton Sands. Inland sits the village itself – a sleepy spot with an atmospheric old pub and a swish modern hotel.

It's also home to one of Devon's best beach-shack eateries, The Beachhouse (☑01548-561144; www. beachhousedevon.com; South Milton Sands; mains £6-18; ☉9am-5pm Apr-Jun, Sep & Oct, to 9pm Jul & Aug, 11am-4pm Sun-Thu, to 9pm Fri & Sat Nov-Mar), a funky, chilled-out place with great seafood and great views. Watch the waves while feasting on cracked crab, seafood linguine and juicy local beef burgers, and follow with scoops of Salcombe Dairy Ice Cream.

Island Cruising Club BOATING
(☑01548-844631; www.islandcruisingclub.co.uk; Island St) Long-established school running RYA (Royal Yachting Association) sailing courses ranging from beginners (per two days £250) to advanced (per five days £525). You must be a member (adult/child £35/50) to sail.

✕ Eating

Casse-Croute DELI £
(☑01548-843003; 10 Clifton Pl; ☉8.30am-5.30pm, to 4.30pm winter) There's more than a whiff of a chic, metropolitan deli about Casse-Croute. Drop by for charcuterie and organic artisanal breads; the sarnie options include chicken with sweet lime chilli.

Salcombe Fishmongers SEAFOOD £
(☑01548-844475; www.salcombeboathire.co.uk; 11 Clifton Pl; snacks from £4.50; ☉9am-5pm Mon-Sat) Offers fresh fish for the BBQ, plus tempting (cooked) seafood platters and classy crab sandwiches (£5.20 to £6.50).

Salcombe Yawl DELI £
(☑01548-842143; 10A Clifton Pl; snacks from £3; ☉9am-5pm) The wide-ranging goodies on offer here span homity pies (open veggie pies), Scotch eggs and huge Cornish pasties.

★Victoria PUB FOOD ££
(☑01548-842604; www.victoriainn-salcombe. co.uk; Fore St; mains £12-17; ☉noon-9pm; 🖥) The Victoria pulls off the trick of being a proper local pub while serving way above average

food. Devon produce packs the menu: beef from within 5 miles, fish from local boats, Salcombe-landed crab and home-laid eggs. Well-kept real ales, champagne by the glass and a sunny, terraced beer garden all make it rather hard to leave.

★Crab Shed SEAFOOD ££
(☑01548-844280; www.crabshed.com; Fish Quay, Gould Rd; mains £12-24) Set plumb on the water's edge, this smart shack has you eating fish and shellfish just yards from its landing spot. Homemade stock ensures bisques and bouillabaisse are intensely flavoured; the fritto misto is beautifully crisp; and the sweet Salcombe crab – of course – is superb.

Winking Prawn BISTRO ££
(☑01548-842326; www.winkingprawn.co.uk; North Sands; mains £15-24; ☉9.30am-4pm & 6-8.30pm Apr-Oct, reduced hours Nov-Mar) Overflowing with distressed driftwood-chic, this brasserie features huge rowing oars, red ensigns and a sea-view deck. It's a perfect spot to sample sautéed scallops with bacon, sea bream with sweet pepper and goats-cheese-themed veggie options. Or work through a pitcher of Pimm's. Summer evenings see staff busy barbecuing mackerel, steaks, haloumi and prawns.

★South Sands Restaurant MODERN BRITISH £££
(☑01548-845900; www.southsands.com; South Sands; lunch mains £15-18, dinner 2/3/6 courses £33/42/65; ☉noon-3pm & 6-9pm) Formerly a chef at Harrods and the Hilton, Allister Bishop brings some serious style to Salcombe's sandy shores. The vibe is relaxed and the food unfussy, but presentation is precise and the cooking assured. Expect bistro classics, plenty of seafood and some surprises: liquorice with salmon, gin soup, and foraged seaweed and flowers.

🍷 Drinking & Nightlife

Ferry Inn PUB
(☑01548-844000; www.theferryinnsalcombe.com; Fore St; ☉11am-11pm Sun-Thu, to midnight Fri & Sat; 🖥) If the sun is shining, this is an unbeatable location: the beer terrace clings to the waterfront, providing cracking harbour views.

Bo's Beach Cafe CAFE
(☑01548-843451; www.southsandssailing.co.uk; South Sands; ☉9am-5pm Apr-Oct) Caffeine-laden espressos, tempting cakes, a chilled vibe, water views and sandy feet. Perfect.

ℹ Information

Salcombe Tourist Office (☏ 01548-843927; www.salcombeinformation.co.uk; Market St; ☺10am-4pm daily Easter-Oct, to 3pm Mon-Sat Nov-Easter).

ℹ Getting There & Away

Bus 606 runs to Kingsbridge (£4, 20 minutes, hourly Monday to Saturday).

Hope Cove

☏ 01548 / POP 500

The charming village of Hope Cove is tucked away between golden beaches and undeveloped cliffs. A couple of pint-sized sandy bays, a tiny harbour, a gathering of thatches, a pub and a couple of eateries – there's not much to Hope, but what's there is utterly delightful.

✗ Eating

★**Cove** PUB FOOD **££**
(☏ 01548-561376; www.thecovedevon.co.uk; mains £10-16; ☺noon-9pm) Live music, a sunny patio and more than 50 craft ales and ciders make this chilled hang-out a hugely popular spot. That and award-winning pub grub, ranging from fish and chips and towering burgers to *moules* (mussels) poached in cider, chorizo scotch eggs and crispy sourdough pizza. Bar stays open till 11pm.

Hope & Anchor PUB FOOD **££**
(☏ 01548-561294; www.hopeandanchor.co.uk; mains £13-20; ☺noon-2pm & 6-8.30pm) The streetside beer terrace here is a favourite with the locals for a pint. The kitchen dishes up good-quality bar food, while the airy, seaview B&B rooms (doubles £70 to £85) are decked out in soft greens and aquamarines.

ℹ Getting There & Away

Bus 162 heads to Kingsbridge (£3.40, 40 minutes, three daily Monday to Saturday). Two buses daily go via Thurlestone (£3.15, 30 minutes).

Bantham

☏ 01548 / POP 200

This pocket-sized village has the best surf spot in South Devon – and hardly anything else. Tucked in at the east side of the River Avon, its scattering of buildings, including an inn and a shop, stretches back from rolling dunes.

⊙ Sights & Activities

Bantham Beach BEACH
(☏ 01548-560897; www.banthamdevon.co.uk; parking per day May-Sep £6, Feb-Apr & Oct-Nov £3.50, Dec & Jan free; ☺8am-dusk or 9pm; P) Bantham is, arguably, South Devon's finest low-tide beach. Set at the mouth of the River Avon, this dune-backed sweep of sand offers a cool cafe, surf hire and lessons, and views onto picturesque Burgh Island on the estuary's other side. Be aware: the rip currents here can be dangerous. Note the warning signs and follow the advice of the (seasonal) lifeguards.

At high tide a ring of sand frames the sea; at low tide it becomes a golden expanse, dotted with pockets of ankle-deep water. Lifeguard are present from 10am to 6pm May to late-September.

**Bantham
Surfing Academy** SURFING
(☏ 01548-853803; www.banthamsurfingacademy.co.uk; Bantham Beach) Offers two-hour surf sessions (£35/125 for one/four lessons) catering to all skill levels, and one-hour sessions for kids (£25), plus stand-up paddleboarding (SUP) lessons (£45 for 90 minutes) and SUP tours (£50 for two hours). The academy hires out surfboards (£10/18 per two hours/day), wetsuits and bodyboards (£5/10 per two hours/day), and SUPs and sit-on-top kayaks (£16/45 per two hours/day).

✗ Eating

★**Gastrobus** FAST FOOD **£**
(www.thegastrobus.co.uk; Bantham Beach car park; snacks from £4; ☺10am-5pm May-Oct; ✐) Superb street food comes to South Devon with this fabulous, funky pop-up alfresco cafe. Tuck into powerful espressos, melting chocolate brownies, gourmet blue-cheese burgers, and goats cheese and grilled veg salads. Leave room for the early-evening charcoal barbecues.

The bus closes (quite rightly) in foul weather.

ℹ Getting There & Away

Buses don't run to Bantham. A (very) part-time passenger ferry (p97) shuttles across the River Avon between Bantham village slipway and the Bigbury-on-Sea side.

Bigbury-on-Sea

From steep cliffs lined with impressive houses, Bigbury-on-Sea rolls down suddenly to a sandy beach (best at low tide), which features a cafe and a watersports-hire outlet. Just offshore sits the intriguing, tidal Burgh Island, home to a jazz-age hotel and an ancient pub.

◉ Sights & Activities

Burgh Island   ISLAND

(www.burghisland.com; Bigbury-on-Sea) A slanting 10-hectare chunk of grass-topped rock, tidal Burgh Island is connected to Bigbury-on-Sea by a stretch of sand at low tide. At high water the journey is made by a sea-tractor (one-way £2), an eccentric device where the passenger platform is perched on stilts 6ft above the tractor's wheels and the waves. Once ashore, it takes around 30 minutes to walk around the island.

Once on the island, bear right, taking the cliff path that edges rocky coves as it heads uphill. At the summit you'll find the remains of a huer's hut, a shelter where lookouts waited to spot lucrative pilchard shoals then raised the alarm (hence the phrase: 'hue and cry').

The gorgeous art deco **Burgh Island Hotel** (☎01548-810514; www.burghisland.com; Burgh Island; s from £350, d £400-680; ☎) sits on the side nearest the shore, with the Pilchard Inn (p97) just alongside. The hotel is not open to nonresidents, except for prebooked, three-course, black-tie dinners).

Discovery Surf School   SURFING

(☎07813-639622; www.discoverysurf.com; lower car park, Bigbury-on-Sea) Offers two-hour sessions of surfing tuition (per one/four lessons £35/120) and stand up paddleboard (SUP) lessons (per one/two hours from £25/50). Also hires out wetsuits (per hour/day £5/10), surfboards (£10/15), SUPs (£16/40) and sit-on-top kayaks (£19/45).

🍴 Eating

Venus   CAFE £

(☎01548-810141; www.lovingthebeach.co.uk; lower car park, Bigbury-on-Sea; snacks from £4; ☺10am-5pm; 🖉) Better-than-average pasties (featuring Cornish ale), Devon beef burgers and Salcombe Dairy ice cream.

★ Oyster Shack   SEAFOOD ££

(☎01548-810876; www.oystershack.co.uk; Stakes Hill, near Bigbury; snacks £4-7, mains £16-30; ☺noon-3pm & 6-9pm, closed Sun dinner) The

ANTB / SHUTTERSTOCK ©

Dittisham

laid-back terrace of this idyllic bistro is *the* place to indulge in local oysters, mussels, monkfish and crab; treatments range from grilled and traditional to spicy and Spanish. Local seafood sizzles on the barbecue; set menus are a bargain (£14/16 for two/three courses); and you can pick up precooked shellfish for picnics. It's just off the tidal road between Bigbury-on-Sea and Aveton Gifford.

Drinking & Nightlife

★Pilchard PUB
(☑01548-810514; www.burghisland.com; Burgh Island; ⊙11am-11pm) What a spot to sip a pint and watch the waters rise. The atmospheric 14th-century Pilchard Inn (think beams and an open fire) sits on the shores of Burgh Island, so it's cut off from the mainland at high tide. All of which somehow makes the real ale and crab baguettes (snacks £6) all the more flavoursome.

❶ Getting There & Away

Bus 875 runs to Plymouth (£5.40, 1¼ hours, one per week) on Fridays only.

River Avon Passenger Ferry (☑07837 361306; £3; ⊙10-11am & 3-4pm Mon-Sat mid-Apr–mid-Sep) runs across the River Avon from the Bigbury-on-Sea side to the Bantham village slipway.

Dittisham

☑01803 / POP 430
Dittisham (pronounce it 'Diti-shm' to feel like a local) is one of those enchanting, waterside villages that makes you wonder why you don't live there yourself. A cluster of rough-stone cottages gathers along a riverbank dotted with yachts, and a pontoon lined with dinghies stretches out from beside a cracking bistro and pub.

Agatha Christie's holiday home, Greenway (p82), sits on the opposite bank, connected by the Dittisham to Greenway Ferry.

Eating

★Anchorstone Café BISTRO ££
(☑01803-722365; www.anchorstonecafe.co.uk; Manor St; mains from £9; ⊙noon-4pm Wed-Sun mid-Mar–Oct) It's hard to know what's best: the food or the view. The dining terrace is right beside the creek, so you can watch the ferry shuttling across the river while tucking into succulent Dartmouth crab, lobster or hand-dived scallops, and sipping local Sharpham wine. During the school summer holidays it's open every day, plus evenings from 7pm to 9pm Wednesday to Sunday.

You can cruise here by ferry (p86) from Dartmouth, too.

Drinking & Nightlife

Ferry Boat Inn PUB
(☑01803-722368; www.ferryboatinndittisham.pub; Manor St; ⊙11am-11pm) Fondly known to locals as the FBI, this is a pub that revels in its unreconstructed air. Expect a friendly waterfront drinking den, serving four real ales and tasty pub grub. It fills up fast on local music nights.

❶ Getting There & Away

The Dartmouth–Dittisham Ferry (p86) runs up- and downriver between the two quays. The **Dittisham–Greenway Ferry** (☑01803-882811; www.greenwayferry.co.uk; Dittisham Quay; adult/child one way £2/1.50; ⊙9am-5pm Easter-Sep) shuttles across the River Dart.

Plymouth & Dartmoor

Best Places to Eat

➡ Gidleigh Park (p117)

➡ Rock Salt (p107)

➡ Old Library (p116)

➡ River Cottage Canteen
(p107)

➡ Horse (p117)

➡ Jacka Bakery (p106)

Best Views

➡ Plymouth Hoe (p104)

➡ The Barbican (p104)

➡ Teign Gorge (p121)

➡ Meldon Viaduct (p120)

➡ Lydford Gorge (p118)

Why Go?

There may only be 10 miles between them, but Plymouth and Dartmoor feel like different worlds. In the vibrant, waterfront city of Plymouth, must-see attractions meet tempting boat trips. Add ranks of restaurants (two headed by celebrity chefs), the region's top theatre, and a lively nightlife and you have a compelling city break.

Then, within a 20-minute drive, there is Dartmoor National Park – a wilderness escape, where gorges cut between hills and ponies roam beside the road. Eat at one of the country's most prestigious restaurants or at an ancient inn warmed by a fire. You can hike, cycle and ride a horse, then doze off in a country house pile – or go wild camping beneath a sky full of stars.

When to Go

➡ **Easter** Plymouth's seasonal ferries resume their runs, bringing more beaches into easy reach.

➡ **Jun** The open-air Tinside Lido opens for unheated saltwater dips.

➡ **Jul** Open-air public pools warm up; wild swimmers head for moorland rivers.

➡ **Aug** Thousands pack Plymouth's shoreline to see the spectacular British Fireworks Championships. Summer days bring plentiful hikers, and warmer nights mean more people camp wild.

➡ **Sep** Tradition-packed Widecombe Fair kicks off, tors turn purple with heather blossom.

➡ **Oct-Mar** The worst of the weather, but the best white-water kayaking season too.

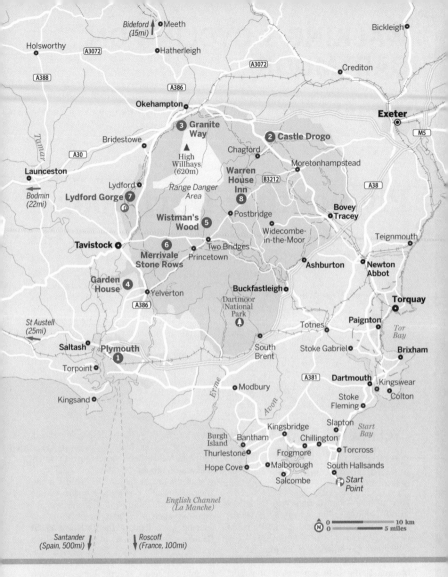

Plymouth & Dartmoor Highlights

1 **Plymouth** (p104)
Delighting in a gin distillery, SUP lessons, boat trips and a 1930s lido in a vibrant waterfront city.

2 **Castle Drogo** (p117)
Wandering the rooms at this exquisite, jazz-age pile.

3 **Granite Way** (p100)
Swooping over a 165m-wide viaduct on an 11-mile cycle trail.

4 **Garden House** (p112)
Savouring the scents amid beguiling floral displays.

5 **Wistman's Wood** (p116)
Getting more than a little bit spooked in this myth-rich, moss-smothered ancient oak forest.

6 **Merrivale Stone Rows** (p118) Playing history

detective amid Bronze Age remains.

7 **Lydford Gorge** (p118)
Scrambling over rocks to a 30m-high waterfall

8 **Warren House Inn** (p116)
Sinking a pint at pub beside a fire that's been lit since 1845.

WALKING & CYCLING ON DARTMOOR

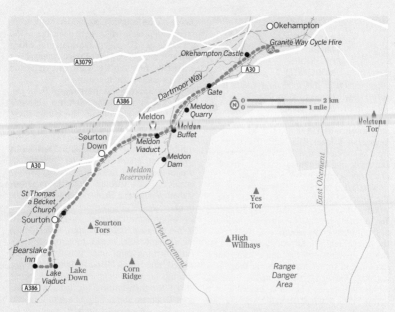

CYCLING THE GRANITE WAY

START/END OKEHAMPTON YHA
DISTANCE 12 MILES (RETURN)
DURATION FOUR HOURS
DIFFICULTY EASY

Hire a bike from **Granite Way Cycle Hire** (p109) before heading downhill, under the railway bridge and turning left onto the Granite Way (part of NCN Route 27).

Shadow the railway line, forking left under a stone bridge; soon the ruins of **Okehampton Castle** (p119) emerge on your right. A bit further on, head left through the **gate** and under the busy A30. The Granite Way traces the route of a railway line, built to shuttle industrial cargoes off the moor – a heritage that's in evidence at **Meldon Quarry**, which is a Dr Who–esque landscape of rocks and waste piles. Next, a ridge of tors emerges, including Dartmoor's highest point: High Wilhays (621m). **Meldon Buffet**, a cafe–visitor centre in former railway carriages sits just before the **Meldon Viaduct**, an impressive 1874 steel structure spanning 165m, which has

views of the deep tor-fringed valley ahead. Detour left (signed Meldon Reservoir) to the 45m-high **Meldon Dam**, a reservoir with waterside walking trails.

Back in the saddle on the main Granite Way, cycle south, dog-legging beside a cattle grid, where the landscape suddenly widens, exposing open moorland sweeping up to Sourton Tors. Explore the 14th-century **St Thomas a Becket** church at Sourton, which pops up beside the track. Eventually the multi-arched granite **Lake Viaduct** appears; it's a stunning structure offering gorse moorland views. Soon, a sign points left towards the Bearslake Inn; head along the steep path onto a rough track that leads under the viaduct, over wooden bridges and beside a stream, before emerging at the **Bearslake Inn** (☎01837-861334; www.bearslakeinn.com; Lake Sourton; mains £8-15; ⊙noon-2.30pm daily & 6.30-9pm Mon-Sat; ℗). Head inside for some classy bar food in snug surrounds. Finally, retrace your steps to the Granite Way for the glorious return pedal to Okehampton. You know you're nearly home when you see Okehampton Castle.

Two Dartmoor adventures: follow a disused railway line by bike from Okehampton via the historic Meldon Viaduct, or drink in stunning views on a moorland walk along the Teign Gorge from Castle Drogo.

WALKING TEIGN GORGE

START/END CASTLE DROGO
DISTANCE 4 MILES
DURATION FIVE HOURS
DIFFICULTY MODERATE

After exploring the intriguing **Castle Drogo** (p116) stately home, pick up Teign Valley Walk signs from the **car park**, heading onto the (signed) Hunter's Path, down the rough-earth steps towards Iron Bridge (which is later signed Dogmarsh Bridge). This skirts the slopes in front of the castle, revealing cracking views of Dartmoor and the plunging gorge – tree-clad and sheer-sided it's a spectacular sight.

Next, head towards Fisherman's Path, past the thatched **Gib House**, ponds and bluebell woods. It's a steep descent around **Hunter's Tor** to the Fisherman's Path (don't cross the bridge); next scramble over tree roots beside the River Teign and head towards Fingle Bridge, looking out for dipper, kingfisher, salmon and trout en route. Soon **Drogo Weir** appears. Designed by Castle Drogo's architect, Sir Edwin Lutyens, it powered the castle's own hydroelectric power station; the weir's **Turbine**

House is a little further on, hidden in the trees on the opposite bank. After a further walk, scramble up the steep steps around **Sharp Tor**. At three-arched **Fingle Bridge**, refuel at the namesake inn – it offers warm fires, riverside terraces and food at lunchtime.

When you're done, head away from the bridge, then switchback left up Hunter's Path to climb sharply up the gorge. Crest a rise and see the steep tree-covered valley, the River Teign far below (listen for its tumblings) and Dartmoor's hills. Now head sharp right, following signs for Drewsteignton, and onto the Drewston/Rectory Woods walk. It leads through conifers to **Drewsteignton** village; a cluster of thatches, traditional stores, a 15th-century church and the Drewe Arms, which serves food at lunch and in the evenings (noon to 4pm on Sundays). Sightseeing done, head towards Hunter's Path, turning right once you reach it (it's signed Road Near Drogo). Drink in more spectacular views before skirting the top of Sharp Tor then cutting up through **Piddledown Common**, and heading back to your car.

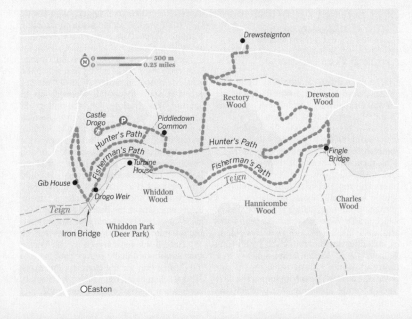

ROAD TRIP >
A DRIVE ON DARTMOOR

Driving across Dartmoor is like being inside a feature film, with compelling 360-degree views being screened all around.

❶ Tavistock

This scenic, west-to-east transmoor traverse sweeps up and through the wilderness, taking in a bleak prison, prehistoric remains, a rustic pub and a unique castle. Some of Dartmoor's lanes are maze-like; a good local map helps when driving this route.

Start by strolling amid the fine 19th-century architecture of **Tavistock** (p112), perhaps dropping by its cavernous Victorian Pannier Market to rummage for antiques.

If you fancy a road-trip picnic, find Warrens Bakery in adjacent Duke St, and one of Devon's best cheese specialists, Country Cheeses, on the east side of the Pannier Market itself.

❷ Merrivale

Shopping done, take the B3357 towards Princetown. It climbs steeply (expect your ears to pop), crosses a cattle grid (always a sign you're on the moor 'proper') and crests

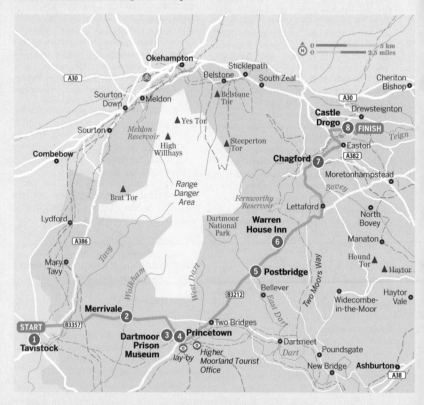

Start Tavistock

End Castle Drogo, near Chagford

Length 20 miles, one day

a hill to reveal swathes of honey-coloured tors. Be aware that much of Dartmoor is unfenced grazing – it's very common to find sheep, cows and sturdy Dartmoor ponies wandering about on the road. The speed limit is often 40mph, but it's wise to slow significantly when passing verge-side animals, as they sometimes dart into the road.

Soon you're at **Merrivale**. Park up on the right, just after the Dartmoor Inn, and stroll over the rise (heading due south). Within minutes you'll discover two parallel, snaking stone rows, the longest of which is 260m. In the middle sits the stacked stones of a compact burial or 'cist' chamber. Carry on walking south (away from the road) for 100m and you'll encounter a small stone circle. Stroll for a further 40m, this time southwest, and you'll come to a slanting 3m menhir (standing stone).

❸ Dartmoor Prison Museum

Back in the car, after climbing a short incline, take the turning right towards Princetown, and glimpse the brooding bulk of Dartmoor Prison. Don't stop here (it's prohibited): there's a much better (and legal) vantage point as you leave Princetown. Instead, call in at the **Dartmoor Prison Museum** (p113) to explore the jail's grim story. Built in the early 19th century, the prison housed French and American prisoners of war, before opening its cells to convicts. The museum's displays include accounts of escape attempts, some of which were successful. The collection of weapons made by modern-day prisoners is particularly gruesome.

❹ Princetown

Motor on into Princetown itself, stopping at the central car park to drop by the **Higher Moorland Tourist Office** (p111), which doubles as Dartmoor's main visitor centre. It features displays focusing on the moor's heritage, environments, industrial past – it was once a significant quarrying and tin-working area – and its myths and legends. The latter helped inspire Sir Arthur Conan

Doyle's Sherlock Holmes story, *The Hound of the Baskervilles*. If you're peckish, Princetown's renowned **Fox Tor Cafe** (p113) will feed you in convivial surrounds; the good food and open fires of the nearby Prince of Wales pub are tempting, too – Jail Ale (appropriately enough) is the local brew.

❺ Postbridge

Head out of Princetown on the B3212 – heading towards Two Bridges; the **lay-by** immediately after you leave Princetown provides prime Dartmoor Prison views. Next, pick up signs for Moretonhampstead. As you do, an expansive landscape unfurls. At **Postbridge** (p113), park and stroll to the 700-year-old bridge. Know as a clapper bridge, it's made up of huge flat slabs perched on columns made out of stones stacked together. It spans the chilly East Dart – more a stream than a river at this point – and has shallows suitable for dunking your feet.

❻ Warren House Inn

Back on the road, the moor opens up again. A few miles further on, **Warren House Inn** (p116) is an atmospheric spot for lunch. A legendary Dartmoor hostelry, this inn has been serving moorland travellers for centuries; its fire has famously (reputedly) been lit since 1845. Expect a warm welcome, snug bars, well-kept ales and hearty local food – the homemade Warreners Pie features rabbit and is named after the men (warreners) who farmed the creatures here.

❼ Chagford

Around **Lettaford** take one of the signed lanes that plunges down into **Chagford** (p117) – keep a look out as it's easy to miss – then explore the town's quaint, thatch-dotted square.

❽ Castle Drogo

Finally head to **Castle Drogo** (p117) to discover a unique 1920s stately home that sits on the side of a plunging, forested gorge – a superb spot for an end-of day-hike.

PLYMOUTH

☑ 01752 / POP 258,000

For decades, some have dismissed Plymouth as sprawling and ugly, pointing to its architectural eyesores and sometimes palpable poverty. But the arrival of high-profile chefs Hugh Fearnley-Whittingstall and Mitch Tonks and an ongoing waterfront regeneration begs a rethink. Yes the city, an important Royal Naval port, suffered heavy WWII bomb damage, and even today it can appear more gritty than pretty, but Plymouth is also packed with possibilities for visitors: swim in an art deco lido; tour a gin distillery; learn to stand-up paddleboard (SUP), kayak and sail; roam an aquarium; take a boat trip across the bay; then see a top-class theatre show and party till dawn. And the aces in the pack? The history-rich Barbican district and Plymouth Hoe – a cafe-dotted, wide, grassy headland offering captivating views of a boat-studded bay.

◉ Sights

★ **Plymouth Hoe**   LANDMARK

Francis Drake supposedly spied the Spanish fleet from this grassy headland overlooking Plymouth Sound (the city's wide bay); the bowling green on which he continued to finish his game after the sighting was probably where his statue now stands. The wide villa-backed promenade features scores of war memorials.

★ **Barbican**   AREA

(www.barbicanwaterfront.com) For a glimpse of ancient Plymouth, head down to this historic harbour area, where part-cobbled streets are lined with Tudor and Jacobean buildings, and old dockside warehouses have been turned into bars, restaurants and art galleries. It's also famous as the point from which the Pilgrim Fathers set sail for the New World in 1620: the Mayflower Steps mark the approximate spot.

★ **National Marine Aquarium**   AQUARIUM

(☑ 0844 893 7938; www.national-aquarium.co.uk; Rope Walk; adult/child £16/12; ☺ 10am-5pm) The sharks here swim in coral seas that teem with moray eels and vividly coloured fish, while huge rays glide over your head as you walk beneath glass arches. The gigantic Atlantic reef tank reveals just what's lurking a few miles offshore. Look out for set events, including shark talks (11am and 3pm), meet the octopuses (1.30pm and 3.30pm) and talks about the coral reef (noon and 4pm).

Tickets are slightly cheaper if you buy in advance, online.

★ **Plymouth Gin Distillery**   DISTILLERY

(☑ 01752-665292; www.plymouthdistillery.com; 60 Southside St; tours £7) This heavily beamed distillery has been concocting gin since 1793, making it the oldest working producer of the spirit in England. Four to six tours per day thread past the stills and take in a tutored tasting before retiring to the beautiful Grade II–listed cocktail bar for a complimentary G&T.

★ **Plymouth Fish Market**   MARKET

(☑ 01752-204738; www.plymouthfishmarket.co.uk; Sutton Harbour) Around 60,000 tonnes of fish pass through this market, making it the second biggest by volume in England after London's Billingsgate. It's an amazing sight when it's in full flow. Tours can be arranged with the harbourmaster (p.bromley@sutton-harbour.co.uk). There are also regular Fish in Sutton Harbour (FISH) guided tours with a local fisher; check www.facebook.com/suttonharbour for the latest.

Smeaton's Tower   LIGHTHOUSE

(☑ 01752-304774; www.plymhearts.org; The Hoe; adult/child £4/2; ☺ 10am-5pm) The red-and-white stripes of Smeaton's Tower rise from the middle of the Plymouth Hoe headland. For an insight into past lighthouse keepers' lives, head up 93 stone steps and through the circular rooms to emerge onto an open-air platform for stunning views of the city, Dartmoor and the sea.

Mayflower Museum   MUSEUM

(☑ 01752-306330; www.visitplymouth.co.uk; The Barbican; adult/child £3/1.50; ☺ 9am-5pm Mon-Sat, 10am-4pm Sun Apr-Oct, 10am-4pm Mon-Sat Nov-Mar) A child-friendly jaunt through the story behind the sailing to America of the Pilgrim Fathers aboard the *Mayflower* in 1620. It makes good use of cartoons, sound effects and hands-on gizmos; the centrepiece is a metre-high 1:11-inch scale model of the vessel itself.

Drake Statue   STATUE

A monument to one of Plymouth's most celebrated sons, Sir Francis Drake – the globetrotting explorer and hero of the battle against the Spanish Armada.

Plymouth

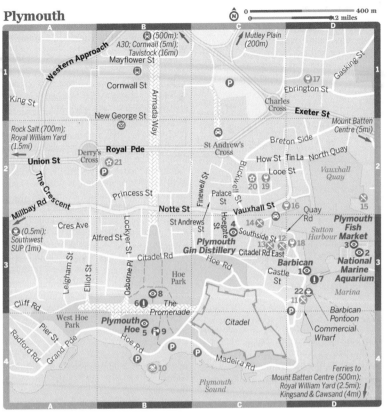

Plymouth

WORTH A TRIP

ROYAL WILLIAM YARD

In the 1840s this collection of waterfront warehouses supplied stores for countless Royal Navy vessels. Today it's home to sleek apartments, a clutch of galleries and shops, and a cluster of restaurants and bars. Highlights include the River Cottage Canteen (p107) and Vignoble (2 01752-222892; www.levignoble.co.uk; Royal William Yard; ☺ noon-11.30pm, to midnight Fri & Sat).

It's an atmospheric spot; roaming past a former slaughterhouse, bakery, brewery and cooperage underlines just how big the supplies operation was.

The yard is 2 miles west of the city centre. Hop on bus 34 (£1.30, nine minutes, half-hourly) or, better still, catch the hourly ferry (p109). A 10-minute walk north of the yard, the Cremyll Ferry (p109) chugs across the Tamar to Cornwall, to the coast walks of the Mount Edgcumbe estate

Plymouth Naval Memorial   MEMORIAL

The immense Plymouth Naval Memorial commemorates Commonwealth WWI and WWII sailors who have no grave but the sea.

🏃 Activities

★ **Tinside Lido**   SWIMMING

(2 01752-261915; www.everyoneactive.com; Hoe Rd; adult/child/family £4.50/3.50/13; ☺ noon-6pm Mon-Fri, from 10am Sat, Sun & school holidays Jun-early Sep) This glorious outdoor swimming pool is one of Plymouth's best-loved sights. Nestled beneath the Hoe with views onto Plymouth Sound, it's a gem of the jazz age: built in 1935, with sleek white curves and candy-striped light- and dark-blue tiles – like something straight out of an F Scott Fitzgerald novel. Tinside's saltwater is unheated, but there are hot showers. It's open until 7.30pm on Wednesdays.

Southwest SUP   WATER SPORTS

(2 07554 419197; www.southwestsup.co.uk; Royal William Yard; lessons per 2hr/day £30/80, hire per day £35) Runs taster sessions, lessons and offers board hire from a water's-edge base in the Royal William Yard.

Mount Batten Centre   WATER SPORTS

(2 01752-404567; www.mount-batten-centre.com; 70 Lawrence Rd) Set on the Mount Batten peninsula and linked to the Barbican by a passenger ferry (p109), this centre offers a range of water-sports tuition, including two-hour taster sessions in sit-on-top kayaks (£19), stand-up paddleboarding and sailing (£20).

👉 Tours

★ **Plymouth Boat Trips**   BOATING

(2 01752-253153; www.plymouthboattrips.co.uk; Barbican Pontoon) The pick of this firm's trips is the Cawsand Ferry, a 30-minute blast across the bay to the quaint, pub-packed Cornish fishing villages of Kingsand and Cawsand (adult/child return £8/4, six daily) from Easter to October. Year-round, regular one-hour excursions head around Plymouth's dockyards and naval base (adult/child £8/4/0.50).

Spring and summer bring longer, 4½-hour trips up the Tamar Valley to the Cornish village of Calstock (adult/child £17.50/12, four per month, April to October), plus sailings to the Plymouth Breakwater (adult/child £15/10) and up the River Yealm (£15/10).

☆ Festivals & Events

★ **British Fireworks Championships**   FIREWORKS

(www.britishfireworks.co.uk; ☺ mid-Aug) Over two nights in mid-August, six professional companies battle it out for the title, with three firms each staging 10-minute displays each night. It's hugely popular, drawing tens of thousands of people to Plymouth's waterfront amid a carnival atmosphere.

🍴 Eating

★ **Jacka Bakery**   BAKERY £

(2 01752-264645; 38 Southside St; snacks £3-8; ☺ 9am-4pm Wed-Mon) Quietly groovy, fantastically friendly and extremely good at baking things, Jacka is much loved by locals. It excels at immense croissants, cinnamon swirls and three type of sourdough loaves. The 'on toast' options are fabulous – the wild mushroom, tarragon and fried egg version is something very fine indeed.

Jacka's can also claim to be one of England's oldest working bakeries (four centuries and counting); it's even said to have provided the ship's biscuits for the Pilgrim Fathers aboard the *Mayflower*.

★ **Supha's Street Emporium**   ASIAN £

(2 01752-228513; www.suphas.co.uk; Unit 1, East Quay House; dishes £6.95-14.95; ☺ noon-9pm Tue & Sun, to 10pm Wed-Sat; 🖉) An exotic new

addition to the up-and-coming area around Sutton Harbour, this joint specialises in spicy, flavourful Thai-style street food: classic massaman curry, steamed sea bass, larb and papaya salads, and much more. Whether you opt for small street plates, platters to share or mix-and-match your curries, you'll enjoy authentic, delicious flavours. It's strong on veggie options, too.

Rockets & Rascals CAFE, SHOP £
(☑01752-221295; www.rocketsandrascals.com; 7 The Parade; snacks £6; ☺8am-6pm Mon-Sat, to 5pm Sun) In this hip 'bicycle emporium', bikes and Tour de France memorabilia hang from the walls and happy customers tuck into punchy coffee, gourmet sarnies and gooey cakes. The shop stocks quality cycles and kit, and hires out bikes, too (£10/15 per three hours/day).

Boathouse Cafe CAFE £
(☑01752-600560; www.theboathousecafe.co.uk; 2 Commercial Wharf; dishes £6-13; ☺9am-5pm Sun-Thu, 8am-9pm Fri & Sat) With a deck enclosed by canvas and clear plastic, and a quayside setting, the Boathouse has a firmly nautical flavour. Fittingly, its chefs delight in showcasing locally caught, sustainable fish dishes (think goujons, fish and chips, and fresh crab), some of which has been caught by its own day boat, the *Fiona Mary*.

★**Rock Salt** MODERN BRITISH ££
(☑01752-225522; www.rocksaltcafe.co.uk; 31 Stonehouse St; mains lunch £13, dinner £14-24; ☺10am-3pm & 5-9.30pm; ☎) Local boy Dave Jenkins has worked wonders at his little brasserie, which has deservedly built up a loyal local following and scooped up foodie awards. It suits all times of day: tuck into fluffy American pancakes for breakfast; enjoy a light artichoke risotto for lunch; and savour confit beef blade for dinner. A local diner par excellence.

River Cottage Canteen MODERN BRITISH ££
(☑01752-252702; www.rivercottage.net; Royal William Yard; mains £12-18; ☺10am-11pm Mon-Sat, to 4pm Sun; ☑) Hugh Fearnley-Whittingstall's cheerful, chilled eatery flies the flag for local, sustainable, seasonal, organic goodies. Expect Devon meats to be roasted beside an open fire, West Country fish to be simply grilled and familiar veg to be given a revelatory makeover. It's in the Royal William Yard, 2 miles west of the city centre. Drive, take the ferry or catch bus 34.

OFF THE BEATEN TRACK

WALKS AROUND PLYMOUTH

Perhaps surprisingly, Plymouth is the springboard for enjoyable coastal hikes that take in a brace of beaches. The Mount Batten Ferry (p109) leaves the Barbican for the Mount Batten peninsula. Walking southeast along the South West Coast Path leads to the compact sandy coves at Jennycliff (1 mile), and then Bovisand (a further 1.5 miles).

From Stonehouse, 2 miles west of the city centre, near the Royal William Yard, the Cremyll Ferry (p109) shuttles over to Cornwall's Mount Edgcumbe estate (p178). From there a gorgeous 3-mile hike leads to the fishing villages and sandy beaches at Kingsand and Cawsand. From there, either loop back inland across the Edgcumbe estate, or catch the Cawsand Ferry (p106), run by Plymouth Boat Trips, back to the Barbican.

Barbican Kitchen MODERN BRITISH ££
(☑01752-604448; www.barbicankitchen.com; 60 Southside St; 2-/3-course lunch menu £13/16, mains £10-20; ☺noon-2.30pm & 6-9.30pm Mon-Sat) Plymouth's chef brothers Chris and James Tanner have brightened up the Barbican with their relaxed-but-refined bistro at the Plymouth Gin Distillery. It's a quirky, fun place to dine – turquoise banquettes and pop-art pics of Yoda and Bruce Lee on the walls – and the food is fresh and contemporary, from devilled whitebait to caramelised cauliflower risotto.

The set menus are super value; the dinner menu (two/three courses £14/17) is served from 6pm to 7.30pm Monday to Thursday, and 5pm to 7pm Friday and Saturday.

Drinking & Nightlife

Like any Royal Navy city, Plymouth has a more than lively nightlife. Union St is clubland; Mutley Plain and North Hill have a studenty vibe; and the Barbican has more restaurants amid the bars. All three areas can get rowdy, especially at weekends.

★**Dolphin** PUB
(☑01752-660876; 14 The Barbican; ☺10am-11pm) This gloriously unreconstructed Barbican boozer is all scuffed tables, padded bench seats and an authentic, no-nonsense atmosphere. Feeling peckish? Get a fish-and-chip takeaway from **Harbourside Fish & Chips**

(www.barbicanfishandchips.co.uk; 35 Southside St; mains £7; ⊙11am-10pm, to 11pm Fri & Sat) two doors down, then settle in with your pint.

Be sure to check out the cheeky paintings by much-loved local artist (and one-time regular) Beryl Cook on the walls.

★**Annabel's** CLUB
(www.annabelscabaret.co.uk; 88 Vauxhall St; ⊙9pm-2am Thu, 8.30pm-3am Fri & Sat) Saucy performances come to the Barbican at this late-night cabaret-cum-nightclub. It's great fun: the DJ sets and lounge-bar vibe is spot on, and you never quite know what the entertainment might be – burlesque or blues, comedy or country.

Bread & Roses PUB
(☑01752-659861; www.breadandrosesplymouth.co.uk; 62 Ebrington St; ⊙4pm-1am Mon-Fri, noon-1am Sat, noon-11pm Sun; 🔊) Plymouth's arty crowd loves this characterful combo of hip boozer, social-enterprise visionary and cultural hub. Amid its Edwardian-meets-modern decor you'll find a good pint, occasional appearances by cool local bands, and lots of people hatching creative plans.

Minerva PUB
(☑01752-223047; www.minervainn.co.uk; 31 Looe St; ⊙11.30am-11pm Sun-Wed, to midnight Thu-Sat; 🔊) Stone walls, wooden benches, parts of wooden sailing ships, real ales, live music and Thursday-night jam sessions make this 16th-century drinking den a locals' favourite.

THE TAMAR BRIDGES

Six miles northwest of the city, two landmark bridges span the majestic River Tamar, linking together the counties of Devon and Cornwall, both symbolically and physically. The first to be built was the Royal Albert Bridge, designed by the visionary architect of the Great Western Railway, Isambard Kingdom Brunel, and opened in 1859. It's still in use to this day, carrying trains to and from Cornwall, and the views across the Tamar are absolutely stunning – and well worth taking the journey.

The more recent Tamar Bridge was opened in 1961, and carries the main A38 road between Devon and Cornwall. It's nowhere near as beautiful as Brunel's masterpiece, but the views are equally impressive – just remember to keep your eyes on the road!

 **Entertainment**

Theatre Royal THEATRE
(TRP; ☑01752-267222; www.theatreroyal.com; Royal Pde) One of England's largest regional theatres, the Theatre Royal features large-scale touring and homegrown productions on the main stage, the Lyric. Its studio space, the Drum, is renowned for featuring new writing.

Plymouth Arts Centre CINEMA
(☑01752-206114; www.plymouthartscentre.org; 38 Looe St; ⊙1-8.30pm Tue-Sat; 🔊) Combines a cracking independent cinema, modern-art exhibitions and a smart cafe-bar (open 5pm to 9pm, Tuesday to Saturday).

ℹ Information

Tourist Office (☑01752-306330; www.visitplymouth.co.uk; 3 The Barbican; ⊙9am-5pm Mon-Sat, 10am-4pm Sun Apr-Oct, 10am-4pm Mon-Sat Nov-Mar) Local leaflets aplenty, plus free accommodation-booking service and advance tickets for many attractions.

ℹ Getting There & Away

BUS

National Express services call at Plymouth's **bus station** (Mayflower St). They include the following:
Bristol £18 to £21, three hours, four to six daily
Exeter £6, one to 1½ hours, four daily
London £28, five to six hours, six daily
Penzance £7, 3¼ hours, five daily

Local services include the following:
Exeter Bus X38 (£7.30, 1¼ hours, six daily Monday to Friday, four on Saturday, two on Sunday).
Totnes Stagecoach Gold (£3.40, one hour, half-hourly Monday to Saturday, hourly on Sunday).

CAR

Plymouth sits just south of the A38 dual carriageway, which leads west to Cornwall and east to Exeter (43 miles), where the motorway network starts.

The quickest route to/from Cornwall is over the Tamar Bridge (www.tamarcrossings.org.uk), six miles' drive from the city centre. There's no toll to cross over from the Devon side, but if you're coming from Cornwall the toll charge is £1.50 for cars and small vans. Motorcycles travel free.

Multistorey car parks include Drake Circus shopping centre (£2.80/4.80 per two/four hours) and the Theatre Royal (£2.40/4.80 per two/four hours). There's also metered parking on the Hoe (in some bays you don't have to pay overnight), and on city streets (£2.80/4.80 per two/four hours).

TRAIN

Services include the following:

Bristol £19 to £29, two hours, two or three hourly

Exeter £8.60, one hour, half-hourly

London Paddington £54, 3¼ hours, half-hourly

Penzance £10, two hours, half-hourly

Totnes £8, 30 minutes, half-hourly to hourly

❶ Getting Around

BOAT

Fleets of foot passenger ferries link different parts of the city. Key routes:

Mount Batten Ferry (☑ 07930 838614; www.mountbattenferry.co.uk; Barbican Pontoon; adult/child return £3/1) Access for water sports activities and beaches.

Royal William Yard Ferry (☑ 07979 152008; www.royalwilliamyardharbour.co.uk/ferry.php; Barbican Pontoon; one way adult/child £3/2; ⊘ 10am-5pm May-Sep) Runs between the Barbican and the yard's eateries and bars.

Cawsand Ferry (p106) Plymouth Boat Trips runs this link to the beaches of the Cornish fishing villages of Kingsand and Cawsand.

Cremyll Ferry (☑ 01752-822105; www.cremyll-ferry.co.uk; Admirals Hard; adult/child return £3/1.50; ⊘ half-hourly) Connects the Stonehouse area with the coastal paths of the **Mount Edgcumbe** (p178) estate in Cornwall.

BUS

Plymouth's **bus station,** (p108) for decades at Bretonside, has moved to a new location beside Mayflower St.

Plymouth City Bus (www.plymouthbus.co.uk) is the main provider; useful services include bus 34, which runs from the city centre to the Royal William Yard (£1.30, nine minutes, half-hourly).

TAXI

Ranks include those on Old Town St, The Parade and outside the train station.

DARTMOOR NATIONAL PARK

Dartmoor is Devon's wild heart. Covering 368 sq miles, this vast national park feels like it's tumbled straight out of a Tolkien tome, with its honey-coloured heaths, moss-smothered boulders, tinkling streams and eerie granite hills (known locally as tors).

On sunny days, Dartmoor is idyllic: ponies wander at will and sheep graze beside the road. It makes for a cinematic location, used to memorable effect in Steven Spiel-

❶ WARNING FOR WALKERS

The military uses three adjoining areas of Dartmoor as training ranges where live ammunition is employed. Tourist offices can outline these locations; they're also marked on Ordnance Survey (OS) maps. You're advised to check if the hiking route you're planning falls within a range; if it does, find out if firing is taking place at the time you plan to walk via the **Firing Information Service** (☑ 0800 458 4868; www.mod.uk/access). During the day, red flags fly at the edges of in-use ranges, while red flares burn at night. Even when there's no firing, beware of unidentified metal objects lying in the grass. Don't touch anything you find: note its position and report it to the **Commandant** (☑ 01837-650010).

berg's WWI epic *War Horse*. But when sleeting rain and swirling mists arrive, you'll understand why Dartmoor is also the setting for Sir Arthur Conan Doyle's *The Hound of the Baskervilles:* the moor morphs into a bleak wilderness where tales of a phantom hound can seem very real indeed.

Dartmoor is an outdoor activities hot spot for hiking, cycling, riding, climbing and white-water kayaking, and has plenty of rustic pubs and country-house hotels where you can hunker down when the fog rolls in.

🏃 Activities

Cycling

Routes include the 11-mile Granite Way (part of NCN Route 27), which runs entirely off-road along a former railway line between Okehampton and Lydford. The 13-mile Princetown & Burrator Mountain Bike Route is a challenging moorland circuit along tracks and bridleways, taking in Princetown, Sheepstor village and Burrator Reservoir.

Tourist offices sell the *Dartmoor for Cyclists Map* (£13).

Devon Cycle Hire CYCLING
(☑ 01837-861141; www.devoncyclehire.co.uk; Sourton Down, near Okehampton; per day adult/child £16/12; ⊘ 9am-5pm Thu-Tue Apr-Sep, plus Wed school holidays) Located on the Granite Way (part of NCN Route 27). Will deliver bikes for a small charge.

Dartmoor National Park

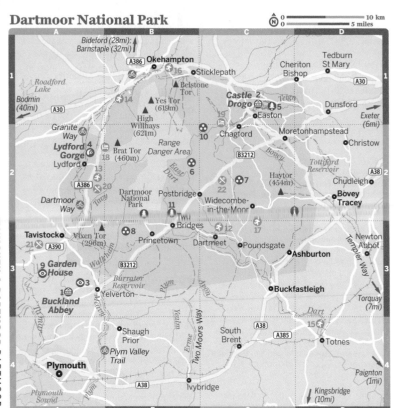

Granite Way Cycle Hire CYCLING
(☎ 01837-650907; www.granitewaycycles.co.uk; YHA Okehampton, Klondyke Rd, Okehampton; adult/child per day £12/10; ⊙9am-5pm Mar-Oct) Based at Adventure Okehampton, this experienced operator offers cycle hire from premises a hundred yards or so from the Granite Way.

Princetown Cycle Hire CYCLING
(☎ 01822-890238; www.princetowncyclehire. co.uk; Fox Tor Cafe, Two Bridges Rd, Princetown; per day adult/child £18.50/10; ⊙9am-5pm) This is handy for the Princetown & Burrator Mountain Bike Route.

Horse Riding

Babeny Farm HORSE RIDING
(☎ 01364-631296; www.babenystables.co.uk; Poundsgate; rides per 30min/1hr £35/50; ⊙Apr-Oct) A friendly, family-run farm that offers rides, lessons and Horse Holidays (ie stabling) for £15 per horse, per night. It's 8 miles northwest of Ashburton.

Cholwell HORSE RIDING
(☎ 01822-810526; www.cholwellridingstables.co.uk; near Mary Tavy; 1/2hr rides £22/40) A family-run stables that caters for novices and experts. It's near an old silver mine on the edge of the moor near the village of Mary Tavy, about halfway between Okehampton and Tavistock.

Eastlake HORSE RIDING
(☎ 01837-52513; www.facebook.com/pg/Eastlake-Riding-Stables; Eastlake, near Okehampton; per 2hr £35; ⊙Easter-Oct) Caters to all skill levels, from novice to expert, at a moorland base near the village of Belstone.

Shilstone Rocks HORSE RIDING
(☎ 01364-621281; www.dartmoorstables.com; Widecombe-in-the-Moor; rides per 1/2hr £40/55) This experienced riding centre offers one- and two-hour rides from its base near Widecombe. Advance bookings are required.

Dartmoor National Park

Hiking

Some 730 miles of public footpaths snake across Dartmoor's open heaths and rocky tors. The Ordnance Survey (OS) Pathfinder *Dartmoor Walks* (£12) guide includes 28 hikes of up to 9 miles, while its *Dartmoor Short Walks* (£8) focuses on family-friendly treks.

★Moorland
Guides   HIKING
(www.moorlandguides.co.uk; adult/child from £2.50/free) A wide range of walks, from one-hour rambles to strenuous all-day hikes, on themes spanning heritage, geology, wildlife, myths and navigation.

Whitewater Rafting

The raging River Dart makes Dartmoor a top spot for thrill seekers. Experienced kayakers can get permits from the Dartmoor National Park Authority. For white-water kayaking, go for Dynamic Adventures (p80), near Totnes. Rivers are only open from October to mid-March.

ⓘ Information

The DNPA's *Enjoy Dartmoor* magazine is packed with details of activities, attractions and campsites. Pick it up at tourist offices and venues across the moor.

Dartmoor National Park Authority (DNPA; www.dartmoor.gov.uk)Comprehensive and informative official website for the park.

DNPA Haytor (☑ 01364-661904; www.dart moor.gov.uk; off B3387; ⊘10am-5pm Apr-Oct, to 3pm Thu-Sun Nov-Mar)

DNPA Postbridge (☑ 01822-880272; www.dart moor.gov.uk; car park beside B3212; ⊘10am-5pm Apr-late Sep, to 3pm Thu-Sun late Sep-Mar)

Higher Moorland Tourist Office (DNPA; ☑ 01822-890414; www.dartmoor.gov.uk; Tavistock Rd; ⊘10am-5pm Apr-Oct, to 3pm Tue & Thu-Sun Nov-Mar)

Visit Dartmoor (www.visitdartmoor.co.uk) Dartmoor's official tourism site has information on accommodation, activities, sights, events and more.

ⓘ Getting There & Away

BUS

The Dartmoor Sunday Rover (adult/child/family £10/7/20) gives unlimited Sunday travel on most moorland bus routes; buy from drivers or at Plymouth train station.

Bus 1 (four per hour Monday to Saturday, hourly Sunday) Shuttles from Plymouth to Tavistock, via Yelverton.

Bus 98 (one daily Monday to Saturday) The only regular bus into the centre of the moor. It runs from Tavistock to Princetown, Two Bridges and Postbridge, then circles back to Yelverton. A couple of afternoon buses repeat the run as far as Princetown and back.

Bus 173 (two per day Monday to Saturday) Runs from Exeter to Moretonhampstead, via Chagford.

Bus 178 (one daily Monday to Saturday) Travels from Newton Abbot to Okehampton, via Bovey Tracey, Moretonhampstead and Chagford.

Bus 6A (four per day Monday to Saturday, one Sunday) Skirts the northern edge of the moor en route from Bude to Exeter, stopping in Okehampton.

Haytor Hoppa Bus 271 Runs Saturdays between late-May and mid-September only, providing four buses between Newton Abbot, Bovey Tracey, Haytor and Widecombe-in-the-Moor (daily fare £5).

CAR

The A38 and A30 dual carriageways frame Dartmoor, while the single-lane B3212 carves a path across the centre, linking Moretonhampstead, Postbridge and Princetown.

Tavistock

📞 01822 / POP 12280

With one metaphorical foot in Cornwall and the other in Devon, the old town of Tavistock has long been a waypoint for travellers heading both east and west. These days it remains a busy little country town, and a handy launch pad for forays onto Dartmoor.

◎ Sights

★ Garden House   GARDENS

(📞 01822-854769; www.thegardenhouse.org.uk; Buckland Monachorum, near Yelverton; adult/child £7.50/3.30; ⏱ 10.30am-5pm Apr-Nov; 🅿) The enchanting blend of landscapes here make this garden one of the best in Devon. Its 3 hectares encompass wildflower meadows and South African planting, Acer glades and a walled cottage garden. Terraces cluster around the picturesque ruins of a medieval vicarage, and clambering up the 16th-century tower will reveal sweeps of blue flax, poppies and buttercups. Everywhere there are tucked-away benches hidden in flower-filled nooks – soothing spots to drink in the fragrance and watch the bees buzz by.

The cafe (mains from £8) serves rustic treats: goats-cheese sandwiches with onion relish, salads scattered with pomegranate seeds, and excellent cakes. The Garden House is 5 miles south of Tavistock.

★ Buckland Abbey   HISTORIC BUILDING

(NT; 📞 01822-853607; www.nationaltrust.org.uk; near Yelverton; adult/child £11/5.50; ⏱ 10am-5pm mid-Feb–Oct, to 4pm Nov & Dec; 🅿) Founded as a Cistercian monastery and abbey-church in the 13th century, Buckland Abbey was one of Henry VIII's 'acquisitions' during the Dissolution of the Monasteries. Sir Richard Grenville bought it from the land-hungry king, before selling it to his cousin and nautical rival Sir Francis Drake. Highlights include Drake's Drum (said to beat by itself when Britain is in danger of being invaded), exquisite modelled ceilings, the Great Barn, fine Elizabethan gardens and woodland walks.

Buckland Abbey is 7 miles south of Tavistock and 11 miles north of Plymouth.

Morwellham Quay   HISTORIC SITE

(📞 01822-832766; www.morwellham-quay.co.uk; Morwellham, near Tavistock; adult/child/family £10/8/35; ⏱ 10am-5pm Easter-Oct, to 4pm Nov-Easter; 🅿) Morwellham Quay is part of the southwest's Mining World Heritage Site and offers intriguing insight into the copper boom that gripped west Devon in the 1860s. Then, this port beside the River Tamar saw tonnes of ore loaded onto masted vessels. Recently, the BBC filmed its series *Edwardian Farm* here. Costumed guides show you around, but the highlight is the atmospheric trip into a copper mine on a little underground train (adult/child £4.50/3.50).

✗ Eating

Elephant's Nest   PUB FOOD ££

(📞 01822-810273; www.elephantsnest.co.uk; Horndon, Mary Tavy; mains £11-25; ⏱ noon-2.15pm & 6.30-9pm) One of those iconic Dartmoor pubs beloved by generations, the Elephant is a 16th-century inn where log burners sit in vast fireplaces, and jugs and glasses dangle from beams. The chefs use top-notch local ingredients to create quality pub-food classics, plus some surprises such as seared scallop, pea and mint risotto. It's 5 miles north of Tavistock.

Cornish Arms   MODERN BRITISH ££

(📞 01822-612145; www.thecornisharmstavistock.co.uk; 15 West St; mains £13-25; ⏱ noon-3pm & 6-9pm) Chef John Hooker has created something special here: a smart but still convivial pub serving creative but unpretentious food that remains true to its West Country roots. So expect the Cornish monkfish to be roasted on the bone and to be doused in seaweed Béarnaise, and the lasagne to feature confit pork cheek.

★ Horn of Plenty   MODERN BRITISH £££

(📞 01822-832528; www.thehornofplenty.co.uk; Gulworthy, near Tavistock; lunch 2/3 courses £20/25, dinner 3 courses £50; ⏱ noon-2pm & 7-9pm) Local foodies love the classic, locally sourced, seasonal cuisine at this country-house hotel 4 miles west of Tavistock. Flavours are rich: choose between black truffle and roasted cauliflower risotto, Brixham red gurnard with lobster agnolotti, or quail breast with wild garlic and Princetown-brewed Jail Ale. Or plump for their memorable five-course tasting menu (£65).

❶ Information

Tavistock Tourist Information Point
(📞 01822-612938; www.visit-tavistock.co.uk; 4 Abbey Pl; ⏱ 7am-10pm)

ℹ Getting There & Away

Bus 1 Heads to Plymouth (£4.80, four per hour Monday to Saturday, hourly on Sunday).

Bus 98 Shuttles from Tavistock to Princetown (£3, 30 minutes, one daily Monday to Saturday), Two Bridges (£3.20, 35 minutes) and Postbridge (£4, 50 minutes). A handful of afternoon buses repeat the run as far as Princetown and back.

Princetown

☑ 01822 / POP 1770

Set in the heart of the remote higher moor, Princetown is dominated by the grey, foreboding bulk of Dartmoor Prison, and on bad-weather days the town can have a remote, even bleak, feel. But it's also an evocative reminder of the harsh realities of moorland life and makes an atmospheric base for some excellent walks.

◉ Sights

Dartmoor Prison Museum   MUSEUM
(☑ 01822-322130; www.dartmoor-prison.co.uk; Princetown; adult/child £3.50/2.50; ⊙ 9.30am-4.30pm Mon-Thu & Sat, to 4pm Fri & Sun; 🅿) In the early 1800s Princetown's jail was home to French and American prisoners of war. It became a convict jail in 1850. Just up from the looming gates, this museum provides a chilling glimpse of life inside. Look out for straitjackets, manacles, escape stories and the makeshift knives made by modern-day prisoners.

The prison itself is still in use: it's currently home to around 640 inmates.

**Higher Moorland
Visitor Centre**   MUSEUM
(DNPA; ☑ 01822-890414; Tavistock Rd; ⊙ 10am-5pm Apr-Sep, to 4pm Mar & Oct, 10.30am-3.30pm Thu-Sun Nov-Feb) FREE At the tourist office–cum–visitor centre, heritage displays include those on tin workings, gunpowder factories, ecology and legends – there's also a stunning time-lapse video.

The building used to be the Duchy Hotel; one former guest was Sir Arthur Conan Doyle, who went on to write *The Hound of the Baskervilles*. Dartmoor lore recounts that local man Henry Baskerville took the novelist on a carriage tour, and the brooding landscape he encountered, coupled with legends of huge phantom dogs, inspired the thriller.

OFF THE BEATEN TRACK

WILD SWIMMING ON DARTMOOR

With 368 sq miles of landlocked hills, Dartmoor may not seem like an ideal spot for an alfresco dip, but in fact Moretonhampstead, Chagford, Bovey Tracey, Buckfastleigh and Ashburton each have small and elegant outdoor pools. These are often solar heated; admission is normally a few pounds and they tend to be open from June to August. Times vary - local tourist offices can advise.

Dartmoor is also increasingly popular with wild swimmers who delight in venturing into rivers, pools and waterfalls. Be aware, though, that the water can be dangerously cold and fast flowing; seek safety advice (p38) from tourist offices and www.devonandcornwallwildswimming.co.uk. The book *Wild Swimming Walks – Dartmoor and South Devon* (£15) by Sophie Pierce and Matt Newbury features 28 hikes and dips.

✕ Eating

★ **Fox Tor Cafe**   CAFE **£**
(☑ 01822-890238; www.foxtorcafe.com; Two Bridges Rd; mains £5-12; ⊙ 9am-5pm Mon-Fri, 7.30am-6pm Sat, 7.30am-5pm Sun; 🛜) Known as FTC to locals, this friendly little cafe is a favourite for hearty breakfasts, doorstep sandwiches and massive chunks of cake, but it does more filling fare, too, such as spicy chilli and mushroom stroganoff. On cold, wet Dartmoor days the two wood-burning stoves are particularly welcoming.

ℹ Getting There & Away

Bus 98 (£3, one daily Monday to Saturday) runs from Tavistock to Princetown, before going on to Two Bridges and Postbridge.

Postbridge

☑ 01822 / POP 170

The quaint hamlet of Postbridge owes its popularity, and its name, to its medieval stone slab or clapper bridge: a 13th-century structure with four, 3m-long slabs propped up on sturdy columns of stacked stones. Walking the bridge takes you across the rushing East Dart; it's a picturesque spot to whip off your boots and plunge your feet

Outdoor Activities

Devon and Cornwall feature Britain's best natural adventure playgrounds, where you can surf amazing waves, hike along spectacular coastal paths, canter across moors or sail between beautiful bays. Whether you're after exhilaration or relaxation, you'll find it here.

2

ANDY STOTHERT / GETTY IMAGES ©

4

STEVE ALLEN / GETTY IMAGES ©

1. Horse Riding (p38)
Horse riding is a popular activity in Exmoor National Park (p126).

2. Cycling (p36)
Varied landscapes and traffic-free paths make the southwest great for cycling.

3. Walking (p35)
The 630-mile South West Coast Path stretches along the coasts of Devon and Cornwall.

4. Surfing (p37)
Newquay (p196) is the self-styled surfing capital.

3

ANTB / SHUTTERSTOCK ©

OFF THE BEATEN TRACK

THE WOODS OF DARTMOOR

While the bleak heaths and twisted tors are undoubtedly the landscapes most people associate with Dartmoor, once upon a time the whole moor would have been covered by a vast forest – until humans arrived, that is. Although much of the moor's ancient woodland has been lost, a few pockets remain – notably at Wistman's Wood, an ancient and mysterious patch of oak woodland near Two Bridges, and Fingle Woods (NT; ☑ 01647-433356; www.finglewoods.org. uk), near Moretonhampstead, where the National Trust and the Woodland Trust have joined forces to restore a huge area of native woodland by removing conifers and planting broadleaf species. Around 28 miles of walking trails are now open to the public, with more still to come.

into water that's quite possibly the coldest you've ever felt.

Eating

★ **Warren House Inn** PUB FOOD ££
(☑ 01822-880208; www.warrenhouseinn.co.uk; near Postbridge; mains £9-15; ◷ noon-8.30pm, bar 11am-11pm, shorter hours winter; ℗) Marooned amid miles of moorland, this Dartmoor institution exudes a hospitality only found in pubs in the middle of nowhere. A fire that's been burning (apparently) since 1845 warms stone floors, trestle tables and hikers munching on robust food; the Warreners' Pie (local rabbit) is legendary. It's on the B3212, some 2 miles northeast of Postbridge.

❶ Getting There & Away

Bus 98 (£2, 20 minutes, one daily Monday to Saturday) runs to Princetown.

Widecombe-in-the-Moor

☑ 01364 / POP 570

With its honey-grey buildings and imposing church tower, this is archetypal Dartmoor, down to the ponies grazing on the village green. The village is commemorated in the traditional English folk song 'Widecombe Fair', a traditional country pageant that takes place on the second Tuesday of September.

The village's St Pancras Church is known locally as the 'Cathedral of the Moor' thanks to its immense 40m tower.

✖ Eating

★ **Rugglestone Inn** PUB FOOD ££
(☑ 01364-621327; www.rugglestoneinn.co.uk; Widecombe-in-the-Moor; mains £11; ◷ noon-2pm & 6.30-9pm) Just one pint at this wisteria-clad pub is enough to make you want to drop everything and move to Dartmoor. It's a classic wood-beamed, low-ceilinged, old-fashioned village boozer, full of local characters and packed with history. There are lots of real ales on tap, and the menu features pies, lasagne, quiches and potted crab.

Ashburton

☑ 01364 / POP 7720

Ashburton is an appealing blend of traditional, edge-of-the-moor town and bordering-on-chic retreat. Elegant terraces and granite cottages line its winding streets, and you can shop for everything from hiking rucksacks to upcycled antiques. It's an all-round pleasant place, and a good base for the southern area of Dartmoor.

✦ Activities

Ashburton Cookery School COOKING
(☑ 1364-652784; www.ashburtoncookeryschool. co.uk; Old Exeter Rd, Ashburton; courses from £75) Long-established cookery school, offering more than 40 courses in everything from breadmaking to teen cuisine, via fish filleting and food photography.

CRS Adventures WATER SPORTS
(☑ 01364-653444; www.crsadventures.co.uk; Holne Park, Ashburton; per person per day from £35) A multi-activity provider offering a huge range of activities: mountain biking (bike hire per day £20), rock climbing, caving, forest skills, kayaking and canoeing, and more.

✖ Eating

★ **Old Library** BISTRO ££
(☑ 01364-652896; www.theoldlibraryrestaurant. co.uk; North St; mains £15-23; ◷ noon-2.30pm & 6-8.30pm Wed-Sat & Mon, noon-2.30pm Sun; ✐) Chefs Joe and Amy describe themselves as 'locally grown' and this idea shines through in their simple but sophisticated food that showcases prime Devon produce. Plump for the likes of Thai-themed tempura fish,

braised beef cheek or twice-baked beetroot and cheese soufflé.

Drop by at breakfast (from 8am to 10am, Wednesday to Monday) for porridge, *huevos rancheros,* or bacon, avocado and scrambled egg.

Moretonhampstead

01647 / POP 1700

Most visitors speed past sleepy Moretonhampstead these days, but this village was once an important stop-off for travellers traversing Dartmoor. The village centre is a muddle of Georgian houses, shops, pubs and restaurants, and its relative bustle can make a welcome change after the remoteness of the higher moor.

Its main site of interest is the ancient Bronze Age village of Grimspound (p118).

✖ Eating

Michael Howard   DELI £
(✆01647-440267; www.michael-howard-butchers.co.uk; 7 Court St; ⊙7.30am-5.30pm Mon-Sat) The perfect moorland refuelling stop: olives and local cheeses sit alongside pasties, pies and tempting cakes. It does takeaway hot drinks, too.

★Horse   GASTROPUB ££
(✆01647-440242; www.thehorsedartmoor.co.uk; 7 George St; mains £8-19; ⊙12.30-2.30pm Tue-Sat, 6.30-9pm daily) You've got to love a place that bills itself as a 'pub and nosebag'. Despite the village location, this is a hip gastropub that wouldn't feel out of place in the big city: it serves simple, well-done food including tapas, mussels, home-cured tuna, chargrilled rib-eye and lots of pizzas.

❶ Getting There & Away

Bus 173 Stops in Moretonhampstead (twice daily Monday to Saturday) on its way from Chagford to Exeter.

Bus 178 Runs from Moretonhampstead to Okehampton (£4, one hour, daily Monday to Saturday), via Chagford (£3, 45 minutes).

Chagford & Around

01647 / POP 1450

Chagford's wonky thatches and cream- and white-fronted buildings cluster on the edge of Dartmoor around a picturesque square. This apparently timeless moorland scene is also home to some stylish places to eat and sleep.

GIDLEIGH PARK

Gidleigh Park (✆01647-432367; www.gidleigh.co.uk; Gidleigh; r £365-545 ste £750-1050; ⊙restaurant noon-2pm & 7-9pm; P🐾) is without doubt Devon's grandest, fanciest and priciest hotel. At the end of a long private drive, the mock-Tudor house is an unashamedly opulent pamper pad: vast suites with wet-room showers, luxurious lounges with crackling fires, and a double Michelin-starred restaurant (3-course lunch menu £60; 10-course dinner £145) overseen by multiple-award-winning Michael Wignall. It's 2 miles west of Chagford.

◉ Sights

★Castle Drogo   HISTORIC BUILDING
(NT; ✆01647-433306; www.nationaltrust.org.uk; near Drewsteignton; adult/child £9/4.45; ⊙11am-5pm mid-Mar–Oct; P) Three miles northeast of Chagford, this outlandish architectural flight of fancy was designed by Sir Edwin Lutyens for self-made food-millionaire Julius Drewe. Built between 1911 and 1931, it was intended to be a modern-day medieval castle, with all the comforts of a country house. Unfortunately, the property hasn't worn well – it's currently the focus of a massive five-year restoration project. Parts of the house remain open, though, and imaginative midrenovation displays include a scaffolding viewing tower.

✖ Eating

Blacks   DELI £
(✆01647-433545; www.blacks-deli.com; 28 The Square; ⊙7.30am-5pm Mon-Sat) Walk into Blacks for one thing and you're likely to leave with half a dozen more. Tempting breads, cheeses and olives are stacked high, along with pies, pasties, and gourmet homemade quiches including leek and Stilton or spicy pepper with chorizo.

Whiddons Bistro   BRITISH ££
(✆01647-433406; www.whiddonsbistro.com; 4 High St; lunch mains £10, dinner 2/3 courses £23/27; ⊙noon-2.30pm Wed-Sun, 6.30-8.30pm Thu-Sat) In this olde worlde tearoom-cum-bistro, traditional tastes rule, with menus full of venison, quail, duck and slow-cooked beef shin. It's all neatly and creatively done and the flavours are intense.

🛈 Getting There & Away

Bus 173 Goes from Chagford to Exeter (£4, one hour, five daily Monday to Saturday), with two services also stopping at Moretonhampstead.

Bus 178 Runs from Moretonhampstead to Okehampton (£4, one hour, one daily Monday to Saturday), via Chagford (£3, 45 minutes).

Lydford

📞 01882 / POP 2050

The little village of Lydford is best known for the dramatic gorge that cuts through the landscape nearby en route to a beautiful waterfall. Once a strategic stronghold, its medieval castle has long since tumbled into ruins. It's 9 miles southwest of Okehampton.

⊙ Sights

⭐**Lydford Gorge** WATERFALL
(NT; 📞 01822-820320; www.nationaltrust.org.uk; Lydford; adult/child £8.90/4/40; ⊙10am-5pm mid-Mar–Oct, 11am-3.30pm Nov & Dec) This plunging gorge is the deepest in the southwest, and can be reached via a 1.5-mile rugged riverside hike past a series of bubbling whirlpools (including the fearsome Devil's Cauldron) to the thundering 30m-high White Lady waterfall.

✕ Eating

⭐**Dartmoor Inn** INN ££
(📞01822-820221; www.dartmoorinn.com; Moorside, Lydford; d £115; ⊙restaurant noon-2.30pm & 6.45-9pm Tue-Sat; 🅿) It looks venerable, but behind the whitewashed exterior, this coaching inn is a thoroughly modern affair: light, bright and bang up to date. Most peo-

ple stop for the superb food, such as slow-cooked oxtail and butterflied lamb rump (mains £12 to £20), but it's worth spending the night: rooms sparkle with Roberts radios, sleigh beds and posh linens.

🛈 Getting There & Away

Bus 46 (seven daily Monday to Saturday) stops in Lydford en route between Tavistock and Okehampton.

Okehampton

📞 01837 / POP 27,500

Okehampton huddles on the edge of an un inhabited tract of bracken-covered slopes and granite tors – the mind-expanding landscape known as the higher moor. The town has a staging-post feel, and its traditional shops and pubs are good places to prepare for a foray into the Dartmoor wilderness.

⊙ Sights

Finch Foundry HISTORIC BUILDING
(NT; 📞01837-840046; www.nationaltrust.org.uk; Sticklepath; adult/child £6.70/3.30; ⊙11am-5pm early Mar-Oct; 🅿) A century ago, this dramatic building would have thundered to the sound of clanging hammers and grinding metal. It was one of the busiest tool factories in the southwest, turning out hundreds of chisels, knives, shears and scythes a day. Though it's not quite the industrial powerhouse of yesteryear, it's still a working forge, powered by three working watermills. You can drive or cycle here, or follow a 4-mile (3½-hour) walk east along the Tarka Trail from Okehampton.

ANCIENT DARTMOOR

With an estimated 11,000 monuments, Dartmoor is ripe for archaeological explorations. It has the largest concentration of Bronze Age (c 2300–700 BC) remains in the country, 75 stone rows (half the national total), 18 stone circles and 5000 huts.

The Merrivale Stone Rows, near Princetown, are a handy one-stop shop for most monument types. The site has a parallel stone row, a stone circle, a menhir, burial chambers and dozens of hut circles.

The biggest site is the Bronze Age village of Grimspound, southwest of Mortonhampstead, just off the B3212, where you can wander inside the circular stone wall that once surrounded an entire village and explore the ruins of several granite roundhouses.

Other sites to look out for are the stone circle at Grey Wethers and the Scorhill Stone Circle at Gidleigh, both near Chagford.

You can buy guides to some sites (£4) from tourist offices.

NIGEL HICKS / GETTY IMAGES ©

PLYMOUTH & DARTMOOR OKEHAMPTON

Okehampton Castle

Okehampton Castle CASTLE
(EH; ☑ 01837-52844; www.english-heritage.org.uk;
Castle Lodge, Okehampton; adult/child £4.50/2.70;
☺ 10am-5pm Apr-Jun, Sep & Oct, to 6pm Jul & Aug)
Okehampton's castle dates back to Norman
times, and is strategically sited on top of a
rocky escarpment. Once Devon's largest castle, it's now a picturesque ruin; little remains
of the interior, but several of the stout exterior walls still stand, some careering off at
improbable angles.

🏃 Activities

Okehampton is the best place to start the
Granite Way; for details on the route, see our
cycling tour (p100).

Adventure Okehampton OUTDOORS
(☑ 01837-53916; www.adventureokehampton.
com; Klondyke Rd, Okehampton; per half-/full day
£25/50; ☺ school holidays only) Runs wall- and
rock-climbing sessions, plus activities including archery, abseiling, kayaking and
gorge scrambling.

🍴 Eating

★ Eat Toast CAFE £
(☑ 01837-54494; www.facebook.com/eattoastuk;
4 Market St; mains from £7; ☺ 9.30am-5pm Mon-
Sat; ☑) It's a winning combination: a quirky
gift shop that shares a cavernous, brick-
lined space with a laid-back cafe. The aroma
of freshly ground coffee fills the air; brightly
coloured trinkets fill the shelves; and the big
leather sofas are the perfect spot for enjoying a superfood salad, olives and sourdough,
or a latte and cake.

ℹ️ Getting There & Away

Bus 6A Runs southbound to Exeter (£3.40,
one hour, six daily Monday to Saturday, three
Sunday).

Bus 6A Heads northbound to Bude (£4.70,
1½ hours, four daily Monday to Saturday, one
Sunday).

Bus 178 Travels from Newton Abbot to Okehampton (one daily Monday to Saturday), via
Bovey Tracey, Moretonhampstead and Chagford.

Exmoor & North Devon

Best Places to Eat

➡ Mason's Arms (p138)

➡ Glorious Oyster (p139)

➡ Olive Branch & Room (p135)

➡ Terra Madre (p137)

➡ Woods (p130)

➡ Cafe Porlock Weir (p133)

Best Wildlife Spots

➡ Lundy Island (p138)

➡ Exmoor (p126)

➡ Braunton Burrows (p137)

➡ Northam Burrows (p137)

➡ Hartland Point (p139)

Why Go?

Thousands of holidaymakers peel past this region on their way to the (undeniably lovely) holiday spots further west. So they miss Exmoor, an enchanting national park, where heather-clad hills are roamed by wild ponies and red deer. Villages huddle cosily beside precipitous cliffs; dramatic headlands plunge towards mossy gorges; and sturdy towns deliver an authentic slice of rural life.

North Devon's charms are also worth the detour: classic surf breaks; a wild, jagged coast with vast expanses of sand; plus pretty villages, striking modern art, fine gardens and stately homes. Everywhere, restaurants serve just-caught seafood and produce fresh from furrow and farm, while sleep options range from comfy camping and vintage caravans to art-packed boutique hotels. That's why your Exmoor and North Devon detour just might end up being your destination.

When to Go

➡ **Apr & May** Vivid bluebells carpet woods; bright yellow gorse dots Exmoor. At Easter, attractions open.

➡ **Jun–Aug** By late-July, blooming heather turns Exmoor into a sea of purple. Expect (possibly) warmer days, but also more demands on accommodation.

➡ **Sep & Oct** Holiday crowds disperse, leaving (hopefully) reasonable weather and warmer seas, and definitely cheaper sleeping bills. Freshly gathered mushrooms enliven restaurant menus.

➡ **Oct** brings the spectacle of stags battling it out, as Exmoor's deer rut begins.

➡ **Dec** Short winter days reveal North Devon and Exmoor's exceptionally dark skies. Enjoy the magical, mischievous Dunster by Candlelight celebrations.

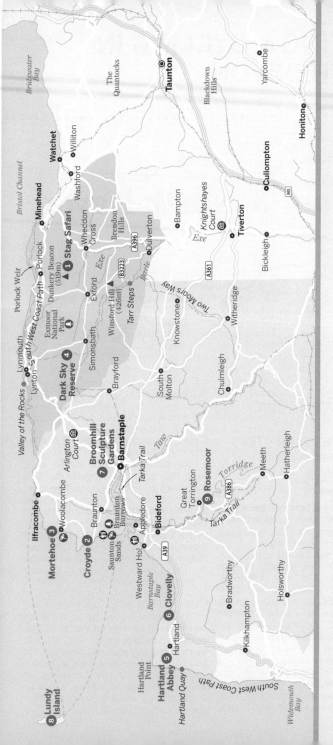

Exmoor & North Devon Highlights

1 Stag Safari (p127)
Heading off-road to spot Exmoor's famous red deer.

2 Croyde (p136) Riding the waves at Devon's uber-cool, thatched surf village.

3 Shepherding Experience (p130) Watching a shepherd and sheepdog herd their flock.

4 Stargazing (p127) Marvelling at constellations in this Dark Sky Reserve.

5 Hartland Abbey (p139) Tracing a timeline spanning centuries at this historic home.

6 Clovelly (p138) Strolling the steep, cobbled streets of a supremely pretty fishing village.

7 Broomhill Sculpture Gardens (p137) Hunting out artworks hidden in acres of magical woods.

8 Lundy Island (p138) Setting sail for your very own offshore, get-away-from-it-all, castaway escape.

9 RHS Rosemoor (p134) Exploring the riot of colour at this exemplar of garden designs.

WALKING & CYCLING IN NORTH DEVON

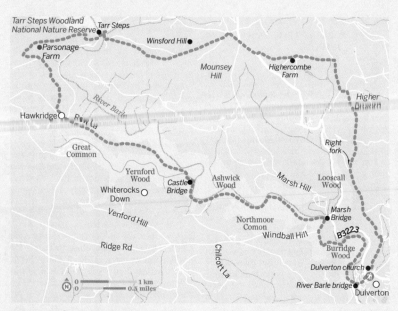

Tarr Steps Woodland National Nature Reserve
Tarr Steps
Parsonage Farm
Winsford Hill
Mounsey Hill
Highercombe Farm
Higher Dunhill
River Barle
Hawkridge
Row La
Right fork
Great Common
Yernford Wood
Castle Bridge
Ashwick Wood
Marsh Hill
Looseall Wood
Whiterocks Down
Marsh Bridge
Venford Hill
Northmoor Comon
Windball Hill
B3223
Ridge Rd
Chilcott La
Burridge Wood
Dulverton church
River Barle bridge
Dulverton
0   1 km
0   0.5 miles

WALKING THE TARR STEPS

START/END DULVERTON CHURCH, FORE ST
DISTANCE 12 MILES
DURATION EIGHT HOURS
DIFFICULTY MODERATE

Skirt the south side of **Dulverton church**, joining the uphill track. Ignore the path leading left to Marsh Bridge; instead, cross the field, take the right fork, then climb to turn left onto a narrow road. Cut left onto a blue-labelled footpath, past **Highercombe Farm** and onto the moor. Head right at the road, then straight on at the cattle grid. Soon there's another road and cattle grid; cut left here, onto the open moorland and **Winsford Hill**'s lower slopes. The valley views are fabulous; look out for the free-roaming Exmoor ponies with anchor brands on their backs.

Eventually high moorland gives way to a wooded river valley, where a right fork leads to the mighty stone slabs of **Tarr Steps** (p127). After an icy paddle (if the river isn't flooded), the **Tarr Farm Inn** (☎01643-851507; www.

tarrfarm.co.uk; Tarr Steps; s £75-90, d £150; [P] [☏]) is an idyllic spot for lunch.

Cross the Barle via those massive stone steps, then peel right following the blue waymarked route up **Parsonage Farm drive**. At the road, go straight on through the fields (by now following yellow waymarks) into the village of **Hawkridge**. Head past the church to fork right down Row Lane, joining the Exe Valley Way to Dulverton. This plunges back into the tranquil woodland framing the river: a mossy, Tolkien-esque landscape of ancient trees that's home to dormice, frogs and otters. As you cross the stone footbridge at **Castle Bridge**, the wood-fringed embankments of the Iron Age hill fort **Mounsey Castle** rise from the opposite bank. The footpath then hugs a river that snakes to **Marsh Bridge**; stay on the south side of the waterway here. Follow it back to Dulverton, walking over the **River Barle bridge**, up Bridge St, then High St and back to Fore St. Ideally, take the Ordnance Survey map *OL9; Exmoor* (£9) on this walk, too.

Take in the quintessential countryside of Exmoor via one of the area's oldest clapper bridges, or cycle beside salt marshes and estuary in the countryside that inspired the classic children's story, Tarka the Otter.

CYCLING THE TARKA TRAIL

START/END BARNSTAPLE TRAIN STATION
DISTANCE 18 MILES
DURATION FOUR HOURS
DIFFICULTY EASY

This tranquil, level, car-free route shadows the immense, sand-fringed River Taw. It traces part of the Tarka Trail, a long-distance route that follows in the paw prints of *Tarka the Otter*, Henry Williamson's classic children's tale.

Hire bikes at **Tarka Trail Cycle Hire** (☑ 01271-324202; www.tarkabikes.co.uk; half-/full day £9/12; ☺ 9am-5pm Mar-Oct) at Barnstaple train station, and pick up Tarka Trail signs south towards Bideford and Meeth. Soon you're amid a lush landscape framed by the Taw and **salt marshes**, prime grazing land and a sea-bass nursery. You're cycling on a disused, late-Victorian railway line, built because larger cargo ships couldn't navigate the Taw. Sweeping into **Fremington Quay** reveals views of that river. Make for the **Fremington Quay Café**, a tea stop set in the old station building; the terrace is an ideal place to watch the world go by. Here, photos reveal the quay's role in exporting the area's high-quality, fine-grained clay, which led to the local pottery industry.

Soon you're beside **Isley Marsh**, an RSPB (Royal Society for the Protection of Birds) reserve of salt marshes and tidal mudflats. Spot oystercatcher, curlew, little egret and grey heron, and maybe kingfisher and osprey. The broad, beautiful estuary views continue at **Instow**, an appealing array of stone shops and cottages lining up beside a sand-fringed shore. Far beyond on the other side of the estuary are the whitewashed houses of Appledore; the massive dunes further north are the tip of **Braunton Burrows**. Dismount to discover more train-related history; Instow's disused railway station comes complete with milk churns on the former platform, and a restored 1873 **signal box**.

Instow's sandy **beach** is perfect for a paddle; next eat at the funky **Instow Arms** (☑ 01271-860608; www.instowarms.com; Marine Pde, Instow; mains £13-16; ☺ 10am-9.30pm) which serves food from noon to 9.30pm. Then saddle up for the view-filled return leg back to Barnstaple train station.

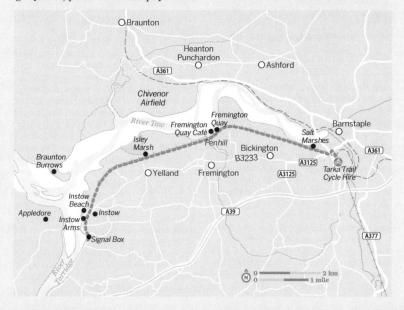

ROAD TRIP >
DUNSTER TO LYNTON

• •

Exmoor is one of the UK's quieter national parks, which makes it brilliant for a backcountry drive – so long as you don't mind tackling a few narrow lanes and sheep-jams.

❶ Dunster

At **Dunster** (p130) take time to explore rusty-red Dunster Castle, which sits on a forested hill in the centre of town. A structure with turrets and robust walls, its most striking features went up in the 1800s, but parts date from the 13th century. Take a quick stroll in the grounds; heading east beside the river leads to a working watermill. Dunster's largely 15th-century church is nearby – once

you're there, track down the 16th-century dovecote just behind it.

❷ Exford

Next motor south down the A396, with Exmoor's hills rising to the west. After turning at Wheddon Cross, the green village of **Exford** (p131) provides an excuse for a stroll. The 16th-century Exmoor White Horse provides the perfect opportunity for refresh-

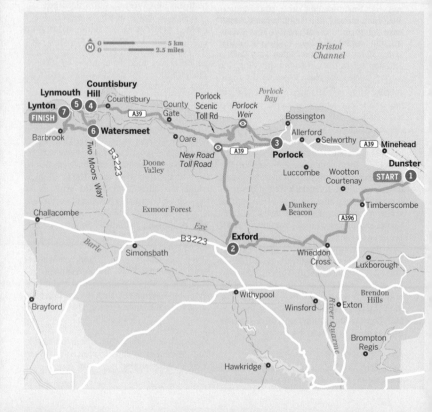

ment; this atmospheric coaching inn has a welcoming bar and an attractive riverside beer terrace.

Drive uphill, past Exford post office, following Porlock signs. After you rattle across a cattle grid, the road climbs, gorse takes over, and buzzards soar. Next comes a long, glorious drive across open moorland; depending on the season, the landscape will be either heather-purple or honey-brown. As you crest a hill, the sea and beach appear far below.

❸ Porlock

Once you reach the A39 you have a choice of two routes to Porlock – both supremely picturesque. The first involves a £2.50 toll. For this turn left, and just under a mile later make a sharp right onto the **New Road Toll Road,** a scenic route that sweeps through pine forests and around U-bends, revealing stretches of shore. Alternatively, to avoid the toll, turn right onto the A39 for a second-gear descent down the infamous 1:4 Porlock Hill; expect hairpin bends, escape lanes and 'try your brakes' signs.

At **Porlock** (p132), park and wander the appealing village's shopping street – perhaps dropping by the tourist office for more info on the local area, or heading into the beam-rich Ship Inn – one-time hang-out of Romantic poet Samuel Taylor Coleridge. Then it's time to drive to **Porlock Weir**, a bewitching pocket-sized stone quay. It's framed by a string of cottages, a shingle beach, a stony harbour approach and sweeping cliffs. Strolling the shingle beach to the west of the weir takes you to the nature reserve of the Porlock Ridge and Saltmarsh SSSI (Site of Special Scientific Interest). Porlock Weir also has a scattering of shops and another great pub – like Porlock's, this one's also called the Ship Inn (they're known locally as Top Ship and Bottom Ship) and has a very popular beer garden.

❹ Countisbury Hill

Next, drive up the lane between the pub and the Cafe on the Weir; the road cuts sharp-

ly right, signed Worthy and Ashley Combe. At the white gate below the thatched stone arch, pay your £2 toll. A bouncing road now climbs beside a wooded stream, and sea glimpses emerge below. At the A39, motor towards Lynmouth through a moorland plateau framed by the sea, wind-bent trees and tufted grass.

First you'll reach **Countisbury Hill,** which plunges down and is a cliff-clinging, brake-burner of a descent. The road signs here speak volumes: 'Rockfalls', '12% gradient' and, chillingly, 'Cyclists Advised to Walk'. A few lay-bys provide safe places to pause and take in the views.

❺ Lynmouth

Eventually you emerge beside the harbour at **Lynmouth** (p133). Look out for the Flood Memorial Hall, which charts the story of the August night in 1952 when torrents of water thundered down Lynmouth's precipitous hills, claiming 34 lives. The Ancient Mariner pub (quality grub) and Rising Sun (akin to restaurant fare) are prime places to eat and drink here. Then stroll west along the seafront to the **Cliff Railway**. This example of Victorian ingenuity sees tiny carriages on rails being powered up (and guided down) the sheer hillside by the force of water alternately being jettisoned and taken on board. Once at the top, stroll to St Mary's Church, where the cliffside graveyard gives views back along Countisbury Hill and your route so far. Hop back onto the cliff railway for your descent and walk back to the car.

❻ Watersmeet

Drive the A39 towards Lynton, via Watersmeet – another first- and second-gear ascent, which hugs the steep-sided and mossy gorge. At **Watersmeet**, stop for the half-mile stroll to the charming waterfalls.

❼ Lynton

Finally, drive up to **Lynton**, where the Vanilla Pod (www.thevanillapodlynton.co.uk) is an ideal spot for supper.

EXMOOR NATIONAL PARK

Exmoor is more than a little addictive, and chances are you won't want to leave its memorable, broad, russet views. In the middle sits the higher moor, an empty, expansive, other-worldly landscape of tawny grasses and huge skies. Here, picturesque Exford makes an ideal village base. In the north, sheer, rock-strewn river valleys cut into the plateau and coal-black cliffs lurch towards the sea.

Amid these towering headlands, charismatic Porlock and the twin villages of Lynton and Lynmouth are atmospheric places to stay. Relaxed Dulverton delivers a country-town vibe, while appealing Dunster boasts cobbled streets and a russet-red castle. Everywhere on Exmoor life is attuned to the rhythms and colours of the seasons – new-born livestock in spring, purple heather in late summer, gold-bronze leaves in autumn, and crisp days and log fires in winter. All this ensures Exmoor delivers insight into an elemental and traditional world.

Activities

Exmoor Adventures   OUTDOORS
(☑07976 208279; www.exmooradventures.co.uk; Porlock Weir) Runs sessions in kayaking and canoeing (£35/70 per half-/full day), mountain biking (from £40 per half-day), coasteering (£35) and rock climbing (£65); caters to skill levels ranging from beginner to advanced. Also rents mountain bikes (£25 per day).

Cycling

Despite (or perhaps because of) the formidable hills, cycling is hugely popular on Exmoor. Several sections of the National Cycle Network (NCN; www.sustrans.org.uk) cross the park, including the West Country Way (NCN Route 3) from Bristol to Padstow, and Devon Coast to Coast (NCN Route 27), between Ilfracombe and Plymouth, via Dartmoor and Exmoor.

Exmoor is also one of the county's most exhilarating off-road cycling destinations, with a wealth of bridleways and permitted tracks. The Exmoor National Park Authority has produced a colour-coded off-road cycle map (£10); buy it at tourist offices.

Exmoor Adventures runs a five-hour mountain-biking skills course (£50) and also rents mountain bikes (£25 per day).

Horse Riding

Brendan Manor Stables   HORSE RIDING
(☑01598-741246; www.ridingonexmoor.co.uk; Brendon Manor) Runs a full range of horse-riding trips, from one to three hours, that head onto the open moor and down into the valleys. Prices start at £30. Based near Lynton.

Burrowhayes Farm   HORSE RIDING
(☑01643-862463; www.burrowhayes.co.uk; West Luccombe; per 1/2hr £23/44; ⊙Apr–mid-Oct) Based near Porlock, Burrowhayes runs a wide range of treks that go into the Horner Valley and onto the moor. Plus special half-hour pony rides for children (£13).

Outovercott Stables   HORSE RIDING
(☑01598-753341; www.outovercott.co.uk; near Lynton; per hr £30) Outovercott's treks onto Exmoor's exposed moorland range from easy one-hour trips for novices to more-challenging excursions for intermediate and experienced riders, which take in views of the Valley of Rocks and the coastline.

Walking

The open moors and a profusion of marked bridleways make Exmoor an excellent area for hiking. The best-known routes are the Somerset & North Devon Coast Path, which is part of the South West Coast Path (www.southwestcoastpath.org.uk), and the Exmoor section of the Two Moors Way, which starts in Lynmouth and travels south to Dartmoor and beyond.

Another superb route is the Coleridge Way (www.coleridgeway.co.uk), which winds for 51 miles through Exmoor, the Brendon Hills and the Quantocks. Part of the 180-mile Tarka Trail cuts through the park: join it at Combe Martin; hike along the cliffs to Lynton and Lynmouth; then head across the moor towards Barnstaple.

Organised walks run by the national park authority are held throughout the year and include deer safaris, nightjar birdwatching walks and dark-sky strolls.

Wildlife Safaris

The Exmoor National Park Authority runs regular wildlife-themed guided walks (free), which include evening deer-spotting hikes. Or head out on an organised jeep safari to combine scenic sightseeing with a couple of hours of off-road wildlife-watching.

Discovery Safaris
OUTDOORS

(📞01643-863444; www.discoverysafaris.com; per person £25) These twice-daily jeep safaris set off from Porlock and head up onto open moorland searching for wildlife, especially Exmoor's famous red deer.

Tours leave from the village hall car park in Porlock.

Exmoor Safari
OUTDOORS

(📞01643-831229; www.exmoorsafari.co.uk; Exford; adult/child £35/16) Long-running wildlife-watching operator that uses 4WD vehicles and local knowledge to search out red deer.

Red Stag Safari
OUTDOORS

(📞01643-841831; www.redstagsafari.co.uk; safaris £30-38) These half-day safaris see you bouncing around Exmoor in a jeep searching for deer. Tours set off from Wheddon Cross, Minehead, Dunster, Porlock, Exford and Dulverton, and depart mornings, afternoons and some evenings.

ℹ️ Information

There are three Exmoor National Park Authority tourist offices, in Dulverton (p130), Dunster (p131) and Lynmouth (p134).

The **Exmoor National Park Authority** (ENPA; 📞01398-323665; www.exmoor-nationalpark. gov.uk) regulates the park.

Active Exmoor (www.visit-exmoor.co.uk/active-exmoor)
Visit Exmoor (www.visit-exmoor.co.uk)
What's On Exmoor (www.whatsonexmoor.com)

ℹ️ Getting There & Away

Exmoor isn't very easy to get around or to get to without your own vehicle. The nearest main-line train stations are around 14 miles away. But with some planning and patience it is possible to travel between many of the moor's main towns and villages by bus.

ℹ️ Getting Around

The **MoorRover** (📞01643-709701; www.atwest. org.uk) is an on-demand minibus that can take you anywhere on Exmoor. Prices range from £10 to £30, depending on distances involved. It'll also carry bikes and provides a luggage-transfer service. Book at least a day ahead.

The website of the Exmoor National Park Authority (p127) lists the moor's bus services. Be aware: some are seasonal, and the more remote services are particularly prone to change.

Bus 28 Shuttles from Taunton to the resort of Minehead (£10, 1¼ hours, at least hourly).

STARGAZING ON EXMOOR

Exmoor holds the distinction of being named Europe's first International Dark Sky Reserve, in recognition of the night-time inky blackness overhead. But what does that mean in practice? Namely, a whole host of local organisations striving to limit light pollution, plus, for visitors, some simply spectacular star displays.

The Exmoor National Park Authority runs occasional moonlit strolls and has produced the *Dark Skies Guide*, which includes star charts and maps pinpointing the best light-free spots. Pick one up at a visitor centre or download it from the authority's website. It also hires out suitable telescopes (£25 per night). For optimum star-gazing, central, higher Exmoor is best – try Brandon Two Gates (on the B3223) or Webber's Post (just north of Dunkery Beacon).

Bus 300 Exmoor Coastal Link Heads along the coast from Minehead to Lynmouth (£10, 55 minutes), via Porlock (£6, 15 minutes). The service is limited to two buses daily between Monday and Saturday, during July and August only.

Bus 309/310 Runs from Barnstaple via Parracombe to Lynton or Lynmouth (£3.40, 55 minutes, eight daily Monday to Saturday).

Bus 467 Runs from Minehead to Dulverton (£3.50, one hour, one daily Monday to Friday), via Dunster (£1) and Wheddon Cross (£2).

Dulverton

📞 01398 / POP 1500

The southern gateway to Exmoor National Park, Dulverton sits at the base of the Barle Valley near the confluence of two key rivers: the Exe and Barle. A traditional country town, it's home to a collection of gun sellers, fishing-tackle stores and gift shops, and makes an attractive edge-of-moor base.

⊙ Sights

⭐Tarr Steps
LANDMARK

Exmoor's most famous landmark is an ancient stone clapper bridge shaded by gnarled old trees. Its huge slabs are propped up on stone columns embedded in the River Barle. Local folklore aside (which declares it was

Seaside Villages

Devon and Cornwall remind you that magical coastal communities are not just figments of your imagination. Cobbled lanes snake down steep hills, cottages cluster beside the shore, floating boats nudge harbour walls, and your fish supper is hauled ashore. Experience it at Clovelly, Mousehole, Fowey, St Mawes, Mevagissey, Port Isaac and Beer.

IAN WOOLCOCK / SHUTTERSTOCK ©

NEALE CLARKE / ROBERTHARDING / GETTY IMAGES ©

1. Clovelly (p138)
A picture-postcard perfect village, Clovelly has quaint B&Bs and pretty inns cascading down the cliffs.

2. Mousehole (p222)
Fishing village Mousehole is packed in summer and deserted in winter.

3. St Mawes (p169)
St Mawes Castle is one of the best preserved of the 16th-century fortresses built by Henry VIII.

4. Beer (p64)
A great base for East Devon, Beer has unusual cave networks and a superb coastal path.

ANDREA PUCCI / GETTY IMAGES ©

THE SHEPHERD'S WAY

For an authentic insight into the lives of those who live and work amid North Devon's extraordinarily craggy scenery, sign up for a memorable two-hour shepherding experience (☑ 01271-870056; www.boroughfarm.co.uk; Borough Farm, near Mortehoe; adult/child £10/5; ☺ Thu evening Jun–mid-Sep). Shepherd David Kennard and adorable collie Fly steer you around the precipitous cliffs at Mortehoe, demonstrating the intricacies of safely herding their sturdy sheep. The human-dog teamwork is touching, the skill levels remarkable, and the scenery breathtaking. Borough Farm is 6 miles southwest of Ilfracombe.

used by the Devil for sunbathing), it first pops into the historical record in the 1600s, and has had to be rebuilt after 21st-century floods. The steps are signed off the B3223 Dulverton–Simonsbath road, 5 miles northwest of Dulverton.

You can also hike there from Dulverton along the banks of the River Barle (12 miles return).

Exmoor
Pony Centre   WILDLIFE RESERVE
(☑ 01398-323093; www.exmoorponycentre.org.uk; Ashwick, near Dulverton; ☺ 10am-4pm Mon, Wed-Fri & Sun Easter-Oct; ℗) **FREE** You'll see them cantering across the open moor, but this is a great way to get up close to Exmoor's stubby ponies. Originally bred as beasts of burden, they're famously hardy despite their diminutive size. A prebooked one-hour taster session (£30) sees you grooming, tacking and riding a pony indoors.

There's also a half-day pony experience; it includes a two-hour moorland hack (for competent riders under 13 stone or 82.5kg only) and costs £45 per person.

✖ Eating

Tantivy   CAFE €
(☑ 01398-323465; www.tantivyexmoor.co.uk; Fore St; snacks from £3; ☺ 9.30am-4.30pm; 🐾) A gift shop, a deli and a tearoom where you can buy a hiking map, peruse the preserves then sip an espresso on the tiny patio.

Exclusive Cake Co   BAKERY €
(☑ 01398-324131; www.exclusivecakecompany. co.uk; 19 High St; snacks from £3; ☺ 9am-4pm

Mon-Fri, to 2pm Sat) Real rarities stack the shelves here: Exmoor ale, cheese and wholegrain-mustard bread; Somerset cider cake; venison and port pie. Note the typically Exmoor warning: 'Game pies may contain lead shot'.

Mortimers   CAFE €
(☑ 01398-323850; 13 High St; mains from £9; ☺ 9.30am-5pm Thu-Tue) Chunky wooden tables and exposed brick defy traditional tearoom expectations; the menu is surprising, too. Expect homemade 'moo burgers' (beef sandwiched between brioche buns) and unusual rarebits – options for cheese-on-toast here include goats cheese or brie with added beer or Somerset cider.

★ **Woods**   BISTRO €€
(☑ 01398-324007; www.woodsdulverton.co.uk; 4 Bank Sq; mains £14-18; ☺ noon-2pm & 7-9.30pm) With its deer antlers, hunting prints and big wood-burning stove, multi-award-winning Woods is Exmoor to its core. No surprise then to find menus full of full-bodied flavours: expect confit leg of guinea fowl, slow-roast lamb shoulder, and asparagus and wild garlic risotto. Book ahead.

ℹ Information

Dulverton Tourist Office (☑ 01398-323841; www.exmoor-nationalpark.gov.uk; 7-9 Fore St; ☺ 10am-5pm Apr-Oct, limited hours Oct-Apr)

ℹ Getting There & Away

Bus 398 Links Dulverton with Tiverton (£5, 45 minutes, two to three daily Monday to Saturday).

Bus 467 Runs from Dulverton to Minehead (one hour, one daily Monday to Friday), via Wheddon Cross and Dunster.

Dunster

☑ 01643 / POP 820

Centred on a scarlet-walled castle and a medieval yarn market, Dunster is one of Exmoor's oldest villages, a tempting tangle of cobbled streets, bubbling brooks and pack-horse bridges.

◉ Sights

★ **Dunster Castle**   CASTLE
(NT; ☑ 01643-821314; www.nationaltrust.org.uk; Castle Hill; adult/child £11/5.50; ☺ 11am-5pm Mar-Oct; ℗) Rosy-hued Dunster Castle crowns a densely wooded hill. Built by the Luttrell

family, which once owned much of northern Exmoor, the oldest sections are 13th century, while the turrets and exterior walls are 19th-century additions. Look out for Tudor furnishings, 17th-century plasterwork and a ridiculously grand staircase. Leave time to explore the colourful terraced gardens, which feature riverside walks, a working watermill and views across Exmoor's shores.

★ Cleeve Abbey   HISTORIC SITE
(EH; ☑ 01984-640377; www.english-heritage.org. uk; Abbey Rd, Washford; adult/child £5/3; ⊙10am-5pm Apr-Jun, Sep & Oct, to 6pm Jul & Aug; P) Most visitors buzz straight past tiny, tumble-down Cleeve Abbey, but it's one of the best examples of traditional Cistercian architecture in southwest England, and offers a fine glimpse into the life of the monks who lived here 800 years ago. It was largely torn down during Henry VIII's dissolution of the monasteries, but you can still see the impressive cloister buildings, the original gatehouse, the refectory and the monks' dormitory. It's 5 miles east of Dunster.

Bakelite Museum   MUSEUM
(☑ 01984-632133; www.bakelitemuseum.co.uk; Bridge St, Williton; adult/child £5/3; ⊙10.30am-5pm Thu-Sun Easter-Jun, Sep & Oct, daily Jul & Aug) The endearingly weird Bakelite Museum, 7 miles east of Dunster, houses the nation's largest collection of Bakelite (otherwise known as polyoxybenzylmethylenglycolanhydride), one of the earliest plastics. The highlight of this treasure trove is the full-sized Bakelite coffin – pity the pall-bearers who had to lug that one.

Other Bakelite items on show include radios, letter openers, egg cups, vacuum cleaners, toasters and even false teeth.

Watermill   HISTORIC BUILDING
(NT; ☑ 01643-821314; www.nationaltrust.org.uk; Mill Lane; ⊙11am-5pm Mar-Oct) Most of the original cogs, wheels and grinding stones continue to rotate in this working 18th-century mill. There's a picturesque riverside tearoom alongside.

Admission to the mill is included in tickets to neighbouring Dunster Castle.

✕ Eating

★ Reeve's   BRITISH €€
(☑ 01643-821414; www.reevesrestaurantdunster. co.uk; 20 High St; mains £18-28; ⊙7-9pm Tue-Sat, noon-2pm Sun) The eponymous chef at seriously stylish Reeve's is an award winner. No wonder: the complex creations here truly showcase Exmoor produce. Opt for seabass on prawn and basil risotto, or meltingly tender lamb roasted with rosemary and garlic. To finish? Some toasted walnut bread with local hard and soft cheeses.

Cobblestones   CAFE €€
(☑ 01643-821595; www.cobblestonesofdunster. co.uk; 24 High St; mains £8-14; ⊙10.30am-3pm Wed-Mon Easter-Oct, 11am-3pm Sat & Sun Nov-Easter) The treats at cosy, friendly Cobblestones range from beef stew to veggie curry, via a belt-busting Somerset cream tea. The cafe also opens some evenings during summer – it's best to book.

🛈 Information

Dunster Tourist Office (☑ 01643-821835; www.exmoor-nationalpark.gov.uk; The Steep; ⊙10am-5pm Apr-Oct, limited hours Oct-Apr)

🛈 Getting There & Away

Bus 467 runs north to Minehead (£1) and south to Dulverton (£3.50, one hour, one daily Monday to Friday), via Wheddon Cross.

The 22-mile **West Somerset Railway** (☑ 01643-704996; www.west-somerset-railway. co.uk; 24hr rover tickets adult/child £20/10) stops at Dunster during summer, with four to seven trains daily from May to October.

EXFORD

Tucked into the banks of the River Exe at the heart of Exmoor, Exford is a delightful medley of cottages and slate-roofed houses clustered around a village green. Step through the door of Exmoor White Horse (☑ 01643-831229; www.exmoor-whitehorse.co.uk; Exford; d £180-205; P 🕾) and find everything you could want from an Exmoor coaching inn: a friendly bar with a real fire, a local produce-packed restaurant (mains £15 to £23) and smoothly comfy rooms. On summer afternoons, the riverside beer terrace is a firm favourite with the locals, and an idyllic spot to watch the horse riders trot by. Bus 198 links Exford with Minehead (£4.20, 45 minutes) and Dulverton (£3.70, 30 minutes) twice daily from Monday to Saturday.

Porlock & Around

☎ 01643

The coastal village of Porlock is one of the prettiest on the Exmoor coast; the huddle of thatched cottages lining its main street is framed on one side by the sea and on the other by steeply sloping hills. Winding lanes lead to the charismatic breakwater of Porlock Weir, 2 miles to the west, with an arching pebble beach and striking coastal views.

👁 Sights

★ Porlock Weir HARBOUR

(P) Porlock Weir's stout granite quay curves around a shingly beach, which is backed by pubs, fisherfolks' storehouses and a scattering of seasonal shops. The weir has been around for almost a thousand years (it's named in the Domesday Book as 'Portloc'). It makes a glorious place for a pub lunch and a stroll, with stirring views across the Vale of Porlock and easy access to the South West Coast Path.

Holnicote Estate ARCHITECTURE

(NT; ☎ 01643-862452; www.nationaltrust.org.uk; near Porlock; P) **FREE** The 50-sq-km Hol-nicote Estate sweeps southeast out of Porlock, taking in a string of impossibly pretty villages. Picturesque Bossington leads to charming Allerford and its 15th-century packhorse bridge. The biggest village, Selworthy offers eye-catching Exmoor views, a cafe, a shop, and cob-and-thatch cottages clustering around the village green.

Exmoor Owl & Hawk Centre WILDLIFE RESERVE

(☎ 01643-862816; www.exmoorfalconry.co.uk; Allerford, near Porlock; adult/child £10/8.50; ⏰ noon-4.30pm Tue-Thu, Sat & Sun Mar-Oct; P) Catch the owl and bird-of-prey flying show (2pm); book your own hour-long private flying session (from £40); or have the kids hitch a half hour ride on the farm's Shetland ponies (£15; bookings essential).

🍴 Eating

Ship Inn PUB FOOD €

(Bottom Ship; ☎ 01643-863288; www.shipinn porlockweir.co.uk; Porlock Weir; mains from £9; ⏰ noon-2.45pm & 6-8.45pm) The floors are flagstone and there's a big wood burner but in the summer you'd be hard-pressed to see them – so crammed at that time is this his-

Porlock Weir

toric Porlock Weir pub with hikers and holi-daymakers. Bag a patio table and join them tucking into hearty chilli, chorizo casserole and cod 'n' chips.

Kitnors CAFE €€
(☑ 01643-862643; www.kitnors.com; Bossington; mains from £5; ☺ 11am-4.30pm Jun-Aug, to 4pm Fri-Tue Oct-May) A quintessential thatched tearoom 1 mile east of Porlock dishing up toasties, soups and afternoon teas featuring homemade scones, proper clotted cream and local jams. The high tea comes with sweet and savoury morsels served on a tiered cake stand.

★**Cafe Porlock Weir** MODERN BRITISH €€
(☑ 01643-863300; www.thecafeporlockweir.co.uk; Porlock Weir; mains £12-18; ☺ noon-8pm Wed-Sun; P 🛜) The food here regularly claims awards, while shore views and an assured, country-house ambience add to the appeal. Ingredients from sea and moor pack the menu; a window table is an atmospheric spot to tuck into oysters, roasted scallops or a tarragon-infused wild-mushroom risotto.

Ship Inn PUB FOOD €€
(Top Ship; ☑ 01643-862507; www.shipinnporlock.co.uk; High St, Porlock; mains £9-18; ☺ noon-2.30pm & 6-8.30pm; P) Romantic poet Samuel Taylor Coleridge and pal Robert Southey both downed pints in this 13th-century thatched Porlock inn – you can even sit in a snug still dubbed 'Southey's Corner'. Substantial pub food – mainly steaks, roasts and stews – is served in the bar.

❶ Information

Porlock Tourist Office (☑ 01643-863150; www.porlock.co.uk; West End, Porlock; ☺ 10am-5pm Mon-Sat Easter-Oct, to 12.30pm Tue-Sat Nov-Easter)

❶ Getting There & Away

Bus 300 heads from Porlock east along the coast to Minehead (£6, 15 minutes), and west to Lynmouth (£10, 55 minutes). It runs in July and August only; there are two buses a day, Monday to Friday only.

Drivers can choose from two picturesque routes into Porlock village. The New Road Toll Road sweeps through pine forests and round U-bends, while Porlock Hill (A39) is a brake-burning 1:4 descent. A further toll road, the Porlock Scenic (Worthy) Toll Road, provides an alternative, bouncing, route up out of Porlock Weir.

Lynton & Lynmouth

Tucked in amid precipitous cliffs and steep, tree-lined slopes, these twin coastal towns are a landscape-painter's dream. Bustling Lynmouth sits beside the shore, a busy harbour lined with pubs and souvenir shops. On the clifftop, Lynton feels much more genteel and well to do. A cliffside railway links the two: it's powered by the rushing West Lyn River, which feeds numerous cascades and waterfalls nearby.

◉ Sights

★**Cliff Railway** HERITAGE RAILWAY
(☑ 01598-753486; www.cliffrailwaylynton.co.uk; The Esplanade, Lynmouth; one way/return adult £2.80/3.80, child £1.70/2.30; ☺ 10am-5pm Feb, Mar & Oct, to 6pm Apr, May & Sep, to 7pm Jun-Aug) This extraordinary piece of Victorian engineering sees two cars, linked by a steel cable, descend and ascend the steeply sloping cliff face according to the weight of water in the cars' tanks. All burnished wood and polished brass, it's been running since 1890 and makes for an unmissable ride.

Flood Memorial MUSEUM
(The Esplanade, Lynmouth; ☺ 9am-6pm Easter-Oct) FREE On 16 August 1952 a huge wave of water swept through Lynmouth following torrential rain. The devastation was immense: 34 people lost their lives, and four bridges and countless houses were washed away. This exhibition features photos of the aftermath and personal testimonies of those involved.

Lyn & Exmoor Museum MUSEUM
(St Vincent's Cottage, Market St, Lynton; adult/child £2/50p; ☺ 10.30am-5pm Tue-Thu & Sat Easter-Oct) This sweet museum's collections include chilling pictures of Lynmouth's devastating 1952 flash flood, which claimed 34 lives. It occupies the town's oldest house.

🏃 Activities

★**Valley of the Rocks** WALKING
The dramatic geology in this valley was described by poet Robert Southey as 'rock reeling upon rock, stone piled upon stone, a huge terrifying reeling mass'. Look out for the formations dubbed the Devil's Cheesewring and Ragged Jack – and also the feral goats that wander the tracks. Its a mile's walk west of Lynton along a cracking coast path.

DON'T MISS

RHS ROSEMOOR

Run by the prestigious Royal Horticultural Society (RHS), Rosemoor (☑01805-624067; www.rhs.org.uk/gardens/rosemoor; Great Torrington; adult/child £11/5.50; ☉10am-6pm Apr-Sep, to 5pm Oct-Mar; ℗) is a must-see source of green-fingered inspiration. One of only four RHS gardens open to the public nationwide, its 25 enchanting hectares are a vivid, fragrant oasis, full of colour, serenity and a wealth of styles ranging from arboreta and croquet lawns to shade, terrace and town gardens.

The fruit and veg section is an object lesson of rows, raised beds and containers. Other highlights include the tree ferns, bananas and ginger lilies in the exotic garden, the sweeps of colour in the cottage garden and Rosemoor's famous, heavily scented rose garden.

Rosemoor is 8 miles south of Bideford, near Great Torrington, off the A3124.

✖ Eating

★**Charlie Friday's**   CAFE €

(☑07544 123324; www.charliefridays.co.uk; Church Hill, Lynton; snacks from £4; ☉10am-6pm Apr-Oct, reduced hours winter; 🛜) A funky, friendly hang-out serving melt-in-your-mouth pastries, thick sarnies, tasty nachos and fair-trade two-shot espresso that really packs a punch.

Esplanade Fish Bar   FISH & CHIPS €

(☑01598-753798; 2 The Esplanade, Lynmouth; mains from £6; ☉noon-7.30pm) An award-winning chippy set a few steps from the shore. Take away and eat on the rough-sand beach, or dine inside within the cheap 'n' cheerful cafe.

★**Rising Sun**   MODERN BRITISH €€

(☑01598-753223; www.risingsunlynmouth.co.uk; Harbourside, Lynmouth; mains £15-28; ☉noon-2.30pm & 6-9pm) At the harbourside Rising Sun, head chef Matthew Rutter focuses on showcasing not only Exmoor meat and vegetables but also the fresh seafood landed along the rugged shore. Seasonal treats might include succulent lobster, fresh sea bass and local mussels, all served up with confidence and more than a dash of élan.

★**Ancient Mariner**   PUB FOOD €€

(☑01598-752238; www.bathhotellynmouth.co.uk; The Harbour, Lynmouth; mains £7-19; ☉noon-3pm & 6-9pm; 🛜) The Mariner brings a burst of shipwreck chic to Lynmouth, thanks to a copper bar top, curved ship's decking and a figurehead that isn't entirely clothed. Drink it all in while tucking into a stacked-high Mariner Burger, complete with Exmoor ale and black-treacle-braised brisket, onion jam and blue-cheese mousse.

ℹ Information

Lynmouth Tourist Office (☑01598-752509; www.exmoor-nationalpark.gov.uk; The Esplanade, Lynmouth; ☉10am-5pm) An Exmoor National Park Authority visitor centre

Lynton Tourist Office (☑0845 4583775; www.lynton-lynmouth-tourism.co.uk; Lynton Town Hall, Lee Rd, Lynton; ☉10am-5pm Mon-Sat, to 2pm Sun Apr-Oct, 10am-3pm Tue-Thu Nov-Mar)

ℹ Getting There & Away

Bus 309/310 Runs year-round from Barnstaple via Parracombe to Lynton or Lynmouth (£3.40, 55 minutes, eight daily Monday to Saturday).

Bus 300 A seasonal, vintage bus (1950s) that shuttles between Minehead and Lynmouth (£10, 55 minutes), via Porlock (£6, 15 minutes), twice daily Monday to Friday, July and August only.

NORTH DEVON

Ilfracombe

☑01271 / POP 11,510

If there's anywhere that sums up the faded grandeur of the British seaside, it's surely Ilfracombe. Framed by precipitous cliffs, elegant town houses, golf greens and a promenade strung with twinkling lights, it's a place that might seem pickled in a bygone age. But look beneath the surface and you'll find there's another side to Ilfracombe – it's a favourite hang-out for the artist Damien Hirst, who's added a controversial statue to the seafront, and is now home to some top-notch eateries. Ilfracombe more than deserves a look.

◉ Sights

★**Verity**   LANDMARK

(The Pier) Pregnant, naked and holding aloft a huge spear, Damien Hirst's 20m statue

Verity towers above Ilfracombe's harbour mouth. On the seaward side her skin is peeled back, revealing sinew, fat and foetus. Critics say she detracts from the scenery; the artist says she's an allegory for truth and justice. Either way, she's drawing the crowds.

Ilfracombe Aquarium   AQUARIUM
(☑ 01271-864533; www.ilfracombeaquarium.co.uk; The Pier; adult/child £4.75/3.75; ☺ 10am-3pm early Feb-late May & Oct, to 5pm late May-Sep) Recreates aquatic environments from Exmoor to the Atlantic, via estuary, rock pool and harbour.

🏃 Activities

★**Tunnelsbeaches**   SWIMMING
(☑ 01271-879882; www.tunnelsbeaches.co.uk; Bath Place; adult/child £2.50/2; ☺ 10am-5pm Apr-Jun, Sep & Oct, to 7pm Jul & Aug) In 1823 hundreds of Welsh miners hacked, by hand, the four tunnels here out of solid rock. It was a remarkable feat. The tunnels lead to a strip of beach where you can plunge into the sea from Victorian tidal bathing pools.

Ilfracombe Princess   BOATING
(☑ 01271-879727; www.ilfracombeprincess.co.uk; The Pier; adult/child £12/6; ☺ 1-4 trips daily Easter-Oct) Hop aboard this cute little yellow tub boat for a 1½-hour Seal Cruise along a dramatic shore.

✗ Eating

★**Grampus**   PUB FOOD £
(☑ 01271-862906; www.thegrampus-inn.co.uk; Lee, near Ilfracombe; mains £8-13; ☺ noon-3pm daily, 7-9pm Mon-Sat) A proper old-fashioned Devonshire pub with a warm welcome, hearty food, an open fire, a raft of pub games and quality beers – try Ilfracombe's own Lundy Gold. It's in the village of Lee, 3 miles west of Ilfracombe. Hiking the coast path is the best way to arrive.

Quay   EUROPEAN ££
(☑ 01271-868090; www.11thequay.co.uk; 11 The Quay; mains £15-25; ☺ noon-2.30pm & 6-9pm daily Apr-Sep, Wed-Sat Oct-Mar) Ilfracombe's hippest harbourside hang-out by far is owned by artist Damien Hirst (he of the cut-in-half cows and pickled sharks). His creations line the walls, so you get to tuck into a cognac-laced lobster bisque or pan-roasted Exmoor chicken breast while studying models of his local statue *Verity* and, with delicious irony, fish in formaldehyde.

La Gendarmerie   MODERN BRITISH ££
(☑ 01271-865984; www.lagendarmerie.co.uk; 63 Fore St; 2/3 courses £25/30; ☺ 7-9pm Thu-Sat) In this dimly lit restaurant imaginative creations are served up with more than a soupçon of French flair. Expect intense flavours: roast pollock with truffle butter and champagne velouté; bouillabaisse-style sea bream; and confit lamb ravioli.

Take Thyme   SEAFOOD ££
(☑ 01271-867622; www.takethymeilfracombe. com; 1 Fore St; mains £14-17; ☺ 7-9pm Tue-Sun, noon-2.30pm Sat) It's the specials board that draws your eye at this intimate bistro; it's full of supremely fresh, locally landed fish. Classic treatments allow the seafood to shine, whether you opt for creamy seafood chowder, plump king scallops or zesty sole baked in lemon and thyme – they're all perfectly cooked. It's popular, so book ahead.

★**Olive Branch & Room**   BISTRO £££
(☑ 01271-867831; www.thomascarrchef.co.uk; 56 Fore St; mains £21-23; ☺ 6.30-9pm Tue-Sat; ☎ ☑) Ilfracombe has added a Michelin-starred eatery to its appeal. Run by Thomas Carr (a protégé of Michelin-starred English chef Nathan Outlaw), this smart bistro-B&B delivers intensely flavoured, complex creations featuring local produce. Perhaps start with local mackerel, Lundy crab and leek tart, before trying the tender Devon steak with

EXMOOR & NORTH DEVON ILFRACOMBE

oxtail fritter and red-wine-infused wild mushrooms. The seven-course taster menu (£68) is sublime. Book ahead.

🍷 Drinking & Nightlife

George & Dragon   PUB
(☑ 01271-863851; www.georgeanddragonilfracombe.co.uk; 5 Fore St; ⊘ 11am-midnight) Ilfracombe's oldest pub (c 1366) has flagstone floors, a beam-crossed ceiling, home-cooked crab on the menu and well-kept Exmoor ales. Food (mains from £9) is served from noon to 3pm and 6.30pm to 9pm.

ℹ Information

Tourist Office (☑ 01271-863001; www.visit ilfracombe.co.uk; The Seafront; ⊘ 9.30am-4.30pm Mon-Fri, from 10.30am Sat & Sun Easter-Oct, closed Sun Nov-Easter) Currently inside the seafront Landmark Theatre building.

ℹ Getting There & Away

Bus 21/21A Runs to Barnstaple (£2.40, 40 minutes, half-hourly) via Braunton (£1.80, 30 minutes).
Bus 300 Runs to Lynmouth in July and August only (£3, two daily Monday to Friday).

Croyde

☑ 01271 / POP 8130

Croyde has the kind of cheerful, chilled vibe you'd expect from its role as North Devon's surf central. The old world meets a new surfing wave here: thatched roofs peep out over racks of wetsuits; crowds of hip wave-riders sip beers outside 17th-century inns; and powerful waves line up to roll in towards acres of sand.

🏃 Activities

Surfing Croyde Bay   SURFING
(☑ 01271-891200; www.surfingcroydebay.co.uk; Baggy Point; per half-/full day £35/70) The pick of the local surf schools, with experienced instructors who can cater for advanced riders with one-on-one tuition as well as for complete novices. It also runs coasteering sessions (per person £40) and stand-up paddleboarding courses (per person £40).

Surf South West   SURFING
(☑ 01271-890400; www.surfsouthwest.com; Croyde Burrows car park; per half-/full day £34/64; ⊘ late Mar-Oct) Experienced and long-standing surf school; the full-day

EXMOOR & NORTH DEVON CROYDE

MANFRED GOTTSCHALK / GETTY IMAGES ©

Damien Hirst's *Verity* (p134) on the pier at Ilfracombe

NORTH DEVON'S BURROWS

North Devon is home to some wild and beautiful natural dune systems, known locally as burrows. The vast expanse at Braunton Burrows (www.explorebraunton.org; near Braunton; **P**) **FREE** is the largest in the UK. Paths wind past sandy hummocks, salt marshes, purple thyme, yellow hawkweed and pyramidal orchids. The burrows fringe an immense sweep of sandy beach, and were the main training area for American troops before D-Day. Mock landing craft are still hidden in the tufted dunes near the car park at its southern tip.

Near Westward Ho!, Northam Burrows (01237-479708; www.torridge.gov.uk/north amburrows; Sandymere Rd, Northam; parking per day £3.50; pedestrians 24hr, cars 7am-10pm Apr-Oct, to 6pm Nov-Mar; **P**) is a wildlife-rich world of grassy plains, sand dunes, sandy shoreline and salt marshes grazed by sheep and horses. Birdwatchers should look out for wheatear, linnet, pied wagtail, stonechat, curlew and little egret. A pebble ridge sits between the burrows and 2-mile-long Westward Ho! beach, forming a natural sea defence.

session is good value, as it includes two lessons and lunch. A full weekend costs £94.

✖ Eating

Hobb's　　　　　　　　　　　BISTRO €€
(01271-890256; www.hobbsbistrocroyde.co.uk; 6 Hobb's Hill; mains £15-28; 6-9.30pm Tue-Sun, to 8.30pm Oct-Mar) Heavily beamed eatery rustling up hearty dishes including steaks, burgers, ribs and a local seafood paella, plus a mildly spiced mint tagine.

❶ Getting There & Away

Bus 21/21A runs from Croyde to Braunton (£1.50, 15 minutes, five daily Monday to Saturday), Barnstaple (£2.50, 45 minutes) and Bideford (£2.80, 1½ hours).

Barnstaple

01271 / POP 54,000

The commercial and administrative centre of North Devon, Barnstaple is also its transport hub. Sitting in a deeply rural region, it's the springboard for two classy attractions: the historic Arlington Court country house and the quirky Broomhill Sculpture Gardens.

◉ Sights

★ **Arlington Court**　　　HISTORIC BUILDING
(NT; 01271-850296; www.nationaltrust.org.uk; Arlington; adult/child £11/5.50; 11am-5pm daily mid-Feb–Oct; **P**) The honey-grey Regency manor house of Arlington Court exudes charm, from the model ships and shells collected by the owners, to the produce-packed walled kitchen garden. Its stables house the National Trust Carriage Collection, and the burnished leather and plush fabrics of

its 40 vehicles summon up an era of stately transport. Arlington Court is 8 miles north of Barnstaple on the A39.

Search out the replica carriages (which you can bounce about in) and the frequent harnessing demonstrations. Also track down the tiny Pony Phaeton, a four-wheeled carriage belonging to Queen Victoria. Her Majesty drove it herself, but a servant walked alongside, ever ready to apply the handbrake (think Billy Connolly's Mr Brown to Judi Dench's Queen Victoria).

★ **Broomhill Sculpture Gardens**　　GARDENS
(01271-850262; www.broomhillart.co.uk; Muddiford Rd; adult/child £4.50/3.50; 11am-4pm; **P**) It's a magical effect: 300 often quirky sculptures hidden away in a 4-hectare wooded valley. There's a fairytale or comic feel to much of it – slivers of burnished steel, painted columns and a series of mystical figures poor out from behind trees; the way they're laid out often invites you to join the composition. Broomhill is 3 miles north of Barnstaple at Muddiford, on the B3230.

✖ Eating

★ **Terra Madre**　　　　　　　　BISTRO €€
(01271-850262; www.broomhillart.co.uk; Muddiford Rd, Muddiford; 3-course lunch/dinner £17/25; 12.15-1.30pm Wed-Sun, 7-8.30pm Wed-Sat) The tables at this slow-food bistro overflow with local, organic produce, including crab and lobster, Red Ruby beef and free-range chicken. Dishes are infused with Mediterranean flavours; Terra Madre even makes its own air-dried chorizo, bacon and salami with local free-range pork. Booking is required for lunch and dinner; tapas (£3.50 to £5) are available daily too (from 12.30pm to 2.30pm).

EXMOOR & NORTH DEVON BARNSTAPLE

★ **Mason's Arms** MODERN EUROPEAN €€€
(☑ 01398-341231; www.masonsarmsdevon.co.uk; Knowstone; mains £24-27; ⊙ noon-2pm Tue-Sun, 7-9pm Tue-Sat) This is a surprise: a Michelin-starred eatery in a thatched 13th-century pub deep in rural North Devon. Modern takes on European classics might include sea bass with smoked eel and clam *ragoût* or wild mushroom *arancini* (risotto balls). Leave room for apricot soufflé with butterscotch ice cream. The Mason's Arms is 20 miles southeast of Barnstaple – it's worth the drive.

ℹ️ Information

Barnstaple Tourist Office (☑ 01271-346747; www.staynorthdevon.co.uk; The Square; ⊙ 10am-5pm Mon-Sat)

ℹ️ Getting There & Away

BUS

National Express Includes services to London, Bristol and Birmingham.

Bus 21 Runs half-hourly to Ilfracombe (£2.40, 40 minutes), via Braunton (£2.30, 30 minutes), and to Bideford in the opposite direction (£2, 30 minutes).

Bus 155 Runs to Exeter (£6.50, two hours, seven daily Monday to Saturday).

TRAIN

The Tarka Line shuttles to Exeter (£10, 75 minutes, hourly Monday to Saturday, six on Sunday).

Clovelly

☑ 01237 / POP 440

Clovelly is the quintessential picture-postcard Devon village. Its cottages cascade down cliffs to meet a curving claw of a harbour that is lined with lobster pots backed by a deep-blue sea. A clutch of impossibly picturesque inns and B&Bs makes it hard to leave.

◉ Sights

★ **Clovelly Historic Village** HISTORIC SITE
(☑ 01237-431781; www.clovelly.co.uk; Clovelly; adult/child £7.25/4.40; ⊙ 9am-6pm Jun-Sep, 9.30am-5pm Apr, May & Oct, 10am-4pm Nov-Mar; Ⓟ) Clovelly is privately owned, and admission is charged at the hilltop visitor centre. The village's cobbled streets are so steep that cars can't cope, so supplies are brought in by sledge; you'll see these big bread baskets on runners leaning outside homes. Charles Kingsley, author of the children's classic *The Water Babies,* spent much of his early life in Clovelly – don't miss his former house, or the highly atmospheric fisherman's cottage and the village's twin chapels.

If you don't feel up to the steep uphill slog – or you're carting luggage to one of the village B&Bs – you can book a space back to the car park on the Land Rover taxi (£2).

Village Tours WALKING
(☑ 07974 134701; www.clovellyvillagetours.co.uk; tours £5) Local expert Jana Edwards leads

---

OFF THE BEATEN TRACK

LUNDY ISLAND

For a castaway, get-away-from-it-all bolthole, try Lundy Island. This slab of granite 3 miles long and half-a-mile wide is anchored on the horizon, a two-hour ferry ride from the North Devon coast. In May and June puffins nest on the 122m-high cliffs; Lundy ponies, sika deer and Soay sheep roam the cliffs; and basking sharks float by offshore. Pack a swimsuit – the wardens here lead snorkelling safaris. There are standing stones, a 13th-century castle and a couple of lighthouses to explore. A car-free island, Lundy is an extraordinarily peaceful place, and its rich star displays lend it a magical quality at night.

The island's only pub, the **Marisco Tavern** (☑ 01237-431831; www.lundyisland.co.uk; mains from £7; ⊙ noon-2pm & 6-8.30pm), serves as the social hub for the community, and feeds and waters day trippers galore.

Between November and March only, a helicopter flies to Lundy from Hartland Point (adult/child return £116/62). It runs on Mondays and Fridays only and can't be taken as a day trip. Between April and October the *MS Oldenburg* sails to the island from Ilfracombe or Bideford (day return adult/child £37/19, two hours, three to four per week). If you stay overnight, the return fare rises to £65 for an adult and £33 for a child.

Transport to the island can be booked through the **Lundy Shore Office** (☑ 01237-477779; www.lundyisland.co.uk; The Quay, Bideford; ⊙ 9am-5pm Mon-Fri) in Bideford.

entertaining walks around the village, pointing out historic houses, intriguing buildings and architectural curiosities along the way – and offering stories about some of the village's former residents.

✖ Eating

The two pubs and the village cafes (including the Visitor Centre cafe) will cater to your eating needs.

★ **Cottage** — CAFE €
(www.clovelly.co.uk; High St; snacks from £4; ⊙ 9am-5pm Easter-Oct) Set halfway up Clovelly's steeply sloping main street, the cluster of tables here are set right into the cliffside. That results in remarkable views to accompany very decent light lunches, tea and cakes.

Cream tea options include Ladies (£7.25), featuring cucumber sandwiches, and Gentleman's (£8.25), which includes salmon sarnies, too.

ⓘ Getting There & Away

Bus 319 runs between Clovelly, Hartland Village, Bideford (£2.20, 40 minutes, four daily Monday to Saturday) and Barnstaple (£3, one hour). It also heads to Bude (£4.20, one daily Monday to Friday) in the opposite direction.

Hartland Peninsula

A rugged right-angle of land, the Hartland Peninsula has the kind of coast that makes you gasp. It feels like the edge of Devon, and it is – the county goes no further west from here and only a few miles south before the cliffs surge off into Cornwall. Tucked away from traffic through-routes, its unspoilt coastline produces gorgeous sunsets and its remoteness ensures stunning star displays at night.

Hartland Quay is around 4 miles by road south of Hartland Point. The village of Hartland, with its shops and pubs, is a few miles inland.

◎ Sights

Hartland Point — AREA
(P) The coast around Hartland Point offers superb hiking. Tucked just under the point is the short white column of a lighthouse,

BEACH EATS

It's ambitiously named, but the Glorious Oyster is one eating experience that definitely lives up to the billing. The idea is to take the street-food ethos and transport it to the beach: tuck into shucked-to-order local oysters, garlicky seared scallops, cider-steamed mussels and griddled lobster with samphire, served on beachside picnic tables with the kind of seaview you'd normally pay a small fortune for. They've got two locations: a **beach shack** (☑ 07843 278521; www.thegloriousoyster.co.uk; Sandhills, Instow; mains from £8; ⊙ 11am-5pm) at Instow Beach, and a pimped-up **horsebox** (☑ 07843-278521; www.thegloriousoyster.co.uk; Golf Links Rd; dishes from £5; ⊙ noon-5pm Thu-Sun) at Westward Ho!

which was built in 1874. You can't go in but there's a viewing platform just to the west, where you can also see the rusting fragments of the coaster *Johanna*.

The coaster came to grief on New Year's Eve in 1982; the crew were rescued by the Clovelly lifeboat.

Hartland Abbey — HISTORIC BUILDING
(☑ 01237-441496; www.hartlandabbey.com; house adult/child £12/5, gardens & grounds £8.50/4.50; ⊙ house 2-5pm, grounds 11am-5pm Sun-Thu Apr-Sep; P) History flows through the walls of this enchanting, warm-grey manor house. Built in the 12th century, it was a monastery until Henry VIII grabbed it in the Dissolution; he then gave it to the sergeant of his wine cellar. Today its sumptuous interiors house vivid murals, the ornate Alhambra Passage and a Regency library designed in the Strawberry Hill Gothic style.

It's 5 miles west of Clovelly, off the A39 between Hartland and Hartland Quay.

ⓘ Getting There & Away

Bus 319 (four daily Monday to Saturday) goes from Hartland village to Bideford (£2.30, 40 minutes) and Barnstaple (£3, one hour), via Clovelly (£1.30, 10 minutes).

Bodmin & East Cornwall

Best Places to Eat

➡ St Tudy Inn (p145)

➡ Woods Cafe (p144)

➡ Rising Sun (p148)

➡ Food@Cowslip (p148)

➡ Hilltop Farm Shop (p145)

Best Activities

➡ Hiking up Brown Willy (p145)

➡ Adrenalin Quarry (p148)

➡ Siblyback Water Park (p149)

➡ Cardinham Bike Trails (p144)

➡ Hallagenna Farm (p145)

Why Go?

Hugging the edge of the Devon border, the stark, barren expanse of Bodmin Moor dominates East Cornwall and is the county's wildest and weirdest landscape. Pockmarked by bogs and treeless heaths, Cornwall's 'roof' is often overlooked by visitors, but it's well worth taking the time to explore: lofty peaks loom on the horizon, stone circles are scattered across the hills, and ancient churches nestle at the foot of granite tors.

It's also home to Cornwall's highest peaks – Brown Willy (420m) and Rough Tor (pronounced row-tor; 400m) – as well as the infamous Beast of Bodmin Moor, a black catlike creature that's been seen for many years but has still not been conclusively captured on camera.

You're unlikely to spy the legendary cat, but on the upside you most likely won't spot many other tourists: Bodmin Moor is an under-explored corner of Cornwall that's unjustly skipped by most visitors.

When to Go

➡ **Apr–Jun** These are often the best months to visit the moor, as they're usually when you'll encounter the most sunshine, along with colourful displays of spring wildflowers.

➡ **Jul & Aug** The summer months can swing either way: it could be hot and sunny one day, or carpeted in thick fog the next. Don't rely on the moor having good weather simply because it's sunny on the coast.

➡ **Sep & Oct** Can also be pleasant months to visit, with a good chance of late sunshine and rich autumnal colours.

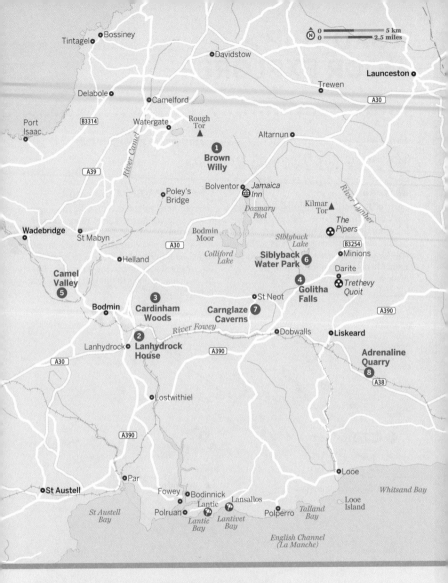

Bodmin & East Cornwall Highlights

1 Brown Willy (p145)
Trekking to the top of Cornwall's loftiest hill for wraparound views of the moor.

2 Lanhydrock (p144)
Stepping back in time at this lavish Cornish country manor.

3 Cardinham Woods (p144)
Hiking or cycling along the forest trails of this tranquil woodland.

4 Golitha Falls (p143)
Having a picnic beside this tumbling, photogenic cascade.

5 Camel Valley (p144)
Sipping a tipple on a tour of Cornwall's premier cru vineyard.

6 Siblyback Water Park (p149) Canoeing or paddleboarding across a moorland lake.

7 Carnglaze Caverns (p149) Delving into the depths of this atmospheric abandoned slate quarry.

8 Adrenalin Quarry (p148) Hurtling off a cliff at 40mph attached to nothing more than a zip wire.

ROAD TRIP >
MOOR EXPLORER

Wild and wonderfully windswept, this drive takes in the stirring sights of Cornwall's rooftop.

① Bodmin

Most of Bodmin Moor can be covered in a day's drive, but a couple of days allows you a bit more time to soak up the views.

The obvious place to start is in **Bodmin** (p144), one of Cornwall's five original stannary towns, and the location of the notoriously haunted Bodmin Jail, now reduced to a spooky ruin.

② Camel Valley Vineyard

From here, take a detour west to sample a few vintages at the **Camel Valley Vineyard** (p144), one of Cornwall's oldest, and many would say, finest vineyards. On weekday afternoons it's possible to take a tour around the vineyard with chief winemaker Sam Lindo, which is well worth doing if you're a real oenophile.

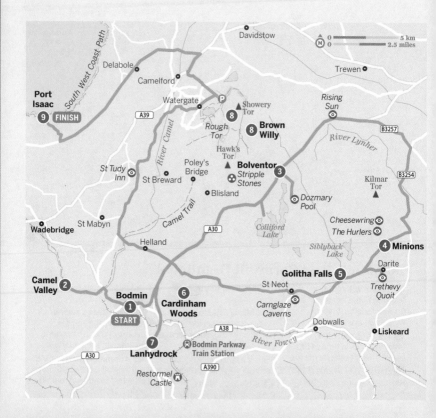

❸ Bolventor

Pick up the A30 again for a drive past the silvery arcs of **Colliford Lake** and **Dozmary Pool** (p149), both rich in fable and folklore – including legendary connections to a giant and to the King Arthur mythos. If you're feeling really brave you could even take a wild dip, but you'll definitely need a wetsuit, whatever the time of year.

As you pass through **Bolventor**, it's worth stopping in for a look around Jamaica Inn, made famous by the novel of the same name – although you'll find the du Maurier connections are pretty thin on the ground these days. A much better option for a pint and a pub lunch is the **Rising Sun** (p148), a cosy pub in nearby Altarnun.

❹ Minions

From here, turn south along the B3257 and the B3254 to the village of **Minions**. Nearby you can hike to two of the moor's prehistoric monuments: **The Hurlers** (p149) and the **Cheesewring** (p149), one made by man, the other by nature. Three miles south, near Darite, is **Trethevy Quoit** (p149), a classic dolmen topped by an enormous flat capstone that's been estimated to weigh an amazing 20 tons. More prehistoric ruins can be found nearby, including hut circles and standing stones, but you'll need an OS map to find most of them.

❺ Golitha Falls

Further west, a narrow backroad winds to the impressive cascade of **Golitha Falls**, which makes a lovely place for a paddle and a picnic on a hot summer's afternoon. Nearby, the parish church of **St Neot** is blessed with some fabulous medieval stained glass that's worth a detour. Otherwise, continue on to the old slate mine at **Carnglaze Caverns** (p149), where you can venture underground to explore the caves and underwater pool.

❻ Cardinham Woods

Finish the day with a walk around the forested trails of **Cardinham Woods** (p144) and a proper Cornish cream tea at the Woods Cafe, nestled in a shady glade in the heart of the forest. Spend the night at **St Benet's Abbey** (☎ 01208-831352; www.stbenetsabbey.co.uk; Truro Rd, Lanivet; d £76-95; ▣ 🛜), a cosy B&B in a former ecclesiastical building that partly dates from the 15th century.

❼ Lanhydrock

On day two, begin by driving south to the magnificent country house of **Lanhydrock** (p144), now owned by the National Trust, but originally built for the Agar-Robartes family. It's a glorious place to explore: you'll need to devote most of the morning to appreciate its secrets. Then head north, skirting onto the northern part of the moor, as you pass through small villages and wide-open moorland en route to St Tudy and a truly memorable lunch at the **St Tudy Inn** (p145), run by chef Emily Scott. The inn's rustic-chic trappings are more than matched by the sophisticated food – you definitely won't find a ploughman's on offer here.

❽ Brown Willy & Rough Tor

After lunch continue across the northern section of the moor towards Camelford. This is the best area of the moor for getting a proper uninterrupted glimpse of **Brown Willy** (p145) and **Rough Tor**, the two highest points of Cornwall: if you're lucky, you'll have a clear view of the twin hills, surrounded by tawny grassland, huge skies and perhaps even a wild pony or two.

Once you've seen enough of Brown Willy, continue through Camelford and follow the road past **Delabole**, renowned for producing some of Cornwall's finest slate; there's a visitor's shop if you feel like picking up a souvenir.

❾ Port Isaac

From here you'll start to get distant glimpses of the sea as you roll onwards to the lovely coastal village of **Port Isaac**, where the TV series *Doc Martin* was set. Stay at the **Old School Hotel** (☎ 01208-880721; www.theoldschoolhotel.co.uk; Fore St; d £119-185; ▣ 🛜), and treat yourself with a world-class seafood supper at **Restaurant Nathan Outlaw** (p189), the only restaurant in Cornwall with two Michelin stars.

BODMIN

☎ 01208 / POP 12,778

On the western side of the moor is the stout market town of Bodmin, which grew up around a large 7th-century monastery founded by St Petroc, and later became one of the county's most important stannary (tin-mining) towns, although much of Bodmin's administrative power shifted to Truro in the late 19th century. The modern town has little to detain you, but it makes a useful launching-pad for venturing out onto nearby Bodmin Moor.

◉ Sights

★ Lanhydrock   HISTORIC BUILDING

(NT; ☎ 01208-265950; www.nationaltrust.org.uk/lanhydrock; adult/child £13.55/6.75; ⊙ house 11am-5.30pm, grounds 10am-5.30pm) This magnificent manor, two-and-a-half miles southeast of Bodmin, offers a fascinating insight into *Upstairs, Downstairs* life in Victorian England. The house was rebuilt after a devastating fire in 1881 as a fashionable home for the Agar-Robartes family, complete with mod-cons such as radiators, roasting ovens, warming cupboards and flushing loos. The centrepieces are the drawing room, packed with artworks and antiques, and the enormous kitchens, complete with a pioneering refrigerator room. The ornate Long Gallery is also famous for its plaster ceiling.

Cardinham Woods   FOREST

(☎ 01208-72577; www.forestry.gov.uk/cardinham) Just outside Bodmin, this large public forest is a great spot for a woody wander, and also has a network of mountain-bike trails if you're feeling more energetic. The Bodmin & Wenford Railway stops at nearby Coleslogget Halt, from where a 1.5-mile trail leads to Cardinham. Beside the main car park, the Woods Cafe (p144) is a lovely place for afternoon tea.

Pencarrow House   HISTORIC BUILDING

(☎ 01208-841369; www.pencarrow.co.uk; house & gardens adult/child £10.75/free, gardens only £5.75/free; ⊙ house tours 11.15am-3pm Sun-Thu) Belonging to the well-to-do Molesworth-St Aubyn family, this wonderful Georgian manor was remodelled in the late 18th century in the best Palladian fashion, aiming to mimic the grandeur and proportions of a Greco-Roman temple. It's certainly an arresting sight, and brimming inside with rococo detailing, sweeping staircases, priceless china and marble busts, as well as a line-up of family portraits (including a couple by Sir Joshua Reynolds). Entry to the house is by guided tour.

✗ Eating

★ Woods Cafe   CAFE ££

(☎ 01208-78111; www.woodscafecornwall.co.uk; Cardinham Woods; mains £6-12; ⊙ 10.30am-4.30pm) In an old woodsman's cottage lost among the trees of Cardinham, this cracking cafe has become a dining destination in its own right – it's locally famous for its home-baked cakes, cockle-warming soups and sausage sarnies (sandwiches).

ⓘ Information

Bodmin Tourist Information Centre

(☎ 01208-76616; www.bodminlive.com; Shire Hall, Mount Folly Sq; ⊙ 8.45am-4pm or 5pm Mon-Fri, 10am-5pm Sat)

BODMIN MOOR

It can't quite boast the wild majesty of Dartmoor, but Bodmin Moor has a bleak beauty all of its own. Pockmarked with heaths and granite hills, including Rough Tor ('row-tor'; 400m) and Cornwall's highest point, Brown Willy (420m), it's a desolate place that works on the imagination; for years there have been reported sightings of the Beast of Bodmin, a large, black catlike creature, although no one's ever managed to snap a decent picture.

The Northern Moor

The northern section of the moor is roughly bordered by the A30 to the south and the A39 to the north. It's mainly visited by hikers and horse-riders, especially people setting out to bag the summit of Brown Willy.

◉ Sights

★ Camel Valley Vineyard   WINERY

(☎ 01208-77959; www.camelvalley.com; ⊙ shop 10am-5pm Mon-Sat, tours 2.30pm Mon-Fri plus 5pm Wed) Cornwall might not seem like an obvious place for winemaking, but father-and-son team Bob and Sam Lindo have been producing award-winning vintages at this Camel Valley Vineyard since 1989. The range includes award-winning whites and rosés, and a bubbly that's Champagne in all but name. Aficionados say the wines have a fresh, light quality that comes from the mild climate and pure sea air. Vineyard tours run regularly and you can taste and buy the goods in the on-site shop.

🏃 Activities

⭐ Brown Willy   HIKING
Now now, stop sniggering at the back. A perennial source of amusement for Cornish schoolkids, Cornwall's highest hill actually gets its name from the Cornish *bronn wennili*, or 'hill of swallows'. From the car park at Poldue Downs, it's a circular tramp of about 5.5 miles: the ascent is steep but straightforward, winding through heathland, bog, gorse and boulders to the 419m summit. The wraparound view is majestic; both Cornish coasts and St Austell's clay hills are visible in clear weather.

Hallagenna Farm   HORSE RIDING
(☑ 01208-851500; www.hallagenna.co.uk; St Breward; per hour £20) One of the best ways to see the moor is from the saddle. This well-established riding stables offers hacks and treks from £20 per hour, plus a three-hour expedition (£60) including a pub stop and lunch at the Blisland Inn.

🍴 Eating

⭐ St Tudy Inn   MODERN BRITISH ££
(☑ 01208-850656; www.sttudyinn.com; St Tudy; mains £14-25; ⊙ meals noon-2.30pm & 6.30-9pm Mon-Sat, noon-2.30pm Sun) Run by the locally lauded chef Emily Scott, whose previous restaurant in Port Isaac received rave reviews, this village pub has fast become one of East Cornwall's top dining destinations. The old pub has been stripped down and sleekened, and Scott's trademark light, fresh, imaginative food takes centre stage. It's a gastropub of the first order – bookings essential.

Hilltop Farm Shop   CAFE £
(☑ 01840-211518; www.hilltopfarmshop.co.uk; Slaughterbridge; teas £3-6) Take your pick from the Cornish fudge, pasties and cheeses in the farm shop, or settle in for scones in the attached tearoom. Staff will also pack you a hamper stuffed with goodies, all with Cornish credentials. It's in Slaughterbridge, 2 miles north of Camelford.

Old Inn   PUB FOOD ££
(☑ 01208-850711; www.theoldinnandrestaurant.co.uk; St Breward; mains £10-26) The main claim to fame of this village pub is that it's the highest in Cornwall (at around 720ft), and sup-

BODMIN & WENFORD RAILWAY

Run by enthusiasts, this **steam railway** (☑ 01208-73555; www.bodminrailway.co.uk; rover pass adult/child £13/6; ⊙ 3-5 daily trains May-Sep, fewer at other times) – the only 'standard gauge' line of its type left in Cornwall – chuffs and clatters for 6.5 miles between Bodmin and Boscarne Junction. Many trains are still decked out in their original 1950s livery. At the Boscarne end, the line links up with the Camel Trail (p191); bikes can be taken on the trains if there's space.

Look out for special trips in summer, including Pullman-style dining trains with a silver-service supper, plus murder mystery and pub quiz trains.

posedly has a heritage that dates back to the 11th century. These days it's mostly a village hang-out: the welcome's warm, there are fires to snuggle by, and the grub's decent – particularly the huge mixed grills.

ℹ Transport

Poldue Downs This is the handiest car park for tackling Brown Willy. Don't leave valuables on show in your car, as break-ins have occurred here from time to time.

Central & Eastern Moor

The wildest parts of the moor can be seen on either side of the main A30 road, which cuts right across its centre, from Bodmin on the east side to Launceston on the west. It's a stark and empty landscape, with few natural features breaking up the plains of tawny grass and tangled gorse – perfect if you prefer to hike in solitude.

⊙ Sights

⭐ Cotehele   HISTORIC BUILDING
(NT; ☑ 01579-351346; www.nationaltrust.org.uk/cotehele; St Dominick; adult/child £11/5.50; ⊙ house 11am-4pm, gardens dawn-dusk) At the head of the Tamar Valley sits the Tudor manor of Cotehele, one of the Edgcumbe dynasty's model country retreats. The cavernous great hall is the centrepiece, and the house has an unparalleled collection of Tudor tapestries, armour and furniture.

West Country Moors

The southwest is famous for its white beaches and rolling fields, but its moors have a harsh beauty all of their own. Treeless, windswept and pockmarked by hills and rocky outcrops, these moors are as close as England gets to wilderness.

RICHIE JOHNS / GETTY IMAGES ©

GAPS / GETTY IMAGES ©

1. Golitha Falls (p148)
River Fowey at Golitha Falls is one of the great beauty spots of Bodmin Moor.

2. Dartmoor National Park (p109)
Rock stacks dot the landscape of Dartmoor, one of the few places where wild camping is still legal.

3. Cheesewring, Bodmin Moor (p149)
Named after the wooden press used to make cheese, this stack of granite rocks seems impossibly balanced.

4. Exmoor National Park (p126)
Sheep graze at Exmoor, which offers extensive hiking and cycling paths.

HELEN HOTSON / SHUTTERSTOCK ©

OFF THE BEATEN TRACK

GOLITHA FALLS

Around 1.25 miles west of St Cleer, these crashing waterfalls are one of the great beauty spots of the moor, and well worth the trip to find. Around the falls are the remains of the ancient oak woodland that once covered much of the moor. There is a car park half a mile's walk from the reserve near Draynes Bridge.

Outside, the gardens sweep down past the 18th-century Prospect Folly to Cotehele Quay, where there's a discovery centre exploring the history of the Tamar Valley and a vintage sailing barge, the Shamrock.

A short walk inland (or a shuttle bus) leads to the restored Cotehele Mill, where you can watch the original waterwheel grinding corn several days a week, and watch a miller and baker at work.

The house is famous for its Christmas wreath, a massive ornamental ring of foliage made from materials gathered on the estate. The house also hosts a large Christmas fair.

⭐ **Tamar Otter Wildlife Centre**   WILDLIFE RESERVE

(☑ 01566-785646; www.tamarotters.co.uk; North Petherwin, near Launceston; adult/child £8.50/5; ⊙ 10.30am-6pm Apr-Oct) Generally, you'll need the skills of Ray Mears to spot otters in the wild, but this wildlife centre 5 miles outside Launceston guarantees a sighting. There's a population of British and Asian short-clawed otters, split between three families, which live in their own naturally constructed holts. Feeding times are noon and 3pm daily. Elsewhere round the reserve you'll have the chance to see fallow deer, muntjac, pheasants and Scottish wildcats. There are birds-of-prey talks at 11.30am and 2.30pm.

Launceston Castle   CASTLE

(EH; www.english-heritage.org.uk/daysout/prop erties/launceston-castle; adult/child £4.30/2.60; ⊙ 10am-6pm) On the eastern edge of the moor is Launceston, a sturdy market town that's mainly worth visiting for the ruins of its 13th-century castle. With its circular keep plonked on top of a grassy hillock, it looks like a stage set from *Monty Python and the Holy Grail*. A spiral staircase leads up to the top for awesome 360-degree views.

🏃 Activities

Adrenalin Quarry   ADVENTURE SPORTS

(☑ 01579-308204; www.adrenalinquarry.co.uk; Lower Clicker Rd, Menheniot; zip wire £12.50, swing £15, coasteering £40; ⊙ 10am-5pm) With the frankly brilliant tag line of 'Throwing people off clifftops since 2009', this octane-fuelled activity centre is based at a flooded quarry near Menheniot. If you love the idea of hurtling down a zip line at 40mph, or struggling not to lose your lunch on a giant swing that simulates the sensation of freefall, then this place will be right up your street.

🍴 Eating

⭐ **Rising Sun**   PUB FOOD **££**

(☎ 01566 86000; www.therisingsuninn.co.uk; Altarnun; mains £9-18; ⊙ 11am-11pm) Posh pub grub and cracking ales from nearby Penpont Brewery are reason enough to visit this 500-year-old inn. It's one of the top places to eat in this corner of the moor, so make sure you book ahead for a table. You're also welcome to camp in the pub's field, but there's a three-night minimum.

Food@Cowslip   CAFE **£**

(☑ 01566-772839; www.cowslipworkshops.co.uk; St Stephens, near Launceston; mains £4-10; ⊙ 10am-5pm) On an old farm just outside Launceston, this homely organic cafe operates alongside craft workshops, and serves delicious farm-style lunches, from a huge ploughman's platter to smoked mackerel salad (the cream tea is a beauty, too). There's also a shop where you can buy fabric and quilting patterns, or sign up for a sewing course.

🍺 Drinking & Nightlife

Blisland Inn   PUB

(☑ 01208-850739; www.bodminmoor.co.uk/blis landinn; Blisland) Popular ale-drinker's pub, with toby jugs, vintage photos and beer mats adorning the walls, and at least six ales and a local scrumpy on tap. Basic pub meals are also served.

The Southern Moor

The southern stretches of the moor are arguably its most beautiful, a wild swath of tawny heaths, wooded copses and blustery lakes. The main town of Liskeard makes a useful access point but, like many of the moorland towns, it's looking a little neglected.

⊙ Sights

Cheesewring ARCHAEOLOGICAL SITE
Looking like a gigantic game of granite Jenga, this stack of rocks is legendarily said to have been the work of giants – but the truth is even stranger. A combination of wind, rain and natural erosion has carved out the rocks' peculiar disc-like shape. The name refers to the formation's similarity to the wooden press that was traditionally used to make cheese.

Cornish Orchards BREWERY
(☑ 01503-269007; www.cornishorchards.co.uk; Duloe, Liskeard; ⊙ 10am-5pm Mon-Fri) This renowned orchard makes fruity apple juices and a range of exotic cider varieties, from traditional heritage scrumpy to raspberry and pear variants. You can pick them all up in the shop and have a free taste; they're in Duloe, 5 miles south from Liskeard.

Carnglaze Caverns CAVE
(☑ 01579-320251; www.carnglaze.com; adult/child £6/4; ⊙ 10am-5pm, to 8pm Aug; 🖫 🏖) Bodmin Moor's slate was once an important local export, and these deep caverns were cut out by hand by local miners, leaving behind a moody network of subterranean caves and a glittering underground pool. Concerts and plays are sometimes held inside the caves in summer. The site is just outside St Neot and well signed.

The Hurlers ARCHAEOLOGICAL SITE
This unusual triple stone circle is said to have been formed by a group of local men who contravened the sabbath and played the local game of hurling (a cross between running and rugby) on a Sunday. In truth, no explanation has settled the mystery of what the trio of circles were for.

Just to the west are the twin standing stones known as **The Pipers** – again, supposedly punishment for playing music on the holy sabbath.

Trethevy Quoit ARCHAEOLOGICAL SITE
Three miles south of Darite is this impressive example of a quoit, or dolmen – a Neolithic burial chamber resembling a flat stone table, supported by three (or in this case, five) standing stones. The capstone has been estimated to weigh around 20 tons, and is tilted at a steep angle, probably as a result of slippage. The structure is thought to date from between 3500 and 2500 BC.

OFF THE BEATEN TRACK

DOZMARY POOL
About a mile south of the A30, this glassy expanse of water has many myths and legends associated with it – including one that claims it's where Arthur was given his famous sword, Excalibur, by the Lady of the Lake. It's also supposedly bottomless: another local legend concerns young Jan Tregeagle, who made a pact with the devil and in return was damned to spend his days emptying the never-ending pool with a leaking limpet shell.

It's generally too cold for swimming and, since there are no trees around its edges, it can be fiercely windy – but it's a mysterious and atmospheric place nonetheless. To the west is **Colliford Lake**, Cornwall's largest and highest reservoir.

🏃 Activities

Siblyback Water Park WATER SPORTS
(☑ 01579-346522; www.swlakestrust.org.uk; ⊙ 9am-5pm) This huge lake offers a wealth of opportunities for getting out on the water, including windsurfing, rowing, waterskiing, wakeboarding, stand-up paddleboarding and kneeboarding. Mixed-use trails also run around the shoreline, and there's a small cafe.

🍴 Eating

Crows Nest Inn PUB FOOD ££
(☑ 01579-345930; near Darite; mains £10-14; ⊙ 11am-3pm & 6-11pm Mon-Fri, 11am-11pm Sat & Sun) Whitewashed walls, a roaring fire and a low-beamed interior make this 16th-century inn a welcome refuge when the moorland weather sets in, especially on Sunday for the generous roast. It's owned by St Austell Brewery, so there's guaranteed to be a pint of Tribute on tap.

Cornish Cheese Company CHEESE
(☑ 01579-363660; www.cornishcheese.co.uk; Upton Cross, near Liskeard; ⊙ 10am-5pm Mon-Sat) Renowned local cheesemaker that has made its name with the powerful, pungent Cornish Blue, which you can buy in the traditional blue-and-white-striped ceramic pots (£18 for 200g).

South Cornwall

Best Places to Eat

➡ Oliver's (p158)

➡ Wheelhouse (p159)

➡ Pandora Inn (p161)

➡ Ferryboat Inn (p165)

➡ Star & Garter (p159)

➡ Hidden Hut (p170)

Best Outdoor Adventures

➡ Fal River Boat Trips (p157)

➡ Salt Air Adventures (p164)

➡ Helford River Boats (p165)

➡ Encounter Cornwall (p174)

➡ Coast to Coast Cycle Trail (p165)

Why Go?

It might lack the rugged granite cliffs and seablown grandeur of the north coast, but Cornwall's southern side has ample charms of its own: gentle creeks, green meadows, quaint harbours and world-renowned gardens such as Trebah, Trelissick, Heligan and Glendurgan, as well as the futuristic biomes of the Eden Project. It feels more pastoral than the craggy beauty of Penwith or the wild emptiness of Bodmin Moor: this is a place for quiet adventures, whether that's touring the back lanes and beaches of the Roseland, mooching around Mevagissey Harbour or kayaking on the Fal and Fowey Rivers.

The remote Rame Peninsula is particularly exploration-worthy. It's a fairly long drive from anywhere, so most visitors never make the effort to explore it, which means its lovely countryside and country houses are relatively quiet. It's also an easy trip from Plymouth thanks to the Torpoint Ferry, which chugs across the scenic Tamar Estuary.

When to Go

➡ **May** The Fowey Festival brings book readings, poetry events and live music to the town.

➡ **Jul** Spectacular gigs light up the biomes during the Eden Sessions, which have become one of the county's top annual music events.

➡ **Sep** The Great Cornish Food Festival, the county's largest food fair, takes place on Truro's Lemon Quay.

➡ **Oct** Falmouth celebrates the mollusc at the annual Oyster Festival with chefs' demos and tasting sessions.

➡ **Dec** Wicker lanterns parade round Truro's streets during the City of Lights procession in the run-up to Christmas.

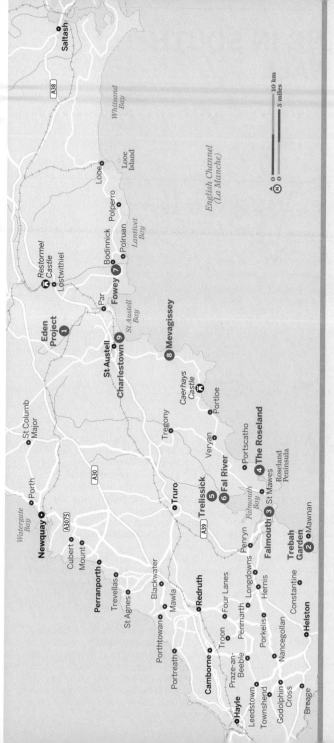

South Cornwall Highlights

1 Eden Project (p171)
Admiring the world's flora in three sci-fi biomes.

2 Trebah Garden (p164)
Marvelling at the horticultural ambition of this great subtropical garden.

3 Falmouth (p156) Exploring the seafaring past of this harbour town with a visit to the National Maritime Museum.

4 The Roseland (p169)
Trekking the coast path in search of a quiet patch of sand.

5 Trelissick (p168) Walking the riverside trails of this fabulous country estate.

6 Fal River (p157) Catching an evening cruise past secret creeks and riverside villages.

7 Fowey (p173) Stopping for a pint on the quayside.

8 Mevagissey (p173)
Continuing the time-honoured pastime of fishing for crabs.

9 Charlestown (p172)
Pretending you're in an episode of *Poldark*.

WALKING IN SOUTH CORNWALL

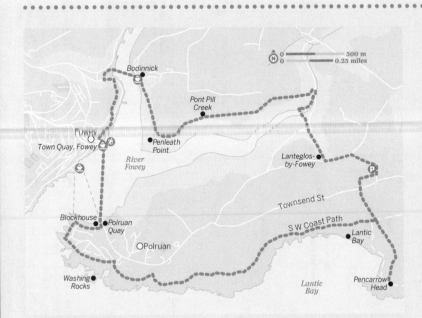

FOWEY, POLRUAN & BODINNICK

START/END FOWEY
DISTANCE 4 MILES
DURATION 2½ HOURS
DIFFICULTY EASY

Start in Fowey (p173) at the town quay, next to the rosy-pink King of Prussia pub. From here, catch the foot ferry across the River Fowey, and disembark in the hugger-mugger village of **Polruan**, a huddle of cottages and narrow streets stacked on a steep coastal cliffside. Take the coast path up to the village's **blockhouse**, one of two such houses built around 1380, which would have enabled a chain to be raised across the harbour to prevent undesirable ships from entering it.

Climb up through town and pick up the path as it heads out past the black reefs known as the **Washing Rocks**. From here, the trail begins to leave the village behind and heads out onto the coast path proper.

After a mile or so, you'll reach the hidden sands of **Lantic Bay** (p174), offering secluded sun-lounging and swimming. Turn right to see the views from **Pencarrow Head**, or turn left to reach the main road and the nearby National Trust car park. Follow the road round till you reach the little church of **Lanteglos-by-Fowey**, and take the path downhill through the churchyard till you reach the creek.

At the bottom of the hill, the road leads across a footbridge to a path that bears left along the banks of **Pont Pill Creek**, offering dreamy views of the river through the overhanging trees. At **Penleath Point**, there's a lovely vantage point back across the river to Polruan and Fowey, as well as a small memorial to the novelist and scholar Sir Arthur Quiller-Couch, who lived in Fowey from 1891 until his death in 1944. From here, the trail winds on to **Bodinnick**, where you can have a pint at the homely **Old Ferry Inn** while waiting for the ferry to carry you back to the northern end of Fowey.

Fowey has coast, countryside and river on its doorstep. This fabulous walk factors in all three, and makes use of a couple of cross-river ferries.

Polruan

ROAD TRIP > THE ROSELAND

With its rolling fields, narrow lanes, quiet beaches and out-of-the-way villages, the rural Roseland makes for an idyllic day's drive.

❶ Truro

Start out in the county's capital city of **Truro** (p166), making time for a morning flat white at the excellent 108 Coffee, followed by a quick spin around the shops and a visit to the city's impressive cathedral. Then head over to the grand estate of **Trelissick** (p168) for a wander around the riverside grounds and a visit to the wonderful rhododendron gardens. If you feel like extending the walk, various trails lead along the creeks leading off the Fal River.

❷ King Harry Ferry

Once you're back in the car, leave Trelissick and turn left, following the road downhill to join the queue of cars waiting for the historic **King Harry Ferry** (p169), a chain-powered ferry that has been transporting passengers and cars over to the Roseland for nigh on a

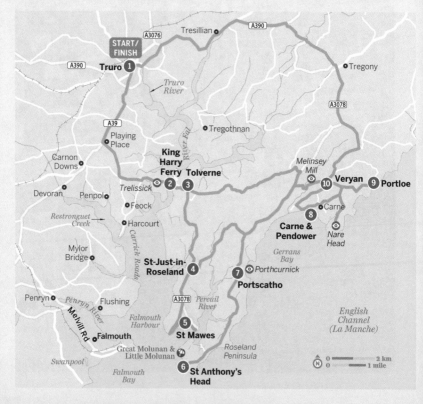

century. It's only a 10-minute journey, but it's a memorable one nonetheless.

❸ Tolverne

On the opposite side of the river, the quay at **Tolverne** is a picture of tranquillity now, surrounded by oak woodland and the lazy waters of the Fal River. But in 1944 it would have been a very different picture: this area of the Fal was a major embarkation point for American troops setting sail for the D-Day landings. If you look closely, a quay marks the spot from where the troops left.

❹ St-Just-in-Roseland

Continue along the B3289 to the flower-filled churchyard of **St-Just-in-Roseland** (p169), one of Cornwall's prettiest: it's well worth stopping for half an hour to wander through the churchyard, peer at some of the gravestones and just sit and admire the lovely river view.

❺ St Mawes

Five miles further south brings you to the chi-chi harbour of **St Mawes**. Stop off for a walk along the harbour-front and a quick visit to St Mawes Castle, followed by a late pub lunch at the Rising Sun, or something more sophisticated at the upmarket Idle Rocks.

❻ St Anthony's Head

From St Mawes, drive all the way around the River Percuil through the village of Gerrans to **St Anthony's Head** (p170), crested by the remains of a Victorian gun battery. Just behind the headland is an impressive lighthouse; if you're of a certain age, you might well recognise it from the opening credits of Jim Henson's children's TV series, *Fraggle Rock*.

❼ Portscatho

Then it's back the way you came for a detour to the quiet fishing village of **Portscatho** (p169) and the nearby beach of **Porthcurnick** (p170), where you can indulge in a cracking cream tea at the beachside Hidden Hut cafe. In summer, the hut also hosts popular feast nights, but you'll need to book way in advance if you want to attend.

❽ Carne & Pendower

Further along the coast, a minor road leads down to the Roseland's most impressive sands at **Carne & Pendower** (p169), a perfect spot to kick off your shoes and have a quick paddle – or if you're feeling brave and the weather's pleasant, perhaps a proper dunk in the sea. Above the beach, the nearby promontory of **Nare Head** is well worth the walk for its views; often you can spot kestrels and buzzards hovering around the headland.

❾ Portloe

Several more pretty fishing villages lie further along the coast, including **Portloe**, once the area's busiest pilchard harbour. The roads are really tiny round here, so be prepared to do a bit of reversing in case you meet oncoming traffic. If you feel like staying overnight, Portloe's lovely **Lugger Hotel** also happens to be one of the Roseland's best places to stay.

❿ Veryan

Inland is the village of **Veryan** (p170), set around a central green and peaceful duck pond. Look out for the two round houses at the top of the village, which are supposedly devil-proof. Stop off at nearby **Melinsey Mill** (p170) to pick up some homemade crafts and cakes, then head back towards Truro; the quickest and most scenic option is to take the shortcut back via the King Harry Ferry, but you can also follow the longer route via the main road between Truro and St Austell.

Reward yourself with dinner: go for the Thomas Daniell if you're in the mood for a gastropub, or the Falmouth Bay Seafood Cafe if you're feeling fishy.

FALMOUTH, TRURO & THE ROSELAND

In contrast to the crags and breakers of the Atlantic coast, the area around Falmouth and the Roseland Peninsula presents a gentler side to the county. Sheltered from the brunt of the biting Atlantic winds, the coastline benefits from a balmy subtropical climate that allows exotic plants and trees to flourish along its valleys; it's no wonder that many of Cornwall's finest gardens and country estates are found here. It's also where you'll find three of Cornwall's great rivers, the Fal, the Helford and the Fowey, which wind their way from the south coast along a maze of wooded creeks and tributaries, and were once the haunt of smugglers.

Falmouth

🖉 01326 / POP 20,775

Few seaside towns in Cornwall boast such an arresting location as Falmouth, overlooking the broad Fal River as it empties into the English Channel. Surrounded by green hills and blue sea, Falmouth is an appealing jumble of cobbled lanes, salty old pubs, slate roofs and trendy cafes. It's an ideal base for exploring Cornwall's south coast, and has a wealth of bars and bistros, a trio of beaches and the nation's foremost maritime museum.

Though it's now mainly supported by students at Falmouth University in nearby Penryn, the town made its fortune during the 18th and 19th centuries thanks to lucrative maritime trade – the deep water offshore is the third-deepest natural harbour in the world, and the town grew rich when tea clippers, trading vessels and mail packets stopped here to unload their cargoes. Falmouth is still an important centre for ship repairs – you can look over the dockyard cranes as you head to Pendennis Point.

◉ Sights

Pendennis Castle   CASTLE

(EH; 🖉 01326-316594; www.english-heritage.org.uk; adult/child £8.40/5; ⊙10am-6pm Mar-Sep, to 5pm Oct, 10am-4pm Sat & Sun Nov-Feb) Designed in tandem with its sister castle in St Mawes across the estuary, this Tudor castle sits proudly on Pendennis Point, and was built as part of Henry VIII's massive castle-building program to reinforce England's coastline. You can wander around the central keep and the Tudor gun deck, as well as the governor's bedroom, a WWI guardhouse and the WWII-era Half-Moon Battery. Listen out for the Noonday Gun, which rings out at 12pm sharp every day throughout July and August.

National Maritime Museum   MUSEUM

(🖉 01326-313388; www.nmmc.co.uk; Discovery Quay; adult/child £12.95/5; ⊙10am-5pm) Falmouth's most high-profile museum is located on the much revamped area around Discovery Quay. It's the sister outpost of the National Maritime Museum in Greenwich, London, and focuses on Falmouth's history as a seafaring port, supplemented by regular nautically themed exhibitions – recent shows covered the history of the Royal National Lifeboat Institution (RNLI), and the tradition of tattooing. The centrepiece is the impressive **Flotilla Gallery**, where an array of small boats is suspended from the ceiling.

From the top floor of the Lookout tower, there's a 360-degree panorama across Falmouth Bay.

Gyllyngvase Beach   BEACH

The nearest beach to town is a flat sandy stretch, known to locals as Gylly. It's about half a mile south of the town centre and is backed by the popular Gylly Beach Cafe (p159). There's also a watersports centre.

Maenporth Beach   BEACH

Maenporth is the quietest of Falmouth's beaches, with facilities including a cafe, kayak centre and restaurant, **The Cove** (🖉 01326-251136; www.thecovemaenporth.co.uk; mains £13-25, 3-course menu £24; ⊙11am-11pm Tue-Sat & to 6pm Sun). The 1978 wreck of the Scottish trawler, the *Ben Asdale*, can be seen along the coast at low tide. The beach is 3 miles south of town. There's no bus service, so you'll either have to drive, cycle or walk.

Swanpool Beach   BEACH

South of Falmouth lies the popular beach of Swanpool, near a small inland lagoon populated by grebes, coots, ducks and mute swans. A coastal path runs here from Gyllyngvase Beach (p156), and there's a decent seafood cafe, **Hooked on the Rocks** (🖉 01326-311886; www.hookedcornwall.com; mains £12-45; ⊙10am-3pm & 5-11pm Mon-Sat, noon-3pm Sun), perched on the point above the beach.

Activities

Gylly Adventures KAYAKING
(☑ 07341 890495; www.gyllyadventures.co.uk; kayak tour per person £40) Based on Gyllyngvase Beach, this watersports company hires the usual kit – stand-up paddleboards, kayaks, bodyboards and the like – but it also offers some great guided kayaking trips. Options include a tour of Falmouth harbour, a trip down the Helford River, a pub paddle and (best of all) a night kayak trip illuminated by LED head torches (£45 per person).

Koru Kayaking KAYAKING
(☑ 07794 321827; www.korukayaking.co.uk; 2hr trip £40) Kayaking trips to Frenchman's Creek from the north bank of the Helford River, as well as from Trevaunance Cove near St Agnes.

Canoe Cornwall CANOEING
(☑ 07749 870923; www.canoecornwall.org.uk; half-/full day £25/30) Operating out of Trelissick Gardens, this well-run company offers trips in traditional open-top wooden canoes (rather than plastic sit-on-top kayaks). Close your eyes and you could almost think you're in Canada. Half-day expeditions last around three hours and run along the Fal River. There are also bushcraft and archery sessions; check the website to see what's happening.

BF Adventure ADVENTURE SPORTS
(☑ 01326-340912; www.bfadventure.org; per half-day from £25) Based on a 24-hectare site near Falmouth, BF runs a wealth of adventure activities, ranging from rock climbing, archery and kayaking to 'quarrysteering' – coasteering (jumping off rock ledges into deep seawater) but in quarries.

Fal River Boat Trips BOATING
Falmouth's main pier is the departure point for boat trips along the Fal River and ferries to Flushing and St Mawes. There are several operators, all offering similar routes: Enterprise Boats (p166) is the best known, and runs regular trips to Truro and St Mawes via Trelissick Gardens.

Festivals & Events

Falmouth Oyster Festival FOOD & DRINK
(www.falmouthoysterfestival.co.uk; ☉ Oct) Feast on fresh oysters, mussels and other crustaceans during this October festival, which also hosts cookery classes and culinary demos.

Falmouth International Sea Shanty Festival MUSIC
(www.falmouthseashanty.co.uk; ☉ Jun) Hearty sailors' songs – accompanied by even heartier drinking – provide the musical backdrop for this lively harbour festival.

Falmouth Week SAILING
(www.falmouthweek.co.uk; ☉ mid-Aug) Held in mid-August, this busy festival is Cornwall's largest sailing regatta.

 Eating

★ **Stone's Bakery** BAKERY £
(☑ 07791 003183; www.stonesbakery.co.uk; 28a High St; breads £1.50-3; ☉ 9am-4pm Mon-Sat) Freshly baked loaves line the window like pieces of art at this gorgeous bakery, which focuses on traditional hand-shaped rustic loaves – the tangy maltster and the organic sourdough are as delicious as you'll ever taste. More tempting treats such as cheese twists, croissants and tarts await on the counter too – we defy you to resist.

The Meat Counter BURGERS £
(☑ 01326-312220; www.facebook.com/themeatcounterfalmouth; 25 Arwenack St; burgers £7-13; ☉ noon-9pm) Perennially popular with Falmouth's hungry student population, this laid-back joint turns out the town's best handmade burgers and hot dawgs. Go for a Philly cheesesteak, a Flat Top Dog or one of the two veggie-friendly options, or brave cardiac arrest with the racily titled MILF (beef, chicken, pork, bacon, four cheese slices, veg and a jalapeno pepper).

Good Vibes Café CAFE £
(☑ 01326-211870; www.facebook.com/GoodVibesCafeFalmouth; 28 Killigrew St; sandwiches & salads £6-8; ☉ 8.30am-5.30pm Mon-Sat) Look no further for lunch than this lovely, contemporary cafe on the Moor, which does a brisk trade from breakfast through to teatime. It's popular for its copious breakfasts, creative sandwiches (which range from pulled spiced chicken to peanut-and-mackerel bagel), crunchy salads and irresistible cakes. There's free cucumber water on tap, plus smoothies and juices galore.

Harbour Lights FISH & CHIPS £
(☑ 01326-316934; www.harbourlights.co.uk; Arwenack St; fish & chips £3-6; ☉ 11.30am-9pm Sun-Thu, to 9.30pm Fri & Sat) Falmouth's classic chippy uses sustainably sourced fish from local boats and was voted Independent Fish

Falmouth

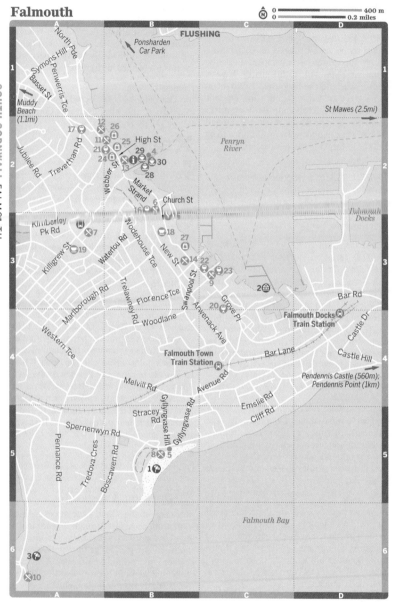

SOUTH CORNWALL FALMOUTH

and Chip Shop of the Year in 2017. Depending on the catch of the day, you might tuck into lemon sole, pollock or hake. You can take away, or there's a pleasant restaurant area with views over the Fal estuary.

★ **Oliver's**   BISTRO **££**

(☎ 01326-218138; www.oliversfalmouth.com; 33 High St; mains £16.50-23.50; ☉ noon-2pm & 7-9pm Tue-Sat) Run by well-respected chef Ken Symons, this little bistro is everyone's tip in Falmouth, but the tiny dining room

Falmouth

means you'll have to book well ahead. White walls and pine tables provide a stripped-back match for Ken's imaginative, Mediterranean-inspired food. Local foragers provide many ingredients.

★**Wheelhouse**   SEAFOOD ££
(☑ 01326-318050; Upton Slip; mains £8-15; ⊙ 6-10pm Wed-Sat) Hidden down a narrow alley off Church St, this backstreet shellfish bar is all about the hands-on dining experience: crab, scallops, mussels and lobsters are served in their shells, complete with cracking tools. There are two sittings, but both are always packed out – you will need to book well ahead, ideally a couple of weeks in advance.

★**Star & Garter**   GASTROPUB ££
(☑ 01326-316663; www.starandgarterfalmouth. com; 52 High St; dinner mains £16-23; ⊙ noon-10pm) At the top of the old High Street among antique shops and health-food stores, this ancient old boozer has been reincarnated as a gourmet gastropub focusing on nose-to-tail dining, locally sourced wherever possible. It's proved a great success, with a bevy of foodie awards and cracking views across the water to Flushing. The menu is meat-heavy, though, so veggies might struggle.

Courtyard Deli   DELI, CAFE ££
(☑ 01326-319526; www.courtyarddeli.co.uk; 2 Bells Ct; mains £8-12; ⊙ 8.30am-5.30pm Mon-Sat, 10.30am-4pm Sun) Small is beautiful, as this cosy deli-diner ably demonstrates. Charcute-

rie, tarts, salads and quiches fill the counter cabinets, and there are regular evening dinner sessions. It's up an easy-to-miss alley, next to Beerwolf Books. Also runs supper clubs.

Gylly Beach Cafe   CAFE ££
(☑ 01326-312884; www.gyllybeach.com; Gyllyngvase Beach; mains £11-17; ⊙ 9am-11pm) When the sun shines, *everyone* heads to the Gylly Beach for coffee or lunch, so it's nigh on impossible to snag an outside table. Sliding doors open onto the glass-fronted patio, perched right above Gyllyngvase's sands. Burgers, kebabs, mussels and salads dominate the menu, and the breakfasts are very good – but it's become a prisoner of its own popularity.

⏻ Drinking & Nightlife

As befits a lively student town, there are lots of drinking choices in Falmouth, from traditional pubs to trendy bars.

★**Espressini**   CAFE
(☑ 01326-236582; www.espressini.co.uk; 39 Killigrew St; ⊙ 8am-6pm Mon-Sat, 10am-4pm Sun;) Cornwall's best coffee house, bar none, run by committed coffee aficionado Rupert Ellis. The choice of blends, roasts and coffees is enough to fill a 2m-long blackboard (literally) and they've recently started serving a small selection of breakfast and lunch dishes too. There's another coffee-only branch across town on Arwenack St.

SECRET GARDENS

The charms of Heligan and Glendurgan are well known, but there are several other secret gardens near Falmouth to discover.

Enys Gardens (☑01326-259885; www.enysgardens.org.uk; Penryn; adult/child £5/2; ⊘2-5pm Tue, Thu & Sun Apr-Sep) is said to be one of the oldest in Cornwall – the area of bluebell woodland known as Parc Lye is believed to have been undisturbed since medieval times. Elsewhere are formal ponds, walkways and rare trees including a Chilean laurel and a huge ginkgo biloba that's allegedly the second largest in Britain.

Penjerrick (☑01872-870105; www.penjerrickgarden.co.uk; Budock Water; adult/child £3/1.50; ⊘1.30-4.30pm Wed, Fri & Sun Mar-Sep) touts itself as Cornwall's 'true' jungle garden (a sly dig at Heligan, perhaps?). It's really two gardens in one: exotic jungle plants in the Valley Garden, and rhododendrons, magnolias and camellias in the Upper Garden. It's in Budock, 3 miles southwest of Falmouth; follow signs on the A39 towards Trebah and Glendurgan, and look out for signs en route.

Potager (☑01326-341258; www.potagergarden.org; suggested donation £3; ⊘10am-5pm Thu-Sun) is well worth the detour. Rescued from dilapidation by its current owners, this gorgeous kitchen garden near the village of Constantine has been renovated by volunteers and modelled on the French 'potager'. Highlights include the 30m greenhouse and the super veggie cafe, which is very popular with lunching locals at weekends (mains £6 to £10).

★ **Beerwolf Books** PUB
(☑01326-618474; www.beerwolfbooks.com; 3 Bells Ct; ⊘noon-midnight) Probably the greatest idea ever, anytime, anywhere: a prime pub and brilliant bookshop rolled into one, meaning you can browse for reading material before settling down for a pint of real ale. Beers change weekly, and you're welcome to bring in food. It feels well worn and welcoming, like a comfy pair of slippers, with old chairs and mix-and-match tables.

Hand Bar BAR
(☑01326-319888; www.facebook.com/HandBeer BarUK; 3 Old Brewery Yard; ⊘noon-1am) Peter Walker's craft-beer bar showcases his knowledge, gained while running Leeds' North Bar: esoteric choices such as New York's Brooklyn Brewery and Bodmin's Harbour Brewing Co are among the regulars on tap – although esoterica equals expensiveness. It's fittingly situated in a former brewery, with a few courtyard tables outside, but space is limited inside.

Dolly's TEAHOUSE
(☑01326-218400; www.dollysbar.co.uk; 21 Church St; ⊘10am-10pm or 11pm Tue-Sat) Frilly and friendly, Dolly's captures the delights of the English tearoom – complete with charity-shop lamps, bone china teapots and cake stands. It kicks into a different gear after dark, with cocktails and jazz.

Boathouse PUB
(☑01326-315425; www.theboathousefalmouth. co.uk; Trevethan Hill; mains £12-16.50; ⊘11am-11pm) Another local's tip, a cosy split-level pub that also serves decent grub and one of the best Sunday roasts in town. The main room has the air of a ship's cabin with views over the river to Flushing. There's also a small covered area, and an outside patio for sunny days.

The Front PUB
(☑01326-212168; Custom House Quay; ⊘11am-11.30pm) The beer-buffs' choice: a cosy spit-and-sawdust pub, with scuffed wood floors and a copious choice of real ales served straight from wooden casks. The entrance is down a small hill off Arwenack St.

Falmouth Townhouse BAR
(☑01326-312009; www.falmouthtownhouse.co.uk; 3 Grove Pl; ⊘11am-11pm; 🛜) Cocktails and continental beers served in a Georgian townhouse, all designer light bulbs and swooshy furniture. There's a wooden patio behind, and hotel rooms upstairs.

Quayside PUB
(☑01326-312113; Arwenack St; ⊘11am-11pm) Along the quay, this is the pub for a sunset pint on a nice day, with plenty of picnic tables beside the harbour.

🛍 Shopping

★ **Jam** MUSIC

(☎01326-211722; 32 High St; ⊙10.30am-5.30pm Mon-Sat) Music aficionados mustn't miss a visit to Falmouth's finest record store, with a just-so selection of vinyl and CDs, leather sofas, magazines to browse and very decent coffee too. New releases are upstairs, vinyl in the basement.

Finisterre CLOTHING

(☎01326-318482; www.finisterre.com; 18 High St; ⊙10am-5pm Mon-Sat) Cornwall's coolest clothing brand, St Agnes-based Finisterre gets its very own end-of-season and end-of-line outlet on Falmouth's old High St. Known for its cold-water surf gear, Finisterre's wool beanies and puffy outdoor jackets are de rigueur for Cornwall's snappiest surfers these days – although their ethical credentials mean they don't come cheap.

Wild Pony VINTAGE

(☎01326-618085; www.wild-pony.co.uk; 19 Arwenack St; ⊙10.30am-5.30pm) A treasure trove for vintage togs, from leather jackets to retro dresses and cowboy boots.

Vintage Warehouse 13 VINTAGE

(☎07545 877622; www.vintagewarehouse13. co.uk; 34 High St; ⊙10.30am-5.30pm Mon-Sat) A bargain-lover's dream, with an ever-changing selection of vintage dresses, lumberjack shirts, used denim and designer furniture. It's worth stopping by just to have a look in the window, which always looks like a work of art.

ℹ Information

Fal River Information Centre (☎01326-741194; www.falriver.co.uk; 11 Market Strand, Prince of Wales Pier; ⊙9.30am-5.30pm Mon-Sat, 10am-4pm Sun) This small information centre by the pier is run by the Fal River Company, and provides useful advice on the Falmouth area. They also operate most of the ferries along the Fal River, and offer an accommodation booking service.

ℹ Getting There & Around

BOAT

St Mawes Ferry (www.falriver.co.uk; adult/child return £10/5.50; ⊙half-hourly Mon-Fri, hourly Sat & Sun) Runs between Falmouth and St Mawes, with great views of the castles. The crossing takes around 20 minutes.

Falmouth Water Taxi (☎07522 446659; www. falmouthwatertaxi.co.uk) Call up a water-based taxi for transport along the Fal. Sample prices are £7/12 for a single/return trip from Falmouth to Penryn or Flushing, or £12/20 for a trip to the Pandora Inn.

Flushing Ferry (www.flushingferry.co.uk; adult/child single £2.50/1; ⊙half-hourly Apr-Oct, hourly Nov-Mar) This little ferry chugs across the river from Prince of Wales Pier to Flushing year-round. It's operated by the Fal River company.

BUS

Falmouth's Moor Bus Station (The Moor) is central. First Kernow (www.firstgroup.com/cornwall) has the following bus routes:

Helston (£5, hourly Monday to Saturday) Bus 35/35A stops at Glendurgan and Trebah Gardens en route.

Penzance (every two hours Monday to Saturday) Bus 2 via Helston.

Redruth (£5, hourly) Bus U2 via Penryn.

Truro (£5, half-hourly Monday to Saturday, hourly Sunday) Bus U1 via Penryn.

To reach Gyllyngvase and Swanpool beaches, bus 367 runs from the station to both (hourly Monday to Friday, four times on Saturday).

TRAIN

Falmouth is at the end of the branch train line from Truro (£4.20, 24 minutes), where you can catch connections with the mainline service from Penzance to stations including Plymouth, Exeter and London Paddington.

DON'T MISS

A PINT BY THE CREEK

At the bottom of a hill by Restronguet Creek, the thatched **Pandora Inn** (☎01326-372678; www.pandorainn.com; Restronguet Creek; dinner mains £12-18; ⊙10.30am-11pm) is one of Cornwall's landmark pubs, in situ since the mid-1600s. It's the picture of a smuggler's pub: inside, blazing hearths, snug alcoves, beams and ships-in-cabinets; outside, whitewashed facade, thatched roof, cob walls and a boat-lined pontoon. The food is great, and there's nowhere prettier for a pint.

Hard to believe it almost burnt to the ground in 2011; thankfully, the ground floor remained largely intact, and it's since been rebuilt in seamless ship-shape fashion. It's owned by St Austell Brewery.

Gardens of the Southwest

Blessed with a balmy climate nurtured by the Gulf Stream, the southwest boasts an array of astonishing gardens. Many, such as Garden House, Heligan, Trelissick and Tresco's Abbey Gardens, date from the 18th and 19th centuries. Others, such as the Eden Project, feel like a vision from a sci-fi future.

SIMON BOND / SHUTTERSTOCK ©

VISITBRITAIN / BRITAIN ON VIEW / GETTY IMAGES ©

1. Eden Project (p171)
One of Cornwall's top attractions, the Eden Project houses weird and wonderful plants from across the globe.

2. Lost Gardens of Heligan (p172)
The *Mud Maid* sculpture, created by artists Pete and Sue Hill, is part of this horticultural wonderland.

3. Buckland Abbey (p112)
Buckland Abbey was originally a Cistercian monastery and abbey-church in the 13th-century.

4 Tresco Abbey Garden (p233)
A must-see gem, this subtropical estate is laid out on the site of a 12th-century Benedictine priory.

OLAF PROTZE / CONTRIBUTOR / GETTY IMAGES ©

SOUTH CORNWALL PENRYN

Penryn

📞 01326 / POP 6810

Just along the river from Falmouth, the small market town of Penryn is effectively a suburb of its bigger neighbour these days, but in centuries past the town was home to Cornwall's great seat of learning, Glasney College, a scholarly monastery which held all the most important books of the Cornish language. The college's disappearance in the Middle Ages following Henry VIII's dissolution of the monasteries effectively marked the beginning of the end of Cornish as a spoken language.

Now home to the main campus of Falmouth University, Penryn nevertheless remains a sleepy and somewhat forgotten town. It's worth a visit though, with a handsome main street lined with 17th- and 18th-century buildings, and some interesting shops and cafes.

✕ Eating

Muddy Beach   CAFE £
(📞 01326-374424; www.muddybeach.com; Jubilee Wharf; lunch mains £5-9, dinner mains £11-14; ⊙ 9.30am-4pm Mon-Wed, to 9pm Thu-Sat, 10am-4pm Sun) This riverside cafe has occupied the space that belonged to Penryn's beloved hang-out, Miss Peapod's. It's a very different proposition, sleek and modern rather than homely and cosy, so it's proved a controversial change. Nevertheless, the location is perfect for lunch, and its weekend 'beach boards' are tempting – choose from meat, seafood and veggie varieties.

ℹ Getting There & Away

Buses including the U2 run half-hourly to Falmouth from Penryn's main street, and all trains between Truro and Falmouth stop here on request.

Flushing & Mylor

📞 01326 / POP 670

Directly across the mouth of the Fal River from Falmouth, the attractive waterfront village of Flushing has survived on its maritime connections for centuries, but it's now mainly the haunt of weekend boaters and yachties rather than fishers or free-traders. Originally known as Nankersey, Flushing became a busy fishing port during the 18th century, and many of the grand houses along the main approach to the village, St Peter's

Hill, belonged to the merchants and captains who grew rich thanks to the Falmouth packet service. It's worth an afternoon stroll, with a handy ferry link across the water to Falmouth,and a couple of pleasant pubs, as well as a pretty riverside trail to the nearby yachting harbour of **Mylor Bridge**.

🏃 Activities

Salt Air Adventures   ADVENTURE SPORTS
(📞 07828 246278; www.saltair.co.uk; Mylor Yacht Harbour) Based at Mylor Harbour, these guys are a good bet for multi-activities – they run stand-up paddleboarding and kayaking from Mylor, surfing and coasteering from their base near Newquay, and also offer climbing sessions in Penwith. They're good value: hiring a single kayak costs £10/45 per hour/day, a coasteering session costs £40 per person, and surfing starts from £25 per half-day.

ℹ Getting There & Away

The **Flushing Ferry** (p161) runs regularly across the water to Falmouth, and is by far the quickest (and prettiest) way to get to the village.

Buse services are pretty limited; about the only option is the 69 (five or six daily), which runs from Falmouth to Mylor Bridge, via Penryn.

Helford River

This is one of Cornwall's prettiest – and priciest – corners, with a tranquil river fringed by coppiced oaks and secret creeks, not to mention some seriously expensive real estate. Two of Cornwall's great subtropical gardens sit side by side along the river's northern bank, about 4 miles south of Falmouth.

The southern bank is actually part of the Lizard Peninsula, and a long drive away by road – but you can take a shortcut thanks to the foot ferry that chugs across the water from the Ferryboat Inn to Helford village.

◉ Sights

Trebah Garden   GARDENS
(📞 01326-252200; www.trebahgarden.co.uk; adult/child £9/3; ⊙ 10.30am-5.30pm, last entry 4.30pm) Trebah Garden was planted in 1840 by Charles Fox, younger brother of Alfred, who established nearby Glendurgan Garden. It's less formal, with gigantic rhododendrons, gunnera and jungle ferns lining the sides of a steep ravine leading down to the quay and shingle beach. There's a pleasant cafe and souvenir shop beside the ticket office.

WORTH A TRIP

THE COAST TO COAST CYCLE TRAIL

Creeping inland from the Fal River along oak-clad banks, Restronguet Creek is perhaps the prettiest of the Fal's many wooded tributaries. It filters all the way to the quaint village of Devoran, once an important site for processing ore from the tin and copper mines ferried here from the north-coast mines aboard the old Redruth and Chacewater tramway – now reinvented as a popular bike route, the Coast to Coast Cycle Trail.

The disused tram track from Devoran to Portreath has been redeveloped as this pretty bike trail, which runs for 11 miles past the old mine workings around Scorrier, Chacewater and the Poldice Valley. It's mostly flat and easy, although there are a few uphill and off-road sections.

Bikes and maps can be hired at the Devoran end from Bike Chain Bissoe (☏ 01872-870341; www.bikechainbissoe.co.uk; Old Conns Works, Bissoe; adult bikes £15-35, child's bikes £10-12; ⏰ 9am-5pm), and from the Portreath end from The Hub (☏ 01209-844666; www.thehubportreath.com; Seafront; bikes per adult/child from £20/12).

Admission to the gardens is half-price from November to February.

Glendurgan GARDENS
(NT; ☏ 01326-250906; www.nationaltrust.org.uk/glendurgan-garden; adult/child £8.10/4.05; ⏰ 10.30am-5.30pm Tue-Sun) Glendurgan was established by Alfred Fox in the 1820s to show off the many weird and wonderful plants being brought back from the far corners of the empire, from Himalayan rhododendrons to Canadian maples and New Zealand tree ferns. Tumbling down a stunning subtropical valley, the garden offers breathtaking views of the Helford, as well as a lovely ornamental maze and a secluded beach near Durgan village. The gardens are now owned by the National Trust.

★ **Cornish Seal Sanctuary** ANIMAL SANCTUARY
(☏ 0871 423 2110; www.visitsealife.com/gweek; adult/child £15.50/12.95; ⏰ 10am-5pm May-Sep, 9am-4pm Oct-Apr) The 'ah' factor goes into overdrive at this sea-life centre, which cares for sick and orphaned seals washed up along the Cornish coastline before returning them to the wild. It's a guaranteed kids favourite, and parents will doubtless find themselves seduced by the seals' antics too. There are regular talks and feeding sessions. Online bookings get a hefty 30% discount.

🏃 Activities

Helford River Boats BOATING
(☏ 01326-250770; www.helford-river-boats.co.uk; Helford Passage; kayak/stand-up paddleboards/rowboat/motorboat per hour £12/15/20/40) There are numerous ways to get out on the water offered here – motorboats, stand-

up paddleboards, rowboats and one- and two-person kayaks. They can also provide a skippered boat service if you're worried about running aground.

Helford River Cruises BOATING
(☏ 07941 027732; www.helfordrivercruises.co.uk; Mawnan Smith; 1½-hr cruise £20) This boat company offers scenic cruises up the Helford River to picturesque areas including Frenchman's Creek and the Helford Passage. It also offers longer trips to Gillan Creek and Falmouth Bay or to Gweek. It's run by the same team as Koru Kayaking (p157), so you can also arrange kayaking-and-cruise combinations. Boats depart from the Budock Vean Hotel in Mawnan Smith.

🍴 Eating

★ **Ferryboat Inn** GASTROPUB ££
(☏ 01326-250625; www.staustellbrewery.co.uk/pub/falmouth/ferryboat-inn; Helford Passage; mains £8-20; ⏰ 11am-11pm) This lovely riverside pub is a Cornish classic. Outside, there are wooden picnic tables with dreamy views over the Helford River; inside, it's all wood, slate and open plan. It's great for food – oysters, shellfish and the Sunday roast are strong points, and a big blackboard is full of fishy specials. Bus 35 passes hourly from Falmouth.

ℹ️ Getting There & Away

The **Helford Ferry** (www.helford-river-boats.co.uk/theferry; adult/child single £5/2, return £6/3, bicycles single £2; ⏰ 9.30am-5pm Apr-Oct) runs regularly across the river from the jetty outside the Ferryboat Inn to the opposite bank at Helford village. Foot passengers, bikes, babies, pushchairs and dogs can all be carried.

Truro

☎ 01872 / POP 17,430

Dominated by the three mighty spires of its 19th-century cathedral, which rises above town like a neo-Gothic supertanker, Truro is Cornwall's capital and its only city. It's the county's main centre for shopping and commerce: the streets here are packed with high-street chains and independent shops, and there are regular weekly markets held on the paved piazza at Lemon Quay (opposite the Hall for Cornwall).

◎ Sights

Truro Cathedral CHURCH

(www.trurocathedral.org.uk; High Cross; suggested donation ⸱⸱; ⸱ ⸱⸱⸱am-⸱pm Mon-Sat, 9am-/pm Sun) Built on the site of a 16th-century parish church in soaring Gothic Revival style, Truro Cathedral was completed in 1910, making it the first cathedral built in England since St Paul's. Inside, the vast nave contains some fine Victorian stained glass and the impressive Father Willis Organ.

Royal Cornwall
Museum MUSEUM

(☎ 01872-272205; www.royalcornwallmuseum.org. uk; River St; ⊗10am-5pm Mon-Sat) FREE Collections at the county's main museum encompass everything from geological specimens to Celtic torques and a ceremonial carriage. Upstairs there's an Egyptian section and a little gallery with some surprising finds: a Turner here, a van Dyck there, and several works by the Newlyn artist Stanhope Forbes.

🏃 Activities

★Enterprise Boats BOATING

(☎ 01326-374241; www.falriver.co.uk/getting-about/ferries/enterprise-boats; day return adult/child £15.30/7.20) Two miles downriver from Truro's city centre, past the green expanse of Boscawen Park, lies the riverside hamlet of Malpas, from where ferries chug out along the Fal River all the way to Falmouth. It's a wonderfully scenic trip that putters past wooded riverbanks and hidden inlets; some boats also stop at Trelissick en route. Depending on the tide, boats either depart from the pontoon at Malpas, or from the harbour-master's office in Truro; double-decker buses link the two locations.

🎊 Festivals & Events

Great Cornish Food Festival FOOD & DRINK

(Lemon Quay; ⊗Sep) This major foodie celebration attracts some of the county's leading food businesses to a covered awning on Lemon Quay. Chefs' demos and freebie tastings are the highlight.

City of Lights FESTIVAL

(www.trurocityoflights.co.uk; ⊗Dec) Giant withy (wicker) lanterns are carried through the city centre during this street parade.

🍴 Eating

Craftworks Street Kitchen STREET FOOD £

(☎ 01872-857117; www.craftworkskitchen.co.uk; Lemon Quay; mains £6-8; ⊗11am-6pm Mon-Thu, to 6pm Fri & Sat, to 4pm Sun) It looks dicey from the outside (it's built from an old shipping container), but this rough-and-ready little diner turns out the best street food in the city. Choose from delicious tacos and burritos like piri-piri chicken and beef brisket, served with taco slaw and red-onion pickle, or go the whole hog with a fish po-boy or a Korean chicken burger.

Cornish Food Box Company CAFE, DELI £

(☎ 01872-211533; www.thecornishfoodboxcompany. co.uk; Walsingham Pl; mains £5-12; ⊗cafe & deli 8am-5pm Mon-Sat) If it's local provenance that's important, then look nowhere other than this backstreet deli-cafe. They started out packing up boxes of veg, meat and treats for customers, but have since branched out with a deli and shop, as well as a quirky cafe where you can tuck into a 100% local lunch while sitting on a haybale.

Hub Box BURGERS £

(☎ 01872-240700; www.hubbox.co.uk; 116 Kenwyn St; burgers £5.75-8.50; ⊗11.30am-9pm) With three locations in Cornwall and another in Exeter, this ever-popular burger joint is definitely doing something right. This is the original and best of the bunch: the setting inside a converted church is fun, and the burgers, sliders and dawgs are generous and inventive – although if you were nitpicking, the chips aren't as crisp as they should be.

Archie Brown's CAFE £

(☎ 01872-278622; www.archiebrowns.co.uk; 105-106 Kenwyn St; mains £8-12; ⊗9am-5pm Mon-Sat; 🖥🍴) 🍴 The Truro outpost of Penzance's much-loved wholefood cafe, Archie Brown's serves up lovely salads and imaginative vegetarian mains, as well as a copious selection of herbal teas. The cafe's upstairs, and there's a wholefood and vitamin shop downstairs.

Truro

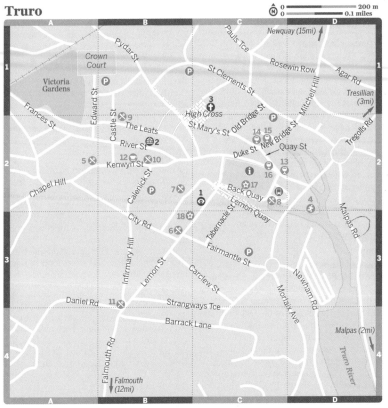

Truro

⊙ Sights
1 Lemon St Market C2
2 Royal Cornwall Museum B2
3 Truro Cathedral C1

➕ Activities, Courses & Tours
4 Enterprise Boats D2

🍴 Eating
5 Archie Brown's A2
6 Bustopher Jones B3
7 Cornish Food Box Company B2
8 Craftworks Street Kitchen C2
9 Falmouth Bay Seafood Café B2

10 Hub Box B2
11 Thomas Daniell B3

🍷 Drinking & Nightlife
12 108 Coffee B2
13 Old Ale House C2
14 Old Grammar School C2
15 Sanctuary C2
16 Sonder C2

🎭 Entertainment
17 Hall for Cornwall C2
18 Plaza Cinema B3

★ **Falmouth Bay Seafood Café** SEAFOOD ££
(☎ 01872-278884; www.falmouthbayseafoodcafe.
com; Castle Villa, 53 Castle St; mains £13-24;
⊙ noon-3.30pm & 5.30-10pm Mon-Sat) Rightly
touted as Truro's top restaurant, this smart
seafooderie focuses on the fruits of the sea –

tuck into fresh Fal oysters or Falmouth
Bay scallops, then go for the seafood platter (£40). The lunch and pre-theatre menu
is good value: £15/18 for two/three courses, served every day at lunchtime, or from
5.30pm to 7pm Tuesday to Thursday.

WORTH A TRIP

TRELISSICK GARDENS

Grandly located at the head of the Fal estuary, 4 miles south of Truro, Trelissick (NT; ☑ 01872-862090; www.nationaltrust.org.uk/trelissick-garden; house & gardens adult/child £10.90/5.45, grounds £4; ⊙ grounds 10.30am-5.30pm, house 11am-5pm) is one of Cornwall's most beautiful aristocratic estates, with a formal garden filled with magnolias and hydrangeas, and a huge expanse of fields and parkland criss-crossed by trails. The main house has only recently been open to the public, and contains a lavish drawing room, solarium and a world class collection of antique china. If you just want to explore the park, parking is £4.

Thomas Daniell　　BRITISH ££

(☑ 01872-858110; www.tdtruro.com; 1 Infirmary Hill; 2-course lunch Mon-Sat £10, dinner mains £10-19; ⊙ lunch noon-5pm daily, dinner 5-10pm Mon-Sat) Run by the owners of the Old Grammar School (p168), this sophisticated gastropub is looking sleek and modern since its recent refurbishment, and it's become one of the city's new favourites. Big wooden tables, local ales on tap and a choice of dining spaces, plus a good wine choice. Food is fairly standard gastropub stuff, like surf-and-turf and battered fish.

Bustopher Jones　　BISTRO ££

(☑ 01872-430000; www.bustophersbarbistro.com; 62 Lemon St; mains £12.50-22.50; ⊙ noon-10pm Mon-Sat) It's been open, closed and open again over recent years, but Bustopher's is back for downtown bistro dining: expect substantial dishes like pan-seared hake with a mussel-butter sauce and duck with dauphinoise potatoes, served up in an attractive, wood-panelled dining room. There's a small patio at the rear.

Heron　　PUB

(☑ 01872-272773; www.heroninnmalpas.co.uk; Malpas; ⊙ 11am-3pm & 6-11pm) If the big city gets too much, head a couple of miles from town to Malpas' delightful creekside pub, which serves good beer and grub (mains £11 to £16), and has outside benches where you can sup your pint overlooking the river. Best of all, combine it with a trip downriver aboard Enterprise Boats (p166) – now there's an afternoon to remember.

🍷 Drinking & Nightlife

★ 108 Coffee　　CAFE

(☑ 07582 339636; www.108coffee.co.uk; 109 Kenwyn St; ⊙ 7am-6pm Mon-Fri, 8am-6pm Sat) Set up by unapologetic coffee nuts Paul and Michelle, this is the premier place for a caffeine fix in Truro. The beans come courtesy of Cornish coffee roasters Origin, and the flat whites and espressos are as good as any the county has to offer (you can even text your order ahead to save waiting). Light bites and cakes are also on offer.

Sonder　　BAR

(☑ 01872-260926; www.sondertruro.co.uk; 6 Princes St; ⊙ 7am-midnight Tue-Sat, 10am-5pm Sun) Truro gets its own craft-beer bar, and it's a cracker; lots of thought has gone into the selection, with local brewers like Black Rock and Padstow Brewing Company sitting alongside guests from the Czech Republic, Scotland, USA and Canada. There's a good cider and cocktail choice too, and street food to snack on like tostados, noodles and jerk chicken.

Old Ale House　　PUB

(☑ 01872-271122; www.old-ale-house.co.uk; 7 Quay St; ⊙ noon-11pm) A proper ale-drinker's pub, with sawdust on the floor, beer mats on the ceiling and a menu of guest ales. Ask at the bar for a handful of peanuts to snack on – they're even happy for you to chuck your shells on the floor. Most of the beers come from Skinner's Brewery.

Old Grammar School　　PUB

(☑ 01872-278559; www.theoldgrammarschool.com; 19 St Mary's St; ⊙ 10am-late Mon-Sat) Open-plan drinking den with big tables and sofas to sink into. Lunch is served from noon to 3pm; later it's all cocktails, candles, and Belgian and Japanese beers.

Sanctuary　　WINE BAR

(☑ 01872-271757; www.facebook.com/TheSanctuaryTruro; 18 Old Bridge St; ⊙ 10am-10pm Mon-Thu, to midnight Fri & Sat) Classy little wine bar that serves several vintages by the glass, and also holds regular film screenings.

☆ Entertainment

Plaza Cinema　　CINEMA

(☑ 01872-272894; www.wtwcinemas.co.uk; Lemon St) Owned by local chain WTW, the city's four-screen cinema is a great space to watch films, and is a favourite of renowned UK film critic Mark Kermode (who occasionally hosts his own special screenings here). At other times, expect the usual mainstream releases.

Hall for Cornwall

THEATRE

(☑ 01872-262466; www.hallforcornwall.co.uk; Lemon Quay; tickets £15-35) In the heart of the city, this is the county's main venue for touring theatre and music. Big-name comedy acts, major touring productions and dance shows all feature on the program, but most events sell out, so book ahead.

🛍 Shopping

Lemon St Market
MARKET

(www.lemonstreetmarket.co.uk; Lemon St; ⊗ 10.30am-5.30pm Mon-Sat) A covered market housing craft shops, cafes, delis and an upstairs gallery. The willow-and-paper lanterns hanging from the ceiling were built for Truro's Christmas street parade, the City of Lights, held in early December.

ℹ Information

Tourist Office (☑ 01872-274555; www.visit truro.org.uk; Boscawen St; ⊗ 9am-5.30pm Mon-Fri, to 5pm Sat) In a small office beside the Hall for Cornwall's rear entrance.

ℹ Transport

BOAT

Enterprise Boats (p166) runs a regular daily ferry service down the Fal River to Falmouth and St Mawes.

There's also a shortcut over to the Roseland Peninsula courtesy of the **King Harry Ferry** (☑ 01872-862312; www.falriver.co.uk/getting-about/ferries/king-harry-ferry; per car one way/return £6/8, bicycles £1, pedestrians free), which crosses over the river near Trelissick Gardens.

BUS

Truro's **bus station** is beside Lemon Quay.

Falmouth (£5, half-hourly Monday to Saturday, hourly Sunday) The U1 bus runs via Penryn.

St Ives (£5, 1½ hours, hourly Monday to Saturday) Bus 14/14A.

Penzance (£5, half-hourly Monday to Saturday, hourly Sunday) Bus 18.

TRAIN

Truro is on the main London Paddington–Penzance line and the branch line to Falmouth.

Bristol £47.30, 3½ hours

Exeter £18.90, 2¼ hours

Falmouth £4.20, 30 minutes

London Paddington £63.70, 4½ hours

Penzance £6.80, 30 minutes

The Roseland

On the opposite side of the Fal estuary from Truro and Falmouth, the Roseland Peninsula gets its name not from flowers but from the Cornish word *ros,* meaning promontory. Greener and gentler than the harsh granite cliffs of the north coast, it's a pastoral place, criss-crossed by hedgerows and quiet lanes, and spotted with quiet villages and fine sandy bays.

⊙ Sights

★ St Mawes Castle
CASTLE

(EH; ☑ 01326-270526; adult/child £5.40/3.20; ⊗ 10am-6pm Apr-Sep, to 5pm Oct-Mar) Strategically sited to command an uninterrupted field of fire over the entrance to Falmouth Bay in tandem with Pendennis Castle (p156), on the opposite side of the estuary, St Mawes is one of the network of 16th-century coastal fortresses built by Henry VIII, and is also among the best preserved. Cloverleaf shaped, with circular towers around a central keep, it's approached via a classic drawbridge, and you can wander freely around the interior chambers and the outside gun decks.

St-Just-in-Roseland
VILLAGE

The creekside church of this sleepy village is quite possibly the prettiest in Cornwall – and in this ecclesiastically minded county, there's no shortage of competition. Surrounded by a jumble of wildflowers and overhanging yews tumbling down to a boat-filled creek, the present church dates from the 13th century, but there was probably an oratory here as far back as the 6th century.

Carne & Pendower
BEACH

These twin side-by-side beaches form one of the Roseland's largest areas of sand at low tide. It's brilliant for beachcombing and rockpooling – look out for mermaids' purses tangled up with the seaweed – but it can get a bit smelly in hot weather when a lot of weed's washed in.

Portscatho
VILLAGE

Portscatho was formerly one of the busiest pilchard ports on Cornwall's south coast. The village boasts one of the county's largest granite breakwaters, alongside a smattering of art galleries, knick-knack shops and lots of second homes (the village is absolutely dead in the middle of winter). It's best reached via a walk along the coast path that includes the nearby beach of Porthcurnick (p170).

Porthcurnick BEACH

A popular family beach near the port of Portscatho, which has become even more frequented thanks to the success of its beachside cafe, the Hidden Hut (p170). Parking here can be tricky – you might be able to find a space on the hill leading down to the beach, otherwise it's often a good idea just to walk over from Portscatho.

St Anthony's Head VIEWPOINT

The remains of a turn-of-the-century gun battery can still be seen along the point at St Anthony's Head. Just along the coast is the peninsula's 1835-built lighthouse, where you can now stay inside the lighthouse keeper's old cottage, Sally Port (☑01386-701177; www.ruralretreats.co.uk; St Anthony; 3 nights from £809; 🅿🖥).

Veryan VILLAGE

Veryan is a sleepy country village, home to a couple of art galleries and an excellent village pub. At the top of the hill above the village are its best-known landmarks: two circular roundhouses, whose lack of corners supposedly made them devil-proof (since there's nowhere to hide in the corners).

🏃 Activities

★ Philleigh Way COOKING

(☑01872-580893; www.philleighway.co.uk; Court Farm, Philleigh; 1-day courses from £95) This fantastic rural cookery school teaches all those culinary skills you've always wanted to learn but have never known who to ask. Filleting fish? Foraging for mushrooms? Baking French bread? Creating curries? All covered, and plenty more esoteric skills besides, such as Argentinian asado and sushi-making. The farm setting is delightful, and the tutors are both knowledgeable and full of fun.

The 'Cornwall in a Day' course covers pasties, saffron buns, hog's pudding, crab-dressing and clotted cream.

7th Rise OUTDOORS

(www.7thrise.co.uk; weekends £275) Founded by forager and outdoorsman Thom Hunt, 7th Rise gives you the opportunity to connect with your wild spirit through full-day or weekend foraging and hunting experiences. Overnight trips run from a hidden cottage and include expeditions to go plant-foraging, mussel-hunting, canoeing on the river and preparing your own wild suppers around the campfire – a fine way to unplug and unwind.

St Mawes Kayaks KAYAKING

(☑07971 846786; www.stmaweskayaks.co.uk; 2hr/day £15/35) Kayaks are ideal for exploring the waters off St Mawes, especially the quiet creeks along the Percuil River, and the nearby beaches of Great and Little Molunan. Single and two-seater sit-on kayaks are available.

✖ Eating

★ Hidden Hut CAFE £

(www.hiddenhut.co.uk; Porthcurnick Beach; meals £5-10; ⊙10am-5pm Mar-Oct) Hidden indeed: this coastal-cabin cafe on Porthcurnick Beach is so tucked away, you might miss it even if you've been here before. The wooden cabin was built as a wartime lookout, but now serves delicious beach food: grilled cheese toasts, hot soups, proper cakes and 'beach salads'. During summer, there are pop-up 'feast nights' once or twice a week.

Melinsey Mill CAFE £

(☑01872-501049; www.melinseymill.co.uk; Veryan; mains £4-10; ⊙10am-5.30pm Tue-Sun Apr-Oct, daily Jul & Aug) Just outside Veryan, this 16th-century watermill has been converted into a delightful cafe and craft shop, where you can pick up wacky withy sculptures and other crafty local items. They also do a cracking cream tea, plus doorstep sandwiches and delicious homemade cakes.

Rising Sun PUB FOOD ££

(☑01326-270233; www.risingsunstmawes.co.uk; St Mawes; mains £7-15) This gabled pub does a roaring trade with visitors straight off the St Ives ferry. It has a little walled patio out front, and serves solid food as well as a decent carvery on Wednesday and Sunday.

Driftwood GASTRONOMY £££

(☑01872-580644; www.driftwoodhotel.co.uk; Rosevine, Portscatho; 3-course menu £65) Chef Chris Eden has worked wonders at this hotel restaurant since taking it over, and it's one of only a handful of places in Cornwall to sport a shiny Michelin star. As such, you can expect seriously fine dining here: creative flavours, top-quality ingredients and presentation that borders on art. It feels formal: white tablecloths, tasteful art, picture windows.

ℹ Getting There & Away

There are hardly any useful buses to the peninsula, but there are other methods – you can catch the **St Mawes Ferry** (p161) directly from Falmouth, or cross over the Fal River via the **King Harry Ferry** (p169) from near Trelissick Gardens to the opposite side at Philleigh. Otherwise it's a drive of around 14 miles from Truro.

SOUTHEAST CORNWALL

Cornwall's southeastern corner presents yet another side to the county, neither as blustery and beachy as the north coast, nor as wild and craggy as the west. It's closer in feel to the area around the Fal River, a landscape characterised by gentle bays and clifftop fields, but it has its fair share of quaint old fishing ports too, of which Mevagissey, Polperro and Looe are the prettiest examples. The area also has two major river estuaries to explore, the Fowey and the Tamar, prime territory for kayaking and country walks, as well as a little-explored peninsula that's home to some of the county's grandest country houses.

But there's one sight here that no one should miss - the sci-fi biomes of the fabulous Eden Project, raised from the dust of a disused Cornish clay pit and now one of the county's most iconic sights.

St Austell & Around

☏ 01726 / POPULATION 19,960

While tin and copper were the minerals that fuelled Cornwall's great industrial heyday during the 19th century, in the area around St Austell it was china clay – or 'white gold', as it was colloquially known. This chalky resource is vital for many industries, from paper-making to porcelain manufacture, and the quality of the clay around St Austell is considered some of the finest on the planet. The effect of this mighty industry can still clearly be seen around St Austell – most notably in the strange landscape of spiky hills and mineral pools known hereabouts as the 'Cornish Alps'.

Sadly, St Austell itself hasn't fared well from industrial decline, and the town centre is looking decidedly down in the dumps (and that's even after the multimillion-pound redevelopment of its town centre). Nevertheless, it's a handy spot for shopping and supplies before further explorations along the southeast coast.

◉ Sights

★ Eden Project   NATURE CENTRE
(☏ 01726-811911; www.edenproject.com; adult/child/family £27.50/14/71, joint ticket with Lost Gardens of Heligan £38/18.50/98; ⊗ 9.30am-6pm, last admission 4.30pm) Lodged at the bottom of an old china clay pit, the giant biomes of the Eden Project – the largest greenhouses in the world – have become Cornwall's most celebrated landmark, and an absolutely essential visit. Looking like a Bond villain's

DOUG MCKINLAY / GETTY IMAGES ©

Inside the tropical dome, Eden Project

SOUTH CORNWALL ST AUSTELL & AROUND

OFF THE BEATEN TRACK

CLAY TRAILS

The Clay Trails (www.claytrails.co.uk) are a network of paths weaving through the weird landscape of spoil heaps, mica dams and turquoise pools left behind by St Austell's clay-quarrying industry. Nature has reclaimed many areas, and you'll probably spot lots of wildflowers and birdlife flitting around the gorse. There are various routes, all suitable for pedestrians, horse riders and cyclists, including one that directly passes next to the Eden Project, one through the Pentewan Valley and another which passes the Wheal Martyn Country Park.

Bikes can be hired from **Pavé Velo** (☑ 01726-64950; www.pavevelo.cc; 22 Grants Walk; adult/child bikes from £15/10; ☉ 9am-5.30pm Mon-Sat) and **Pentewan Cycle Hire** (☑ 01726-844242; www. pentewanvalleycyclehire.co.uk; 1 West End, Pentewan; adult/child per day £14/9).

lair, Eden's bubble-shaped biomes maintain miniature ecosystems that enable all kinds of weird and wonderful plants to flourish – from stinking rafflesia flowers and banana trees in the Rainforest Biome to cacti and soaring palms in the Mediterranean Biome. The Eden site is at Bodelva, about 5 miles' drive from St Austell. There are 10% discounts for buying tickets online and arriving by public transport, and joint tickets with the Lost Gardens of Heligan. Local tourist offices also sell discounted tickets. Bus 101 runs hourly from St Austell train station.

★**Lost Gardens of Heligan** GARDENS (☑ 01726-845100; www.heligan.com; Pentewan; adult/child £14.50/6.50; ☉ 10am-6pm Mar-Oct, to 5pm Nov-Feb) This is Cornwall's real-life secret garden. Formerly the family estate of the Tremaynes, Heligan's magnificent 19th-century gardens fell into disrepair following WWI, but have been splendidly restored by the brains behind the Eden Project, Tim Smit, and a huge army of gardeners and volunteers. It's a horticultural wonderland: wandering round you'll encounter formal lawns, working kitchen gardens, fruit-filled greenhouses, a secret grotto and a 25m-high rhododendron, plus a lost-world Jungle Valley of ferns, palms and tropical blooms.

Heligan is 7 miles from St Austell. Bus 24 links Heligan with Mevagissey and St Austell train station.

★**Port of Charlestown** HISTORIC SITE (☑ 01726-69897; www.shipwreckcharlestown.com/ historic-port; Quay Rd; adult/child £5/2.50; joint ticket with shipwreck heritage centre £10/5; ☉ 10am-5pm Apr-Oct) It's been off-limits for many years to everyone except film crews, but since spring 2017 Charlestown's historic port has finally reopened to the public. You can now wander round the Georgian quays, and with a bit of luck, step on board a tall ship docked alongside the harbour (assuming there's one in port, that is). Joint tickets with the **Charlestown Shipwreck and Heritage Centre** (☑ 01726-69807; www.shipwreck charlestown.com; Quay Rd; adult/child £6/£3, joint ticket with harbour £10/5; ☉ 10am-5pm Apr-Oct) are available.

Restormel Castle CASTLE (Lostwithiel; adult/child £3.60/2.20; ☉ 10am-6pm Jul & Aug, to 5pm Apr-Jun & Sep, to 4pm Oct) High on a hilltop above Lostwithiel, 9 miles from St Austell on the A390, the ruined castle of Restormel was built by Edward the Black Prince (the first Duke of Cornwall), although he only stayed there twice during his life. It's one of the best-preserved circular keeps in the country, and affords brilliant views across the river and fields from its crenellated battlements. Almost nothing remains of the interior, apart from a few side rooms and a medieval garderobe (storage room).

Roche Rock RUINS (Roche) Clinging to a spur of contorted rock surrounded by barren heath, the curious tumbledown chapel on top of Roche Rock looks like a forgotten set from Monty Python's *Life of Brian*. The present chapel is thought to date from around the 15th century, although there was an oratory here long before.

The site is just outside Roche village; watch for the signs as you drive east on the A30 from Fraddon.

❶ Getting There & Away

BUS

Eden Project Bus 101 (20 minutes, hourly).
Fowey Bus 24 (45 minutes, hourly Monday to Saturday, six on Sunday) Via Charlestown and Par.

Mevagissey Bus 24 (20 minutes, hourly Monday to Saturday, six on Sunday) Via Heligan Gardens.

TRAIN

St Austell's train station is on the main Penzance–London Paddington line. To get to Newquay, you need to change at Par, one stop west from St Austell.

Truro (£5.60, 15 minutes)
Penzance (£10.20, one hour)
Plymouth (£10.20, one hour)

Mevagissey

📞 01726

Slender alleyways, flower-fronted cottages and a grand double-walled quay make the little coastal village of Mevagissey one of the most authentically pretty ports in southeast Cornwall. Its character has changed little since the days when it earned its keep from the sea; higgledy-piggledy buildings line the old streets leading inland from the harbour, and fishing boats bob on the incoming tide.

⊙ Sights

Caerhays Castle   GARDENS
(📞 01872-501310; www.caerhays.co.uk; Porthluney; adult/child £8.50/4.50; ⊙ 10am-5pm mid-Feb–mid-Jun) On the hills above the gentle crescent of Porthluney Beach, this crenellated country mansion was originally built for the Trevanions and later remodelled under the guidance of John Nash (who designed Buckingham Palace and Brighton Pavilion). The house is still a private residence, and is open for guided tours in spring, while the gardens are worth visiting for their wonderful displays of camellias, rhododendrons and magnolias.

Dodman Point   NATURAL FEATURE
(NT) Thrusting into the English Channel, the Dodman (or the rather more macabre Deadman, as it's nicknamed by shipwreck-wary sailors) is the highest headland for miles around, and well off most visitors' radar. From the point, there are huge views east and west – which is probably why Iron Age builders decided to build a great fort here, 66m long and over 6m high, enclosing the entire point. There's also a large Celtic cross, placed here in 1896 as a navigational aid for seafarers.

Vault Beach   BEACH
For acres of sand near Mevagissey, Vault is the choice, but it's not everyone's cup of tea. The walk down from the nearby NT car park is long and steep; the sand is grey and rather pebbly; and flies can be a problem here thanks to the copious seaweed deposited by the incoming tide. In its favour, the beach is huge and feels fantastically secluded, and the far end is reserved for people who prefer to sunbathe *au naturel*.

ⓘ Getting There & Away

St Austell (20 minutes, hourly Monday to Saturday, six on Sunday) Bus 24 runs past Heligan Gardens.

Fowey

📞 01726 / POP 2275

In many ways, Fowey feels like Padstow's south-coast sister; a workaday port turned well-heeled holiday town, with a tumble of pastel-coloured houses, portside pubs and tiered terraces overlooking the wooded banks of the Fowey River. The town's wealth was founded on the export of china clay from the St Austell pits, but it's been an important port since Elizabethan times, and later became the adopted home of the thriller writer Daphne du Maurier, who used the nearby house at Menabilly Barton as the inspiration for *Rebecca*.

Today it's an attractive and increasingly upmarket town, handy for exploring Cornwall's southeastern corner.

A few miles north along the creek, the riverside hamlet of Golant is also well worth a detour, with a waterfront pub for lunch and excellent kayaking opportunities.

⊙ Sights

Polkerris Beach   BEACH
(www.polkerrisbeach.com) A couple of miles west of Fowey, this is the area's largest and busiest beach. Sailing lessons, windsurfing and stand-up paddleboarding are all available.

Readymoney Cove   BEACH
From the town centre, the Esplanade leads down to this little cove and the remains of the small Tudor fort of St Catherine's Castle (Readymoney Cove; free).

Fowey

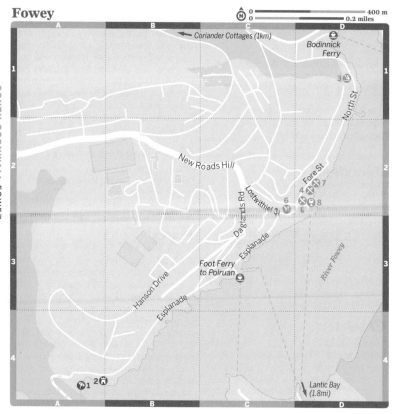

Lansallos BEACH
There are several little-known beaches strung along the coastline between Polruan and Looe, but they can be tricky to find without a decent map. Lansallos is a small patch of sand and shingle reached by a half-mile trail from Lansallos village; a second, even more remote beach called Palace Cove can be reached along the coast path.

Lantic Bay BEACH
The twin beaches of Great and Little Lantic sit side by side on the coastline between Polruan and Looe. They're remote, but worth the effort to reach, with soft sand, good wild swimming and usually not too many people. Access is via a steep trail from the coast path.

🏃 Activities

★ **Encounter Cornwall** KAYAKING
(☑ 07976 466123; www.encountercornwall. com; Golant; adult/child £28/15) Three-hour guided kayaking trips from Golant, just north of Fowey, with a choice of exploring creek or coastline. It also offers two-hour 'sundowner' expeditions and stand-up paddleboarding trips.

Fowey River Expeditions   KAYAKING
(☑ 01726-833627; www.foweyexpeditions.co.uk;
47 Fore St; adult/child £30/15) Guided trips in
single- and double-seater open-top canoes,
which are ideal for beginners. Standard trips
last about three hours and leave from Fowey.

★ Festivals & Events

Fowey Festival   LITERATURE
(www.foweyfestival.com; ⊘ early May) A week-
long celebration of art and literature brings
big-name speakers from the cultural world
to the town. It's run by the du Maurier Festival Society, so there's usually a few events
exploring the author's work.

✖ Eating

Lifebuoy Cafe   CAFE £
(☑ 07715 075869; www.thelifebuoycafe.co.uk; 8
Lostwithiel St; mains £5-10; ⊘ 8am-5pm) Everyone's favourite brekkie stop in Fowey, this
friendly cafe is a riot of character, from the
brightly coloured furniture and polka-dot
bunting to the vintage Action Men on the
shelves. Wolf down a Fat Buoy brekkie or a
classic fish-finger butty, washed down with a
mug of good old English tea.

Dwelling House   CAFE £
(☑ 01726-833662; 6 Fore St; tea £3-6; ⊘ 10am-
6.30pm May-Sep, to 5.30pm Wed-Sun Oct-Apr) Top
spot for tea (20-plus varieties) and dainty
cakes (decorated with sprinkles and icing
swirls, and served on a proper cake stand).

Lazy Jack's Kitchen   ICE CREAM £
(☑ 01726-832689; 4a Webb St; ice-creams £2-3;
⊘ 10am-5pm) The owners of the Lifebuoy
Cafe have branched out with a coffee bar
and ice-cream shop, selling delicious Moo-
maid of Zennor ice-cream.

Sam's   BISTRO ££
(☑ 01726-832273; www.samscornwall.co.uk/fowey;
20 Fore St; mains £12-17; ⊘ noon-9pm) Sam's has
been a stalwart in Fowey for years. Booth
seats, day-glo menus and a lively local vibe
keep the feel laid-back, and the menu of
burgers, fish, salads and steaks proves perennially popular. No bookings.

Sam's on the Beach   DINER ££
(☑ 01726-812255; www.samscornwall.co.uk/on-the-
beach/on-the-beach-about; Polkerris; mains £12-16;
⊘ 9am-11pm) Lodged in the old lifeboat house
on Polkerris, this beachside outpost of the
all-conquering Sam's empire is handy for
post-swim snacks. Pizza is a speciality thanks
to the homemade wood-fired oven, but there

are big bowls of mussels, plates of prawns
and seafood platters too. Sliding windows
open up on sunny days to let the outside in.

☕ Drinking & Nightlife

King of Prussia   PUB
(☑ 01726-833694; www.kingofprussia.co.uk; Town
Quay; ⊘ 11am-11pm) Fowey has lots of pubs,
but you might as well go for the one with
the best harbour view, named after notorious 'free trader' (otherwise known as smuggler) John Carter. Head up the steps into the
candy-pink building, and aim to get one of
the river-view tables.

ℹ Information

Fowey Tourist Information Centre (☑ 01726-
833616; www.fowey.co.uk; 5 South St;
⊘ 9.30am-5pm Mon-Sat, 10am-4pm Sun)
Lots of information on Fowey and southeast
Cornwall.

ℹ Getting There & Away

Bus services are limited: the only really useful
service is bus 24 (hourly Monday to Saturday, six
on Sunday), which runs to St Austell, Heligan and
Mevagissey. It also stops at Par train station,
where you can catch trains on the main London–
Penzance line.

There are two ferry services from Fowey: the
Bodinnick Ferry (www.ctomsandson.co.uk/
bodinnick-ferry; car & 2 passengers/pedes-
trian/bicycle £4.60/1.80/free; ⊘ last ferry
8.45pm Apr-Oct, 7pm Nov-Mar) which carries
cars over the river to Bodinnick en route to
Polruan, and the pedestrian-only **Polruan Ferry**
(www.ctomsandson.co.uk/polruan-ferry; adult/
child/bicycle/dog £2.80/0.80/1/0.40; ⊘ last
ferry 11pm May-Sep, 7pm Oct-Apr).

Polperro
☑ 01503

Even in a county where picturesque fishing
harbours seem to fill every cove, it's hard not
to fall for Polperro – a warren of cottages,
boat stores and alleyways, all set around a
stout granite harbour. Unsurprisingly, this
was once a smugglers' hideout, and it's still
a place with a salty, sea-dog atmosphere,
despite the inevitable summer crowds. The
coast path between Polperro and Looe is
particularly scenic.

Apart from the village's old fashioned
Heritage Museum (☑ 01503-272423; The Warren; adult/child £2/0.50; ⊘ 10am-4.30pm or 5pm
Mar-Oct), there are no sights as such – but it's
a charming spot.

The main car park is 750m uphill from the village, from where it's a 15-minute stroll down to the quayside.

Looe

🗷 01503 / POP 5280

Nestled in the crook of a steep-sided valley, the twin towns of East and West Looe stand on either side of a broad river estuary, connected by a multi-arched Victorian bridge built in 1853. There's been a settlement here since the days of the Domesday Book, and the town thrived as a medieval port before reinventing itself as a holiday resort for well-to-do Victorians – famously, the town installed one of the county's first 'bathing machines' beside Banjo Pier (named for its circular shape) in around 1800, and it's been a popular beach retreat ever since.

In contrast to Fowey, Looe still feels a little behind-the-times – chip shops, souvenir sellers and chintzy B&Bs still very much rule the roost here – but if it's a classic bucket-and-spade seaside town you're looking for, you've definitely found it in Looe.

◉ Sights

Looe Island   ISLAND
(www.cornwallwildlifetrust.org.uk/looeisland; ☺ guided walks £25) A mile offshore from Hannafore Point is the densely wooded Looe Island (officially known as St George's Island), a 9-hectare nature reserve and a haven for marine wildlife. You can explore on foot, or book a guided walk with the island ranger, who can help spot local wildlife including grey seals, cormorants, shags and oyster-catchers.

Between April and September, trips are offered by the **Moonraker** (🗷 07814-264514; Buller Quay; return adult/child £7/5, plus landing fee £4/1) from Buller Quay, but they're dependent on the weather and tides.

Talland Bay   BEACH
Along the coast path between Looe and Polperro is this small sheltered beach, which makes a great spot for swimming at both low and high tide, with inlets and tidal pools to explore. The beach is a bit pebbly above the strand-line, but there's sand and rock-pools to explore at low tide. It's not very big, though, and parking is limited.

Porfell Wildlife Park   ZOO
(🗷 01503-220211; www.porfell.co.uk; Lanreath; adult/child £9.50/6.50; ☺10am-5pm Apr-Sep,

11am-4pm Feb & Oct, closed Nov-Mar; ⭐) A lively animal park a couple of miles outside Looe, with wild denizens including macaws, parakeets, owls, lemurs, meerkats and zebras, as well as a venerable capybara called Bert.

Wild Futures
Monkey Sanctuary   WILDLIFE RESERVE
(🗷 01503-262532; www.monkeysanctuary.org; St Martins; adult/child/family £9/6/27; ☺11am-4.30pm Sat-Thu) Half a mile east of Looe, this wildlife centre is guaranteed to raise some 'aaahhhhs' over its woolly and capuchin monkeys, many of which were rescued from captivity. They're all contained in wire-mesh cages, so it's not quite an 'in-the-wild' experience, but it's still bound to please the kids – and the charity is involved in some important conservation work and breeding programs.

🏃 Activities

Boat Trips   BOATING
(Buller Quay) Various boats set out from Buller Quay for destinations along the coast – just head along to the quay and check out the chalkboards, where the next sailings will be chalked up. In summer, there are frequent sailings to Fowey and Polperro. Fishing trips also run regularly – mackerel, conger and various reef species are all regularly caught here.

🍴 Eating

Sarah's Pasty Shop   BAKERY £
(🗷 01503-263973; www.sarahspastyshop.com; 6 Buller St; pasties £3-5; ☺9am-4pm Mon-Sat, 10am-4pm Sun) Much-loved Looe pasty shop, now run by Sarah's daughter Lucy, with some non-standard variations including lamb, mint and leek, chickpea and lentil, and a 'breakfast fry-up' (with sausage, beans, egg, bacon and tomato). As usual, the traditional pasties are the best – but it's worth turning up on 'Fishy Friday' for the rather good mackerel, horseradish and pea pasty.

Talland Bay Beach Cafe   CAFE £
(🗷 01503-272088; www.tallandbaybeachcafe.co.uk; Talland; mains £4-8; ☺9am-5pm Mar-Oct) This fun seaside cafe has little dining booths made out of beach huts, where you can settle down for a crab ciabatta, a brie-and-cranberry panini, an indulgent cake or an ice-cream courtesy of Roskilly's. There are also plenty of picnic tables outside, and a beach shop and kayak hire.

PJ PHOTOGRAPHY / SHUTTERSTOCK ©

Talland Bay

ℹ️ Information

Looe Tourist Office (☎ 01503-262072; www.looeguide.co.uk; Guildhall, Fore St; ☑ 10am-5pm Easter-Oct) Looe's efficient and well-staffed visitor centre is the hub for all tourist things: accommodation, activities, restaurant recommendations and so on.

ℹ️ Getting There & Away

BUS

All buses to Looe cross over the main bridge between East and West Looe.

Plymouth (one hour, hourly, six to eight on Sunday) Plymouth Citybus 72 via St Germans.

Polperro (20 minutes, hourly, six on Sunday) Plymouth Citybus 73; runs to Liskeard in the opposite direction.

TRAIN

The branch line from Liskeard to Looe is almost a day out in itself, tracking through wooded valleys all the way out to the seaside. The Looe Valley Line Day Ranger ticket (adult/child £4.30/2.15) allows one day's unlimited travel; the journey from Liskeard to Looe takes about 40 minutes.

Rame Peninsula

Often called 'Cornwall's forgotten corner', the Rame Peninsula remains one of the county's most unspoilt pockets, and it's a fine place to head when you want to give the crowds the slip. This area was once parcelled up between some of Cornwall's old aristocratic families, and several grand country estates are open to the public. The coastline is worth exploring too, particularly the huge beach at Whitesand Bay.

◎ Sights

⭐ **Whitesand Bay**   BEACH

Small coves dot the coastline of the Rame Peninsula, but for a proper stretch of sand, this huge – and under-visited – bay is the place. Pronounced *whitsand* (and not to be confused with its namesake near Sennen), it's a vast 3-mile expanse that's actually made up of four distinct beaches, backed by dunes, and accessed via cliff paths and steps. It's mostly covered at high tide, but the reliable swells make it popular with surfers whatever the weather.

OFF THE BEATEN TRACK

RAME HEAD

A great bulk of rock topped by a picturesque clifftop chapel, Rame Head is another of Cornwall's most majestic coastal viewpoints, with a jaw-dropping 360-degree panorama stretching east towards Plymouth Sound and the South Hams, and west to Dodman Point, the Roseland and even the Lizard on a really clear day. It was occupied by an Iron Age hill fort and an early Christian oratory, but the present chapel was built in the late 14th century, dedicated to St Michael.

Generations of sailors and seafarers have used this rocky headland and its chapel as a waymarker; it's traditionally one of the last sights of England as they chart a course south, and the first sight when they return. It even features in an old sea shanty, 'Spanish Ladies': 'Now the first land we made it is called the Deadman, Next Ram Head off Plymouth, off Portland the Wight...'.

It's a little out of the way compared to Cornwall's main sights of interest, so it's a good bet if you want to escape the summer crowds – and it's an easy day trip from Plymouth.

Offshore, a naval frigate called HMS *Scylla* was sunk here in 2004 to create an artificial reef for divers.

Cawsand & Kingsand VILLAGE

While many of the coastal villages have become gentrified to the point of unrecognisability, these twin villages still genuinely feel like the fishing ports they were of old. A string of stout-walled granite cottages run along the seafront, overlooked by a Victorian clock tower, and fronting a few small beaches that are great for a paddle. In bygone days, both villages were a notorious haven for smugglers, and secret tunnels are still said to run beneath the towns' streets.

The seafront also doubled as Margate in Mike Leigh's film *Mr Turner*, a testament to their traditional and unspoilt architecture. Fittingly, there's also a large and active artistic community here, and you might well run into someone painting *en plein air* down by the beach.

In summer, a ferry runs from Cawsand Beach to the Mayflower Steps in Plymouth. You can also walk to the village through the grounds of Mount Edgcumbe estate (p178).

Mount Edgcumbe HISTORIC BUILDING

(☑ 01752-822236; www.mountedgcumbe.gov.uk; Cremyll; adult/child £7.20/3.75; ⏰ 11am-4.30pm Sun-Thu Mar-Sep) Encompassing 350 hectares, this Grade I-listed estate was built for the Earls of Edgcumbe, but is now owned by Cornwall and Plymouth City Councils. It's one of the earliest of Cornwall's estates, liberally sprinkled with follies, chapels, grottoes, pavilions and formal gardens. The house was built between 1547 and 1553, but was practically destroyed by German bombing in 1941. It's since been restored in lavish 18th-century style. The gardens are particularly lovely.

Antony House HISTORIC BUILDING

(NT; ☑ 01752-812191; www.nationaltrust.org.uk/antony; Torpoint; adult/child £9.60/4.80, grounds only £5.30/2.65; ⏰ house 12.30-4.30pm, garden noon-5pm Tue-Thu, Sat & Sun) Owned by the National Trust and occupied by the Carew-Pole family, this house's main claim to fame is its decorative gardens, designed by the 18th-century landscape architect Humphry Repton and filled with outlandish topiary, some of which featured in Tim Burton's *Alice in Wonderland*. It's 9 miles east of Looe or 6 miles west of Plymouth.

Port Eliot HISTORIC BUILDING

(☑ 01503-230211; www.porteliot.co.uk; St Germans; house & grounds adult/child £8/4, grounds only £5/2; ⏰ 2-5pm Sun-Fri mid-Mar–Jun) This glorious country estate is the family seat of the Earl of St Germans. The Grade I-listed house is open for three months of the year; guided tours of the kitchen, basements, library, wine cellars and the famous Round Room (with an original mural by the Plymouth painter Robert Lenkiewicz) are included in the admission price. The estate also has lots and lots of fabulous walks.

The house is still occupied by the St Germans family; the present earl (Albert Clarence) is the 11th to have inherited the title, following the death of his father Perry in 2016.

The annual Port Eliot Festival (p257) of music and literature is held here in July, and the house is sometimes open for special events – so check the website for details.

Eating

★ The View MODERN BRITISH ££

(☑ 01752-822345; www.theview-restaurant. co.uk; Treninnow Cliff Rd, Torpoint; dinner mains £16.50-22.50; ⏰ lunch noon-2pm Wed-Sun, dinner 7-8.45pm Wed-Sun) The name says it all. This restaurant sits in a stunning position on the cliffs above Whitsand Bay, offering an amazing panorama of Rame Head and the Eddystone lighthouse. Chef Matt Corner was classically trained, but prefers a simpler, un-fussier style these days – classic flavours, artful presentation and premium local ingredients.

Halfway House Inn   PUB FOOD **££**
(☑ 01752-822279; www.halfwayinnkingsand.co.uk; Fore St, Kingsand; mains £12.50-16.50; ⊙ 11am-11pm) A posh corner pub near the front in Kingsand, serving Sharp's ales and an upscale menu (pan-seared scallops with pancetta, trio of pork with cider jus). Don't expect too much low-beamed atmosphere – it's light, bright and modern inside, a theme which runs into the small-but-smart upstairs rooms (doubles £80 to £100).

The Old Bakery   BAKERY **£**
(☑ 01752-656215; www.theoldbakery-cawsand. co.uk; Garrett St, Cawsand; mains £5.50-8.50; ⊙ 9am-5pm) An artisan bakery that's renowned in the village for its sourdough (if you want to learn the secrets, you can sign up for a breadmaking course). They also serve delicious lunches – our tip is the rarebit, liberally spiced with Worcester sauce – and they do pizza nights once a week. There are two cosy B&B rooms upstairs.

🚗 Getting There & Away

Two historic ferry services chug between Plymouth and the Rame Peninsula.

Torpoint Ferry (www.tamarcrossings.org.uk; 2 Ferry St, Torpoint; car/motorbike/pedestrians & cyclists £1.50/0.30/free; ⊙ 24hr) Carries cars, bikes and passengers; it runs 24 hours a day, with a half-hourly service from 9.30pm to 6.30am.

Cremyll Ferry (www.plymouthboattrips.co.uk/ ferries/cremyll-ferry; adult/child £1.50/0.75, bicycles £0.75) Pedestrian ferry from Admirals Hard quay in Plymouth to Cremyll Quay on the Mount Edgcumbe estate.

Tamar Valley

Cutting a swathe through a gentle landscape of fields and woods, the mighty Tamar has marked the age-old dividing line between Devon and Cornwall for over a thousand years; it was officially declared as Cornwall's

eastern edge in 936 by King Athelstan, the first unified English king.

Though it's spanned by around 20 bridges – including Brunel's Royal Albert rail bridge (built in 1859) and the more recent Tamar Bridge for cars (1961) – the Tamar is still an important psychological boundary for the Cornish, as demonstrated by the recent proposals to create a new cross-county 'Devonwall' constituency, which predictably met with howls of protest.

For most people, their only view of the Tamar is from the bridges as they travel in or out of the county, but the river is a deliciously peaceful area to explore if you have the time.

🏃 Activities

⭐ **Tamar Trails**   CYCLING
(☑ 01822-833409; www.tamartrails.co.uk; Gulworthy; ⊙ dawn-dusk) This new project has opened up 25km of hiking and biking trails which were previously off-limits to the public. The trails start at the visitor centre just off the A390 between Gunnislake and Tavistock, and wind their way along the banks of the river, passing through riverside copses and several disused mine workings. They're ideal for mountain bikes, on foot or even by segway. There are also other activities including archery and 'tree surfing' at the main visitor centre.

Canoe Tamar   CANOEING
(☑ 01822-833409; www.tamartrails.co.uk/canoe-tamar; adult/child £30/24) It'd be a shame to come to the Tamar and not see the river scenery close-up. Canoe Tamar leads daily expeditions up to the river's tidal limits in beautiful wooden Canadian canoes. The departure point is Cotehele Quay.

ℹ️ Information

Tamar Valley Information Centre (☑ 01822-835030; www.tamarvalley.org.uk; Cemetery Rd, Drakewalls, Gunnislake; ⊙ 10.30am-3.30pm Mon-Fri) Offers general info on the Tamar area in Drakewalls, near Gunnislake.

ℹ️ Transport

Buses from Tavistock stop near the entrance to the visitor centre.

The Torpoint Ferry crosses over the Tamar from Torpoint to Plymouth.

Newquay & North Cornwall

Best Places to Eat

➡ Restaurant Nathan Outlaw (p189)

➡ Paul Ainsworth at No 6 (p192)

➡ Appleton's at the Vineyard (p192)

➡ Mariners (p193)

➡ Fresh from the Sea (p189)

Best Beaches

➡ Watergate Bay (p196)

➡ Crackington Haven (p186)

➡ Constantine (p189)

➡ Porthcothan (p190)

➡ Holywell Bay (p197)

➡ Perranporth (p200)

Why Go?

If it's the classic Cornish combination of lofty cliffs, sweeping bays and white-horse surf you're after, then Cornwall's north coast fits the bill. Battered by Atlantic breakers and whipped by sea winds, the shoreline between St Ives in the south and Bude to the north is arguably the county's most dramatic stretch of coast. Unsurprisingly, this was poet John Betjeman's favourite part of Cornwall, but it's far from a well-kept secret; you'll be sharing the scenery with everyone from weekend surfers to coasteerers and celebrity chefs.

The heart of the action is Newquay, North Cornwall's long-standing party town and the capital of the county's surf scene. The beaches here are spectacular. If you prefer your sands quieter, head west towards the coastal villages of St Agnes and Perranporth, or east towards Padstow and its booming culinary culture. Even quieter are the out-of-the-way beaches east of the Camel Estuary towards Tintagel and Boscastle.

When to Go

➡ **May** Join the throngs for Padstow's raucous 'oss-themed May Day celebrations, but remember to book your accommodation early – or better still, stay out of town.

➡ **Aug** Watch the pros in action at the Boardmasters surf and music festival, the largest event of its kind in the UK. The action centres around Fistral Beach.

➡ **Late Sep** This is a great time of year to enjoy the north coast's beaches in relative peace and quiet – with a bit of luck, you might even get some early-autumn sun.

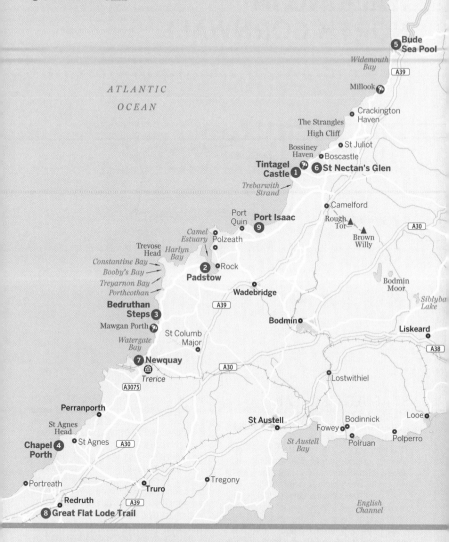

Newquay & North Cornwall Highlights

1 **Tintagel Castle** (p188) Pondering the legend of King Arthur at this clifftop ruin.

2 **Padstow** (p189) Chowing down in Cornwall's culinary capital.

3 **Bedruthan Steps** (p199) Walking along the beach underneath these impressive rock stacks.

4 **Chapel Porth** (p201) Wandering along the cliffs to one of Cornwall's most photographed engine houses.

5 **Bude Sea Pool** (p186) Enjoying a dip in a saltwater pool at Summerleaze beach.

6 **St Nectan's Glen** (p187) Seeking out a secret valley waterfall for a bracing shower.

7 **Surfing** (p196) Catching a wave on one of the many beaches around Newquay.

8 **Great Flat Lode Trail** (p203) Cycling past engine houses and mine stacks along this great mineral seam.

9 **Port Isaac** (p188) Dining at Nathan Outlaw's stellar seafooderie.

WALKING IN NORTH CORNWALL

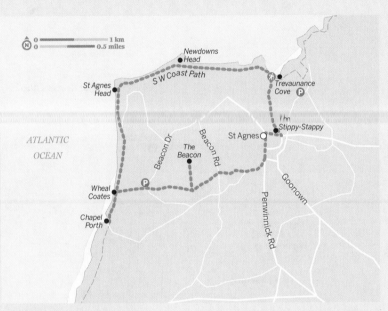

ST AGNES CIRCULAR

START/END TREVAUNANCE COVE
DURATION/DISTANCE 3-4 HOURS, 5 MILES
DIFFICULTY MODERATE

This walk takes in the beautiful, windblown scenery around the old mining village of St Agnes, with panoramic coastal views and a trip to the area's highest point, the Beacon.

Start at **Trevaunance Cove** (p201), where you can park in the car park opposite the Driftwood Spars pub. From here follow the coast path as it climbs steeply around the clifftops to **Newdowns Head**. Offshore there are two rocks known locally as the Bawden Rocks, or the Cow and Calf, which according to local legend were hurled there by the local giant, Bolster. From here, the coast path tracks round to **St Agnes Head**, travelling through thick heather and gorse.

The trail then swings south, opening out onto the exposed cliffs around **Tubby's Head** before dropping down to the picturesque mine workings and chimney stacks at **Wheal Coates**, one of the most photographed old

mines in Cornwall. From here it's a steep walk downhill to the cove of **Chapel Porth** (p201), where you can fuel up with a hot tea and hedgehog ice cream from the shack cafe.

From here, backtrack to the Wheal Coates mine ruins, and this time turn inland along the uphill path, which leads to a **car park** beside Beacon Dr. Turn left, then immediately right through Beacon Cottage Touring Park, where you'll see signs to the **Beacon** (p201). The path climbs sharply up the heathery hilltop, giving truly majestic views of St Agnes and the surrounding coastline, and inland towards Carn Brea.

From the top, there are several trails leading back towards Goonvrea Rd, from where it's an easy downhill stroll back into the centre of **St Agnes** (p201) village. Follow the road down through town past the St Agnes Hotel, and take the footpath down past the terraced houses known as the Stippy Stappy, which leads back down to **Trevaunance Cove.** Reward yourself with a well-earned pint of homebrewed ale and a ploughman's lunch at the **Driftwood Spars** (p202).

Mine stacks, sea cliffs and huge views await on this stunning coastal hike.

IANWOOL / GETTY IMAGES ©

Trevaunance Cove (p201)

ROAD TRIP >
NORTH COAST CRUISER

* *

Wind down your windows and let the sea breeze roll in for this classic coastal adventure.

❶ Bude

For a top-down, wind-in-your-hair, non-stop-scenery kind of road trip, the north Cornish coast is hard to beat. You could spend weeks exploring and still not see all that's on offer, but this whistle-stop tour is a good way to pack in the sights. Begin in **Bude** (p186), a busy beach town tucked into the far northeast of the region. It's surrounded by beaches, but to reach the best patches of sand you'll need to head out of town. Cruise

south along the main A39 till you reach the village of Wainhouse Corner and the turn-off signed to **Crackington Haven** (p186). The narrow road dips down towards the rocky beach, from where you can follow the coast path to High Cliff, the highest in Cornwall.

❷ Strangles

From here it's a short spin south to the **Strangles** (p186), a rather macabre name for a rather beautiful beach. This is an ideal spot to stretch your legs: the coast path

Start Bude

End Newquay

Length 65 to 70 miles, two days

• •

around here is fabulous, with unbroken coastal views extending in all directions.

❸ Boscastle

Follow the road as it loops back to the B3263, which runs past the church of St Juliot, known for its Thomas Hardy connections (he met his wife-to-be, the rector's daughter, here). From here, the road drops into the pretty harbour of **Boscastle** (p187); don't miss a walk along the harbour, a visit to the weird and wonderful Witchcraft Museum, and a superb cream tea and an ice cream at the Boscastle Farm Shop. From Boscastle, the coast road runs west through Trethevy, where trails lead to the pool of **St Nectan's Glen** (p187) and the remote beach of **Bossiney Haven** (p188), well worth a stop if you like your beaches wild and quiet.

❹ Tintagel

Next comes **Tintagel** (p188) and its crumbling clifftop castle. It's worth devoting at least a couple of hours to exploring: a dizzying staircase leads up the cliff-side to the oldest part of the castle, and you'll be treated to majestic views on the way up and down. Down underneath the castle is Merlin's Cave, a spooky underground passage where the wizard is said to have dabbled with magic.

❺ Port Isaac

Continue onto the B3314, which runs through the old slate-mining village of Delabole and passes the turning to **Port Isaac** (p188), a seaside village that doubles as the village of Portwenn in the TV series *Doc Martin*. Port Isaac has also become renowned for its food since chef Nathan Outlaw set up his main venture in town – a visit to his stellar double-Michelin-starred restaurant is an absolute must. The village also has some pleasant hotels and B&Bs, making it good for an overnight stop.

❻ Polzeath

On day two, continue west until you reach the turn-off to the surfy village of **Polzeath** (p193), where you can stop for brunch, or pass on

through to the lovely beach of **Daymer Bay**, a favourite of the poet John Betjeman.

❼ Wadebridge

South of Daymer, the road loops through **Rock** (p193), the second-home capital of Cornwall, then heads to **Wadebridge** (p193). This is an attractive little town with some great cafes; it's also the best place to start a bike ride along the famous Camel Trail; bikes are cheaper, and the trail is quieter, if you start from the Wadebridge end.

❽ Padstow

If you're not up for a bike ride, continue till you reach a roundabout signed to **Padstow** (p189), and turn off onto the B3274. Padstow is another of Cornwall's foodie hot spots, and there are some superb restaurants to try – but for now, head onwards to explore Padstow's 'Seven Bays'. Of these, **Trevone** and **Harlyn** are nearest to town, and have the most facilities. As you continue west, it's worth making a detour out to **Trevose Head** (p190), where there's a historic lighthouse and a wraparound view of the bay.

❾ Constantine

West of Trevose are four other bays: tiny **Booby's Bay** and **Constantine** (p189) are essentially one beach at low tide, and nearby **Treyarnon** (p191) is a surfers' favourite. Last comes **Porthcothan** (p190), perhaps the loveliest of all, and generally fairly quiet, even in summer.

❿ Bedruthan Steps

South of Porthcothan, the B3276 unfurls past another of the north coast's classic photo stops: the rock towers at **Bedruthan Steps** (p199), formed by erosion over the course of tens of thousands of years. It's an epic spot for a selfie.

⓫ Newquay

From here, you'll pass more beaches, including **Mawgan Porth** (p197) and **Watergate Bay** (p196), before reaching journey's end in Newquay.

THE ATLANTIC HIGHWAY

This grandly named stretch of road (known more prosaically as the A39) stretches all the way from the Devon border into Cornwall's northeastern corner. It's an area that feels a little cut off from the rest of Cornwall, but it gives access to some of the county's prettiest fishing villages – there's a good reason that the hit TV series *Doc Martin* was filmed here. Elsewhere, there's a string of impressive beaches to explore around Bude, and a stunning clifftop castle at Tintagel that's rife with Arthurian connections.

Bude

📞 01288 / POP 9240

A scant few miles across the Devon border, Bude is a breezy seaside town with a bevy of impressive beaches, as well as a lovely seawater lido built in the 1930s. The town itself isn't much to look at, but the stunning coastline on its doorstep makes it worthy of a stop.

◉ Sights

★ **Bude Sea Pool** SWIMMING
(www.budeseapool.org; ⊙24hrs) **FREE** Built in the 1930s, this handsome seawater pool sits behind Summerleaze beach to provide a safe place for sea swimming, without the danger of tides or waves. It's perfect for kids and reticent swimmers, and has the added benefit of warming up fast on a sunny day.

Summerleaze BEACH
Bude's main family beach is a classic bucket-and-spade affair, with its proximity to town ensuring it's awash with windbreaks in summer. it's also home to the beautiful Bude Sea Pool.

Crackington Haven BEACH
Probably the most dramatic of Bude's beaches, it has rock shelves and pebbly sand bordered by black cliffs, speckled by a blaze of wildflowers in spring. Once considered for industrial exploitation, the beach is a bit off the main tourist radar, making it a simpler, wilder alternative to the sandy family beaches nearer town. There are lifeguards in season, and there's a small beach cafe and shop. It's 11 miles southwest of Bude.

Widemouth Bay BEACH
If you're travelling with kids, the best idea for a sunny day is to head to Widemouth (pronounced *wid*-muth). It has acres of sand at low tide, plenty of facilities, good safe swimming and lifeguarding throughout the summer. Though it looks like one long continuous stretch at low tide, it's officially two beaches (North and South) divided by the spiny spur of Black Rock. It's about 3 miles south of town.

Strangles BEACH
Precious few people make the effort to seek out this remote cove, and to be fair, it's a bit rocky and pebble-strewn, not to mention quite a trek down from the coast path – and the trail in some places is crumbly and slippery underfoot. But if you're looking to leave the crowds behind, the Strangles is a perfect spot to do it.

🏄 Activities

Bude Canal CYCLING
A 19th-century canal is probably not what you'd expect to find in Bude. Disused for more than a century, it has been restored along the first 2 miles from the sea-lock to Helebridge, and it's lovely for a walk or bike ride. The 2-mile gravel towpath is also suitable for wheelchairs and buggies. Boats can be hired from **Bude Boat Hire** (📞07968 688782; www.budeboathire.co.uk; rowboats/canoes & pedalos per hr £10/15; ⊙10am-dusk Apr-Sep).

Bude Cycle Centre CYCLING
(📞01288-353748; www.budebikes.co.uk; Petherick Mill; adult/child per day £14/10; ⊙9am-5pm) Hire a bike from this friendly company and pick a route: seven have been designed from scratch, all downloadable for free from the website. The most popular ones follow the Bude Canal, but longer routes explore local villages and the Tamar Lakes.

Big Blue Surf School SURFING
(📞01288-331764; www.bigbluesurfschool.co.uk; per lesson £30) A recommended school that offers lessons mainly to beginner and intermediate surfers. Special lessons for surfers with disabilities, and a 'women's club' on Tuesday evenings and Saturday mornings are some of its main attractions. Look for the trailer in the Summerleaze beach car park.

🍴 Eating

Life's a Beach CAFE **££**
(📞01288-355222; www.lifesabeach.info; Summerleaze; mains lunch £8-12, dinner £16.50-22.50; ⊙10.30am-3pm & 7-10pm Mon-Sat, 10.30am-3pm Sun) This beachside bistro overlooking Sum-

merleaze has a split personality: by day it's a beach cafe serving coffee, panini and ice cream; by night it's a smart seafood restaurant. It's the most popular place to eat in town, so book ahead.

Scrummies   CAFE £
(☎ 07902 140691; Lansdown Rd; mains £6-8; ☺ 9am-5pm) The best place for fish and chips in town – most of the daily catch is caught by the owner's boat, *Dreamcatcher*. If you're lucky, you might be able to tuck into some wild sea bass or half a lobster, sold for bargain-basement prices. Well worth a meal.

ℹ Information

Bude Tourist Office (☎ 01288-354240; www. visitbude.info; The Crescent; ☺ 10am-5pm Mon-Sat, plus 10am-4pm Sun summer) Beside the main car park near Bude Castle.

ℹ Getting There & Away

First Kernow bus 95 (£3.20 to £5.20, six daily Monday to Saturday, four on Sunday) leaves Bude and travels southwest via Boscastle (30 minutes), Tintagel (40 minutes), Camelford (1 hour) and Wadebridge (1½ hours).

From Camelford, you can catch the 96 bus (four daily Monday to Saturday) for onward travel to Port Isaac, Polzeath and Rock. Note that on Sunday, the 95 service stops at all the places normally served by the 96.

Boscastle

☎ 01840 / POP 640

Nestled in the crook of a steep coombe (valley) at the confluence of three rivers, Boscastle's seafaring heritage stretches back to Elizabethan times. With its quaint cottages, flower-clad cliffs, tinkling streams and a sturdy quay, it's almost impossibly photogenic.

But the peaceful setting belies some turbulent history: in 2004 Boscastle was hit by one of Britain's largest-ever flash floods, which carried away cars, bridges and buildings. Happily, the village has since been rebuilt, but look closely even now and you'll be able to spot reminders of the floods dotted around the village.

◉ Sights

Museum of Witchcraft & Magic   MUSEUM
(☎ 01840-250111; www.museumofwitchcraftand magic.co.uk; The Harbour; adult/child £5/4; ☺ 10.30am-6pm Mon-Sat, 11.30am-6pm Sun Mar-Nov) This oddball museum has been a

OFF THE BEATEN TRACK

ST NECTAN'S GLEN

Hidden away in a secret valley, this little glen (www.st-nectansglen.co.uk; near Trethevy; adult/child £5.95/4.70; ☺ 9.30am-5pm Apr-Oct, 10.30am-3pm Nov-Mar) feels like something from a fairy tale. Fringed by climbing ivy and shrubs, a 60ft waterfall tumbles across the slate into a kieve (plunge pool). It's a mystical spot, supposedly frequented by Cornish piskies (pixies), and legendarily associated with King Arthur – you'll see ribbons and offerings dangling from the trees around the pool. It's also a bracing spot for a dip – though be warned, the water's icy cold year-round. A new walkway has opened up two smaller waterfalls nearby, and the walk through the woodland is bewitchingly pretty.

To find it, take the B3263 coast road from Tintagel towards Boscastle, and look out for the car park at Trethevy. From here, signs lead down to the glen.

fixture in Boscastle since 1960, and apparently houses the world's largest collection of witchy memorabilia, from haunted skulls to hags' bridles and voodoo dolls (known as poppets). It's half-tacky, half-spooky, and some of the more 'controversial' exhibits might perturb kids of a sensitive disposition (and some adults, for that matter).

✕ Eating

★ **Boscastle Farm Shop**   CAFE £
(☎ 01840-250827; www.boscastlefarmshop.co.uk; cakes & teas £3-5; ☺ 10am-5pm; 🅿) Half a mile from the harbour on the B3263, this excellent farm shop sells its own produce, including ruby-red beef and possibly the best sausages on the north coast. In the cafe, tall windows look out onto fields and the coast – the perfect setting for a superb cream tea.

ℹ Information

Boscastle Tourist Office (☎ 01840-250010; www.visitboscastleandtintagel.com; The Harbour; ☺ 10am-5pm Mar-Oct, 10.30am-4pm Nov-Feb) Not far from the quay, and with some useful leaflets on local history and walks.

ℹ Getting There & Away

Coastal bus 95 (£3.20 to £5.20, six daily Monday to Saturday, four on Sunday) stops in Boscastle

BOSSINEY HAVEN & TREBARWITH STRAND

A secluded and secret(ish) beach within easy reach of Tintagel, the tiny, tucked-away cove of **Bossiney Haven** is accessible via farmland and steep steps cut into the cliff. The beach is practically submerged at high tide, and a tough walk up and down, so it usually stays pretty quiet. It's a great place for a picnic and an out-of-the-way dip, but beware – the tide rolls in fast.

A little further south is **Trebarwith Strand**, a small beach at the end of a gently sloping valley road that's all but claimed by the sea at high tide. Access is across some rocks, so flip flops or surf shoes are a good idea. There's a big public car park, plus a surf shop and cafe.

on its way from Bude (30 minutes), then continues on to Tintagel (13 minutes), Camelford (30 minutes) and Wadebridge (1 hour).

From Camelford, you can catch the connecting bus 96 to Port Isaac.

Tintagel

📞 01840 / POP 1820

The spectre of legendary King Arthur looms large over Tintagel and its dramatic clifftop castle. Though the present-day ruins mostly date from the 13th century, archaeological digs have revealed the foundations of a much earlier fortress, fuelling speculation that Arthur may indeed have been born at the castle, as locals like to claim. It's a stunningly romantic sight, with its crumbling walls teetering precariously above the sheer cliffs, and well worth devoting at least half a day to exploring.

The village itself isn't terribly exciting, but if you're looking for cheesy King Arthur souvenirs, you'll find them in ample supply.

◎ Sights

★ **Tintagel Castle**   CASTLE
(EH; 📞 01840-770328; www.english-heritage.org.uk; adult/child £8.40/5; ⊙10am-6pm Apr-Sep, to 5pm Oct, to 4pm Nov-Mar) Famous as the supposed birthplace of King Arthur, Tintagel's epic clifftop castle has been occupied since Roman times and once served as a residence for Cornwall's Celtic kings. The present castle is largely the work of Richard, Earl of Cornwall, who built a castle here during the 1230s. Though the Arthurian links may be tenuous, it's certainly a fine spot for a fortress: clinging to black granite cliffs, surrounded by booming surf and wheeling gulls, it's the classic fairy-tale castle.

King Arthur notwithstanding, it's hard to think of a more soul-stirring spot for a stronghold. Though much of the castle has long since crumbled, it's still possible to make out the footprint of the Great Hall and several other rooms.

Part of the castle stands on a rock tower known as 'The Island', cut off from the mainland, and accessed via a wooden bridge and a dizzying set of cliff steps (vertigo sufferers beware). There's also a curious tunnel that's still puzzling archaeologists; it may have been used as a larder or cold store.

Trails lead along the headland to the atmospheric medieval chapel of **St Materiana**, and down on the beach below the castle the rocky mouth of **Merlin's Cave** is exposed at low tide – local legend claims it's where the wizard once wove his spells.

It's a steep walk down to the castle from the village car parks; in summer, Land Rover taxis shuttle up and down throughout the day.

Old Post Office   HISTORIC BUILDING
(NT; 📞 01840-770024; www.nationaltrust.org.uk; Fore St; adult/child £4/2; ⊙10.30am-5.30pm mid-Mar–Sep, 11am-4pm Oct) This is one of the best-preserved examples of a traditional 16th-century Cornish longhouse, topped by pepper-pot chimneys and a higgledy-piggledy roof, and riddled with tiny rooms. As its name suggests, it was used as a post office during the 19th century.

❶ Getting There & Away

First Kernow bus 95/96 (£3.20 to £5.20, six daily Monday to Saturday, four on Sunday) stops in Tintagel en route from Camelford (15 minutes) to Bude (50 minutes).

Port Isaac

📞 01208 / POP 720

If you're looking for a classic Cornish fishing town, you've found it in Port Isaac, where a cluster of cobbled alleyways, slender opes (lanes) and cob-walled cottages collect around a medieval harbour and slipway.

Though still a working harbour, Port Isaac is best known as a filming location: the hit TV series *Doc Martin* has used the village as a ready-made backdrop. A sign near the quayside directs visitors straight to Doc Martin's cottage. A short walk along the coast path leads to the neighbouring harbour of **Port Gaverne**, while a couple of miles west is **Port Quin**, now owned by the National Trust.

Cornwall's chef *du jour* Nathan Outlaw has recently made the village his culinary centre of operations.

✖ Eating

Outlaw's Fish Kitchen   SEAFOOD £
(☑01208-881183; www.outlaws.co.uk/fishkitchen; 1 Middle St; mains £6.50-12; ☉noon-3pm & 6-9pm Mon-Sat Jun-Sep, Tue-Sat Oct-May) Nathan Outlaw's newest venture is this tiny fish restaurant down beside the harbour. It specialises in small seafood plates, designed to share. The exact menu is dictated by whatever's brought in on the day by Port Isaac's fishers, and the restaurant is tiny – literally just a few tables – so bookings are essential.

Fresh from the Sea   SEAFOOD ££
(☑01208-880849; www.freshfromthesea.co.uk; 18 New Rd; sandwiches £5.50-9.50, mains £10.50-20; ☉9am-4pm Mon-Sat) Local man Callum Greenhalgh takes out his boat daily in search of crab and lobster, then brings back the catch to sell at his dinky Port Isaac shop. Seafood doesn't get any fresher – a crab salad with glass of wine costs £12.50, and a whole lobster is £20. Depending on the season, oysters from nearby Porthilly cost £1.50 each.

★**Restaurant**
Nathan Outlaw   SEAFOOD £££
(☑01208-862737; www.nathan-outlaw.com; 6 New Rd; tasting menu £125; ☉7-9pm Wed-Sat, plus noon-2pm Fri & Sat) Port Isaac's prestige has skyrocketed since Cornwall's top chef, Nathan Outlaw, moved his main operation here from Rock. This is the place to experience Outlaw's passion for Cornish fish and seafood. His style is surprisingly classic, relying on top-notch ingredients rather than cheffy tricks. As you'd expect of a twice-Michelin-starred restaurant, you'll pay top dollar, but it's very much a tell-your-friends experience.

Vegetarians are well catered for, and there's a good-value four-course menu available at lunchtime on Friday and Saturday (£62).

THE NORTH COAST

Padstow
☑ 01841 / POP 3160

If anywhere symbolises Cornwall's changing character, it's Padstow. This once-sleepy fishing port has been transformed into one of the county's most cosmopolitan corners thanks to celebrity chef Rick Stein, whose property portfolio encompasses several restaurants, shops and hotels, as well as a seafood school and fish-and-chip bar.

The 'Stein Effect' has certainly changed the place: Padstow feels more Kensington chic than Cornish quaint these days, with fancy restaurants and boutiques sitting alongside the old pubs and pasty shops. Whether the town's managed to hold onto its soul in the process is debatable, but it's still hard not to be charmed by the setting.

Across the Camel Estuary from Padstow is Rock (p193), a once-quiet village that's been reinvented as an uber-exclusive holiday destination. Nearby lies the long sweep of **Daymer Bay**, and between the two resorts is the treacherous sandbank known as the Doom Bar.

◉ Sights

★**Trevibban Mill**   VINEYARD
(☑01841-541413; www.trevibbanmill.com; Dark Lane, St Issey; ☉noon-5pm Wed-Thu & Sun, to 10pm Fri & Sat) This young vineyard has a fast-growing reputation in the wine world, and it's a fine place to sample vintages in a dreamy Cornish setting. In total there are some 11,000 vines and 1700 apple trees spread across the estate, producing a range of whites and rosés in both still and sparkling versions (there are even a couple of fruity reds on the roster). The ciders and juices are delicious, too.

Guided tours (£30) exploring the art of winemaking and the estate's organic ethos take place on Sundays and include a tasting. There's also a lovely restaurant, Appleton's at the Vineyard, and a wine-tasting bar.

★**Constantine Bay**   BEACH
Arcing along the west side of the headland from Trevose Head, Constantine is one of the most impressive sweeps of sand near Padstow. It's a long, west-facing, gently sloping shelf of sand, separated by a rocky point from another beach known as **Booby's Bay**.

Padstow

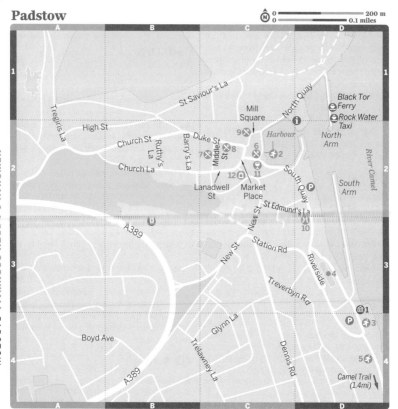

Padstow

◉ Sights
1 National Lobster Hatchery D3

◆ Activities, Courses & Tours
   Jubilee Queen ....(see 2)
2 Padstow Boat Trips C2
3 Padstow Cycle Hire.......................... D4
4 Padstow Seafood School D3
   Padstow Sealife Safaris...............(see 2)
5 Trail Bike Hire D4

⊗ Eating
6 Chough Bakery................................ C2
7 Paul Ainsworth at No 6...................... C2
8 Prawn on the Lawn........................... C2
9 Rojano's in the Square...................... C2
10 Seafood Restaurant........................ D3

● Drinking & Nightlife
11 BinTwo.. C2

◉ Shopping
12 Padstow Brewing Tasting Room........ C2

Porthcothan   BEACH
A long, narrow, northwest-facing beach backed by grass-covered dunes, tall cliffs and divided by a tidal stream. It's best visited at low tide, when there's a huge area of sand to wander, and several small coves to explore to the north and south. There's a little shop at the rear of the beach, and loos next to the car park.

Trevose Head   NATURAL FEATURE
Four miles west of Padstow town is the distinctive outcrop of Trevose Head, a notorious shipping hazard that was once used as a quarry, and has been topped by a lighthouse since the mid-19th century. It's accessed via a private toll road (£3 per car); the wonderful coastal views are probably worth it.

Tregirls Beach   BEACH
Given how close it is to Padstow, this grand beach stays surprisingly quiet most of the year. It looks out over the mouth of the

Camel Estuary and, thanks to its position in the lee of Stepper Point, it's usually fairly sheltered. The beach runs from Gun Point west to the small inlets of Harbour Cove and Hawkers Cove, a total area of more than a mile of sand at low tide. There are no facilities, and no lifeguard cover.

Harlyn Bay   BEACH

For a proper surf, this wide, sandy beach is the best option within easy reach of Padstow. There's a surf school based here, and summer-long lifeguarding. It's a lively and popular spot, and can be a bit overcrowded in summer.

Treyarnon   BEACH

A good family beach, with easy access from the car park, lots of fine sand at low tide and a small area for swimming, that's framed by rocks on either side. It's an easy walk from nearby Constantine Bay (p189).

National Lobster Hatchery   MUSEUM

(☑ 01841-533877; www.nationallobsterhatchery.co.uk; South Quay; adult/child £3.95/1.85; ⊙ 10am-7.30pm Jul & Aug, to 4pm or 5pm Sep-Jun) 🖉 In an effort to combat falling lobster stocks, this harbourside hatchery rears baby lobsters in tanks before returning them to the wild. Displays detail the crustaceans' life cycle, and there are viewing tanks where you can watch the residents in action. Booking a 30-minute 'Meet the Expert' tour (adult/child £12/6) allows you a glimpse into work behind the scenes.

🏃 Activities

⭐ **Camel Trail**   CYCLING

(www.cornwall.gov.uk/cameltrail) Closed in the 1950s, the old Padstow–Bodmin railway has been turned into Cornwall's most popular bike trail. The main section starts in Padstow and runs east through Wadebridge (5.75 miles); the trail then runs on all the way to Poley Bridge on Bodmin Moor (18.3 miles).

Bikes can be hired from **Padstow Cycle Hire** (☑ 01841-533533; www.padstowcyclehire.com; South Quay; per day adult/child £15/7; ⊙ 9am-5pm, to 9pm summer) or **Trail Bike Hire** (☑ 01841-532594; www.trailbikehire.co.uk; Unit 6, South Quay; adult £14, child £5-8; ⊙ 9am-6pm) at the Padstow end, or from Bridge Bike Hire (p196) at the Wadebridge end.

Pumps and helmets are usually included. Tandems and kids' trailers cost extra.

Most people do the route from Padstow and back, so it's often quieter (and much easier to find parking) if you start from the Wadebridge side.

Padstow Boat Trips   BOATING

(www.padstowboattrips.com; South Quay) Between Easter and October, the Jubilee Queen runs scenic trips along the coastline, while Padstow Sealife Safaris visits local seal and seabird colonies.

For something racier, 15-minute **speedboat trips** (£7) zip past the treacherous sandbank of Doom Bar and the beaches of Daymer Bay, Polzeath, Hawkers Cove and Tregirls.

The main Padstow Boat Trips website keeps listings of all the local operators.

Jubilee Queen   BOATING

(☑ 0/836-798457; www.padstowboattrips.co.uk; South Quay; adult/child £12/7) Built in 1977, this stately old vessel is the oldest hand in Padstow's harbour, conducting scenic tours around the bay in the company of experienced skipper Brian Chapman. Seabirds are guaranteed, and if you're lucky you might even spot a dolphin in the estuary. On high tides, some trips continue upriver to Wadebridge.

Padstow Sealife Safaris   BOATING

(☑ 01841-521613; www.padstowsealifesafaris.co.uk; 2hr cruises adult/child £39/25) Scenic trips to see the local seabird colonies and offshore islands around Padstow. A shorter one-hour tour to a seal cave costs £22.50/15 per adult/child.

🍴 Courses

Padstow

Seafood School   COOKING

(☑ 01841-532700; www.rickstein.com; Riverside, The Harbour; 1-day courses from £198) Masterclasses in everything from French fish to perfect sushi are on offer at chef Rick Stein's cookery school, which is above Stein's Fish & Chips. Courses are usually booked out months in advance; check the website for late availability.

🎪 Festivals & Events

May Day   CULTURAL

(⊙ 1 May) Also known as 'Obby 'Oss Day, Padstow's biggest party is said to have its roots in an ancient pagan fertility rite, and sees two coloured 'osses (red and blue) twirl through the streets before meeting up beneath the maypole. It attracts thousands of visitors, so plan well ahead.

✗ Eating

Chough Bakery BAKERY £

(☑ 01841-533361; www.thechoughbakery.co.uk; 1-3 The Strand; pasties £3-5; ⊙ 9am-5pm Mon-Sat) A family-run bakery right in the heart of town, renowned for its traditionally made pasties – they're among the best in the county, and several times have scooped top honours in the World Pasty Championships.

Appleton's at the Vineyard BISTRO ££

(☑ 01841-541413; www.trevibbanmill.com/apple tons-at-the-vineyard; St Issey; mains £17-24; ⊙ noon-5pm Wed-Sun, 6.30-10.30pm Fri & Sat) Having headed up Jamie Oliver's Fifteen at Watergate Bay, chef Andy Appleton has now set up his own venture at Trevibban Mill Vineyard – and, suitably enough, it's an ab solute corker. It's an Italian-meets-Cornish menu – think octopus carpaccio and roasted sardines with panzanella – with a strong seasonal focus and a great wine list.

Prawn on the Lawn BISTRO ££

(☑ 01841-532223; www.prawnonthelawn.com; 11 Duke St; mains £7.50-29; ⊙ noon-midnight Tue-Sat) An offshoot of a London original, this tiny seafood bar is a new addition to Padstow's dining line-up. It's a simple one-room affair, with bare brick, white tiles and blackboards, and a handful of tables lined up along one wall. But frills aren't important here: the seafood is what counts, served as small plates, sharing platters or by weight.

Rojano's in the Square ITALIAN ££

(☑ 01841-532796; www.paul-ainsworth.co.uk; 9 Mill Sq; pizza & pasta £8.50-18; ⊙ 10am-10pm Mon-Sun) Now under the stewardship of Michelin-starred chef Paul Ainsworth, this excellent little Italian bistro turns out fantastic wood-fired pizza, spicy pasta and antipasti. It's a fun and laid-back place to dine, and prices are very reasonable.

Cornish Arms GASTROPUB ££

(☑ 01841-520288; www.rickstein.com/the-cornish-arms.html; St Merryn; mains £7-18; ⊙ 11.30am-11pm) This country pub near the village of St Merryn is now owned by chef Rick Stein's foodie empire, and offers updated pub classics such as scampi and chips, and a pint of prawns, with a characteristically creative spin. The Sunday roast is phenomenally popular, so arrive early. It's a 3-mile drive from Padstow.

★ Seafood Restaurant SEAFOOD £££

(☑ 01841-532700; www.rickstein.com; Riverside, Padstow; 3-course lunch £40, mains £19.50-65.50; ⊙ noon-2pm & 6.30-10pm) Now run by chef Rick Stein's son Jack (a talented chef in his own right), this world-famous seafood restaurant is the address that kick-started Padstow's foodie revolution. It's an elegant place to dine, with a spacious, light-filled dining room, and a conservatory overlooking the harbour. Fish is the raison d'être, from fresh lobster to turbot, John Dory and *fruits de mer.*

You'll generally need to book months in advance, although last-minute lunch tables sometimes crop up.

★ Paul Ainsworth at No 6 BRITISH £££

(☑ 01841-532093; www.paul-ainsworth.co.uk/number6; 6 Middle St; 2-/3-course lunch £19/26, dinner mains £29-40; ⊙ noon-2.30pm & 6-10pm Tue-Sat) Famous telly chef Rick Stein might be the household name, but Paul Ainsworth is rightly touted as Padstow's top chef. His food combines surprising flavours and impeccable presentation with a refreshingly unpretentious approach, and the townhouse setting is a relaxed, unfussy place to dine. Now Michelin-starred, this is Padstow's prime table – and the set lunch is a bit of a bargain.

☕ Drinking & Nightlife

BinTwo WINE BAR

(☑ 01841-532022; www.bintwo.com; The Drang; ⊙ 10am-6pm Mon-Thu, to 9pm Fri & Sat, 11am-6pm Sun) A top-notch wine merchant where you can order fine vintages by the glass, and chase them down with Padstow's best espresso. Young owner David McWilliam is a mine of oenological info.

Padstow Brewing Tasting Room BREWERY

(☑ 01841-533886; www.padstowbrewing.co.uk; 6 Broad St; bottled beers £2-3; ⊙ 11am-8pm) This craft-brew company has taken off like a bottle rocket over the last couple of years, and has recently opened a tasting room and retail shop in town. Tutored beer tastings are available, and you can buy individual bottles and gift packs to take home. Its range runs from light and hoppy Kor' Degel to nut-brown, malty Stormrunner.

ℹ Information

Padstow Tourist Office (☑ 01841-533449; www.padstowlive.com; North Quay; ⊙ 10am-5pm Mon-Sat, to 4pm Sun Apr-Sep, 10am-4pm Mon-Sat Oct-Mar) In a red-brick building on the quayside.

Transport

BOAT

Black Tor Ferry (www.padstow-harbour.co.uk/phc_ferry.html; adult/child return £4/2, bikes £4, dogs £1) Shuttles across the estuary to Rock.

Rock Water Taxi (☑ 07778 105297; www.rock-watertaxi.com; adult/child one way £5/3, return £7/4; ☺ 7am-midnight Easter-Oct) The late-night option once the ferry stops.

BUS

The only useful bus serving Padstow is First Kernow bus 56 to Newquay (hourly Monday to Saturday, five on Sunday, one hour 25 minutes), which runs along the coast via Harlyn Bay, Constantine Bay, Porthcothan, Mawgan Porth, Newquay Cornwall Airport and Porth Beach.

Rock

☑ 01841

The exclusive enclave of Rock, directly across the Camel Estuary from Padstow, is now one of Cornwall's priciest postcodes – hence the area's bevy of disparaging nicknames (Cornwall's St-Tropez, Kensington-on-Sea etc). It's a far cry from the sleepy seaside backwater recalled so fondly by poet John Betjeman, who regularly holidayed here between the 1930s and 1960s. The coastline and countryside around Rock featured in many of his poems, notably in *Trebetherick*, while in his poetic autobiography *Summoned by Bells* he recounts the delights of arriving here on the coastal railway (now the Camel Trail).

While it's certainly changed, Betjeman's Rock hasn't disappeared entirely. The dune-backed white sands of **Daymer Bay** are as glorious as ever, and outside the main holiday season of June to August they often largely deserted. Betjeman himself lies buried at **St Enodoc Church**, on the dunes above the bay.

Just along the coast is **Polzeath**, the area's main surfing beach and a lively location for some beach-lounging or adrenaline-fuelled outdoor activities.

Activities

Era Adventures OUTDOORS
(☑ 01208-862963; www.era-adventures.co.uk) One of the best multi-activity operators on the north coast, offering packages covering coasteering, surfing, sea-kayaking and guided mountain biking. The guides all have a background in lifeguarding or medical

training, so you'll be in safe hands. It's based down a lane from Polzeath village, signed to Valley Caravan Park & Era Adventures.

Eating

Mariners GASTROPUB **££**
(☑ 01208-863679; www.themarinersrock.com; mains £13.50-17.50; ☺ 11am-11pm) A joint venture between local brewer Sharp's and renowned chef Nathan Outlaw, this gourmet gastropub serves up some of the best grub anywhere in Rock. Easygoing dishes such as Portobello mushroom pie, breaded hake and potted duck on toast are the order of the day here, and staff will happily recommend the perfect beer to accompany your main.

Surfside Polzeath CAFE **££**
(☑ 01208-862931; www.surfsidepolzeath.com; Polzeath; mains £8-24; ☺ 10am-11pm) Surf-themed inside and out, this lively cafe is everyone's favourite down-by-the-beach hang-out. For lunch, there are hot-dogs, lobster rolls and burgers; for dinner, fancier dishes of fresh fish, Porthilly mussels and a Frut an Mor seafood platter.

Getting There & Away

The easiest way to get to Rock is aboard the Black Tor Ferry (p193) from Padstow. Alternatively, bus 95/96 (five daily Monday to Saturday, four on Sunday) stops in Polzeath (£4.20, 30 minutes) on its way from Wadebridge to Port Isaac.

Wadebridge

☑ 01208 / POP 7900

Tucked at the eastern end of the Camel Estuary, the market town of Wadebridge grew up around its eponymous bridge, which was for centuries the only crossing over the River Camel. It receives less attention than its starry coastal neighbours these days, particularly nearby Padstow, but it's an attractive town in its own right, with a growing number of shops and eateries to explore.

It makes a useful alternative to starting the Camel Trail at the more popular Padstow end; bikes can be hired from Bridge Bike Hire (p196).

Eating

Relish DELI, CAFE **£**
(☑ 01208-814214; www.relishcornwall.co.uk; Foundry Court; mains £4-10; ☺ 9am-5pm Tue-Sat) Wadebridge locals make a beeline for

LAZY DAYS

There's no shortage of ways to fill your days in Cornwall, but sometimes it's important to take a breather, sit back and just chill. Here are a few ideas.

A PINT AT A PUB

Riverside inns like the **Pandora** (p161) on Restronguet Creek, the **Ferryboat** (p165) and the **Shipwrights Arms** (p230) on the Helford River, are ideal for sipping pints and watching the world go by.

BEACH TIME

If you like to bask all day long, **Crantock** (p197) and **Holywell Bay** (p197), near Newquay, are good options: they're flat, accessible and have loads of space. Remoter coves like **Porth Joke** (p200) and **Lantic Bay** (p174) are good for escaping the crowds, while **Porthcurnick** (p170), **Gyllyngvase** (p156) and **Porthminster** (p212) have all got cracking cafes nearby.

BOAT TRIPS

A boat cruise makes a relaxed, easy day out. **Enterprise Boats** (p166) chugs along the River Fal between Truro and Falmouth, or you can hire boats from **Helford River Boats** (p165). For coastal trips, cruises depart from **Padstow** (p191), **St Ives** (p212) and **Looe** (p176).

GREEN SPACES

Another option is to pack a picnic and find some unspoilt countryside. **Trelissick** (p168) has acres of rolling fields, and a small beach for paddling. The grounds of **Lanhydrock** (p144), **Glendurgan** (p165) and **Godolphin** (p226) are glorious, and lesser-known gardens like **Enys** (p160) or **Penjerrick** (p160) seem made for lazy exploring.

1. Porthminster Beach, St Ives (p212)
2. Lantic Bay, Fowey (p174)
3. Lanhydrock, Bodmin (p144)

MIKE CHARLES / SHUTTERSTOCK ©

3

Hugh Hercod's super little cafe-deli when they're after their morning coffee. He won the UK barista championships in 2008 – so the cappuccinos and espressos here are top-notch. He also runs coffee courses, covering everything from bean selection to milk-frothing. Relish makes a great lunch spot, with delicious salads, sandwiches and tarts.

Tim's Place   CAFE £

(☑ 01208-812550; 1 Foundry St; mains £6-12; ☺ 9am-5pm Mon-Sat, 10am-3pm Sun) At this modest but friendly cafe, local lad Tim provides honest food such as fish-finger butties, bacon and brie sandwiches, and spring mackerel salad, plus a good selection of homemade cakes. There are comfy leather sofas to relax on and magazines to browse, and the hot chocolate is thick enough to stand your spoon up in.

Strong Adolfo's   CAFE ££

(☑ 01208-816949; www.strongadolfos.com; A39, Hawksfield, near Wadebridge; mains £7-10; ☺ 8.30am-4.30pm Mon-Fri, 9am-5pm Sat, to 4.30pm Sun) On the main road into Wadebridge, this sleek Scandi-style cafe makes for a fine lunch stop. Plate glass, chrome and blackboard menus conjure a contemporary feel, and the specials take in everything from Moroccan stew to homemade dhal and deli sandwiches. The owner is Swedish, so the coffee and cakes are tops, too.

🏃 Activities

Bridge Bike Hire   CYCLING

(☑ 01208-813050; www.bridgebikehire.co.uk; The Camel Trail; adult £12-14, child £6-9; ☺ 10am-5pm) Offers a large range of bikes, including cruisers and tandems, as well as tag-a-longs and trailers for kids.

❶ Getting There & Away

Several First Kernow buses stop in Wadebridge:
Bodmin Bus 55 (£5.20, one daily Monday to Saturday).
Newquay Bus 94 (£4.20, one hour, two daily Monday to Saturday).
Port Isaac Bus 96/95 (£4.20, 50 minutes, five daily Monday to Saturday, four on Sunday) runs north via Rock and Polzeath. It then stops in Camelford and connects onwards to Boscastle, Tintagel and Bude.
Truro Bus 95 (£5.20, one hour, three daily Monday to Saturday).

Newquay

☑ 01637 / POP 19,420

Newquay has had a bad rap over the years. The unofficial capital of Cornish surfing is also the north coast's busiest, brashest town: a favourite hang-out of beer boys, beach bums and backpackers, it has a well-earned reputation for the county's rowdiest nightlife thanks to a surfeit of pubs, bars and clubs.

And while that certainly holds true, the town has been making a concerted effort to steer itself in a different direction. It has a fast-growing foodie scene: bistros, coffee bars and health-food shops have sprung up in the town centre, while several fancy boutique hotels have opened along the coastline. The town's cluster of beaches remains as glorious as ever, and if you're looking to learn how to brave the waves, this is the place to do it.

◉ Sights

Watergate Bay   BEACH

This magnificent sweep of sand presents what is undoubtedly the finest panorama of any beach near to Newquay. Travelling north from town, as the road crosses over the crest of the hill and drops towards the beach, you'll find sand that arcs beneath grassy cliffs like a golden crescent. It's an arresting sight, and looks completely different in all weathers. It's a great spot for trying out water-based activities such as surfing and stand-up paddleboarding, thanks to the Extreme Academy (p198).

Lunch is covered too, thanks to Jamie Oliver's Fifteen Cornwall (p200) and the Beach Hut (p199), both just behind the sand.

The beach's northern end at Fox Hole is often much quieter than the rest of the bay, but it gets cut off at high tide, so make sure you've checked the tide times if you're going exploring.

Fistral   BEACH

Probably the most famous stretch of sand in Cornwall, and definitely Newquay's best-known beach, Fistral has become synonymous with Cornish surfing thanks to its reliable waves. Purists scoff that it's way too busy to be worth surfing these days – and they may be right – but its consistent swell and close-to-town facilities make it a fine place for beginners and novices. Just don't expect to be on your own.

Newquay

There's a surf school right on the beach, as well as a cafe and a shop complex.

Holywell Bay
BEACH

Two miles southwest of Newquay as the crow flies (but more like five by road), Holywell is a wonderful expanse of white sand, dotted with tidal pools and rocky towers. It's as flat as a pancake, and vast at low tide, but also fairly exposed, so it can feel windy even in a light breeze.

Crantock
BEACH

Around Pentire Head lies this big, broad shelf of golden sand, backed by grassy dunes and set alongside a river called the Gannel. It's one of the most spacious of Newquay's beaches, and the swimming is generally excellent – with lifeguard duty throughout the summer months. Make sure to stay inside the flags, and take extra care to avoid the area where the Gannel empties out into the sea, as the currents here can be very strong.

Mawgan Porth
BEACH

Five miles northeast of Newquay, this wide, arc-shaped bay is often quieter than its neighbours. The beach is lovely, and less developed than those nearer town. Two of the north coast's swishest hotels, the Scarlet (☑ 01637-861600; www.scarlethotel.co.uk; Maw-

gan Porth; r from £250; P ⬤ ❄) and the Bedruthan Hotel (☑ 01637-860555; www.bedruthan.com; Mawgan Porth; d from £156; P ⬤ ❄), are just inland.

Lusty Glaze
BEACH

(www.lustyglaze.co.uk) Probably the least hectic of Newquay's beaches, this is a sheltered wedge of sand framed by cliffs. It has a good adventure-sports centre, and also hosts live music gigs in summer.

Trerice
HISTORIC BUILDING

(NT; ☑ 01637-875404; www.nationaltrust.org.uk; adult/child £9.45/4.75; ⊙ house 11am-5pm, gardens 10.30am-5pm) Built in 1751, this National Trust–owned Elizabethan manor is most famous for the elaborate barrel-roofed ceiling of the Great Chamber, and some fantastic original 16th-century stained glass among the 576 panes that make up the great window. It's 3.3 miles southeast of Newquay.

Newquay Zoo
ZOO

(☑ 01637-873342; www.newquayzoo.org.uk; Trenance Gardens; adult/child/family £13.20/9.90/41.35; ⊙ 10am-5pm; ⊛) Newquay's pint-sized zoo isn't a world-beater, but its population of penguins, lemurs, parrots and snakes will keep the kids happy. The Tropical House and Toad Hall are particularly good fun, and key events include penguin feeding at noon and lion feeding at 2.30pm.

Blue Reef Aquarium AQUARIUM
(☎ 01637-878134; www.bluereefaquarium.co.uk/newquay; Towan Promenade; adult/child/family £10.75/8.25/35.50; ☉10am-6pm; ♿) A small aquarium on Towan beach, with touch pools and various deep-sea denizens, including reef sharks, loggerhead turtles and a giant Pacific octopus. There's a discount for online bookings.

🏃 Activities

EboAdventure OUTDOORS
(☎ 0800 781 6861; www.eboadventure.co.uk) Surfing's not the only sport on offer: you can also try kite-buggying, kayaking, stand up paddleboarding and coasteering (a mix of rock climbing, scrambling and wild swimming). This multi-activity centre is based at the Penhale Training Camp, at the northern end of Holywell Bay.

Adventure Centre ADVENTURE SPORTS
(☎ 01637-872444; www.adventure-centre.org; Lusty Glaze) On Lusty Glaze beach, the Adventure Centre runs multi-activity sessions

on land, sea and cliff-face. There's loads on offer: jet-skiing, paddleboat rides, abseiling, tightrope walking and, of course, surfing. Note that some activities, such as zip-lining, aren't suitable for younger children.

**Newquay
Watersports Centre** WATER SPORTS
(☎ 01637-498200; www.newquaywatersportscentre.co.uk) In addition to surfing, this watersports company based on the old harbour offers options such as kayaking, wave-ski and stand-up paddleboarding (on both regular and monster-sized boards), as well as fishing, coasteering and power-kiting.

Extreme Academy ADVENTURE SPORTS
(☎ 01637-860840; www.extremeacademy.co.uk; Watergate Bay) Owned by the Watergate Bay Hotel, this is a large and efficient operation that offers the full gamut of watersports: surfing, of course, as well as more unusual options such as stand-up paddleboarding and hand-planing (which involves catching a wave with a miniature surfboard attached to your wrist).

A 2½-hour beginners' surf lesson costs £35, or it's £25 for bodyboarding and £40 for SUP.

MIKE CHARLES / SHUTTERSTOCK ©

Trerice (p197)

English Surfing Federation
Surf School
SURFING

(☑ 01637-879571; www.englishsurfschool.com; lessons from £35) One of the most experienced and efficient large schools, linked with Rip Curl and staffed by fully English Surfing Federation–approved instructors (including the British team coach). Also offers coasteering and bodyboarding.

Fistral Beach Surf School
SURFING

(☑ 01637-850737; www.fistralbeachsurfschool.co.uk; lessons from £35) This is the only school based on Fistral beach, so it's ideal for a last-minute booking if you feel like having a go.

Cornwall Zorbing Park
ADVENTURE SPORTS

(☑ 01637-800273; www.cornwallzorbingpark. co.uk; 2 zorb runs £30; ☺ 10am-6pm Sat & Sun year-round, plus weekdays Jul & Aug) Ever wondered what it feels like to hurtle downhill in a gigantic plastic bubble with no ability to either steer or stop yourself? Well, wonder no longer – the lunatic activity known as zorbing is the speciality here, and you can zorb till your money runs out or you're sick. Or possibly both.

☆ Festivals & Events

Boardmasters
SURFING

(www.relentlessboardmasters.com; ☺ Aug) Surf and sports hit Fistral beach, while bands strut stages on Watergate Bay in early August.

✘ Eating

★ Sprout
VEGETARIAN £

(☑ 01637-875845; www.sprouthealth.co.uk; Crescent Lane; mains £3.50-5.50; ☺ 9am-5pm Mon-Sat; ☑) If you like your food organic and your ingredients fair trade, then this excellent wholefood shop is the only address in town. The one-pot veggie meals (think vegan African peanut stew and hearty Moroccan stew) are delicious and sell out fast – almost as fast as the delectable gluten-free cakes.

Box & Barber
CAFE £

(82 Fore St; cakes & pastries £2-4, mains £6-9; ☺ 8am-4pm) Everyone's top spot for a flat white in town, this fine coffeehouse has a loyal following, and covers all the trendy coffee bases, from V60 drip to Aeropress. It also does great breakfasts, plus salads and toasties for lunch (our tip: try the avocado, cheese and chilli). Needless to say, you'll find plenty of sweet-and-sticky things to go with your afternoon espresso, too.

BEDRUTHAN STEPS

Roughly halfway between Newquay and Padstow loom the stately rock stacks of Bedruthan (Carnewas; NT; www.national trust.org.uk). These mighty granite pillars have been carved out by the relentless action of thousands of years of wind and waves, and now provide a stirring spot for a stroll. The area is owned by the National Trust (NT), which also runs the car park and cafe. Admission to the site is free, but non-NT members have to pay for parking.

The beach itself is accessed via a steep staircase and is submerged at high tide. Towards the northern end is a rocky shelf known as Diggory's Island, which separates the main beach from another cove.

Café Irie
CAFE £

(☑ 01637-859200; www.cafeirie.co.uk; 38 Fore St; lunch £5-10; ☺ 9am-5.30pm Mon-Sat) A surfers' favourite in the centre of Newquay that's perfect for hot chocolates, sticky cakes and jacket spuds after hitting the waves. The beach-shack vibe and reclaimed furniture are right on the money.

Zacry's
MODERN BRITISH ££

(☑ 01637-861231; www.watergatebay.co.uk/food-and-drink/zacrys; Watergate Bay; 2-/3-course menu £32/38; ☺ 6.30-9.30pm) The newest offering at the Watergate Bay Hotel: a smart bistro-diner with wooden booths arranged in a gentle curve, overlooking a semi-open-plan kitchen. Head chef Neil Haydock has a taste for Italian and Stateside flavours, so expect things like chargrilled flat-iron steak, caponata and shellfish succotash, alongside plenty of Cornish fish. The food is great, but kids aren't encouraged.

Beach Hut
BISTRO ££

(☑ 01637-860877; Watergate Bay; mains £10-18; ☺ 9am-9pm) A recent refit has left this beachside cafe looking really smart, with bleached blonde wood and big glass windows to make the most of the view. The food's relaxed: order a stacked-up burger, spicy seafood curry or a bowl of mussels, or pop in post-surf for a mug of hot chocolate or a freshly mixed Bramble cocktail.

It's underneath Fifteen Restaurant, but is owned by the Watergate Bay Hotel.

OFF THE BEATEN TRACK

PORTH JOKE

Not quite the off-the-radar secret it once was, Porth Joke remains a good spot to escape (most) of the crowds. Known as Polly Joke to locals, the main point in its favour is its remoteness: it's hard to find by road; there's precious little parking, and few facilities. But it you're after a wild beach with water to swim in and sand to lounge on, it's hard to beat.

It's about 5 miles southwest of Newquay, sandwiched between Crantock and Holywell Bay.

Lewinnick Lodge BISTRO ££

(☑ 01637-878117; www.lewinnicklodge.co.uk; Pentire Head, Newquay; mains £12.50-20; ⊘ 8am-10pm) For lunch with a view, this smart cafe-bistro is the choice. It's perched right on the cliffs of Pentire Head, giving a knockout perspective on the coastline around Newquay. The decor is modern – all bleached wood and plate glass – and the food is decent: gourmet burgers, mussels and Thaistyle salads are on the menu. Rooms (from £170) are extremely pleasant.

Fifteen Cornwall ITALIAN £££

(☑ 01637-861000; www.fifteencornwall.com; Watergate Bay; 2-/3-course lunch menu £26/32, 5-course dinner menu £65; ⊘ 8.30am-10am, noon-2.30pm & 6.15-9.15pm) With its street-art decor, beach-view windows and shamelessly surfy vibe, this canteen-with-a-conscience is run by celeb chef Jamie Oliver, and trains up young apprentices while turning out Jamie's trademark Italian-influenced food. It's an admirable enterprise, and very well known, which means everyone wants to dine here – but in truth it's very expensive and standards can be extremely variable.

ℹ Information

Newquay Tourist Office (☑ 01637-854020; www.visitnewquay.org; Marcus Hill; ⊘ 9.15am-5.30pm Mon-Fri, 10am-4pm Sat & Sun) Small but well-stocked office, which can help you arrange everything from accommodation to surf lessons.

ℹ Getting There & Away

AIR

Five miles from town, **Newquay Cornwall Airport** (p272) offers direct daily flights to Man-chester and London Gatwick with Flybe (www.flybe.com) and the Isles of Scilly with Isles of Scilly Skybus (p230). Various seasonal destinations around the UK and Europe are offered during summer.

BUS

Newquay's bus station is on Manor Rd. Useful destinations:

Padstow Bus 56 (90 minutes, hourly Monday to Friday, five to seven on Saturday and Sunday) stops at the airport and then trundles up the coast via Mawgan Porth, Porthcothan, Constantine Bay and Harlyn Bay. Note that only a few buses a day stop at Bedruthan Steps.

St Agnes Bus 87 (50 minutes, hourly Monday to Saturday, five on Sunday) stops at Crantock, Holywell Bay and Perranporth en route to St Agnes, and continues to Truro.

Truro Bus 90/92/93 (70 minutes, half-hourly Monday to Saturday, five on Sunday); the various routes travel via different villages but all terminate in Truro.

Wadebridge Bus 95 (50 minutes, five daily Monday to Saturday).

TRAIN

Newquay is on the branch line between Newquay and Par (Atlantic Coast Line; £6.30, 45 minutes), from where you can hop aboard the main London–Penzance line.

Perranporth

☑ 01872 / POP 4270

Perranporth is one of North Cornwall's classic seaside resorts. It's famous for its epic beach – nearly a mile long, banked by grassy dunes, and an enduring favourite for surfers and wind-buggiers. With one main street lined by the usual greasy-spoon cafes, surf shops and souvenir stalls, the town itself has little to recommend – life here is all about the beach.

🍷 Drinking & Nightlife

Watering Hole BAR

(☑ 01872-572888; www.the-wateringhole.co.uk; Perranporth Beach; ⊘ 10am-11pm) Generations of Cornish youth have passed through this venerable beach bar, and it's still going strong, despite nearly being swept away during recent storms. It's a bit rough and ready, but it makes a pleasant spot for a morning coffee or an evening beer as the sun goes down. It's also good for live music.

❶ Getting There & Away

First Kernow bus 87 (£3.20 to £5.20) from Newquay stops hourly in Perranporth as it trundles along the coast via Crantock and Holywell Bay. It then continues to St Agnes (15 minutes) and on to Truro (50 minutes).

St Agnes

📞 01872 / POP 2230

Abandoned engine houses litter the hilltops around the town of St Agnes, which once resounded to the thump and clang of mine pumps and steam engines, and now echoes only to the strains of crashing surf and calling gulls. Slate-roofed houses hint at the town's former prosperity as one of Cornwall's tin-mining boom towns: the local landmark Stippy Stappy consists of a terrace of miners' cottages built in a steeply stepped pattern down the hill to Trevaunance Cove.

Known to locals as Aggie, it's a lively village these days with a very active surf scene, and some great beaches and walks nearby.

◉ Sights

★Chapel Porth   BAY

(NT; www.nationaltrust.org.uk; P) Two miles from St Agnes is one of Cornwall's most beautiful coves, Chapel Porth, a wild, rocky beach framed by steep, gorse-covered cliffs, owned by the National Trust. Above the cove is the ruined engine stack of Wheal Coates, which still boasts its chimney and winding house, from where the coast path winds all the way to the blustery outcrop of St Agnes Head. It's a panorama that graces many a postcard; don't forget your camera.

Trevaunance Cove   BAY

St Agnes' main beach is great for paddling and rock-pooling, and has old-fashioned beach huts where you can get changed. Koru Kayaking (p157) runs trips from the cove.

Beacon   VIEWPOINT

If you're feeling energetic, climb up to the area's highest viewpoint. The panorama from the top of the Beacon stretches across most of Cornwall on a clear day; look out for the dark tors of Bodmin Moor to the east

Chapel Porth

and the distinctive summit of Carn Brea in the west. It's just over a mile's walk (about an hour) from St Agnes town, and fairly well signposted from the village square.

Trevellas Porth
BAY

This former mining valley near Trevaunance Cove is locally known as Blue Hills, a reference to the vivid blue heather that grows here in summer. There's a small sandy beach at the bottom of the valley, lots of rock pools to explore, and the offshore stacks offer great snorkelling. It's a mile east of St Agnes, off the B3285 (signed to Wheal Kitty). Road access is steep and parking limited; better to park at the top and walk down.

The valley is littered with mine workings and chimneys, one of which is home to Cornwall's last remaining tin workshop, Blue Hills Tin Stream (☑01872-553341; www.cornishtin.com; adult/child £6.50/3; ☺10am-2pm Tue-Sat mid-Apr–mid-Oct).

North of the beach, the coast path leads up to Perranporth Airfield, built during WWII but now used by local flying clubs. Along the way, you'll be rewarded with spectacular views back towards St Agnes.

✗ Eating

Chapel Porth Cafe
CAFE £

(Chapel Porth; sandwiches & cakes £2-5; ☺10am-5pm) This cafe down on the edge of Chapel Porth beach is a local institution, serving hot chocolate, cheesy baguettes, flapjacks and the house speciality: hedgehog ice cream (vanilla ice cream topped with clotted cream and hazelnuts).

Genki
CAFE £

(☑01872-555858; Quay Rd; mains £4-8; ☺9am-5pm) This shack cafe on the road to Trevaunance Cove is perfect for quick paninis, homemade soups and cheese platters. The smoothies and coffee are pretty fancy too. There are only a couple of picnic tables to sit at.

Taste
BISTRO ££

(☑01872-552194; 40 Pengarth; mains £13.50-24; ☺10am-2pm & 6-9pm) Every village needs its own homely bistro where the owners greet you by name. Taste majors on classic bistro dishes served with minimal frills – homemade fish cakes, herb-crusted lamb rack, and a plate of pan-seared scallops. It's fairly simple, yes, but reassuringly unpretentious, a vibe mirrored in the plain tables and unfussy grey-and-white colour palette.

Sorting Office
COFFEE

(☑07807 324085; Churchtown; ☺8.30am-4.30pm) You can tell St Agnes is getting uber-trendy these days: it even has its own artisan coffee shop. Sorting Office serves delicious pastries and cakes, plus the usual selection of espresso-based treats and a few more unusual options (gingerbread latte anyone?). The smoothies are killer, too.

Driftwood Spars
PUB FOOD ££

(☑01872-552428; www.driftwoodspars.com; Trevaunance Cove; mains £8-16; ☺11am-11pm; ℗) This whitewashed pub has served generations of St Agnes drinkers, and you'll join a largely local crowd downing pints here. The downstairs area has the most character, with a huge, higgledy wooden bar, upturned barrels and bench seats to hunker in; upstairs the restaurant is lighter and brighter, and serves surf-and-turf dishes. The pub also brews its own ales.

On the upper floors there's a good selection of pleasant, vaguely maritime-themed rooms (doubles from £90), nearly all of which have glorious views over Trevaunance Cove.

ⓘ Getting There & Away

Bus 87 (£6, 45 minutes, hourly in summer) stops in St Agnes on its way from Newquay, via Crantock, Holywell, Perranporth and Trevellas, to Truro.

Porthtowan & Portreath

It's not the prettiest beach on the north coast, but Porthtowan is an old stalwart for local surfers. It offers reliable swell and a popular post-wave hang-out, the Blue Bar.

There's also a tidal seawater pool that makes a fine place for a dip.

Portreath is a busy and popular harbour town set around a broad sandy beach, 4 miles southwest of Porthtowan. In truth, it's not the best place for sunbathing, but it's fun for families, and there's usually enough swell for bodyboarding.

◎ Sights

Mount Pleasant Eco Park
COMMUNITY

(☑01209-891500; www.mpecopark.co.uk; Chapel Hill) Up on the hill above Porthtowan, this community-focused eco-centre and organic farm is a catch-all venue, hosting everything from vegan food fairs to green weddings. It regularly runs workshops on the likes of running your own allotment, sustainable building and hedge-laying; check the website to see what's on.

The park also hosts the rootsy Tropical Pressure (www.tropicalpressure.co.uk) music festival in July.

There's a back-to-basics campsite – standard sites cost £12, or £20 with car, plus £4 for electric hook-up.

Eating

★ **Blue Bar** BISTRO ££
(☎01209-890329; www.blue-bar.co.uk; Porthtowan; mains £8-16; ☉10am-11pm) For a seaside sundowner or a lunchtime burger by the sand, this Porthtowan cafe is tough to beat. It's a social hub for the north coast, and everyone knows each other, which can make it feel a little cliquey. Everyone also knows about it, so arrive early.

Camborne & Redruth

☎01209 / POP 55,400
Though they rarely figure on the radar of visitors, in many ways the gritty twin towns of Redruth and Camborne represent Cornwall's tin-seamed soul. A century-and-a-half ago, these towns were at the centre of the county's mining industry, and their hilltops would have thrummed and pounded with the sound of mine wheels and engine stacks. Sadly, the decline of the mining industry has been mirrored in the towns' fortunes – they're now among the most deprived areas in Cornwall.

The area received a boost in 2006 following the designation of Unesco World Heritage status for the Cornwall & West Devon Mining Landscape (www.cornish-mining.co.uk), and there are various sites that explore the county's industrial past and future.

Looming above town is the unmistakable landmark of Carn Brea, a rocky hill topped by a Celtic cross. The views from here stretch all the way to both coasts on a clear day.

◉ Sights

Tehidy Woods FOREST
(www.cornwall.gov.uk) The 101-hectare country park of Tehidy formerly belonged to the Bassets, one of Cornwall's four richest tin-mining families, who made their fortune from exploiting mineral rights across west and central Cornwall. The estate has been owned by the council since 1983 and is run as public woodland, criss-crossed by trails, lakes, wildlife reserves and a golf course. There's a good cafe for lunch (mains £4 to £8). Local theatre company Rogue Theatre also presents live performances here several times a year.

East Pool Mine MINE
(NT; ☎01209-315027; www.nationaltrust.org.uk; adult/child £7.70/4.05; ☉10.30am-5pm) This mining centre near Redruth is an ideal place to get acquainted with Cornwall's once-great industry. At the heart of the complex are two massive working beam engines, both once powered by steam boilers designed by local engineer Richard Trevithick (who was born in Redruth in 1771). You can wander round both of the engine houses, and guides are on hand to provide backstory.

King Edward Mine MINE
(☎01209-61468; www.kingedwardmine.co.uk; Troon, near Camborne; adult/child £8/2; ☉10am-5pm Wed-Mon Jul-Sep, Wed-Sun Jun, Wed, Thu, Sat & Sun May) If you're into mining heritage, this historic mine is a must-see. It's changed little over the last hundred years, largely because it was used as a teaching facility for the nearby Camborne School of Mines, and is packed with all kinds of machinery (like a Heath Robinson illustration) used to dress and sort the ore. Engineer nerds will appreciate details such as the pioneering Holzer rock drill, invented by Camborne-based mining company Holman Brothers and later exported all over the world.

🏃 Activities

Great Flat Lode Trail CYCLING
A 7.5-mile circular hiking-and-biking trail that forms part of the Mineral Tramways network, and winds past several engine houses and mining ruins dotted around Carn Brea.

The trail roughly follows the course of the Great Flat Lode – a rich seam of tin ore discovered here in the 1860s, so-called because it ran at a gradient of 30 degrees, rather than the usual 70, and was thus much easier to mine.

West Cornwall & the Isles of Scilly

Best Places to Eat

➡ Shore (p219)

➡ Tolcarne Inn (p222)

➡ Gurnard's Head (p218)

➡ Ben's Cornish Kitchen (p223)

➡ Kota (p227)

➡ Porthminster Beach Café (p212)

Best Views

➡ Gwithian and Godrevy (p213)

➡ Porthcurno (p216)

➡ Lizard Point (p229)

➡ Hell's Mouth (p213)

➡ Kynance Cove (p228)

➡ Land's End (p215)

Why Go?

While most visitors head for the tourist honey pots of the north coast, the wild west of Cornwall receives fewer visitors outside the major draws of St Ives and Land's End. But the real beauty of this corner lies off the beaten track: it's a land where stone monuments rise up from the hilltops, ancient moorland butts up against gorse-topped cliffs, and forgotten mine stacks stand out in relief against the skyline.

With its sparkling seaside setting and artistic connections, the attractions of St Ives are very well known, and the town can feel uncomfortably crowded between July and September; visit in early spring or autumn and you'll find things quieter. Similarly, the main beaches around Gwithian, Sennen and the Lizard can be very busy, but many more remote coves can be reached via the coast path. And for a real escape, the lesser-visited islands of Scilly feel like a whole different world.

When to Go

➡ **Apr** Porthleven celebrates Cornwall's food culture with a big festival, when top chefs and suppliers set up stalls by the harbour.

➡ **May** St Mary's on the Isles of Scilly hosts the World Pilot Gig Championships over a weekend in early May. Accommodation is almost impossible to find, so you'll need to book at least six months ahead

➡ **Jun** Penzance stages its big summer street celebration during the Golowan Festival in June: try to visit on Mazey Day if you can, when the whole town turns out to party.

➡ **Dec** Christmas lights cover the harbour around Mousehole, and Penzance's pagan Montol Festival provides a slightly more alternative view of the festive season.

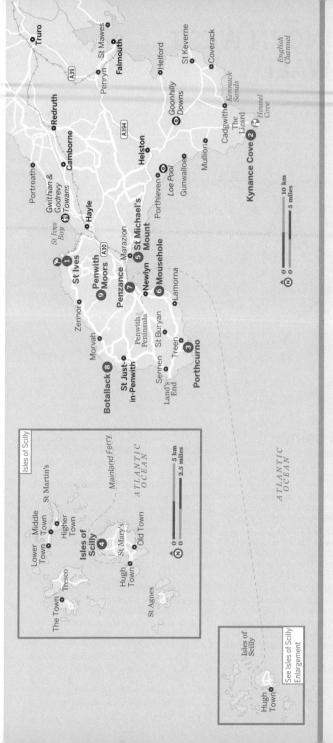

West Cornwall & The Isles of Scilly Highlights

1 St Ives (p210) Celebrating Cornwall's artistic heritage at Tate St Ives.

2 Kynance Cove (p228) Wild swimming, walking the cliffs and scanning for choughs.

3 Porthcurno (p216) Catching a clifftop play with a breathtaking Atlantic backdrop.

4 Isles of Scilly (p230) Swimming with wild seals on this island archipelago.

5 St Michael's Mount (p223) Crossing the cobbled causeway to an island abbey.

6 Mousehole (p222) Wandering the cobbled alleys of this pretty fishing village.

7 Penzance (p218) Admiring fine Georgian architecture in Chapel St, then taking a dip in Jubilee Pool.

8 Botallack (p216) Clambering down the cliffs

to one of Cornwall's most photogenic mines.

9 Penwith Moors (p214) Wandering round stone circles and Iron Age villages on this wild, windy heath.

WALKING IN WEST CORNWALL

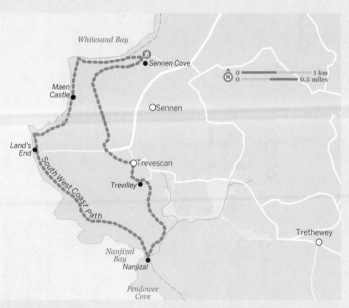

Whitesand Bay

Sennen Cove

Maen Castle

Sennen

Land's End

South West Coast Path

Trevescan

Trevilley

Trethewey

Nanjizal Bay
Nanjizal

Pendower Cove

1 km
0.5 miles

LAST STOP CORNWALL

START/END SENNEN
DURATION 3-4 HOURS
DISTANCE 6- 7 MILES

This hike is as far west as you can walk on mainland Britain; it starts at the lovely cove of Sennen and circles round via the end-of-everything headland of Land's End, taking in some of the wildest coastal scenery in all of Cornwall. A few of the tracks are easy to miss, so an Ordnance Survey (OS) map will come in handy.

Leave the car at the car park at Sennen (p216), and head west along the coast path, which climbs steeply past an old lookout station that's been refurbished by the National Trust. Head on along the coast path, and look out for the remains of **Maen Castle** on your right, a prehistoric hillfort dramatically sited on the cliffs. The surrounding area has been inhabited since Neolithic times; it's thought that many of the field boundaries were established by ancient settlers. This section is particularly spectacular in summer, when

the wildflowers are a blaze of colour, and seabirds wheel and circle over the clifftops.

Continue on the coast path till you reach **Land's End**, (p215) where you can snap your picture next to the famous sign: 28 miles to Scilly, 874 miles to John O'Groats, 3147 to New York, and 1.5 miles out to sea to the famous Longships Lighthouse. From here it's another mile or so along the rather precarious coast path to the secluded beach of **Nanjizal**, reached by wooden steps. It's great for swimming, but the waves can be powerful so take care.

After your dip, take the path leading inland up the hillside; turn left when you reach a junction, and cross the fields till you arrive at **Trevilley Farm** and the nearby village of Trevescan, where you can reward yourself with a cream tea at the delightful **Apple Tree Cafe** (01736-872753; www.appletreecafe.co.uk; Trevescan; mains £6-12; 10am-5pm Wed-Sun). From here, head along the road till you come to the junction with the A30. You'll see a sign for a public bridleway directly opposite the turning, which leads all the way back down to Sennen.

A fine ramble along the wild west coast via surfy Sennen, Land's End and the remote beach of Nanjizal.

ANDY COX / SHUTTERSTOCK ©

Land's End (p215)

ROAD TRIP >
PENWITH'S PREHISTORY

Take a trip into the ancient past on this drive to visit some of Penwith's mysterious prehistoric monuments – some of which predate Stonehenge.

❶ St Ives

Penwith has an astonishing concentration of ancient sites – more than practically anywhere else in northern Europe, in fact – suggesting there was a thriving community in this wild landscape as long ago as the building of Stonehenge.

This road trip takes in the highlights. It begins in **St Ives** (p210), the centre of Cornwall's buzzing art scene, then veers out into the wonderful B3306 coast road, signed to **Zennor** (p212), a twisting corkscrew of a road that winds past moorland, granite tors, ancient fields and drystone walls: the land here is thought to have been farmed since the Iron Age, and probably long before. It's worth hiking past the village church to the craggy cliffs above Pendour Cove, said to be the home of the fabled Mermaid of Zennor.

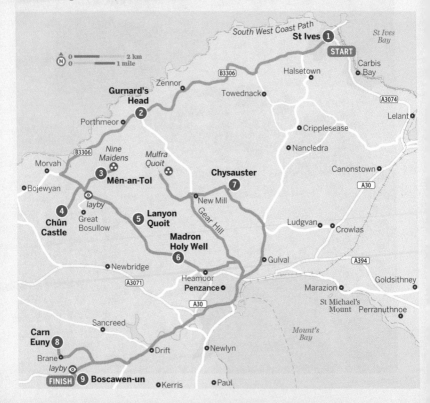

➋ Gurnard's Head

Continue along the B3306 to renowned gastropub the **Gurnard's Head** (p218), which makes a great stop for an early lunch.

➌ Mên-an-tol

Alternatively, stay on the road till you reach the next left-hand turn, signed to Penzance/Madron (you'll see a white cottage next to the turning). Stay on this road until you reach a small **layby** and farm gate on the left; it's easy to miss, so keep your eyes peeled. From here, an unsigned trail leads up to the ring-shaped stone known as the **Mên-an-tol** (p214) – it's worth taking the opportunity to crawl through as, according to local lore, you'll either a) fall pregnant or b) get cured of rickets, depending on which legend you choose to believe. From here, you can hike along a side-trail to the **Nine Maidens** stone circle. It's a mile there and back from the layby.

➍ Chûn Castle

Back in the car, backtrack a little the way you came, and take the left-hand turning signed to **Chûn Castle**. Though there's little physically left of it these days, this was once perhaps the greatest Iron Age hillfort in the whole of Penwith; most of the walls and stones have been plundered, but you can still make out the enclosing ditch, and the view from the top is super.

➎ Lanyon Quoit

Return to the main road, drive past the Mên-an-tol layby and continue for half a mile. Before too long, you'll pass **Lanyon Quoit** (p214) on your left, one of the largest and best-preserved of Penwith's dolmens, or burial chambers. It's clearly visible from the road, but it's worth hopping over the wall to stand next to it and appreciate its size – and the inexplicably massive effort it must have required to lift the 20-tonne capstone into place.

➏ Madron

From here, it's another couple of miles to the village of Madron and its ancient **holy well** (p219), one of many dotted across Penwith. These ancient springs have a long and mysterious heritage that stretches back to pagan times, and probably long before; the water is said to have all kinds of curative properties, but it's a pretty spot even if you decide not to taste it.

➐ Chysauster

Continue downhill towards Penzance. When you reach the village of Heamoor, take the minor road signed left towards Gulval. Continue through the village and onto the B3311 towards Nancledra. Climb the hill to Badger's Cross, and take the next left signed to **Chysauster** (p214), 0.75 miles after the turning. This is the southwest's most important Iron Age village, and you can wander freely around the remains of a complex of roundhouses where several families must once have lived.

Follow the road from Chysauster on to the nearby village of Mulfra, where you can see another impressive dolmen, **Mulfra Quoit**.

➑ Carn Euny

For the last stage of the drive, another Iron Age village awaits at **Carn Euny**. Head to Penzance and take the A30 road west out of town, heading for Land's End. Pass through Drift; you can take the first brown sign to Carn Euny if you wish, but it's easier to stay on the A30 till you see the next sign on the right, signed 'Carn Euny 1½ miles'. Follow this minor road to the hamlet of Brane. Park up and follow the track up for about 500m to find the remains of another impressive Iron Age village and a mysterious stone passage known as a *fougou*.

➒ Boscawen-un

Backtrack the way you came to the A30, turn right towards Land's End, and look out for the turning on the left to Boscawenoon Farm. Continue west till you see a small **layby** on the left; from here, a track leads to perhaps Penwith's most impressive stone circle of all, **Boscawen-un**. It makes a fitting end to your ancient tour.

WEST CORNWALL

St Ives

📞 01736 / POP 9870

Even if you've seen St Ives many times before, it's still hard not to be dazzled as you gaze across its improbably pretty jumble of slate roofs, church towers and turquoise bays. Once a busy pilchard harbour, St Ives later became the centre of Cornwall's arts scene in the 1920s and '30s, and the town is still an artistic centre, with numerous galleries and craft shops lining its winding cobbled streets, as well as the southwestern outpost of the renowned Tate Museum.

Unfortunately, change has come at a price – St Ives is packed throughout summer, and prices here are substantially higher than in other parts of Cornwall. To see it at its best, avoid school holidays and July and August.

◉ Sights

★ Tate St Ives   GALLERY

(📞 01736-796226; www.tate.org.uk/stives; Porthmeor Beach; adult/child £7.50/6) After an 18-month, multimillion-pound refit, St Ives' most illustrious gallery has finally reopened its doors, although the long-awaited gallery extension wasn't open at the time of writing. The present space is dedicated to revolving exhibitions exploring the work of artists with a Cornish connection. It's a fabulous space, hovering like a concrete curl above the sands of Porthmeor Beach; inside, the gallery is luminous with light and painted stark white to place the focus firmly on the artworks.

The new gallery space will provide permanent room for exploring the work of some of the key figures who placed St Ives on the artistic map – you can expect to see work from Barbara Hepworth, Ben Nicholson, Peter Lanyon and Terry Frost, as well as more unfamiliar names such as Naum Gabo and Wilhelmina Barns-Graham.

There's also a top-floor cafe with cracking views over the beach.

Barbara Hepworth Museum   MUSEUM

(📞 01736-796226; Barnoon Hill; adult/child £6.60/5.50, joint ticket with Tate St Ives £10/8; ⊙10am-5.20pm Mar-Oct, to 4pm Nov-Feb) Barbara Hepworth (1903–75) was one of the leading abstract sculptors of the 20th century and a key figure in the St Ives art scene. Her studio on Barnoon Hill has remained almost untouched since her death and the adjoining garden contains several of her most notable sculptures, many of which were inspired by the elemental forces she discovered in her adopted Cornish home: rock, sea, sand, wind, sky. Free private tours are also available to provide extra context.

Leach Pottery   GALLERY

(📞 01736-796398; www.leachpottery.com; Higher Stennack; adult/child £6/free; ⊙10am-5pm Mon-Sat, 11am-4pm Sun) While other St Ives artists broke new ground in sculpture and abstract art, potter Bernard Leach was hard at work reinventing British ceramics in his studio in Higher Stennack. Drawing inspiration from Japanese and oriental sculpture, and using a unique hand-built 'climbing' kiln based on ones he had seen in Japan, Leach's pottery created a unique fusion of Western and Eastern ideas.

Porthmeor Beach   BEACH

Stretched out beneath Tate St Ives is the sandy beach of Porthmeor, a good choice for swimmers and novice surfers thanks to its gentle swells. There's a beach cafe for post-swim sustenance.

St Ives

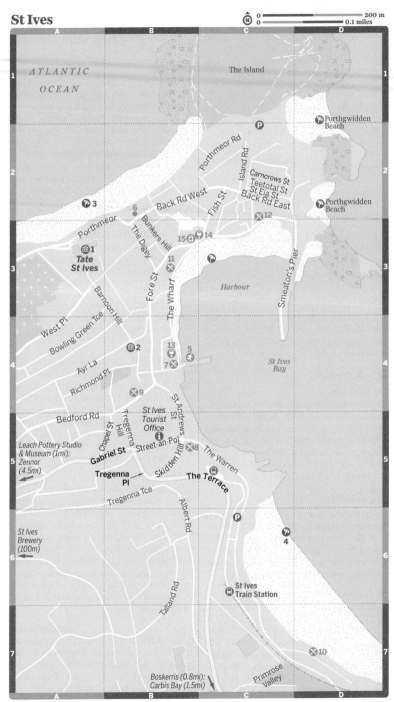

ATLANTIC
OCEAN

The Island

Porthgwidden
Beach

Porthmeor Rd

Island Rd

Carncrows St
Teetotal St
St Eia St
Back Rd East

Back Rd West

Fish St

Porthgwidden
Beach

Porthmeor

The Digey

Bunkers Hill

Tate
St Ives

Fore St

The Wharf

Harbour

Smeaton's Pier

West Pl

Barnoon Hill

Bowling Green Tce

Ayr La

Richmond Pl

St Ives
Bay

Bedford Rd

Tregenna Hill

Chapel St

St Andrews St

St Ives
Tourist
Office

Street-an-Pol

The Warren

Gabriel St

Tregenna
Pl

Skidden Hill

The Terrace

Leach Pottery Studio
& Museum (1mi);
Zennor
(4.5mi)

Tregenna Tce

Albert Rd

St Ives
Brewery
(100m)

St Ives
Train Station

Talland Rd

Primrose
Valley

Boskerris (0.8mi);
Carbis Bay (1.5mi)

OFF THE BEATEN TRACK

HAYLE ESTUARY

The huge expanse of **tidal flats** (www.
rspb.org.uk; Hayle) FREE around Hayle
is a twitchers' paradise, and an important Royal Society for the Protection of
Birds (RSPB) reserve. It's worth visiting
whatever the season: in winter, more
than 18,000 birds come here to sit out
the cold. Spring and autumn is great for
curlews, egrets, oystercatchers, gulls
and terns, and in summer ospreys have
been known to hunt here.

There are various access points: the
easiest trail circles round Carnsew Pool,
a short walk from Foundry Sq in Hayle's
town centre.

For lunch, it's well stopping by **Philps**
(☑ 01736-755661; www.philpspasties.co.uk;
1 East Quay; pasties from £3.50), one of
Cornwall's most renowned pasty-
makers, just outside the town centre.

Porthminster Beach   BEACH
The most impressive of the town beaches,
with an attractive arc of soft golden sand
that's usually sheltered from the wind by the
cliffs. It inevitably gets busy on warm days.

Activities

St Ives Boats   BOATING
(☑ 0777 300 8000; www.stivesboats.co.uk; adult/
child £10/8) St Ives Boats is one of several
operators along the harbour front to offer
fishing trips and scenic cruises, including to
the grey seal colony on Seal Island. If you're
really lucky, you might even spot a porpoise
or a basking shark in summer.

Eating

Pengenna Pasties   BAKERY £
(www.pengennapasties.co.uk; 9 High St; pasties £3-
5; ⊙ 10am-5pm Mon-Sat) Generously stuffed
pasties, with a controversial top crimp (not
sanctioned by the official Cornish Pasty Association) and a slightly flakier texture.

 **Porthminster
Beach Café**   BISTRO ££
(☑ 01736-795352; www.porthminstercafe.co.uk;
Porthminster Beach; mains £15-22; ⊙ 9am-10pm)
This is no ordinary beach cafe: it's a full-
blown bistro with a gorgeous sun-trap terrace and a superb Mediterranean-influenced
menu, specialising in seafood. Tuck into rich
bouillabaisse, seafood curry or Provençal

fish soup, and settle back to enjoy the breezy
beach vistas. It's published its own cook-
book, too, if you fancy taking the recipes
home.

Searoom   CAFE ££
(☑ 01736-794325; www.thesearoomstives.co.uk;
1 Wharf House; mains £9.50-15; ⊙ 9.30am-10pm
Mon-Sat) A fine bet for a light bite for lunch –
tuck into one of the yummy-looking lunchtime tarts or copious seafood salads, or ask
for one of the fun sharing boards (available
in cheese, charcuterie or seafood pâté varieties). It's a relaxed space, with leaded windows peeping out towards the harbour, and
a young and friendly staff. No bookings.

Porthminster Kitchen   BISTRO ££
(☑ 01736-799874; www.porthminster.kitchen; The
Wharf; mains lunch £7.50-15, dinner £11-17; ⊙ 9am-
10pm) Run by the same team as Porthminster
Beach Café, this is a welcome new addition
to the harbourside in St Ives. It showcases
fresh, zingy, fusion food, from tuna sashi-
mi and sea trout with Asian mushrooms to
Malay veggie curry – there's an emphasis on
minimising gluten and dairy too. The quay-
view dining room is lovely.

Blas Burgerworks   CAFE ££
(☑ 01736-797272; The Warren; burgers £10-12.50;
⊙ noon-9.30pm Jul & Aug, 5.30-9.30pm rest of
year) 🌿 St Ives' boutique burger joint, with
an ecofriendly manifesto and an imaginative
menu. Go for a 6oz Classic Blasburger, or
branch out with a guacamole and corn salsa–
topped Rancheros, or a Smokey with beetroot, aged cheddar and homemade piccalilli
(there are plenty of veggie options, too).

Halsetown Inn   PUB FOOD ££
(☑ 01736-795583; www.halsetowninn.co.uk; Halsetown; mains £13-22.50; ⊙ noon-2pm & 6-9pm)
Prime pub grub a mile from St Ives in tiny
Halsetown. It's still the village boozer –
local ales, first-name bar staff, cosy crannies to hunker down in – but the food is a
notch above the norm thanks to the owners, who also run Blas Burgerworks. Expect
posh mains such as chicken pithivier and
cider-baked ham, plus a excellent Sunday
roast.

Alba   MODERN BRITISH £££
(☑ 01736-797222; www.thealbarestaurant.com; Old
Lifeboat House; 2-/3-course dinner menu £24/28;
mains £16-28.95; ⊙ 6-10pm) Other restaurants
come and go, but this harbourside bistro
beside the old lifeboat station continues to

excel. It's in a converted boathouse, with a split-level layout: dining is upstairs, with picture windows looking over the harbour; downstairs is the sleek A-Bar. Head chef Grant Nethercott has a Michelin-starred background, so standards are high: first-class fish and seafood are the mainstays.

The set dinner menu is available from 6pm to 7.30pm.

Drinking & Nightlife

St Ives Brewery   MICROBREWERY
(☑ 01736-793467; www.stives-brewery.co.uk; Trewidden Rd; mains £3-8; ☺ 9am-5pm Mon-Sat, 10am-4pm Sun) St Ives' own microbrewery has had a vintage time since its foundation in 2010: it's expanded operations and has recently opened its own cafe and tasting room. The flagships are Boiler's, a golden session ale, and the hoppy IPA-style Knill By Mouth; you can sample both in the cafe while enjoying an absolutely stunning outlook over the town's rooftops.

Sloop Inn   PUB
(☑ 01736-796584; www.sloop-inn.co.uk; The Wharf; ☺ 11am-11pm) This beam-ceilinged boozer is as comfy as an old pair of slippers, with a few tables on the harbour and lots of local ales.

Hub   BAR
(www.hub-stives.co.uk; The Wharf; ☺ 9am-11pm) The open-plan Hub is the heart of St Ives' (limited) nightlife: coffee and burgers by day, cocktails after dark.

Shopping

Sloop Craft Market   ARTS & CRAFTS
(☑ 01736-796051; Back Lane) Just off the harbour, this little mews holds the workshops and exhibition spaces for several local artists, creating everything from driftwood furniture to handmade jewellery. if you're after an affordable piece of art to take home as a souvenir, this is a great place to do it.

ⓘ Information

St Ives Tourist Office (☑ 01736-796297; www.visitstives.org.uk; Street-an-Pol; ☺ 9am-5.30pm Mon-Fri, 9am-5pm Sat, 10am-4pm Sun) Inside the Guildhall.

ⓘ Getting There & Away

The **bus** (Station Hill) and train stations are located near each other at the top of Tregenna Hill.

Bus 17/17A/17B (£5, 30 minutes, half-hourly Monday to Saturday, hourly Sunday) The quickest route to Penzance, via Lelant and Marazion.

Bus 16/16A (£5, hourly Monday to Saturday) An alternative route to Penzance; bus 16A travels via Zennor and the Gurnard's Head pub, while bus 16 goes via Halsetown, Ludgvan and Gulval.

The branch train line from St Ives is worth taking just for the coastal views.

Trains shuttle between St Ives train station and St Erth (£3, 14 minutes, half-hourly), where you can catch connections along the Penzance–London Paddington main line.

Gwithian & Godrevy Towans

Four miles' drive east of St Ives, the dune-backed flats of Gwithian and Godrevy unfurl in a glimmering golden curve that joins together at low tide to form Hayle's '3 miles of golden sand'. This is one of Cornwall's most glorious beach panoramas, fringed by acres of rockpools and grassy dunes (known in Cornish as *towans*), beloved by everyone from surfers to dog-walkers. At the northern end of the beach is Godrevy Island, topped by a 19th-century lighthouse that inspired Virginia Woolf's stream-of-consciousness classic *To The Lighthouse*.

The cliffs here are an important wildlife habitat: they're carpeted with wildflowers in summer, and provide nesting sites for seabirds including cormorants, guillemots and several gull species. Around the headland from Godrevy, there's also a small cove where you can usually spot grey seals basking on the beach. Occasionally, you might even spot bottlenose dolphins riding the surf.

Nearby, on the road from Portreath to Gwithian, is the spectacular stretch of cliffs known as Hell's Mouth. It's the steepest cliff drop in Cornwall: 88m of sheer granite plunging from grassy clifftop into churning surf. It's notoriously prone to landslides: in 2011 a massive 110,000-ton chunk fell off into the sea (you find a video of it online).

✗ Eating

Godrevy Café   CAFE £
(☑ 01736-757999; www.godrevycafe.com; lunch £6-10; ☺ 10am-5pm) This is everyone's favourite place to snack after a beach walk or a surf – a stylish split-level cafe beside the National

WILD FOOD FORAGING

If you can't tell your wild sorrel from your samphire, then **Fat Hen** (☑ 01736-810156; www.fathen.org; Boscawen-noon Farm, St Buryan; 1-day course £95) – aka forager-ecologist Caroline Davey – can help. From her base near St Buryan, she leads foraging courses in search of wild goodies, before retiring to headquarters to see the raw materials transformed into something tasty by the Fat Hen chefs. There are one-day courses, as well as a fun one-day wild food cycling and foraging excursion.

Or you can opt for a longer wild food weekend (£195 not including accommodation), which includes three slap-up meals in the Goat Barn. Hedgerow cocktails, anyone?

Other courses include skills such as shellfish cooking, bread-making and game.

Trust car park, serving great sandwiches, salads, breakfasts and coffee. Arrive early if you want to bag a table on the top-deck patio overlooking the beach.

Trevaskis Farm FOOD
(☑ 01209-713931; www.trevaskisfarm.co.uk; 12 Gwinear Rd, Hayle; ⊙ 9am-6pm Jun-Aug, to 5pm Sep-May) Near Gwithian, this farm shop sells meats, homemade chutneys and fresh fruit and veg. The restaurant also does vast Sunday roasts.

Penwith Peninsula

Taking its name from two Cornish words – *penn* (headland) and *wydh* (end) – Penwith juts like a crooked finger into the wild waters of the Atlantic, stretching from St Ives to the most westerly point on the British mainland at Land's End. Wild and remote, spotted with mine stacks, ancient farmland and windswept moor, this is a truly wild corner of Cornwall, and feels a long way from the county's pretty harbour towns and neatly kept beaches.

The twisting B3306 coast road is a rollercoaster, winding through a panorama of granite-strewn moorland and patchwork fields, some of which date back to medieval times. Craggy tors and auburn heaths dominate the horizon, and broken cliffs tumble down into booming surf. It's scarcely populated now, but during Neolithic times this empty landscape was home to a string of ancient settlements, the remains of which can still be seen scattered among the granite rocks.

◉ Sights

For more on Penwith's ancient sites, see the road trip Penwith's Prehistory (p208).

★ **Chysauster** ARCHAEOLOGICAL SITE
(EH; www.english-heritage.org.uk/visit/places/chysauster-ancient-village; Newmill; adult/child £4.60/2.80; ⊙ 10am-6pm daily) Two thousand years ago, Penwith's moors would have been littered with Iron Age settlements. Most have vanished, but a few remain – and Chysauster is the best-preserved of them all. Consisting of around eight stone-walled houses, each with its own central courtyard, it gives you a real sense of daily life during the Iron Age – you can still see the stone hearths used to grind corn, and wander around the field system where the residents kept livestock and grew crops.

Lanyon Quoit ARCHAEOLOGICAL SITE
Perhaps the most impressive of all of the ancient sites in this part of Penwith, this is a classic example of a quoit, or dolmen – a table-like structure consisting of several uprights and a capstone, which probably marked an ancient burial site. In the 18th century the monument was tall enough to shelter a man on horseback, but an 1815 storm blew the quoit down and broke one of the four uprights; it was re-erected nine years later.

It's in a field beside the road between Madron and Morvah, but it's easy to miss, so keep your eyes peeled.

Mên-an-tol ARCHAEOLOGICAL SITE
This baffling monument is the only one of its kind in Cornwall, consisting of two upright menhirs flanking a hollow, ring-shaped stone. Squeezing through the stone was said to be a cure for infertility and rickets, but quite what the original purpose of the stone was is still a complete mystery. Its name derives from the Cornish for 'stone of the hole'.

The site is situated along a side track 5 miles south of Morvah – look out for the turning signed to Chûn Castle, and park in the next layby. The track leads from here.

Land's End

The clue's in the name. This wild, craggy headland is where Cornwall (and, by extension, the rest of Britain) comes to a screeching halt, and the black granite cliffs fall away into thundering white surf and sea-spray. The views are truly epic: the restless Atlantic seems to wrap itself around the horizon, shimmering and flashing in the late-afternoon light, and when the weather's clear you can often glimpse the faint outlines of the Isles of Scilly, 28 miles out to sea.

Famous as the last port of call for charity walkers on the 874-mile slog from John O'Groats in Scotland, Land's End is a special spot – which makes the decision to build a tacky theme park here in the 1980s all the more inexplicable. Still, once you bypass the tat, the coast path which runs south from Land's End remains as wild and beautiful as any in Cornwall.

◎ Sights

Longships Lighthouse LIGHTHOUSE

Perched on a rocky reef, 1.25 miles out to sea from Land's End, this famous lighthouse is a marvel of maritime engineering. Built to warn ships away from this infamously dangerous stretch of coastline, the first structure was built in 1795 but was swamped by waves, and subsequently replaced in 1873 at the considerable cost of £43,870. Since then it's somehow withstood even the worst of the Atlantic storms, and has been unmanned since 1988.

Nanjizal BEACH

It's a bit of a walk from Land's End, but this remote, rocky cove is an old favourite if you fancy a bit of seclusion away from the crowds (or most of them, at least). Head south from the headland for about 1.6 miles, and you'll spy the stony path down into the cove. The swimming is generally good, but

WEST CORNWALL & THE ISLES OF SCILLY PENWITH PENINSULA

Penwith Peninsula & Land's End

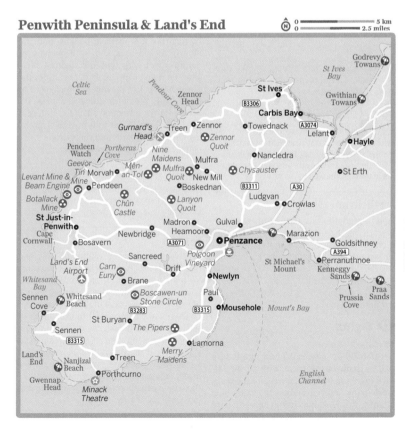

WORTH A TRIP

BOTALLACK

Clinging to the cliffs near Levant, a dramatic complex of mine-workings near **Botallack** (NT; www.nationaltrust.org.uk/botallack) is a powerful reminder of Cornwall's industrial past. The main mine stack, properly known as **The Crowns**, teeters picturesquely on the cliff edge above a cauldron of boiling surf. It's famously photogenic and a frequent filming location, most recently used by the BBC's latest version of *Poldark*. It's a steep walk down, but well worth the trek; an audio guide can be downloaded from the NT website.

During its 19th-century heyday, the mine was one of the county's richest and deepest, producing 14,500 tonnes of tin and 20,000 tonnes of copper ore from shafts that snaked nearly half a mile out to sea. You can explore the site's history at the Count House workshop, which once contained the stables that housed the mine's pit ponies.

the waves can be very strong, so take care. Otherwise, there's plenty of sand and rock-pools to investigate.

ⓘ Getting There & Away

Bus 1/1A (eight daily Monday to Friday, seven on Saturday, six on Sunday) travels from Penzance to Land's End via Sennen, Treen and Porthcurno; in summer, the service often uses an open-top bus to max out the views.

Porthcurno

Teetering right out on Cornwall's far-western tip, the sandy wedge of Porthcurno is one of the best beaches in west Cornwall for swimming and sunbathing, and around the headland, the lesser-known beach of **Pednvounder** nearby is good if you like to sunbathe au naturel – it's one of Cornwall's few naturist beaches.

◉ Sights

★**Minack Theatre**　　　　THEATRE
(☑01736-810181; www.minack.com; tickets from £10) In terms of theatrical settings, the Minack takes top billing. Carved into the crags overlooking Porthcurno and the azure-blue Atlantic, this amazing clifftop amphitheatre

was the lifelong passion of theatre-lover Rowena Cade, who dreamt up the idea in the 1930s. It's now a hugely popular place for alfresco theatre, with plays staged from mid-May to mid-September.

**Porthcurno
Telegraph Museum**　　　　MUSEUM
(☑01736-810966; www.telegraphmuseum.org; adult/child £8.95/5; ⓣ10am-5pm) This fascinating museum charts the unlikely tale of Porthcurno's role in transatlantic telecommunications. In 1870 an underwater cable was laid here, which enabled telegraph messages to be sent as far away as Bombay in less than a minute. Over the next century, a total of 14 cables ran into Porthcurno, carrying a good chunk of Britain's global telecommunications. The telegraph station was decommissioned in 1970. The museum explores the story in imaginative ways, with interactive morse-code kits, vintage equipment, archive footage and so on.

Logan Rock　　　　NATURAL FEATURE
Perched on the end of the headland above Porthcurno, this massive boulder once famously rocked back and forth on its own natural pivot with only the slightest pressure; its name supposedly derives from the Cornish verb 'log', meaning 'to rock', used to denote the motion of a drunken man. It's been a tourist attraction since the 18th century, but the path out to it involves traversing narrow cliff paths and sheer drops, so it's better appreciated from a distance.

ⓘ Getting There & Away

Porthcurno is 3 miles from Land's End and 9 miles from Penzance. Bus 1/1A from Penzance stops here several times daily.

Sennen

Tucked into the arc of Whitesand Bay, Sennen Cove boasts Penwith's best surf and sand. With vivid blue waters and a mile of beach backed by dunes and marram grass, it's one of west Cornwall's most impressive bays.

There's not a great deal to the village itself save for the lifeboat station (in operation since 1853), a handful of shops, cafes and galleries and the venerable village pub. But when you've finished lazing about on the beach, Sennen makes a super spot for walks – the coast path allows access to several fabulous beaches nearby.

🏃 Activities

Sennen Surfing Centre   SURFING
(☑ 01736-871227; www.sennensurfingcentre.com; single lesson £30; ⊙ Apr-Oct) Learning to surf in the wild waves of west Cornwall isn't always easy, but it's a lot more fun than among the overcrowded waves of the north coast. This local outfit is friendly, approachable and experienced, and will have you standing upright in no time. There are discounts if you book multiple lessons; a one-on-one session costs £60.

✕ Eating

Ben Tunnicliffe Sennen Cove   BISTRO ££
(☑ 01736-871191; www.benatsennen.com; mains £12.50-17.25; ⊙ 10.30am-8.30pm) Renowned local chef Ben Tunnicliffe brings his skills to this beachside bistro, which boasts a glorious glass-walled balcony overlooking Sennen's shining sands. It's a considerable cut above your average beach food – think crab bisque, River Exe mussels and Indonesian seafood curry, plus a blackboard of fish specials. It's pricey, and gets very busy, but is usually worth the wait.

❶ Getting There & Away

Bus 1/1A travels from Penzance (£5, one hour, eight daily Monday to Friday, seven on Saturday, six on Sunday).

St Just-in-Penwith

☑ 01736 / POP 4812
The old granite village of St Just has been linked with mining and quarrying for centuries, but these days it's mainly known as a hub for artists, sculptors and creative types. It's a stout, stern village, hewn from stone and granite – look out for the village green, known as the Plen-an-Gwary, where 'mummers' plays' would have been staged during medieval times.

◎ Sights

★ Geevor Tin Mine   MINE
(☑ 01736-788662; www.geevor.com; adult/child £13.95/8; ⊙ 9am-5pm Sun-Fri Mar-Oct, to 4pm Nov-Feb) Just north of St Just near Pendeen, this historic mine closed in 1990 and now provides a powerful insight into the dark, dingy and dangerous conditions in which Cornwall's miners worked. Above ground, you can view the dressing floors and the original machinery used to sort the minerals and ores, before taking a guided tour into some of the underground shafts. Claustrophobes need not apply.

Levant Mine & Beam Engine   HISTORIC SITE
(www.nationaltrust.org.uk/levant-mine-and-beam-engine; adult/child £7.70/3.85; ⊙ 10.30am-5pm) At this clifftop site, one of the world's only working beam engines is still in thunderous action. Built in 1840, these great engines were the powerhouses behind the Cornish mining boom, powering mineral trains, running lifts down into the mine shafts, and pumping water from the underground tunnels. Closed in 1930, it's since been lovingly restored by a team of enthusiasts, and is a sight to behold when it's in full steam.

Cape Cornwall   LANDMARK
Jutting out from the cliffs near St Just is Cornwall's only cape, a craggy outcrop of land topped by an abandoned mine stack. Below the cape is the rocky beach of **Priest's Cove**, while nearby are the ruins of **St Helen's Oratory**, supposedly one of the first Christian chapels built in West Cornwall.

❶ Getting There & Away

St Just is 6 miles north of Land's End. Bus 10/10A (£5, hourly Monday to Saturday, six on Sunday) runs a circular route from Penzance via Madron, St Just and Botallack.

Zennor

☑ 01736 / POP 217
The B3306 coast road between St Ives and Zennor ventures into a wild corner of Cornwall, a long way from the prettified harbour towns and manicured beaches. This tiny village is set around the medieval Church of St Senara. Its main claim to fame is as the home of the legend of the Mermaid of Zennor, but

---

OLD SUCCESS INN

Owned by local beer barons St Austell Brewery, the venerable whitewashed pub **Old Success Inn** (☑ 01736-871232; www.oldsuccess.co.uk; Cove Hill, Sennen Cove; rooms £95-185; 🅿 🗊 🐾) dates from the 17th century, but it's looking 21st-century trendy these days. The 12 rooms offer 'contemporary coastal style' – sea views, nautical colours and bleached wood, plus in-room bathtubs in the suites. Grub is good too – try a shellfish platter, summer picnic board or whole lobster.

it has another literary connection too: the writer DH Lawrence sojourned here between 1915 and 1917, but his liberal habits and metropolitan tastes (not to mention a wild party or two) earned short shrift from the locals, and the writer was drummed out of the village as a suspected communist spy (an episode recounted in his novel *Kangaroo*).

Sights

Church of St Senara
CHURCH
This little church in the hamlet of Zennor dates from at least 1150. Inside, a famous carved chair depicts the legendary Mermaid of Zennor, who is said to have fallen in love with the singing voice of local lad Matthew Trewhella. Locals say you can still sometimes hear them singing down at nearby Pendour Cove – and even if you don't, the views along the coast path are reward enough.

Zennor Hill
NATURAL FEATURE
Looming high above the village, the hilltop above Zennor is littered with strange rock formations, runnels, hollows and stacks that are imbued with many myths and legends. The surrounding moors are also scattered with ancient tumuli, hut circles and a large dolmen, Zennor Quoit, suggesting the site was very important to ancient people.

It's a good target for a walk, although unsurprisingly it's pretty steep – but the view of the coast from the top is absolutely eye-popping.

Eating

Gurnard's Head
BRITISH ££
(01736-796928; www.gurnardshead.co.uk; near Zennor; mains £12-19.95, r £115-180; P🐾📶🍽) On the wonderful coast road between Zennor and St Just, you can't possibly miss the Gurnard's – its name is emblazoned on the roof. This is quite possibly the quintessential Cornish country pub, with wooden furniture, book-lined shelves and sepia prints conjuring a cosy, lived-in feel. It's also rightly renowned for its food – rich and sophisticated dishes fill the menu.

Tinner's Arms
PUB
(01736-796927; www.tinnersarms.com; mains £11-18; ⊗10am-11pm) The Tinner's may well be able to claim the title as Cornwall's oldest boozer; it's believed to have been built c 1271 by the masons who constructed the village church. It's a real beauty: whitewashed and slate-roofed, with a beamed main bar, a crackling fire, bench seats, and

thoroughly decent grub and ale. Local folk musicians play regularly.

Getting There & Away

Bus 17/17A (£5, half-hourly Monday to Saturday, hourly on Sunday) stops in Zennor en route from St Ives to Pendeen. The 16/16A round-robin bus between Penzance and St Ives also runs through Zennor a few times daily.

Penzance

01736 / POP 21,168
Overlooking the majestic sweep of Mount's Bay, the old harbour of Penzance has a salty, sea-blown charm that feels altogether more authentic than many of Cornwall's polished up ports. Its streets and shopping arcades still feel real and a touch ramshackle, and there's nowhere better for a windy-day walk than the town's seafront Victorian promenade.

Sights

Chapel Street
HISTORIC SITE
The cream of Penzance's heritage architecture can be seen along Chapel St, which is lined with a wealth of beautifully preserved Georgian buildings.

Exchange
GALLERY
(01736-363715; www.newlynartgallery.co.uk; Princes St; ⊗10am-5pm Mon-Sat Easter-Sep, Tue-Sat Oct-Easter) **FREE** Housed in Penzance's former telecoms building, this gallery hosts regular exhibitions of contemporary art. It's the sister gallery to the Newlyn Art Gallery (p221), a mile west along Penzance's prom.

Penlee House Gallery & Museum
GALLERY
(01736-363625; www.penleehouse.org.uk; Morrab Rd; adult/child £5/4; ⊗10am-5pm Mon-Sat Easter-Sep, 10.30am-4.30pm Mon-Sat Oct-Easter) Penzance's historic art gallery displays paintings by artists of the Newlyn School (including Stanhope Forbes and Lamorna Birch) and hosts regular exhibitions. The nearby Penlee Gardens are well worth a stroll.

Trengwainton
GARDENS
(NT; 01736-363148; trengwainton@nationaltrust.org.uk; Madron; adult/child £8.10/4.05; ⊗10.30am-5pm Sun-Thu mid-Feb–Nov) Two miles north of Penzance near Madron is the walled garden of Trengwainton, which has a subtropical collection of ferns, shrubs, magnolias and rhododendrons.

Tremenheere Sculpture Garden GARDENS
(☑01736-448089; www.tremenheere.co.uk; adult/
child £8/4.50; ⊙gardens 10am-5pm; 🎫) This
inventive garden opened just outside Penzance in 2012. The landscaped gardens sit in
a sheltered valley awash with artworks and
installations: look out for a 'sky-view' chamber by James Turrell; 'Black Mound', a pile of
tree stumps by David Nash; and a 'Camera
Obscura' by Billy Wynter, offering a unique
panorama of the gardens and Mount's Bay.

There's also a super cafe, Tremenheere
Kitchen (lunches £8 to £14), and family
events such as den-building and art workshops during school holidays.

🏃 Activities

⭐ **Jubilee Pool** SWIMMING
(☑01736-369224; www.jubileepool.co.uk; Western
Promenade Rd; adult/child £5/3.50; ⊙10.30am-
6pm, to 8pm Tue, early June-late Sep) After being
thoroughly battered during recent winter
storms, Penzance's glorious seawater lido
has reopened and regained its place as the
town's pride and joy. Built in 1935, it's a bold
statement of art-deco styling, sleek, sharp
and whitewashed – the perfect backdrop
for sea bathing in style. There's discounted
entry after 3.30pm (adult/child £3.15/2.50).

Polgoon WINERY
(☑01736-333946; www.polgoon.com; Rosehill,
Penzance) This up-and-coming vineyard just
outside Penzance is earning a sparkling
reputation for its rosés and whites, which
come in both still and bubbly varieties. It's
also recently added juices and ciders to its
range. Informative tours are offered at 2pm
from Wednesday to Friday, and cost £10 per
person.

🎊 Festivals & Events

Golowan Festival ART & CULTURE
(www.golowan.com; ⊙mid-late Jun) Ten days of
music, art and Cornish culture, plus a big
street parade on Mazey Day (mid-June).

Newlyn Fish Festival FOOD
(www.newlynfishfestival.org.uk; ⊙Aug) Newlyn
celebrates its piscatorial heritage at this festival, held over the August Bank Holiday.

🍴 Eating

Honey Pot CAFE £
(☑01736-368686; 5 Parade St; mains £5-12;
⊙9am-5pm Mon-Sat) For afternoon tea and
crumbly cakes, there's nowhere better in

OFF THE BEATEN TRACK

MADRON HOLY WELL

Down a muddy track lined by hawthorn
hedges, this natural spring has been
revered since ancient times, and its
waters are reputed to have magical and
healing properties. In bygone days people would come here to bathe in the waters, leaving behind a strip of cloth from
their clothing (known as a cloutie); it
was said that, as the rag deteriorated, so
would their affliction. The trees around
the well are still decorated with colourful
cloth strips and other offerings.

Near the well are the remains of a
12th-century chapel, supposedly built
on a much more ancient site of worship
(the well's name is believed to derive
from Modron, the Celtic goddess of
motherhood). You can just about make
out the chapel's old font and altar
half-buried in the undergrowth.

Madron is about 2 miles from Penzance; the track to the well begins in
the village.

Penzance than the Honey Pot, opposite the
Acorn Arts Centre. It attracts punters across
the Penzance spectrum, from arty types
supping cappuccinos to earth-mums tucking into fruit teas and homity (cheese) pie.
Naturally, nearly everything's homemade
and local.

Archie Brown's CAFE £
(☑01736-362828; Bread St; mains £7-10; ⊙9am-
5pm Mon-Sat; 🍴) 🌿 A much-loved veggie
cafe and health shop, serving quiches, homity pies and salads to Penzance's arty crowd.
Stock up on supplements, organic teas and
fair-trade chocolate downstairs, then head
up the stairs for soups, salads, frittatas and
other veggie-friendly mains.

⭐ **Shore** MODERN BRITISH ££
(☑01736-362444; www.theshorerestaurant.uk;
13/14 Alverton St; 2-/3-course lunch £19/23, dinner
mains £17.50-20; ⊙12.30-1.30pm Fri-Sat & 6.30-
9pm Tue-Sat) This brilliant seafood bistro is
overseen by chef Bruce Rennie, a veteran
of many a Michelin-starred kitchen. It's all
about classic fish and shellfish here, sourced
from the Newlyn day boats and served with
a strong French-Italian influence. Odds are
that this is the next address in Cornwall to
bag a Michelin star; get in while you can.

WEST CORNWALL & THE ISLES OF SCILLY PENZANCE

Penzance

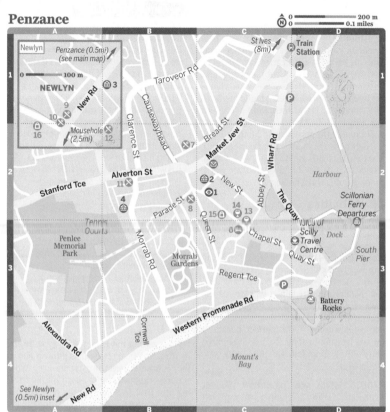

Cornish Barn BISTRO ££
(☑ 01736-365664; www.artistresidencecornwall.
co.uk/food-and-drink; 20 Chapel St; dishes £8-
16; ⊗ 8am-10pm) On the ground floor of the
Artist Residence Penzance (☑ 01736-
365664; www.arthotelcornwall.co.uk; 20 Chapel
St; d £130-190, deluxe ste from £310; ⃰), this
funky cafe-diner has become a firm favourite. Rough wood, bare bulbs and an outdoor
bar conjure the hipster vibe, and the menu
offers both tapas-style tasting plates (think
chilli-lime squid or parsnip rosti with goat's
cheese) and heartier dishes from the smoker
(think pulled pork ribs or beer-can chicken).

Coldstreamer Inn PUB FOOD ££
(☑ 01736-362072; www.coldstreamer-penzance.
co.uk; Gulval; mains £11-17.95; ⊗ from 10am) This
village inn in Gulval is a real corker. Chef-
patron Tom Penhaul has a strong local pedigree, and his stylish food has earned many
admirers, including a mention in the Michelin pub guide. It's traditionally decorated in-

side, with a choice of dining areas: main bar
or restaurant. Seafood is the cornerstone,
but there are tasty meat and veg options too.

🍷 Drinking & Nightlife

Admiral Benbow PUB
(☑ 01736-363448; 46 Chapel St; ⊗ 11am-11pm)
On historic Chapel St, the salty old Benbow
looks as if it's dropped from the pages of
Treasure Island, with nautical decor mostly
reclaimed from shipwrecks: anchors, lanterns, figureheads and all.

Turk's Head PUB
(☑ 01736-363093; Chapel St; ⊗ 11am-11pm) Pur-
portedly the town's oldest pub; there's been
a tavern here since the 13th century, and
it was supposedly a favourite hangout for
Penzance's 'free traders' (aka smugglers);
a subterranean tunnel once led straight to
the harbour from the cellar (now the dining
room). Skinner's and Sharp's ales on tap,

Penzance

and a seafood-dominated menu that features crab sandwiches and grilled lobster.

🛍 Shopping

★**Steckfensters**   VINTAGE
(☑ 01736-363545; 10 Chapel St; ⊙ 10am-5pm Mon-Sat) A real dig-and-delve treasure trove, overflowing with all kinds of bric-a-brac, vintage clothes, retro lamps, secondhand vinyl and other bits of who-knows-what ephemera. You could spend hours of happy browsing in here.

❶ Getting There & Away

AIR
Land's End Airport (http://www.landsendairport.co.uk/) is 5 miles from Penzance, and handles all flights to the Isles of Scilly.

BOAT
The Scillonian III (p230) to the Isles of Scilly leaves from Penzance harbour for St Mary's between April and September.

For bookings to the Isles of Scilly (both by air and by sea), contact the **Isles of Scilly Travel Centre** (☑ 0845 710 5555; www.islesofscilly-travel.co.uk; Quay St; ⊙ 8am-6.30pm Mon-Sat).

BUS
Buses depart from the **bus station** (Wharf Rd). Local destinations include the following:
Helston (bus 2/2A; £5, hourly Monday to Saturday, two hourly Sunday) Travels via Marazion and connects onwards to Falmouth.
St Ives (bus 17/17A/17B; £5, 30 minutes, half-hourly Monday to Saturday, hourly Sunday).

TRAIN
Penzance is the last stop on the line from London Paddington.
Truro £6.80, 30 minutes
St Ives £4.30, 50 minutes Change at St Erth.
Exeter £21, three hours
London Paddington £63.70, 5½ hours

Newlyn

☑ 01736 / POP 4432
Two miles along the Penzance promenade, the salty old harbour of Newlyn has weathered the storms in the wider fishing industry and clung on as Britain's busiest working port. It's a briny old town where trawlers and day boats bob in the harbour, and fishermen's stores and processing factories still occupy many of the harbour buildings.

The old Cornish staple, the pilchard, has recently received a rebrand as the 'Cornish sardine' in an effort to boost consumer appeal (it's not entirely sleight of hand: pilchards are in fact simply juvenile sardines). Although the town's last pilchard cannery closed in 2005, ending a tradition stretching back over three centuries, Newlyn still has many suppliers where you can pick up fish literally straight off the boats.

◎ Sights

Newlyn Art Gallery   GALLERY
(☑ 01736-363715; www.newlynartgallery.co.uk; New Rd; ⊙ 10am-5pm Mon-Sat Easter-Sep, Wed-Sat Oct-Easter) 🆓 On the edge of Newlyn, this historic gallery was founded in 1895 to display the work of the artists of the Newlyn School, but since 2007 the gallery's focus has been on contemporary art. There's usually a main exhibition dedicated to the work of one artist, showcased in the gallery's light-filled rooms. The upstairs cafe has wonderful bay views, too.

🍴 Eating

Mackerel Sky Seafood Bar   CAFE £
(☑ 01736-448982; www.mackerelskycafe.co.uk; New Rd; mains £6.50-8.50; ⊙ noon-3pm & 6-9pm

DON'T MISS

OLD COASTGUARD HOTEL

Run by the owners of the Gurnard's Head, the coastal beauty Old Coastguard Hotel (☑ 01736-731222; www.old coastguardhotel.co.uk; The Parade, Mousehole; d £140-225; P 🛜 🐾) has a much more relaxed atmosphere than it used to. Rooms are still classic – restrained colour schemes, stately beds – and the best ones obviously have a sea view. Seafood takes prominence in the sea-view restaurant (mains £13.50 to £18.50), and there's a cliff garden for soaking up the rays. There are also some good deals for room-and-dinner stays.

The Old Coastguard is located in Mousehole, 20 minutes' drive from Penzance.

Tue-Sun) Small but perfectly formed, this cute little cafe sits a stone's throw from the harbour, on the humpbacked bridge. It's a bright, airy spot for tucking into fishy snacks – mackerel pâté on hot toast, scallops in herby butter or an excellent crab ciabatta sandwich. No bookings.

Jelbert's Ices ICE CREAM £

(2 New Rd, Newlyn; ⊙ 10am-3pm Mon-Sat) This traditional ice-cream maker still does things the old-fashioned way. There's only one flavour (vanilla), made with Cornish clotted cream and served in old-school wafer cones. You won't need a flake; it's yummy enough as is.

★ Tolcarne Inn PUB FOOD ££

(☑ 01736-363074; www.tolcarneinn.co.uk; Tolcarne Pl; mains £15-22; ⊙ noon-2.15pm & 7-9pm Tue-Sat, noon-2.15pm Sun) This Newlyn inn is run by chef Ben Tunnicliffe, a long-standing name on the Cornish dining scene. The ethos here is refreshingly honest – top-quality fish, seafood and locally sourced meat, served with minimal fuss. It's a snug space, full of smuggler's pub charm – blackboard menus, whitewashed walls and views of the harbour. Bookings advisable, especially for Sunday lunch.

🛍 Shopping

★ W Harvey & Sons FOOD

(☑ 01736-362983; www.crabmeat.co.uk; The Coombe, Newlyn; ⊙ 8am-4.45pm Mon-Fri, 8am-11.45am Sat) If it's fresh crab and lobster you're after, this wharf warehouse is the best place in Cornwall – you can buy unpicked whole hens and cocks or, if you'd rather avoid the hard work, there are prepackaged sachets of dressed white and dark meat, too. Depending on the season, you can also pick up mussels, anchovies, crevettes and more.

It's always worth phoning ahead to check what is in stock.

PJ Tonkin & Co FOOD

(☑ 01736-360779; www.fresh-cornish-fish.co.uk; 38-40 The Strand; ⊙ 9am-3pm Mon-Fri) A reliable all-round Newlyn fish merchant, with stocks of whatever happens to have been landed off the boats that day – dover sole, lemon sole, hake, pollack and more besides. It also offers fish selection boxes if you can't choose.

ⓘ Getting There & Away

Bus 1/1A stops in Newlyn on its way from Penzance (10 minutes, every two hours Monday to Saturday, four on Sunday) to Land's End.

Mousehole

☑ 01736 / POP 697

With a tight tangle of cottages and alleyways gathered behind the granite breakwater, Mousehole (pronounced *mowzle*) looks like something from a children's storybook (a fact not unnoticed by author Antonia Barber, who set her much-loved fairy tale *The Mousehole Cat* here). In centuries past this was Cornwall's busiest pilchard port, but the fish dried up in the late 19th century, and the village now survives mostly on tourist traffic. Packed in summer and deserted in winter (Mousehole is renowned for its high proportion of second homes), it's ripe for a wander, with a maze of slips, net lofts and courtyards.

🍴 Eating

2 Fore St FRENCH ££

(☑ 01736-731164; www.2forestreet.co.uk; Fore St; dinner mains £14.25-18; ⊙ noon-2pm & 7-9pm) Not in the very top rank of Cornwall's bistros perhaps, but a deeply pleasant place to dine, nonetheless. This laid-back bistro is squeezed into a small space along Mousehole's backstreets, and majors on French-inspired classics – unsurprising, given the head chef trained under Raymond Blanc. There's a small dining room, a sweet garden and a locally focused menu strong on seafood.

♀ Drinking & Nightlife

Ship Inn PUB

(☑ 01736-731234; www.shipmousehole.co.uk; South Cliff; ⊙ 10am-11pm) The old Ship dates (at least in parts) back to the 1700s and has lashings of period charm, with hefty fireplaces and leaded glass windows (double room £80 to £120). Food is standard pub grub – steak pie, veggie chilli (mains £9.95 to £15.95).

❶ Getting There & Away

Bus 6/6A makes the 20-minute journey along the seafront to Penzance (£3, half-hourly), stopping in Newlyn along the way.

Marazion

☑ 01736 / POP 1440

Little Marazion is a pretty seaside village lined with seafront houses and Victorian villas with a truly epic view across Mount's Bay. A couple of miles east along the coast from Penzance, past the sandy curve of Long Rock, Marazion is a friendly, arty little town, with a smattering of galleries and cafes along the main street, but the main site of interest is quite impossible to miss – the rocky island-topped abbey that dominates the skyline out to sea, and is otherwise known as St Michael's Mount.

◎ Sights

★ **St Michael's Mount** LANDMARK

(NT; ☑ 01736-710507; www.stmichaelsmount. co.uk; house & gardens adult/child £14/6.50; ⊙ house 10.30am-5.30pm Sun-Fri Jul-Sep, 10.30am-5pm Mar-Jun & Oct) Looming up in the middle of Mount's Bay and connected to the mainland at Marazion via a cobbled causeway, this abbey-crowned island is an unforgettable sight, and one of Cornwall's most iconic images. Initially a Benedictine monastery, and later the seat of the St Aubyn family, it's a must-visit. You can catch the ferry (adult/child £2/1) from Marazion at high tide, but it's worth arriving at low tide so you can walk across the causeway, as pilgrims did centuries ago.

✗ Eating

★ **Ben's Cornish Kitchen** BRITISH ££

(☑ 01736-719200; www.benscornishkitchen.com; Marazion; 2-/3-course dinner £27/33; ⊙ noon-1.30pm & 7-8.30pm Tue-Sat; ☑) Blink and you'll miss Ben Prior's restaurant as you zip along Marazion's main street, but diners travel from far and wide to taste his superlative cooking, which majors in meaty Cornish flavours with a French influence. Ben's cooking has earned glowing reviews, and awards from Waitrose, *The Good Food Guide* and the *Trencherman's Guide*, so tables are scarce – book ahead.

❶ Getting There & Away

Bus 2 trundles through Marazion from Penzance (14 minutes, hourly Monday to Saturday, six on Sunday) before continuing on to Helston (45 minutes). A few buses also continue onwards to Falmouth.

THE LIZARD

Cornwall's southern coastline takes a sudden wild turn around the Lizard Peninsula, where fields and heaths plunge into a melee of black cliffs, churning surf and saw-tooth rocks. Cut off from the rest of Cornwall by the River Helford, and ringed by treacherous seas, the Lizard was once an ill-famed graveyard for ships, and the peninsula still has a raw, untamed edge. Wind-lashed in winter, in summer its clifftops blaze with wildflowers, and its beaches and coves are perfect for a bracing wild swim.

It's also a stronghold for the Cornish chough, the red-billed, crow-like bird which features on the county's coat-of-arms. Once

ART COURSES IN PENWITH

Two local art schools offer a range of painting and sculpture courses if you feel inspired to explore your inner artist. The **Newlyn School of Art** (☑ 01736-365557; www.newlynartschool. co.uk; Chywoone Hill) offers everything from experimental landscape painting to screen printing – and the roster of tutors reads like a *Who's Who* of the Cornish art scene. The **St Ives School of Painting** (☑ 01736-797180; www. schoolofpainting.co.uk; workshops from £40) overlooks Porthmeor Beach, and has been offering artistic training since 1938. Courses focus mainly on painting in watercolour, gouache, oils and other media, covering everything from landscapes to life drawing. There are short two-hour workshops, plus longer courses lasting from two to six days.

Historic Southwest

The southwest packs nearly 5000 years of history into its rugged landscapes. From strange quoits and stone circles left behind by neolithic people to a catalogue of castles, churches and country houses, it's a place where the past is never too far away.

1. Tintagel Castle (p188)
The supposed birthplace of King Arthur, part of Tintagel Castle stands on a rock tower known as 'The Island'.

2. Lanyon Quoit (p214)
This classic example of a quoit (a table-like structure) is thought to have marked an ancient burial site.

3. Merrivale Stone Rows (p118)
Merrivale is a one-stop shop for prehistoric monuments.

4. Buckland Abbey (p112)
Founded in the 13th century, Buckland Abbey houses Drake's Drum (said to beat by itself when Britain is in danger of being invaded).

OFF THE BEATEN TRACK

THE LOE

A mile south of Helston is Loe Pool, Cornwall's largest freshwater lake, said by some to be the resting place of King Arthur's magical blade, Excalibur. It's cut off from the sea by the treacherous sandbank of Loe Bar – scene of many a shipwreck down the centuries. Walking trails wind their way around the lakeshore and the surrounding Penrose Estate, but swimming is dangerous due to unpredictable rip currents.

all but extinct, it's slowly re-establishing itself around the Lizard's rugged cliffs.

You may catch sight of slow worms and even an adder here in summer, but the peninsula's peculiar name actually has no reptilian connections; it comes from the old Celtic words 'lys ardh', meaning 'high court'.

Helston

☏ 01326

The Lizard's main town is Helston, which started life as a bustling river port and one of the county's stannary towns, where local tin was assayed and stamped. The town received another lease of life with the arrival of the naval airbase at Culdrose, which hosts a popular annual air-display day in late July.

It's a sleepy, traditional little town, with a couple of pleasant cafes and pubs to while away a few hours. It's also handy for supplies if you're venturing deeper onto the Lizard.

◉ Sights

★Godolphin   HOUSE

(NT; ☏01736-763194; www.nationaltrust.org.uk/godolphin; adult/child house & garden £8.10/4.05, garden only £6.80/3.60; ☉house 10am-5pm Mon-Thu, garden 10am-5pm daily) This wonderful medieval house and garden was the family seat of the Godolphin family who, during the 17th and 18th centuries, were one of Cornwall's great mining dynasties. The main house is still undergoing restoration by the National Trust: tours of the interior run on most days (check ahead), but the wider estate can be explored on your own. With acres of woodland, riverside walks and lawns to roam, it's hard to think of a more tranquil place for a stroll.

Helston Folk Museum   MUSEUM

(☏01326-564027; Market Pl; ☉10am-1pm Mon-Sat) FREE There's plenty of background on the Furry Dance at the town's quirky museum, where the displays include replica shopfronts, a 5-tonne cider press and a display on local hero Bob Fitzsimmons, the first man to simultaneously hold the world titles for middleweight, light heavyweight and heavyweight boxing.

✰ Festivals & Events

Flora Day   PARADE

(☉8 May) The biggest day of the year in Helston, this peculiar street parade is believed to derive from a pagan celebration marking the coming of spring. It's a mix of street dance, musical parade and floral pageant: the town is always packed, so arrive as early as possible.

The two main events of the day are the Hal-An-Tow, in which St Michael and the devil do battle; and the Furry Dance, which kicks off at noon and proceeds around the town's streets (participants take part by invitation only, and the dance is always led by a local couple).

☙ Drinking & Nightlife

Blue Anchor   PUB

(☏01326-562821; www.spingoales.com; 50 Coinagehall St; ☉10am-midnight) If it's brass taps, old tables and banter you like from your pub, then you'll be right at home at the Anchor. It's a local favourite, and brews its own Spingo beer – the traditional fuel for Flora Day. There's also a small skittle alley out the back.

❶ Getting There & Away

Helston is the main bus hub for getting to and from the Lizard, serving the following destinations:

Penzance Bus 2/2A (£6, hourly Monday to Saturday, six on Sunday), stopping at Porthleven and Marazion on the way.

Falmouth Bus 2/2A (£5, seven Monday to Friday, six on Saturday).

Truro Bus 36 (£6, five daily Monday to Saturday, three on Sunday). In the opposite direction, the same bus also runs to St Keverne and Lizard Point, but only from Monday to Friday.

Lizard Point Bus 37 (£5, hourly Monday to Saturday, five on Sunday), stopping at Mullion on the way.

Redruth Bus 37 (£5, hourly Monday to Saturday, five on Sunday).

Porthleven

📞 01326 / POP 3190

Three miles southwest of Helston is Porthleven, a small port set around the massive walls of its stone quay, built to shelter the harbour from winter storms. It's a town with a fast-growing foodie scene that has led many to claim it's set to become the south coast's version of Padstow (a claim that looks to have been underlined since Rick Stein installed one of his franchise restaurants along the quay). There's a big annual food festival, held every year in April, but it's a pretty place to visit at any time of year.

✦ Festivals & Events

⭐ **Porthleven Food Festival**   FOOD & DRINK
(www.porthlevenfoodfestival.com; ⊘ Apr) This yearly food fair runs over three days in late April, and attracts big-name chefs to town for cooking demonstrations and talks, along with some 30,000 peckish punters. Many of the county's top producers also display their wares along the quayside.

✖ Eating

⭐ **Kota**   INTERNATIONAL ££
(📞 01326-562407;   www.kotarestaurant.co.uk; 2-/3-course menu £20/25, mains £14-22; ⊘ 6-9pm Tue-Sat) Half Maori, half Chinese-Malay, chef Jude Kereama takes his culinary inspiration from his globetrotting travels, and his menu is spiced with exotic flavours, from Szechuan to Thai and Malaysian. This is seriously fine dining – dishes are impeccably presented and sizzle with unusual flavour combinations, and the setting inside a converted mill has tons of charm. Staff are efficient and friendly, too.

Kota Kai   CAFE ££
(📞 01326-574411; www.kotakai.co.uk; mains £8-19; ⊘ noon-2pm Thu-Tue, 5.30-9.30pm Mon-Sat; 📶) On the 1st floor of a quaysider, this zingy cafe is chef Jude Kereama's second restaurant in Porthleven. It's a more relaxed affair, but still showcases his taste for spicy, exotic dishes: laksa curry, tom yum soup, five-spiced squid. The dining room is full of light, and the picture-window views over the quay are super.

Amélie's   BRITISH ££
(📞 01326-554000; www.ameliesporthleven.co.uk; mains £11-18; ⊘ 10.30am-9pm) This popular harbourside hang-out has a little bit of everything: pizzas, burgers, sharing platters (known here as 'planks') and plenty of seafood. It's a pleasant space in which to dine: a big, high blue shack with bench seats and a covered patio on the side. The food is fairly simple, and doesn't always live up to the prices, though.

❶ Getting There & Away

Bus 2 (13 minutes, hourly Monday to Saturday, six on Sunday) runs down into Porthleven on its way from Helston to Marazion (30 minutes) and Penzance (40 minutes).

Gunwalloe

This remote village on the edge of the Lizard Peninsula is a great spot to feel far from the crowds, especially on a foggy day in winter, when it feels like the ends of the earth. It's sited at the southern end of Loe Bar, which terminates in the hulking 60m mass of Halzephron Cliff. A little way south is the pretty Church Cove, named after the medieval church of St Winwaloe half-buried in the sand. It's also home to a large golf course.

✖ Eating

Halzephron Inn   PUB FOOD ££
(📞 01326-240406;   www.halzephron-inn.co.uk; mains £10-22; ⊘ 11am-11pm) On the cliffs above the cove of Gunwalloe, 5 miles south of Helston, this is a historic Cornish local, whitewashed and slate-topped, with brassy trinkets above the bar, stout beams and a menu of beer-battered fish, grilled gammon steak, duck breast and the like. It's cosy and stone-walled, with lots of nooks and crannies, and a small patio outside.

Mullion

📞 01326 / POP 2114

Tucked away on the Lizard's west side is the friendly old fishing village of Mullion, which is pretty much the only hamlet of note on this side of the coast before you reach Lizard Point. It's a tiny place, but worth a morning wander – the best idea is to stock up with supplies at the village shop, go for a paddle down by the town harbour, then set out for the pretty beaches of Polurrian and Poldhu to the north.

⊙ Sights

Predannack Wollas   VIEWPOINT

Mullion's beaches are inevitably busy in summer, so if you're after a bit of solitude then you're best off hiking south along the coast path from Mullion Cove along this dramatic expanse of windy, wild clifftops. It's full of scenic drama, and good for spotting seabirds, and you're likely to have it pretty much to yourself.

Poldhu Cove   BEACH

A west-facing beach bordered by gently sloping fields, this is a family-friendly stretch of sand that's easily reached from Mullion, which means you won't be alone here. There's plenty of space at low tide, offering ample opportunity for sandcastles and sunbathing, and the swimming is generally very safe. There's also a very good beach cafe.

Poldhu's other claim to fame is as the site of the world's first ever radio transmission, sent from Poldhu Point across 2000 miles of the Atlantic to St John's in Newfoundland by Italian engineer Guglielmo Marconi in 1901. A plaque on the clifftop marks the site of the original transmission station.

Goonhilly Downs   WILDLIFE RESERVE

Across the centre of the Lizard sprawls the barren Goonhilly Downs, a flat, grassy heathland which – rather improbably – also happens to be home to one of the UK's largest satellite stations. Not too long ago, these massive dishes (all named after Arthurian characters) transmitted a fair proportion of

---

ROSKILLYS FARM

Just outside the village of St Keverne, Roskillys Farm (☑ 01326-280479; www. roskillys.co.uk; lunch mains £6-10; ⊙10am-7pm) produces some of Cornwall's most delicious ice cream, in flavours like ginger fairing, golden fudge and cream tea. It's a lovely spot to spend an afternoon: there are walking trails to wander, and you can watch the cows being milked, followed by lunch at the Croust House cafe. In summer, the farm stays open till 9pm and serves wood-fired pizzas from its outdoor oven. The farm is at Tregallast Barton, about a mile south of St Keverne.

---

the UK's satellite traffic, but the dishes were decommissioned by owners British Telecom in 2010, and now their future is uncertain.

The area of heathland around the satellite station is an important SSSI (Site of Special Scientific Interest), and an excellent spot to see rare butterflies, slow-worms and even the occasional adder in summer.

✕ Eating

Poldhu Beach Cafe   CAFE £

(☑ 01326-240530; www.poldhu.com; Poldhu Cove; lunch mains £4-7.50; ⊙9.30-5pm or 6pm Apr-Oct, 9.30am-4pm Nov-Mar) If you're peckish after a swim or a hike, this charming beach cafe will come as a welcome break. There's a limited menu – veggie or full English breakfasts, bacon baps and smoked salmon bagels, plus burgers or ciabatta melts for lunch – but they're extremely generous and will keep you well fuelled for the day's activities.

❶ Getting There & Away

Bus 37 (£5, eight daily Monday to Saturday, five on Sunday) stops in the village en route from Helston to Lizard Point.

Lizard Point

Five miles south from Mullion, the British mainland reaches its southernmost tip at Lizard Point, historically one of Britain's deadliest headlands. Hundreds of ships have come to grief around the point itself or the many submerged reefs over the centuries, from Spanish treasure galleons to naval frigates. It's a mecca for scuba divers, as well as coastal walkers who flock to the clifftops to bask in the majestic coastal scenery.

With its conglomeration of fudge-sellers and souvenir shops, Lizard village makes a pretty disappointing gateway, so most people just park in the village and take the mile-long stroll down to the point itself.

⊙ Sights

★ Kynance Cove   BEACH

A mile north of Lizard Point, this National Trust-owned inlet is an absolute show-stopper, studded with craggy offshore islands rising out of searingly blue seas that seem almost tropical in colour. The cliffs around the cove are rich in serpentine, a red-green rock popular with Victorian trinket-makers. It's an impossibly beautiful spot and, when the seas aren't too rough, an exhilarating place for a wild swim. Drinks and snacks are available at the eco-friendly beach cafe.

The island opposite the cove is called **Asparagus Island**, as wild asparagus can be foraged here in spring and summer.

Lizard Point   NATURAL FEATURE
Trekking out to Lizard Point is a fine way to while away an hour or two. A trail leads here from the village, past the lighthouse to the point itself, where another steep track winds down to the long-disused lifeboat station and shingly cove. At the time of writing, a landslip meant that the cove path had been closed for public access, so you might just have to admire the view from the cliffs instead.

Lizard Lighthouse
Heritage Centre   MUSEUM
(☑ 01326-290202; www.lizardlighthouse.co.uk; adult/child £3.50/2.50; ☺ 11am-5pm Sun-Thu Mar-Oct) Rising above Lizard Point, the white-washed lighthouse was built in 1751 and has protected ships from the treacherous rocks ever since. Although it's now automated, like all the UK's lighthouses, you can still visit the heritage centre to learn more about its mechanics and the many ships that have come to grief nearby. It's also the only lighthouse in Cornwall you can actually climb; guided tours (adult/child £8.50/5) ascend into the tower to see the lamp room and foghorn.

Cadgwith   VILLAGE
This titchy village is truly a postcard come to life. With its idyllic huddle of thatched houses and fishermen's cottages, set at the foot of a lung-bustingly steep hill, it's many people's ideal picture of what a Cornish fishing village should look like. But it's not just for show: fishing boats still run out from the cove in pursuit of local crabs and lobsters, and you'll see their pots piled up beside the village beach.

There's a car park halfway down the hill, but spaces are limited, so it's best to arrive early. Whatever you do, don't head on blindly into the village in search of a space – there aren't any, and you'll probably end up scraping the side of your car on the fiendishly narrow lanes.

 Eating

⭐ **Ann's Pasties**   BAKERY £
(☑ 01326-290889; Beacon Tce; pasties from £3.50; ☺ 9am-5pm) Are Ann Muller's pasties the best in Cornwall? Well, according to Rick Stein they are – and judging by the queues stretching out the door at lunchtime, locals seem to agree. Traditionally made and prodigiously sized, these pasties are nigh-on perfect – there's a classic meat and even a (delicious) vegan version.

Kynance Cove
Cafe   CAFE
(☑ 01326-290436; www.kynancecovecafe.co.uk; mains £5-14; ☺ 9am-5.30pm) There can be few beachside cafes in Cornwall – or Britain, for that matter – with a finer location than this one, huddled among the rocks on the edge of Kynance Cove. For lunch you'll find pasties, crab sandwiches and burgers, chased down with classic cream teas and yummy cakes, all best savoured at one of the outside picnic tables.

Cadgwith Cove Inn   PUB FOOD ££
(☑ 01326-290513; www.cadgwithcoveinn.com; mains £8-16; ☺ 11am-11pm) Cadgwith's fishermen have been congregating in this thatched pub since time immemorial, and if you're lucky you might be treated to a traditional sea shanty or two if the boys are in the mood. If not, you'll just have to soak up the pub's low-ceilinged atmosphere, or sup a pint of Otter or Sharp's ale.

ℹ **Getting There & Away**
Bus 37 (£5, hourly Monday to Saturday, five on Sunday) runs from Helston to Lizard Point, stopping at Mullion on the way.

The Helford

Flowing along the Lizard's northern edge, lined with overhanging oaks and hidden creeks, the Helford River feels far removed from the rest of the Lizard peninsula. There are few corners of Cornwall which have remained as naturally unspoilt, and it's a haven for marine wildlife, as well as one of Cornwall's last remaining oyster fisheries at Porth Navas. Trails wind along the riverbanks, including one to the inlet of Frenchman's Creek, made famous by Daphne du Maurier's classic smuggling tale.

◉ Sights

Helford Village VILLAGE

If you were to sit down and design the perfect riverside village from scratch, chances are you'd come up with something pretty close to Helford. It's a winning combination of old cottages, quiet lanes, river views, old woodland and bobbing boats. There's nothing much to see – it's just a place to sit and soak up the vibe.

Frenchman's Creek RIVER

This famous creek is an easy walk from Helford village, but it's much more evocative to explore by kayak or rowboat. Fringed by overhanging trees and small muddy beaches, the creek gets its name from smuggling days – the secluded creeks round the Helford were perfect for stashing goods smuggled in from France (especially brandy, tobacco and lace) to avoid customs duties.

✕ Eating

★ New Yard BISTRO ££

(☑ 01326-221595; www.newyardrestaurant.co.uk; 2-/3-course lunch £14.50/18.85, dinner mains £14-24; ⊙ 8.30-12.30pm daily & 6.30-9.30pm Mon-Sat) Run by a new chef, Jeff Robinson, this upmarket bistro on the Trelowarren Estate is passionate about local sourcing: fish comes from a Cadgwith boat, meat is from Warrens in Launceston, and most veg is grown on the estate. The converted barn space is light and airy, and the food bang on trend – artfully presented and flavoured with foraged ingredients.

★ Shipwright Arms PUB FOOD ££

(☑ 01326-231235; www.shipwrighthelford.co.uk; Helford; mains £9-18; ⊙ 11am-11pm) Thatched on top, beamed inside, with to-die-for river views, the Helford's waterfront pub is a riverside beauty. Nautical knick-knacks adorn the bar, and there are outside tables right on the water. It's hard to think of a more idyllic place for an afternoon pint, and the menu's tempting too: local fishermen supply crab, lobster, monkfish, mussels, mackerel and more besides.

❶ Getting There & Away

There's no useful public transport to this remote part of the Lizard, but you can catch the **Helford Ferry** (p165) over from the river's northern bank.

ISLES OF SCILLY

While only 28 miles west of the mainland, in many ways the Isles of Scilly feels like a different world. Life on this archipelago of around 140 tiny islands seems hardly to have changed in decades: there are no traffic jams, no supermarkets, no multinational hotels, and the only noise pollution comes from breaking waves and cawing gulls. That's not to say that Scilly is behind the times – you'll find a mobile phone signal and broadband internet on the main islands – but life ticks along at its own island pace. Renowned for its glorious beaches, there are few places better to escape.

Only five islands are inhabited: St Mary's is the largest, followed by Tresco, while only a few hardy souls remain on Bryher, St Martin's and St Agnes. Regular ferry boats run between all five islands.

Unsurprisingly, summer is by far the busiest time. Many businesses shut down completely in winter.

❶ Getting There & Away

Bookings for flights and ferries are handled by the Isles of Scilly Travel Centre (p221) in Penzance. There's also a small enquiries office (p233) in Hugh Town on St Mary's.

Bad weather and fog often play havoc with the islands' travel schedules, so it's worth checking on the latest status before you set out – the Ios Travel Twitter account is very useful (@IoSTravel).

AIR

Isles of Scilly Skybus (☑ 01736-334220; www.islesofscilly-travel.co.uk) provides the air link to the islands from Land's End and Newquay, which runs from Monday to Saturday, weather permitting. Planes land at **St Mary's Airport** (ISC; ☑ 01720-424330; www.scilly.gov.uk), about a mile east of Hugh Town. Bus transfers connect with every flight. The flight time is just 20 minutes.

Note that flights are often cancelled during bad weather.

BOAT

The cheapest – and slowest – way to reach the islands is aboard the **Scillonian III** (☑ 0845 710 5555; www.islesofscilly-travel.co.uk; ⊙ Apr-Oct) passenger ferry from Penzance to St Mary's, but be prepared for a rough ride in choppy weather. The ferry service only runs between April and October. The crossing takes about three hours.

There's also boats to the other islands with the St Mary's Boatmen's Association (p233).

Isles of Scilly

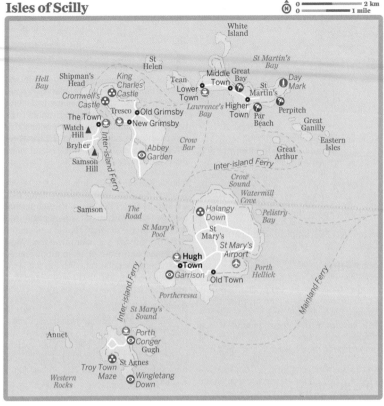

DAY TRIPS

Special day-trip fares (£105) allow you to fly out to the islands early from Land's End Airport, and return on the last flight home (generally around 5pm or 6pm depending on the time of year).

You can also choose a fly-sail combo ticket (£72) which works out cheaper, but the last ferry of the day usually departs at 4.30pm.

St Mary's

☑ 01720 / POP 2200

First stop for every visitor to Scilly (unless you're arriving aboard your own private yacht) is St Mary's, the largest and busiest of the islands, and home to the vast majority of hotels, shops, restaurants and B&Bs. Just over 3 miles at its widest point, St Mary's is shaped like a crooked circle, with a claw-shaped peninsula at its southwestern edge – home to the island's capital, Hugh Town, and the docking point for the Scillonian ferry. The main airport is a mile east near Old Town.

⊙ Sights

Isles of Scilly Museum　　　　　　MUSEUM

(☑ 01720-422337; www.iosmuseum.org; Church St, Hugh Town; adult/child £3.50/1; ⊙ 10am-4.30pm Mon-Fri, 10am-noon Sat Easter-Sep, 10am-noon Mon-Sat Oct-Easter) The small Isles of Scilly Museum explores the islands' history, with an eclectic mix of archaeological finds and artefacts from shipwrecks. Among the collection are Neolithic remains such as tools and jewellery, clay pipes left behind by generations of sailors, a couple of sailing boats and a small exhibition on Ted Heath, the British prime minister who loved Scilly so much he was buried here.

Porthcressa　　　　　　　　　　BEACH

For many day-trippers to St Mary's, Hugh Town's big, sandy, south-facing beach is as far as they ever explore – and it's hard to blame them. It's a fine beach, good for sunbathing and swimming, and close to all the facilities you could wish for – although obviously it's a busy old place in summer.

Pelistry Bay
BEACH

A secluded beach on the east side of St Mary's, accessible from the coast path. It's generally quieter than the island's other beaches, and has a mix of rock pools and sand to explore, as well as little Toll's Island just offshore.

Halangy Down
ARCHAEOLOGICAL SITE

While Neolithic settlers probably only visited Scilly sporadically, by the Iron Age settlers had arrived on Scilly and made a life here, ekeing out a living by fishing and farming. The remains of one of their villages can still be seen on the edge of Halangy Down, consisting of one large courtyard house and several smaller roundhouses dating from around 200 BC, complete with hearths and exterior walls.

Bant's Carn
ARCHAEOLOGICAL SITE

(EH) One of the best-preserved Neolithic chamber tombs in the Scilly Islands, on the northwest side of the island on the edge of Halangy Down. It's still largely in its original form, covered with a grassy mound, with a hobbit-sized entrance – and an interesting comparison to the exposed tombs you'll find on the mainland around the Penwith Peninsula. It dates from between 3000 and 4500 BC, and was probably the burial site of an important chieftain or notable family.

🏃 Activities

Book a Bike
CYCLING

(☑ 01720-422661; www.bookabikeonscilly.co.uk; adult/child £12.50/8 per day) Cycling is the best way to explore St Mary's. You can circumnavigate the island in about four hours. This company (also called St Mary's Bike Hire) allows you to pre-book your bikes, and offers daily and weekly rates.

Island Wildlife Tours
WALKING

(☑ 01720-422212; www.islandwildlifetours.co.uk; half-/full day £6/12) Regular birdwatching and wildlife walks with local character and resident twitcher Will Wagstaff, the undisputed authority on Scilly's natural history. Most tours start at 9.45am or 10am on St Mary's, but there are regular tours on other islands too; you need to add on the cost of the boat transfer.

Scilly Walks
WALKING

(☑ 01720-423326; www.scillywalks.co.uk; adult/child £6/3) Three-hour archaeological and historical tours of St Mary's, plus regular guided walking trips to other islands, conducted by local historian and archaeologist Katherine Sawyer.

Island Sea Safaris
BOATING

(☑ 01720-422732; www.islandseasafaris.co.uk) Trips to see local seabird and seal colonies (adult/child £34/25), plus one-hour 'island taster' tours (£25 per person). Also rents wetsuits and snorkelling gear.

🍴 Eating

Juliet's Garden Restaurant
BISTRO ££

(☑ 01720-422228; www.julietsgardenrestaurant. co.uk; lunch mains £7-15, dinner mains £14-24.95; ⊙ lunch noon-4pm, dinner 6-9pm) St Mary's long-standing bistro, in business for three decades, is still the best place to eat. It's in a converted barn 15 minutes' walk from town: expect gourmet salads and sandwiches by day, plus classier plates of pan-roasted bream, slow-roast lamb and lobster after dark, served by candlelight. The garden is glorious on a sunny day, but it gets busy.

Dibble & Grub
CAFE ££

(☑ 01720-423719; www.dibbleandgrub.com; lunch £6-12, dinner £10-16; ⊙ 10am-10pm Apr-

---

GIG ROWING

The six-oared wooden boats known as pilot gigs were once a common sight around Cornwall's shores, used for transporting goods and passengers from tall ships too large to moor in the shallow coastal harbours. These days the boats are used for gig racing, a highly competitive and physically demanding sport. Every April or May St Mary's hosts the World Pilot Gig Championships (www.worldgigs.co.uk; ⊙ late April or early May), the largest gig-rowing event in the world.

Teams come to the islands from as far afield as the Netherlands, Canada and Australia: there's not a bed to be found during the championships, so book well ahead if you want to attend.

Even if you're not here for the championships, you'll often spot local teams practising in the waters around St Mary's. Organised races are held most weekends.

Sep) Smart beachside cafe beside Porth-cressa, housed in the island's old fire station. The menu dabbles in tapas and Mediterranean-style classics.

Kaffeehaus Salbei   CAFE **£**
(☑ 01720-422440; www.scillyguesthouse.co.uk/kaffeehaus; Sage House, High Lanes; £4-7; ☺ 11am-5pm Mar-Oct) A little slice of Germany on Scilly courtesy of owner Sabine, who runs this coffee shop at her guesthouse. She serves traditional Teutonic treats such as rye bread, würst, cold meats and hearty soups, followed by a prodigious line-up of sweet cakes. The coffee and meats are both sourced from small-scale suppliers in the motherland.

ℹ Information

Isles of Scilly Tourist Information Centre
(☑ 01720-424031; www.visitislesofscilly.com; Porthcressa Beach, St Mary's; ☺ 9am-5.30pm Mon-Sat, 9am-2pm Sun Mar-Oct, 10am-2pm Mon-Fri Nov-Feb) The islands' only tourist office.

IoS Travel Enquiries Office (☑ 01720-424220; www.islesofscilly-travel.co.uk; Hugh St) This small enquiries office handles travel to/from the islands (the main travel centre is in Penzance). It handles bookings for the *Scillonian III* ferry, and also coordinates flights. In periods of bad weather when planes are grounded, most customers will be shifted to the next ferry service (assuming it's not already too late in the day).

ℹ Getting There & Away

St Mary's is the main transport hub for the islands. Flights from Land's End Airport, Newquay and Exeter land at St Mary's Airport (p230), about a mile east of Hugh Town.

The island ferry service from Penzance, the Scillonian III (p230), docks in Hugh Town, where you'll also be able to catch boats to the five other inhabited islands with the St Mary's Boatmen's Association.

ℹ Getting Around

BOAT
St Mary's Boatmen's Association (☑ 01720-423999; www.scillyboating.co.uk) The association co-ordinates the ferries that shuttle between St Mary's and the smaller islands surrounding it. Services run at least daily between April and October, leaving St Mary's in the morning and returning in the afternoon. Adult/child returns cost £9.00/4.50 direct to any island, or £15/7.50 for a circular ticket which allows you to island-hop.

In season, it also offers a two-island trip (adult/child £13/6.50), a supper boat to St Agnes (£7.60/3.80) and an evening trip to watch gig-racing on Wednesday and Friday (£6/3).

There's also a wildlife-watching trip out to Bishop Rock (£17/8.50).

BUS
Paulgers Transport (☑ 01720-423701; adult/child return £7.50/3.50) Provides transport to either your accommodation or the quayside if you're travelling straight to another island.

Island Rover (☑ 01720-422131; www.islandrover.co.uk; tickets £8) St Mary's bus service runs circular tours from Holgate's Green in Hugh Town at 10.15am and 3.30pm, plus extra tours in high summer.

TAXI
For taxis on St Mary's, try **Island Taxis** (☑ 01720-422126), **Scilly Cabs** (☑ 01720-422901) or **St Mary's Taxis** (☑ 01720-422142), or airport taxi Paulgers Transport (p233).

Tresco
01720 / 175

A short boat hop across the channel from St Mary's brings you to Tresco, the second-largest island, once owned by the monks of Tavistock Abbey, and now privately leased by the Dorrien-Smith family from the Duchy of Cornwall.

The main attraction here is the island's fabulous subtropical garden, but the rest of the island is a lovely place just to explore by bike – although since the whole place is privately leased, it feels a little more manicured and packaged than the other, more community-driven islands, especially since the focus here is very much on high-end visitors.

◉ Sights

★ **Tresco Abbey Garden**   GARDENS
(☑ 01720-424105; www.tresco.co.uk/enjoying/abbey-garden; adult/child £15/free; ☺ 10am-4pm) Tresco's key attraction – and one of Scilly's must-see gems – is this subtropical estate, laid out in 1834 on the site of a 12th-century Benedictine priory by the horticultural visionary Augustus Smith. The 7-hectare gardens are now home to more than 20,000 exotic species, from towering palms to desert cacti and crimson flame trees, all nurtured by the temperate Gulf Stream. Admission also covers the Valhalla collection, made up of figureheads and nameplates salvaged from ships wrecked off Tresco.

Activities

Tresco Bike Hire CYCLING

(☑ 01720-422849; adult/child per day £12/9; ⏱ 8.30am-12.30pm & 1.30-5.30pm Mon-Fri, 10am-noon Sat) Everyone gets around on two wheels on Tresco, and bikes can be hired from the bike store next to Tresco Stores. They can be a bit rickety, so check that the gears and brakes work, and the saddle is comfy, before you set out round the island. It's worth pre-booking in summer, but you won't need a lock – there's no one on the island to steal it.

✕ Eating

Ruin Beach CAFE **££**

(☑ 01720-424849; mains £12-10, pizzas £10-12; ⏱ 8am-10.30pm) Named after a ruined smuggler's cottage nearby, this red-tiled beach cafe makes a fine place to stow away for a lazy island lunch. It's big on grilling and baking thanks to its impressive wood-fired oven, equally adept at producing pork belly and sea bream as perfectly crisped pizza. It's relaxed and popular: beachside tables go fast, so come early.

🛍 Shopping

Tresco Stores FOOD

(☑ 01720-422806; shop@tresco.co.uk; ⏱ 9am-5.30pm Mon-Sat, 10am-1pm Sun) The island's well-stocked shop sells a full range of supplies, as well as island treats such as pasties, smoked fish, island beef and ice cream from Troytown Farm on Bryher.

ℹ Getting There & Away

Tresco has the most frequent boat service of all the islands from St Mary's; in summer there are five boats a day provided by St Mary's Boatmen's Association (p233). The island also has its own boat service, **Tresco Boats** (☑ 01720-423373; per person £5.50), which picks up guests staying on the island and also runs occasional sightseeing trips to the other islands.

Bryher

☑ 01720 / POP 84

Only around 80 people live on Bryher, Scilly's smallest and wildest inhabited island. Covered by rough bracken and heather, and fringed by white sand, this slender chunk of rock takes a fearsome battering from the

Pony on Bryher

Atlantic – Hell Bay hasn't earned its name for nothing. But on a bright sunny day, it's an island idyll par excellence, ideal for exploring on foot.

It's an island with a strong sense of community; you'll see little stalls around the island selling freshly cut flowers, homegrown veg, jams and packets of fudge.

◉ Sights

★ Rushy Bay
BEACH

Bryher is fringed by fabulous beaches, but Rushy Bay is the largest – and many would say the loveliest. South-facing and sheltered by the hummock of Watch Hill, it has powder-soft sand and super swimming.

★ Watch Hill
HILL

For the best views on the island, hike up to the top of Watch Hill, from where you can drink in a panorama right across the archipelago. It's a truly glorious spot to sit and watch the sunset, but – in the words of the locals – it can be hellish windy up top.

The hill gets its name from the days of the tall ships, when watchers would sit on the summit and look out for masts, and then signal down to pilots who would row out to meet the ships.

Great Par
BEACH

A grand curve of sand on the west side of Bryher, super for rock-pooling and paddling.

Samson
ISLAND

This tiny island really is for Robinson Crusoes. It's been abandoned since 1855, and now the only signs that anyone ever lived here are a few crumbling cottages, all but swallowed up by the bracken and gorse. It feels fantastically isolated, and is a great location for bird-spotting. Day trips over to the island can be arranged through the boatyard on Bryher.

🏃 Activities

Bennett Boatyard
BOATING

(☑07979-393206; www.bennettboatyard.com; single/double kayak per day £30/45; ⊙9.30am-6pm) This mixed-use boatyard rents out all kinds of vessels for exploring Bryher's waters: kayaks, stand-up paddleboards, rowboats and larger sailing vessels.

🍴 Eating

Vine Cafe
CAFE £

(☑01720-423168; bryhercath@hotmail.co.uk; mains £4-10; ⊙noon-4pm Mon-Sat, 7-9pm Sat-

NEW INN
· ·
By Tresco standards, the New Inn (☑01720-422849; www.tresco.co.uk; r £120-320; 🛰📶) is a bargain. The rooms are soothingly finished in buttery yellows and pale blues, although inevitably you'll have to fork out for a view. The inn itself serves good food (mains £10 to £18), mainly standards such as pollock and chips, steaks, burgers and the like, and the low-beamed bar is full of island atmosphere.

Wed) Bryher's eating options are limited, which makes this cosy little caff all the more welcome. It's housed in an old flower shed, and serves up toasted sandwiches and baps by day, plus more generous plates of lasagna, curries and the like by night. There's always at least one veggie option, and a generous roast on Sunday.

Crab Shack
SEAFOOD ££

(☑01720-422947; www.hellbay.co.uk; crab £20-40, mussels & scallops £12-24; ⊙noon-8pm May-Sep) This seafood shack in the grounds of the Hell Bay Hotel serves just three dishes: mussels, scallops and Bryher crab. It's a hands-on place where you're expected to get your hands dirty – crabs come with clawcrackers and picks to get the meat out. There are fries, salad and bread for sides, and cheese or Eton mess for afters.

Fraggle Rock
CAFE ££

(☑01720-422222; www.bryher.co; mains £8-15; ⊙9am-9pm; 🛰) This relaxed cafe also doubles as Bryher's pub. The menu's mainly quiches, salads and burgers, ideally served in the front garden, where chickens scratch around and there are views out to Hangman's Rock. It's a lively evening hang-out in season. There are a few timber-clad cabins (£620 to £1090 per week) if you feel like staying.

Island Fish
SEAFOOD

(☑01720-423880; www.islandfish.co.uk; ⊙9.30am-5.30pm Mon-Sat) Many generations of Mike Pender's family have been fishermen on Scilly, so it seems entirely fitting that he's started up one of the best fish suppliers on the islands. Started in 2015, it sells linecaught mackerel, pollock and mullet, as well as fantastic crab and lobster. There's a takeaway paella night once a week.

🛍 Shopping

Veronica Farm Fudge SWEETS
(☑ 01720-422862; www.veronicafarmfudge.co.uk;
bags of fudge from £4) Veronica Farm's wonderful fudge is almost worth a trip to Bryher on its own. It's made using butter, milk and clotted cream (all sourced from the farm's cows, of course). You can pick up a bag at the little honesty stall outside the farmhouse, or buy it in Bryher's shop, as well as several shops on St Mary's.

Bryher Shop DELI
(☑ 01720-423601; www.bryhershop.co.uk; ☺ 9am-5.30pm Mon-Sat, 10am-1pm Sun) Pick up all your essential supplies at the island's charming general store, which also has a post office.

ℹ Information

Bryher's useful website (www.bryher-islesof scilly.co.uk) covers various aspects of visiting the island. There's a downloadable walking leaflet.

ℹ Getting There & Away

Bryher is very close to Tresco, which means it's very easy to combine the two islands in a single day trip.

There are two direct boats a day to Bryher from St Mary's in summer, courtesy of the St Mary's Boatmen's Association (p233). Some boats offer a two-island itinerary, allowing you to visit both Tresco and Bryher.

OFF THE BEATEN TRACK

THE OFF ISLANDS

To explore the more remote islands, you'll need to employ the services of a local boatman. St Agnes Boating offers day trips to Scilly's most secret corners, including the deserted beaches of the Eastern Isles, the many shipwreck spots around the Western Rocks, and the Bishops Rock Lighthouse, a marvel of 19th-century engineering raised on a sliver of rock barely 46m long by 16m wide.

It also offers fantastic wildlife-spotting tours to see local colonies of puffins, shearwaters and seals. If you're really lucky, you might even see a dolphin.

St Agnes

☑ 01720 / POP 170

Scilly's southernmost island feels really remote, with a string of empty coves and a scattering of prehistoric sites. Visitors disembark at Porth Conger, near the old lighthouse, from where you wander along the coast path around the whole island.

At low tide, a narrow sand bar appears and provides a bridge to the neighbouring island of Gugh, where many ancient burial sites and a few chamber tombs can be found.

◉ Sights

Gugh ISLAND
Pronounced gew, this small island can be reached from St Agnes via a sandbar at low tide. It's famous for its Bronze Age remains and the slanting 3m-high menhir known as the Old Man of Gugh. Take care not to be cut off by the rising tide, which comes in fast and is too strong for swimming.

Troytown Maze MONUMENT
The coast path around St Agnes leads to this concentric maze of stones that's thought to be around two centuries old, but might be based on a prehistoric original.

Wingletang Down NATURE RESERVE
Covering much of the southern part of St Agnes, this bracken-strewn heath is littered with prehistoric remains, although they can be tricky to find among the undergrowth.

🏃 Activities

St Agnes Boating BOATING
(☑ 07990-742982; www.stagnesboating.co.uk) Scenic boat trips to the main islands (adult/child return £9.20/4.60) as well as the Western Rocks and Bishop's Rock lighthouse (£16/8). All boats leave from the island's quay.

🍴 Eating & Drinking

★ **Troytown Farm Ice Cream** ICE CREAM £
(☑ 01720-422360; www.troytown.co.uk/troytown -farm-dairy; ice cream £2-4) Troytown Farm's exceptional ice cream and sorbets are sold across the islands, but there's nothing quite like tasting it at source. Made in small batches with milk from the farm's dairy herd, it's seriously delicious. Try the rose geranium (your tastebuds will thank you) or go for 'The Works', a two-scoop cone with a fudge stick and a dollop of clotted cream.

STEPHEN REES / SHUTTERSTOCK ©

Troytown Maze

Coastguards Cafe CAFE £

(📞 01720-422197; mains £3-8; ☺ Apr-Sep) Local boy Tristan Hicks has breathed fresh life into this island cafe. With wooden tables and homespun decor inside, and outside seating making the most of the views, it's a fine place for a crab sandwich, some smoked mackerel pâté or a teatime cake. Breads are homemade, and hot chocolate comes with stirrers from the Little Island Chocolate Company.

It's located in the same building as **High Tide** (📞 01720-423869; www.hightide-seafood. com; mains £14-18; ☺ dinner 6.30-10pm Tue-Sat Jun-Aug, shorter hours rest of year) restaurant.

⭐ **Turk's Head** PUB ££

(📞 01720-422434; mains £8-14; ☺ 11am-11pm Mon-Sat, noon-10.30pm Sun) You can almost smell the history at Britain's most southerly alehouse. It's covered in maritime memorabilia – model ships in glass cabinets, vintage maps of the islands, black-and-white photos of seafarers – and there are few finer places to sup a pint. You might even be treated to a sea shanty if the local lads are in the mood.

❶ Getting There & Away

The **St Mary's Boatmen's Association** (p233) runs three boats a day between St Agnes and St Mary's.

St Martin's

📞 01720 / POP 136

The third-largest and furthest north of the islands, St Martin's is the main centre for Scilly's flower-growing industry, and the island's fields are a riot of colourful blooms in season. It's also blessed with gin-clear waters and the kind of untouched sands you'd more usually associate with St Lucia than Cornwall.

The main settlement is Higher Town, where you'll find the village shop and diving operation, but there are small clusters of cottages in nearby Middle and Lower Towns.

❍ Sights

⭐ **Great Bay** BEACH

On the remote north side of the island, this large expanse of sand is aptly named – it's great indeed, both in size and scenery. It feels wonderfully unspoilt, and the quality of the water is incredible. At low tide it joins up with its neighbour Little Bay, and from the western end you can cross to White Island.

Along the cliffs from Great Bay is the island's famous red-and-white-striped Day Mark, a navigation aid dating back to 1683.

St Martin's Vineyard
WINERY

(☑ 01720-423418; www.stmartinsvineyard.co.uk; ⊙ 10.45am-4pm Tue-Thu, conducted tours 11am) The UK's smallest and most southwesterly vineyard produces its own range of white wines. Tours are conducted by owners Val and Graham Thomas.

🏃 Activities

★ Scilly Seal Snorkelling
SWIMMING

(☑ 01720-422848; www.scillysealsnorkelling.com; per person £46; ⊙ Mar-Sep) Now here's an experience to remember – the chance to swim with wild grey seals in the clear waters off St Martin's. the more inquisitive ones come right up close – and the boldest have even been known to nibble your fins. Trips last about three hours.

It'll collect you from your accommodation on St Martin's, but it also provides a morning transfer from Tresco or St Mary's harbour.

St Martin's Dive School
DIVING

(☑ 01720-422848; www.scillydiving.com; per dive from £50) This diving company allows qualified divers to explore the fabulous underwater scenery that lies on the seabed around Scilly. The islands' waters are a degree or two warmer than the UK average, allowing many submarine species to flourish – from jewel anemones to fan corals and technicolour sponges. Unsurprisingly, the wreck-diving is also world class. It also offers snorkelling safaris (£25).

Freedom Hire
KAYAKING

(☑ 07925-762856; www.stmartinsfreedomhire. com/; single/double kayaks £30/40 per day; ⊙ May-Sep) Sit-on-top kayaks for hire, allowing you to paddle out on a day trip to the uninhabited islands of Tean or Samson.

🍴 Eating

Adam's Fish & Chips
SEAFOOD £

(☑ 01720-422457; www.adamsfishandchips.co.uk; fish & chips takeaway £9, dine-in £10.50; ⊙ 6-8.30pm Tue-Thu & Sat, noon-2pm Sun Jul & Aug, 6-8.30pm Tue, Thu & Sat Easter-Jun & Sep) The fish here is about as fresh as it gets – whatever's caught on the day is what ends up in your batter. It's run by Adam and Emma, who live and work on Little Arthur Farm nearby. Takeaway is available, but you'll need to book if you want one of the six tables.

Little Arthur Farm
CAFE £

(☑ 01720-422457; www.littlearthur.co.uk; cafe meals £6 0, ⊙ 10 11am-4pm) 🌱 A little slice of the good life on tiny St Martin's, this small-scale farm has diversified in all kinds of imaginative directions. There's a cafe-bistro, it grows its own produce and even makes environmentally-friendly shoes – and there's an eco-cabin to stay in too (£280 to £380 per week).

Island Bakery
BAKERY £

(☑ 01720-42211; www.theislandbakery-stmartins. com; bread & cakes £2-5; ⊙ 9am-5pm Mon-Sat) This homespun bakery run by Barney and Ella McLachlan turns out fresh bread, pizzas and, of course, scrumptious homemade pasties.

🍸 Drinking & Nightlife

Seven Stones
PUB

(☑ 01720-423777; sevenstonesinn@gmail.com; ⊙ 10am-11pm) A fine pub and the island's only boozer, so it's the heart of the action every night of the week. Decent grub (mains £8 to £14), Cornish ales and super views of the other islands from the terrace.

❶ Getting There & Away

Ferry services to the islands are provided by St Mary's Boatmen's Association (p233) and Tresco Boats (p234). There are at least three sailings a day in summer.

Understand Devon & Cornwall

Devon & Cornwall Today

Welcome to the southwest, a land of beaches, countryside and coastline – as well as sky-high house prices and rock-bottom wages. It has more Blue Flag beaches than practically anywhere, as well as a higher proportion of second homes. Coastal communities are changing, towns are gentrifying, and not everywhere is sharing in the spoils. Will this all change post-Brexit? Only time will tell.

Best in Music

Word of Mouth (Seth Lakeman; 2014) Devon's foremost folk artist explores his West Country roots.

Year of the Clown (3 Daft Monkeys; 2017) Playful pop-folk with a political edge courtesy of this longstanding Cornish band.

Making Waves (People's String Foundation; 2009) Heart-warming, multi-instrumental and huge amounts of fun from this folk orchestra.

Every Kingdom (Ben Howard; 2011) The classic post-surf soundtrack from this chilled singer-songwriter.

Best in Print

Vanishing Cornwall (Daphne du Maurier; 1967) A lyrical history exploring various aspects of old Cornwall.

Collected Poems (Charles Causley; 2000) Cornwall's de facto poet laureate lived most of his life in Launceston.

The Levelling Sea (Philip Marsden; 2012) Fascinating account of Falmouth's seafaring heyday.

The Cornish Overseas (Philip Payton; 1999) A readable account of Cornwall's post-mining migration.

Jamaica Inn (Daphne du Maurier; 1936) The classic thriller, set on Bodmin Moor.

House Prices & Second Homes

Spiralling house prices and the ever-increasing number of second homes and retirement apartments continue to be thorny topics. With the average house price now more than 10 times the average wage in Cornwall and Devon, this region is officially one of the UK's most unaffordable areas, especially for young people and first-time buyers in picturesque places such as Salcombe, St Mawes, Perranporth, Padstow, Fowey and Falmouth. Cornwall and Devon also top the league for the number of holiday homes (50,000-plus, and growing), but the debate rumbles on about how much these homes-away-from-home actually contribute to the local economy. One solution is to let locals decide: a recent vote in St Ives to limit new-build homes to residents working locally met with widespread approval, and may point the way forward in years to come.

Fine Food & Sustainable Fish

Food and drink continue to be major growth areas. From Michelin-starred restaurants to microbreweries, coffee-roasters to chocolate makers, vineyards to gin distilleries and street-food vans to food-box schemes, the southwest's producers are leading the way when it comes to culinary innovation – and, in a world where local sourcing and seasonal ingredients are becoming ever more important, that's a really positive sign. Similarly, the southwest's fisheries are pioneering more sustainable fishing practices – since 2012, the 90-sq-mile Lyme Bay Fisheries and Conservation Reserve has enabled conservationists to work with fishers to preserve fish stocks and ensure the health of the marine environment.

Energy & Industry

Green energy remains a contentious topic within the southwest. With large areas of open farmland, the region has become a magnet for solar farms and wind turbines. To some, a field covered in solar panels or turbine blades is a blot on the landscape; to others, it's a sign of a southwest looking towards a greener, cleaner future. Unfortunately, other experimental energy projects, like the Wave Hub tidal-power scheme, and attempts to generate geothermal energy in some of Cornwall's disused mines, have yet to prove financially viable. There have also been attempts to revive some of Cornwall's mines, buoyed by rising mineral prices and a growing demand for rare earth metals (for microchips) and lithium (for batteries) – but these projects are unpopular with Unesco, which claims the area's heritage status depends on the mines remaining closed.

Grockles & Emmets

A century ago it was farming and fishing, but tourism is now far and away the region's top-grossing industry. Recent figures indicate that tourism adds somewhere between £5 to £8 billion to the region's coffers, and it's estimated that around one in five jobs now depend on the tourism industry, directly or indirectly. The region's residents have a mixed relationship with the summer influx of grockles and emmets (as tourists are called in Devon and Cornwall, respectively): traffic jams, litter, pollution and overcrowded beaches are problems, but many towns and villages would find it impossible to survive without the cash injection visitors bring.

The Brexit Question

The biggest issue looming on the horizon is what the 2016 vote to leave the EU means for the southwest. Cornwall and Devon both voted in favour of leaving the European Union by some margin. The region has a large conservative base, along with a high number of older residents (who are statistically more likely to vote and tend to favour Brexit), and the vote can also be seen as a cry of protest in a perennially deprived area, where seasonal work is the norm, traditional industries have collapsed, and conventional politics has failed to solve enduring problems such as low wages, unpredictable work patterns and unaffordable housing.

Yet the southwest has arguably benefited more than most from EU membership, through farming subsidies, environmental grants and Objective One funding in Cornwall, which has financed regeneration initiatives and funded flagship projects such as the Eden Project and Falmouth University. In an area that relies heavily on agriculture, seasonal work and tourism – all industries guaranteed to be affected by Brexit – what the future holds for the southwest outside the EU is on everyone's minds.

POPULATION: **1,720,900**

AREA: **10,270 SQ KM**

MILES OF COASTLINE: **530**

UNEMPLOYMENT: **4%**

NUMBER OF CORNISH PASTIES MADE PER YEAR: **120 MILLION**

if Devon & Cornwall were 100 people

20 would work in tourism
8 would work in manufacturing
5 would work in agriculture or fishing
1 would work in mining or quarrying
66 would work in another job

belief systems
(% of population)

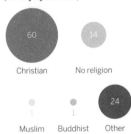

60 Christian
14 No religion
1 Muslim
1 Buddhist
24 Other

population per sq km

DEVON & CORNWALL   UK   USA

☗ ≈ 30 people

History

Wherever you travel, history seems to be written into the southwest's landscape. Hillforts and stone circles stand out along the skyline. Crenellated castles loom on the hilltops. Abandoned engine houses crumble along the clifftops. From aristocratic estates, landscaped gardens and ancient ruins to a rich legacy of mining, agriculture and industry, it's a living textbook waiting to be read.

Ancient History

It's thought that humans have inhabited southwest England for more than 100,000 years, but the first definitive evidence of human settlement is a jawbone dating from around 35,000 BC, unearthed in Kents Cavern, near Torquay, during an excavation in 1927 (academic opinion is still divided as to whether the bone belongs to a Neanderthal or prehistoric ancestors of Homo sapiens). A similar argument continues to rage over the controversial issue of cannibalism: some evidence has emerged that suggests early humans had no qualms about eating their deceased relatives, and may even have used their bones to make drinking vessels and dining implements.

The earliest settlers were tribes of hunter-gatherers, living seasonally from the land and travelling in pursuit of seasonal game. The first signs of organised farming and animal domestication emerged around 4000 BC. Around this time prehistoric builders developed their taste for eye-catching architecture, and built many stone circles, menhirs, quoits and barrows across Devon, Dartmoor, Bodmin Moor, Penwith and the Isles of Scilly.

By 1800 BC there was already a thriving trade in gold, tin, bronze and copper between southwest mines and many parts of Europe and the Mediterranean. This trade continued following the arrival of the Celts, who established themselves in southwest Britain from around 1000 BC.

The Celts quickly conquered much of the area, establishing themselves in hilltop forts and coastal strongholds. The remains of several Bronze and Iron Age 'villages' can still be seen in many areas, including

The last native speaker of the Cornish language, *kernewek*, was Dolly Pentreath, who died in 1777, but the language has since undergone a modest revival; around 500 people are thought to be fluent, although several thousand speak at least some words.

TIMELINE	4000–1500 BC	1000–500 BC	55 BC
	First evidence of organised farming. Neolithic builders construct dolmens, quoits, stone circles and menhirs.	Arrival of the Celts, who establish hillforts and fortified settlements across the region, and gradually integrate with native Britons.	Roman legions under Julius Caesar land in Britain and defeat native tribes, although some areas of west Cornwall and Devon remain effectively independent kingdoms.

Dartmoor and Penwith: Chysauster, Carn Euny and Grimspound are per-haps the best preserved.

Over the next few centuries, Celtic society flourished in southwest Britain and developed its own culture, architecture and language, but by the 1st century BC a new wave of invaders had landed and brushed all but the hardiest Celtic defenders aside. *Veni, vidi, vici* – the Romans had arrived.

Roman Rule

The first Roman landings in Britain were led by Julius Caesar in 55 BC. In AD 43 Aulus Plautius invaded Britain with around 20,000 troops, who were backed by reinforcements from the stuttering Emperor Claudius. Over the next five years, under the orders of their commander Vespasian, the legions rampaged through southern England.

Having wrested control of the area from the ruling Celtic tribes (the Durotriges in Dorset and Somerset, and the Dumnonii in Devon and Cornwall), the Romans set about building a network of roads, settle-ments, ports, temples and forts. A key garrison was stationed at Exeter (Isca Dumnoniorum to the Romans), which marked the western end of the Roman road to Lincoln known as the Fosse Way. Further west, pock-ets of Celtic culture survived, and it's thought that at least a few tribes remained unconquered.

The Romans' grip on power lasted until the 4th century, when mil-itary pressures and dwindling resources forced their withdrawal from many of the empire's more far-flung outposts. By 410 the last legions had returned to Rome, and the so-called 'Dark Ages' had begun.

The Dark Ages

Over the next 500 years, southwest Britain was invaded by Anglo-Saxon settlers, mainly tribes of Angles, Saxons, Jutes and Frisians from modern-day Germany, who first came as mercenaries in the Roman army. The native Celts were pushed back into their core strongholds in Wales, Dart-moor and Cornwall, creating pockets of Celtic culture, while the rest of the region was largely colonised by the Anglo-Saxons. Around this time a fearsome war leader – supposedly named Arthur or Arthurus – is said to have emerged to lead a counter-attack against the invading Saxons, checking their progress over 12 great battles, and launching the enduring legend of King Arthur.

The first Christian saints arrived in the southwest around this time, probably from Ireland, although their vessels were a little unconventional – St Ia is supposed to have sailed to the north Cornish coast on a giant leaf, while St Piran, patron saint of Cornwall, allegedly arrived aboard a granite millstone.

Ancient Sites

·····················

Chysauster Iron Age Village, near Penzance

·····················

Grimspound Bronze Age Village, Dartmoor

·····················

Grey Wethers Stone Rows, Dartmoor

·····················

The Hurlers, Bodmin Moor

·····················

The Merry Maid-ens, near Penzance

·····················

Mên-an-tol Stone, Penwith

HISTORY ROMAN RULE

AD 410–600	899	927	1050
Christianity is brought to the southwest by Irish missionaries (many of whom are subsequently made saints, including St Piran, the patron saint of Cornwall).	Having led a successful resistance against the Vikings, Alfred the Great, the King of Wessex, dies and is buried at Winchester Cathedral.	King Alfred's grandson, Athelstan, defeats the last remaining Viking kingdom of York, making him the first Anglo-Saxon ruler of the whole of England.	Foundation of the first cathedral at Exeter, although the original building is substantially remodelled by succes-sive bishops in the 12th and 13th centuries.

Classic Castles

....

Tintagel

....

Restormel

....

Pendennis

....

St Mawes

....

Totnes

....

Powderham

....

Launceston

In the early 9th century, King Egbert and the armies of Wessex swept west and brought the whole of the southwest under Anglo-Saxon control. His grandson, King Alfred, led a series of campaigns against Viking incursions (and famously burnt some cakes while hiding on the island of Athelney). After a series of power struggles between various Anglo-Saxon kingdoms over the next century, King Edward (the Peacemaker) was the first monarch to be crowned king of a unified England, at Bath Abbey in 973.

The Middle Ages

Following the Norman conquest of 1066, the region came under the sway of feudal lords, who developed the area's potential for trade, agriculture and industry. Wool, tin and minerals became important exports, and ports grew along the southwest coastline, notably at Fowey, Bristol, Looe, Saltash and Plymouth.

In 1305 Edward I recognised the importance of tin mining to the area by granting official charters to the Stannaries (tin-mining districts) and establishing five stannary towns in Cornwall (Truro, Lostwithiel, Launceston, Helston and Bodmin) and three more in Devon (Chagford, Ashburton and Tavistock). Among other functions, these towns had the right to assay tin to determine its quality before export. Cornwall also had its own Stannary Parliament, governed by its own system of taxes and laws; tin miners were effectively exempt from civil jurisdiction, and had the right to be tried according to Stannary law. In 1337, Edward III established the Duchy of Cornwall for his son Edward, the 'Black Prince', a title that is still traditionally inherited by the heir to the throne.

The long-held rights of the Stannaries were a major factor in the 1497 'An Gof' rebellion, a popular uprising against taxes levied by Henry VII to fund a war against the Scots, which many believed eroded the Stannaries' right to govern their own affairs. Under leaders Thomas Flamank, a Bodmin lawyer, and Michael Joseph, a blacksmith (*an gof* in Cornish) from St Keverne, an army of 15,000 Cornishmen marched on London. Despite a series of battles, it was outclassed by the king's forces, and Flamank and Joseph were hanged, drawn and quartered before having their heads impaled on pikes on London Bridge.

A similarly brutal end awaited the region's ecclesiastical institutions during Henry VIII's Dissolution of the Monasteries. Nearly all of the region's abbeys, including Buckfast, Bodmin and Glasney College in Penryn, were abolished. Assets were stripped, buildings dismantled and most of the monks were forcibly retired or, in many cases, put to death. In the absence of the abbeys, the cathedral of Exeter flourished alongside smaller chapels and churches.

The Levelling Sea is a fascinating account of Falmouth's seafaring heyday, written by local author Philip Marsden. It's packed with salty sea-dogs and tales of derring-do on the Cornish seas.

1201	1337	1348	1497
King John grants the first charter to the Stannaries (tin-mining districts) of Cornwall. Further charters are granted in the early 14th century by Edward I.	The Duchy of Cornwall is established, and Edward the 'Black Prince' becomes the first Duke of Cornwall.	The Black Death, a form of flea-borne bubonic plague spread by rats and other rodents, kills an estimated one-third of the population.	The 'An Gof' rebellion against Henry VII marches on London, but is quashed and its leaders executed. A second Cornish rebellion under Perkin Warbeck fails later the same year.

The Reformation also abolished the use of Latin in church services and introduced a new all-English Book of Common Prayer. This was the final straw for many devout worshippers in Cornwall and Devon, but the so-called Prayer Book Rebellion of 1549 was put down in similarly bloody fashion to the 'An Gof' rebellion 52 years before; the West Country armies were summarily crushed outside Exeter, and the leaders executed.

The Age of Exploration

Surrounded on three sides by the sea, it's unsurprising that the southwest became famous as a land of explorers and seafarers. Several of Britain's foremost medieval seamen were born here – iconic names like the Cornish nobleman Sir Richard Grenville (born at Buckland Abbey in Devon); his cousin, Sir Walter Raleigh (born in Hayes Barton, East Devon); Sir John Hawkins (Plymouth); and his cousin, Sir Francis Drake (Tavistock). Drake launched his epoch-making circumnavigation of the globe from Plymouth in 1577: a replica of his ship, the *Pelican*, renamed the *Golden Hind*, can be seen on Brixham Harbour.

The southwest's sea captains also proved crucial during a great crisis of the late 16th century: the invasion of the Spanish Armada. Tensions between Catholic Spain and Protestant England boiled over in 1588, when Philip II of Spain dispatched a fleet of 130 warships to bring England under Catholic rule. The Armada was sighted off the Lizard on 19 July, and the message was carried to London via a series of beacons along the south coast. Famously, Drake is supposed to have spied the ships from Plymouth Hoe, but refused to set sail until he'd finished his game of bowls. Regardless of the truth of the tale, his response was swift and decisive: he set sail from Plymouth with a fleet of 55 ships and, over

Devon is thought to be the last place in England to execute women on suspicion of witchcraft: Temperance Lloyd, Susannah Edwards and Mary Trembles in Bideford in 1682, and Alice Molland in Heavitree in 1685 in Heavitree. All four were hanged.

TITANS OF INDUSTRY

As this area was massively transformed during the Industrial Revolution, it's perhaps unsurprising to discover that several local engineers played a key role in this era of technological change. First came Dartmouth-born Thomas Newcomen (1664–1729), the pioneer of the earliest steam engines, which were subsequently used to power the pumps that extracted water from Devon and Cornwall's deep-shaft mines, greatly improving the mines' safety and efficiency. Then came Redruth-born Richard Trevithick (1771–1833), who devised the first steam-powered locomotive, which he named his 'Puffing Devil', first demonstrated to an amazed Cornish crowd in 1801. Another gifted Cornishman also did much to improve the miners' lot: the genius chemist Humphry Davy (1778–1829), who invented the safety lamp (sometimes known as the Davy lamp) in 1815, which prevented the lethal underground explosions caused by flammable gases being ignited by the miners' candles.

1588	1620	1720	1743
The Spanish Armada invasion fleet, first sighted off the Lizard Peninsula, is defeated by the Royal Navy fleet under the command of Sir Francis Drake, stationed at Plymouth.	The Pilgrim Fathers set sail from Plymouth aboard the *Mayflower*, founding the colony of New Plymouth in Massachusetts in November the same year.	Thomas Newcomen builds an 'atmospheric engine' at Wheal Fortune Mine, in the Gwennap mining district, heralding the arrival of mechanised mining.	The preacher and theologian John Wesley delivers his first sermon in Cornwall, and begins the long process of Methodist conversion in the county.

In the mid-18th century a pound of tea cost at least 8 shillings – roughly the same as a bottle of champagne and the average weekly wage of a manual labourer.

the next two weeks, Drake fought a series of engagements against the Spanish fleet, culminating in the Battle of Gravelines on 29 July, in which 11 Spanish galleons were destroyed and the rest put to flight.

Drake and Hawkins' subsequent exploits were rather less commendation-worthy: they were instrumental in establishing the first slave-trafficking routes with Africa, a trade that underpinned the growth of several southwest ports (especially Bristol and Plymouth) over the next two centuries.

The southwest was also an important launchpad in the move from Old to New World. Following Sir Francis Drake's circumnavigation of the globe from Plymouth, the city also witnessed the first voyage of the Pilgrim Fathers, who set sail from the Barbican on 16 September 1620 aboard the *Mayflower*. The pilgrims landed at Provincetown Harbour in present-day Massachusetts and founded the colony of New Plymouth, marking the start of modern America.

SMUGGLERS AND FREE TRADERS

In the late-18th century, in an effort to fund an ongoing (and hugely costly) war with France, the government imposed customs duty on imported goods (especially luxury items such as brandy, gin and tea). This led to a huge growth in smuggling along the southwest coastline. Cornwall's remote coves were perfect hideouts for the enterprising 'free traders', and the sight of government 'preventive' boats in pursuit of smuggling vessels off the southern Cornish coastline became commonplace. But the government operatives were often fighting a losing battle. Widespread opposition to the taxes, coupled with the lucrative returns that could be made from handling contraband goods, meant that collusion between the smugglers and onshore communities was widespread.

Smuggling rapidly became a hugely profitable industry – according to some estimates, as much as four-fifths of the tea drunk in England in the late-19th century had escaped official duty – and some smugglers, such as Harry Carter and Jack Rattenbury, became local celebrities. Harry Carter even published his own autobiography, and Daphne du Maurier penned several rollicking tales on the subject, including the classic *Frenchman's Creek* (which is based on a real place near Helford village on the Lizard).

Another smuggling-related activity that's often associated with the southwest is wrecking. According to some accounts, a few communities deliberately lured ships onto the rocks, using lanterns and fires to disorientate their navigation, before plundering the wrecks for their booty (and disposing of any survivors). In truth, there's no hard evidence that wrecking was ever a widespread activity: what's much more likely is that the ships were wrecked by bad weather or bad navigation (or a combination of both), and local communities subsequently helped themselves to the spoils washed up on shore.

1801	1833	1850	1859
Redruth-born Richard Trevithick demonstrates his groundbreaking steam locomotive on Fore St in Camborne.	Isambard Kingdom Brunel begins construction of the groundbreaking Great Western Railway line from London. The final section to Penzance is completed in 1867.	The pioneering Packet Service from Falmouth comes to an end, marking the transition from the age of sail to the age of steam.	The Brunel-designed Royal Albert Bridge over the River Tamar connects Cornwall to Devon.

The Industrial Age

From the Middle Ages onwards, there was one industry that was to shape the region's fortunes more than any other – and that was mining. There is evidence that mining has been an important industry here as far back as neolithic times – and by the time of the Bronze Age, it's certain that there was a well-established trading link with the southwest and many other European cultures: mineral analysis has shown that metals used by Mediterranean societies were forged using minerals mined in Cornwall and Devon.

But it was during the great era of industrial expansion in the 17th and 18th centuries that the region's mines came into their own. The huge demand for minerals (particularly tin, iron and copper, but also tungsten and arsenic) heralded the beginning of the great age of mining in Cornwall and west Devon, and the advent of new technologies such as steam power, beam engines and 'blast' extraction enabled the region's miners to reach previously inaccessible lodes of high-quality metals.

Mining in Cornwall boomed: in 1800 the county boasted 75 mines employing 16,000 people, but by 1837 this had mushroomed to 200 mines employing some 30,000 workers. The industry flourished until the mid-19th century, when mineral lodes in many mines were already beginning to fail, turning them into *knackt bals* (exhausted mines). Much worse was to follow: a great financial panic in 1866 bankrupted many investors, while the discovery of huge mineral deposits in other areas of the globe – particularly Australia, Mexico and the western US – led to a crash in commodity prices and forced the closure of huge numbers of mines. Faced with joblessness and starvation, entire communities upped sticks and emigrated to Australia, Mexico and the western United States (a phenomenon referred to as the 'Cornish Diaspora'). It's thought that around a third of Cornwall's mining community had emigrated overseas by the end of the 19th century: collectively they became known as 'Cousin Jacks', a wry joke based on the fact that practically every family in Cornwall had at least one relative who had emigrated overseas, likely never to return.

The West Country's industrial boom also had a surprising by-product: it made many families fabulously rich, enabling them to lavish huge sums on creating grand country estates that showcased their newfound wealth and prestige. Many of the region's country houses and gardens were established around this time.

Mining was also responsible for the growth of Methodism, a form of Protestantism that preached the virtues of temperance, piety and self-reliance – a practical, down-to-earth religion that found fertile ground

History Museums

National Maritime Museum

RAMM, Exeter

Royal Cornwall Museum

Porthcurno Telegraph Museum

Lizard Lighthouse Heritage Centre

Dartmouth Museum

Plymouth Museum (reopening 2020)

1919	1940–42	1951	1973
Thirty-one men are killed at Levant Mine, when a link attached to the 'man engine' carrying miners up and down the shaft snaps – the worst disaster in Cornwall's mining history.	Plymouth endures heavy bombing raids by the Luftwaffe, and sustains heavy damage. Exeter is damaged during the Baedeker Blitz.	Dartmoor becomes the southwest's first designated national park, followed three years later by Exmoor.	Britain joins the EEC (European Economic Community), opening up the region's fishing grounds to foreign trawlers for the first time.

in a hard-working land of miners, farmers and fishermen. Methodism flourished, and preachers such as John Wesley and Billy Bray (an ex-miner) became household names. By 1851 more than 60% of Cornwall's population classed themselves as Methodists.

The main online resource for the Unesco Cornwall and West Devon Mining World Heritage Site is www.cornish-mining.org.uk, which has a list of all the key sites and a good potted history.

The Arrival of the Railway

As the Industrial Revolution rolled on, pioneering engineers set about reinventing Britain's infrastructure, constructing tunnels, canals and railways to link Britain's industrial bases. Foremost among them was Isambard Kingdom Brunel, one of England's brightest engineering minds, who built everything from groundbreaking bridges to the first great transatlantic steamers. Perhaps Brunel's greatest achievement was the development of the Great Western Railway, which provided the first rapid link between London and Bristol in 1841, and was later extended into Devon and Cornwall.

The railway also brought a new phenomenon to the southwest: tourism. Rising living standards and better wages, coupled with the expanding rail network, brought swaths of trippers from the region's smog-choked cities to the southwest's shores. Many towns were quick to seize the opportunity: Torquay, Paignton, Ilfracombe and Penzance grew rapidly to cater for the booming tourist trade, adding a plethora of promenades, piers and seaside villas. Over a century later, tourism remains one of the southwest's biggest industries, accounting for around 20% of the region's total income.

Mining Sites

Wheal Crowns, Botallack
....
Wheal Coates, St Agnes
....
Levant Mine, Penwith
....
Geevor Tin Mine, St Just
....
Great Flat Lode Trail, Camborne

The World Wars

As with many corners of England, the southwest suffered heavily during the Great War. Many rural regiments recruited men en masse from local villages, which meant that entire populations could be wiped out in the space of just a few hours of fighting.

The region fared little better in WWII, when its ports and manufacturing bases became key targets for the Luftwaffe. Plymouth fared the worst, and by the end of the Blitz huge swaths of the city centre had been reduced to rubble, while Exeter had been heavily damaged during the so-called Baedeker raids (which deliberately targeted historic cities in an effort to dent British morale).

Later in the war, the deep-water harbours around Falmouth and the Carrick Roads played a pivotal role in the preparations for D-Day, and marked the embarkation point for millions of American troops setting sail for the Normandy beaches.

1998	1999	2001	2006
The closure of South Crofty, the last working mine in Cornwall, results in thousands of job losses and an end to over 4000 years of metal mining in Cornwall.	Cornwall qualifies for Objective One funding from the European Union, recognising its status as one of the southwest's poorest counties.	Foot-and-mouth disease strikes the southwest. The Eden Project opens in a disused Cornish clay pit. The Jurassic Coast becomes the UK's first natural World Heritage Site.	The Cornwall and West Devon Mining Landscape is recognised by Unesco for its cultural and historical importance.

Modern History

The last 50 years has been a period of fluctuating fortunes for the southwest. Traditional industries such as fishing and mining have almost completely disappeared (since the closure of South Crofty near Camborne in 1998, there are now no working mines in the region), and only Brixham and Newlyn retain sizeable fishing fleets. But the area's naval associations have continued, and Falmouth and Devonport Dockyard in Plymouth have both retained their shipyards – with 15 dry-docks and 4 miles of waterfront, Devonport is the largest naval base in Western Europe.

But the region's great growth industry over recent years has been tourism. Depending on which statistic you listen to, tourism adds between £5 and £8 billion to the region's coffers every year, and in some areas over half of all jobs are related to the wider tourist industry. Despite tourism's dominance, the southwest is slowly making the transition towards a more diversified economy: culture, food and the environment are particularly strong areas of growth. Exciting developments such as the Eden Project, as well as the conferment of Unesco World Heritage status on the Jurassic Coast and the Cornwall and West Devon Mining Landscape, have helped refocus attention on the region's history, heritage and creativity.

In 2001 Cornwall also qualified for Objective One status from the European Union, recognising it as one of the country's poorest areas – which makes the county's decision to vote to leave the EU during the 2016 'Brexit' referendum (a decision shared by Devon) even more surprising.

In 2014 Cornish people were granted official status as an ethnic minority in the UK, allowing them to state Cornish as their ethnic identity, as the Welsh, Scots and Northern Irish can.

2011	2012	2014	2016
After a long campaign, the Cornish pasty finally receives 'protected geographical indication' (PGI) status.	On 19 May 2012, the Olympic Torch arrives at Land's End before making its journey around Britain.	Severe storms batter the southwest, flooding many coastal communities and washing away part of the railway line at Dawlish.	Devon and Cornwall both return a majority vote in favour of exiting the European Union.

Food & Drink

The southwest is Britain's happening foodie hot spot. Whisk together superb produce with a scattering of celebrity chefs and you get a perfect culinary storm. To cream teas and pasties add just-caught seafood, rich cheeses, fine wines and an array of scenic restaurants, beach cafes and farm shops showcasing the best of the west.

Local Produce

The organic sector is strong in Devon and Cornwall. A whopping 28% of the UK's organic farmland is in the wider southwest; a little over 8% of the region's total agricultural land. And all over the two counties producers and eateries are promoting the slow food ethos of placing importance on seasonality, taste, quality and the production process itself.

Twice winner of the BBC Farmer of the Year award, Guy Watson has been pioneering organic food at Riverford Farm (www.riverford.co.uk), near Totnes, for more than 20 years. It's now one of the UK's biggest organic delivery schemes, dropping off veg grown at local farms at more than 47,000 doors nationwide. Its innovative, on-farm field kitchen (p81) in Devon sees you eat produce harvested to order from just outside. Other top delivery schemes are the Cornish Food Box Company (www.thecornishfoodboxcompany.co.uk) and the Cornish Food Market (www.cornishfoodmarket.co.uk).

> **Cream Teas**
>
> A classic afternoon treat featuring scones, jam and fresh clotted cream, cream teas are a source of heated debate. The Cornish insist the jam must be spread on the scones first; while in Devon, it's the cream.

Celebrity Chefs

When Rick Stein opened a restaurant in the quaint Cornish fishing village of Padstow in 1975, few realised he was about to transform the culinary landscape. By 1995 Stein's *Taste of the Sea* TV series had placed Cornwall firmly in the foodie spotlight; his show *Food Heroes* brought local produce to mainstream attention.

Others followed. Hugh Fearnley-Whittingstall set up River Cottage on the Devon–Dorset border in 1998; now you can dine at his farm River Cottage HQ (p60) and his canteens in east Devon (p60) and Plymouth (p107), and learn how to grow vegetables, make bread and butcher meat.

Along with creating a small-screen lifestyle idyll, Fearnley-Whittingstall has also pushed for real change; more than 870,000 people signed up to Fish Fight, which called for cuts in the number of dead fish being thrown back into the sea.

Jamie Oliver, who battled for quality school dinners, brought Fifteen (p200) to a Newquay beach in 2006. This gourmet restaurant is also a social enterprise, dedicated to making a real difference to the lives of its young apprentices.

And then there are chefs, famed in foodie circles, who dish up superb food: Nathan Outlaw (p189) in Port Isaac; Paul Ainsworth (p192) in Padstow and Mitch Tonks (p86) in Dartmouth.

Regional Specialities

Devon and Cornwall's specialities speak eloquently of the counties' pasts, and form a key part of the region's current cultural identity: the Cornish pasty is a miner's lunch turned cultural icon; fish pies, once a meal wrought of hard times, are these days a seaside staple; and cider, born of the region's subsistence economy, is now a trendy craft tipple.

Fish & Seafood

The fruits of the southwest's seas provide a tasty, tangible link between food and place. Eating fish that's been landed a few yards away is special – still in buckets, it's sometimes even carried past diners by waterproofs-clad fishermen.

Rejoice in these negligible-food-mile eateries in the ports of Newlyn, Falmouth, Padstow and Mevagissey in Cornwall; and Brixham, Torquay and Dartmouth in Devon. Some 40-plus species are still hauled in locally. Highlights include superb oysters, mussels, crab and lobster, line-caught sea bass and mackerel, and the freshest monkfish, John Dory and Dover sole.

Then there's the classic fish and chips. Wrapped in paper, dripping with vinegar and scattered with salt, it can be surprisingly good, especially in ports where the day's catch ends up in batter.

Meat & Game

The southwest is famous for its dairy herds, with top-quality milk, cream, ice cream and, especially in Cornwall, cheese. Beef and lamb are other regional highlights – look out for South Devon and Red Ruby Devon beef, and lamb reared in the valley of the River Exe. You'll also find a wealth of excellent local poultry, pork, cured meats and, of course, the world-famous Cornish pasties .

Top Cream Teas

Boscastle Farm Shop *(near Tintagel)*

Brimpts Farm *(Dartmoor)*

Roskillys Farm *(The Lizard)*

Cottage *(Clovelly)*

FOOD & DRINK REGIONAL SPECIALITIES

THE CORNISH PASTY

In the 13th century, these crinkly-edged half-moons of carbohydrate consisted of vegetables wrapped in pastry – many experts say originally no meat was actually involved. This creation delivered a portable, durable two-course lunch, and over the centuries pasties became a staple of tin-mining communities. Those working underground in grim, arsenic-laced conditions didn't eat the crimped seam; instead it allowed them to hold their food without contaminating it.

When waves of impoverished Cornish miners emigrated in the mid-1800s, they took their pasty techniques with them, particularly to Australia and the US. Today, you can still pop out for a pasty in places as far from Cornwall as Adelaide and Arizona.

Annually, pasty production employs thousands of people and brings millions of pounds into Cornwall's economy. In 2011 the savoury was finally awarded protected status by the European Commission, meaning only pasties with the following characteristics can be called 'Cornish pasties':

➡ crimped on one side, never on top

➡ must have at least 12.5% meat

➡ must include swede, potato and onion, and a light peppery seasoning

➡ has no flavourings or additives

➡ must be made in Cornwall

For more, see the Cornish Pasty Association (www.cornishpastyassociation.co.uk).

Top Traditional Devon cream tea with scones, strawberry jam and clotted cream.

Bottom Cornish Brie cheese and red wine.

Venison and game, particularly pheasant, features on many rural menus and especially on Dartmoor and Exmoor. You may also see signs in local bakeries warning of the possibility of 'shot' (gun pellets) in produce such as game pies.

The Tamar Valley, straddling the border between Cornwall and Devon, has a tradition of fruit farming. Although it's a much less important sector than it was in the 19th century, you'll still see early season strawberries, apples and cherries region-wide. Dittisham on the River Dart in south Devon is renowned for its plums. The region is also famous for organic produce, a sector in which it is particularly strong (p250).

Cheese

Creamy, tangy, soft and hard: the southwest offers cheese lovers countless slices of gourmet heaven. Look out for these highlights:

Blue Cheeses (aka the 'Blues') Exmoor (cow), Devon (cow), Harbourne (goat) and Beenleigh (sheep).

Brie Try Cornish Country Larder, and Sharpham (Devon).

Cornish Blue A Gorgonzola-esque, gooey offering from the fringes of Bodmin Moor.

Cornish Yarg Gentle, nettle-wrapped and semi-hard.

Davidstow Creamery Award-winning cheddar, with a 60-year heritage.

Quicke's Mouth-puckeringly strong cheddar, made near Exeter.

Drinks

Cider

The southwest is rightly famous for ciders that conjure images of golden summers and hazy days. Centuries ago no farm would have been without its orchard; apples were pressed and then fermented to form the 'scrumpy', which was often drunk instead of water (then, the H_2O was more toxic than the alcohol). Dazed but delighted labourers were paid partly in this golden currency – an average four-pint (2.25L) daily allowance increasing to a staggering eight pints during hay-making.

This deeply flavoured elixir was evocatively dubbed 'wine of wild orchards' by the writer Laurie Lee. The apple names alone are enough to give you a warm, fuzzy glow: Slack ma Girdle, Sops in Wine and Quench.

Excellent small-scale producers include southeast Cornwall–based Cornish Orchards; south Devon–based Luscombe; and Helford Creek, near Helston.

Wine

The mild southwest weather ensures good conditions for vineyards, and sipping a chilled glass of white on a sun-drenched terrace, overlooking rows of vines, feels more like Chablis than the southwest. These wineries are worth seeking out:

Sharpham (☑01803-732203; www.sharpham.com; from £2.50; ☉10am-6pm May-Sep, to 5pm Mar & Apr, to 3pm Mon-Sat Oct-Dec; ℗) Set in 200 stunning south-Devon hectares; wine ranges from £13 for a decent zesty white to £26 for bottle of fizz.

Camel Valley (p144) A north-Cornwall award-winner; try its aromatic and appropriately named Bacchus (£13).

Polgoon (p219) Near Penzance, produces award-winning still rosé and a sparkling apple wine.

Yearlstone (☑01884-855700; www.yearlstone.co.uk; Bickleigh; ℗) Take a tour, then eat and drink beside these east-Devon vines.

Trevibban Mill (p189) A newly-founded vineyard just outside Padstow.

Unusual Foods

Laverbread
Patties of seaweed, oats and bacon, from north Devon and Exmoor.

Salcombe Smokies *Salcombe's famous smoked mackerel.*

Samphire
A salty, fragrant coastal plant often partnered with seafood.

Stargazy Pie
Mousehole's famous fish pie.

FOOD & DRINK REGIONAL SPECIALITIES

Breweries

The southwest has a long and illustrious brewing heritage, but in recent years it's witnessed an explosion in small breweries catering to the craft-beer crowd.

Plymouth Gin is the oldest producing distillery in the world, and for 200 years was the staple pick-me-up for the Royal Navy. Today you can take tasting tours at the distillery.

Beer Engine (p57) Devon microbrewery-cum-pub beside a railway; hence the brews, Rail Ale and Sleeper Heavy.

Harbour (www.harbourbrewing.com) North Cornwall–based contemporary craft brewery; try the caramel-meets-toffee Amber Ale, or the citrusy India Pale.

Keltek (http://keltekbrewery.co.uk) Cornish offerings include mild Even Keel (3.4%) and superstrong Beheaded (7.6%).

Sharp's (www.sharpsbrewery.co.uk) A Rock-based brewery producing Atlantic, Wolf Rock and the best-selling Doom Bar.

Skinners (www.skinnersbrewery.com) Truro operation with cheekily named tipples: Cornish Knocker, Ginger Tosser and Keel Over.

St Austell (☑01726-66022; www.staustellbrewery.co.uk; 63 Trevarthian Rd; beer tour £12; ☺9am-5.30pm) Runs 150 southwest pubs; brews Tribute, Proper Job and Tinners.

Padstow Brewing (p192) A north-coast newcomer: try coppery Windjammer, nutty Storm Runner or hoppy Kor' Degel.

St Ives Brewery (p213) Far-west brewery known for its crisp, hoppy brews such as Boiler's and Knill By Mouth.

Where to Eat & Drink

Devon and Cornwall have a fine range of eating options (p250). It's wise to book ahead for midrange restaurants, especially at weekends and during holiday periods. Top-end restaurants should be booked at least a couple of weeks in advance, some run by celebrity chefs fill up six months to a year ahead of time.

Restaurants Ranging from cheap-and-cheerful to Michelin-starred; many delight in serving local, seasonal and organic produce.

Cafes Open during the daytime (rarely after 6pm), cafes are good for a casual breakfast or lunch, or simply a cup of coffee.

Pubs Most southwest pubs serve reasonably priced meals; the best compete with restaurants on quality.

Best Beach Cafes

Glorious Oyster (p139) A shabby-chic seafood pop-up, set right beside north Devon's sand dunes.

Beachhouse (p94) Seafood and sea views on the south-Devon shore.

Porthminster Beach Café (p212) St Ives' beachside seafood bistro serving up a taste of the Med.

Hidden Hut (p170) A secret shore-side Cornish cabin rustling up fabulous beach fare.

COOKING CLASSES

River Cottage (p60) Hugh Fearnley-Whittingstall's east Devon HQ. Learn butchery, baking or allotment gardening.

Fat Hen (p214) Wild food foraging in Cornwall's rugged far-western tip.

Padstow Seafood School (p191) Rick Stein's kitchen classroom.

Ashburton Cookery School (p116) An award-winning school offering 40 courses.

Etherington Meats (☑01209-890555; www.etherington-meats.co.uk; Wheal Rose, Scorrier; courses from £60) Teaches butchery.

FARMERS MARKETS

Crediton Held on the first and third Saturday every month.

Sennen Hugely popular market, staged every Tuesday morning.

Totnes Good Food Sunday One of Devon's biggest, held on the third Sunday of each month.

Penzance On Friday mornings, showcasing produce from the far west.

Tavistock Sets up shop on the second and fourth Saturday of each month.

Gastrobus (p95) Gourmet burgers, diet-busting brownies and punchy espressos at a south-Devon surfers' beach.

Kynance Cove Cafe (p229) Classic seaside offerings at one of Cornwall's most picturesque bays.

Top Dining Pubs

St Tudy Inn (p145) One of east Cornwall's top dining destinations, tucked into a Bodmin Moor inn.

Rusty Bike (p54) Rustic-themed dishes served up in a shabby-chic Exeter local.

Pandora Inn (p161) Thatched, creekside Cornish pub, serving up quality grub.

Horse (p117) Excellent gastro-pub bringing a dash of foodie elan to market-town Dartmoor.

Gurnard's Head (p218) Classy cooking in a picture-postcard Cornish pub.

Rugglestone (p116) As traditional as it comes: real fires and hearty dishes in an ancient Dartmoor inn.

Seafood Addresses

Britannia @ the Beach (p88) The fish has been landed just yards away from this south Devon shack.

Restaurant Nathan Outlaw (p189) Superb seafood in quaint Port Isaac from one of Cornwall's top chefs.

Seahorse (p86) One of Devon's top restaurants, this Dartmouth establishment specialises in perfectly charcoal-grilled fish.

Wheelhouse (p159) A Falmouth shellfish bar where it's all about the hands-on experience.

Crab Shed (p94) Eat crab beside the picking plant at this smart Salcombe shed.

Tolcarne Inn (p222) Unfussy smuggler's pub dishing up fine market-fresh Newlyn fish.

Vegetarians & Vegans

In general vegetarians should encounter enough possibilities to make their stay enjoyable. As ever, the cities and bigger towns will cater to their needs better; in some rural and coastal areas, meat and fish dominate menus.

Predictably vegans fare worse except in larger towns and cities, but ethnic restaurants and counter-culture hubs such as Totnes and Falmouth boost prospects considerably.

The Arts

The southwest has inspired artists of all persuasions, from poets, painters and sculptors to novelists, dramatists and children's authors. Cornwall is especially known for its thriving art scene: it's more than a century since the well-known Newlyn and St Ives Schools were first established here, and the area remains a magnet for artists, with lots of local galleries hosting exhibitions.

Painting & Sculpture

Art Courses
....
St Ives School of Painting
....
Dartington International Summer School (Totnes)
....
Newlyn School of Art
....
East Devon Art Academy (Sidmouth)

Early Years

Cornwall's role as an artistic magnet arguably began when JMW Turner toured the southwest in 1811 while painting watercolours for the engravings *Picturesque Views on the Southern Coast of England*. Turner travelled widely, but it was under Cornwall's wide-open skies that his passion for dreamy, ethereal landscapes found fullest expression. He was an observer of contemporary society and many of his paintings provide an insight into early 19th-century Cornish life. *St Mawes at the Pilchard Season* (1812) depicts a chaotic harbour filled with pilchard boats and bustling villagers, backed by a St Mawes Castle bathed in Turneresque sunlight.

The Great Western Railway edging west of the Tamar in 1877 opened up the region's landscapes to artists – particularly Impressionists, who came to the southwest to paint *en plein air* (on location, rather than working from sketches in a studio).

The Newlyn School

In the early 1880s a group of artists settled around the fishing port of Newlyn, spearheaded by Birmingham-born Walter Langley, Dubliner Stanhope Forbes and the Lincolnshire artist Frank Bramley. Inspired by the naturalistic French Barbizon School, they set out to depict the day-to-day reality of people's lives. They became particularly fascinated by Newlyn's fishermen, depicting everyday tasks like net repair, sail rigging or fish sales on the quayside. Other artists exploited the natural drama and pathos of the fishermen's lot: poverty, hardship, storms and the ever-present danger of shipwrecks. Characteristic works include Stanhope Forbes' *The Health of the Bride*, depicting the marriage of a young sailor and his wife in a Newlyn inn; and Bramley's *A Hopeless Dawn*, which shows a distraught wife receiving the news that her husband has been lost at sea.

By 1884 there were at least 30 artists working either in Newlyn or the nearby towns of St Ives, Lelant and Falmouth. In 1889 Forbes and his wife Elizabeth formally established the first Newlyn School of Artists; a second colony of artists later developed in the nearby cove of Lamorna, forming the Lamorna Group (often referred to as the later Newlyn School).

The work of many of the key Newlyn and Lamorna artists – particularly Forbes, Bramley, Henry Scott-Tuke, Samuel John (Lamorna) Birch, Thomas Cooper Gotch and Walter Langley, as well as female artists Laura Johnson, Dod Procter and Elizabeth Forbes – was highly influential, and exhibited by the Royal Academy and the National Gallery.

The St Ives School

The next generation of artists reacted powerfully against the figurative concerns of their predecessors. The advent of modernism in the 1920s opened up the canvas far beyond the confines of representational painting – soon Cornwall became identified with a much more radical style of art.

Links between St Ives and the avant-garde go back to the mid-1920s, when the ground-breaking potter Bernard Leach established his first workshop in St Ives, in partnership with the Japanese ceramics artist Shoji Hamada. Leach was fascinated with the functions, shapes and forms of oriental pottery and went on to develop a highly influential style, fusing Eastern philosophies with Western materials.

By the mid-1920s the painters Cedric Morris, Christopher 'Kit' Wood and Ben Nicholson had followed in Leach's wake. During one visit to St Ives, Wood and Nicholson stumbled across the work of an entirely self-taught Cornish fisherman and painter, Alfred Wallis, whose naive style – which paid little heed to conventional rules of perspective, scale or composition – proved a powerful influence on the modernist artists, many of whom were seeking a return to the more primitive style of art that Wallis' work seemed to embody.

Within a few years Wallis found himself surrounded by a new artistic community that established itself in St Ives throughout the 1930s and early 1940s. At the forefront of this new movement were Nicholson and his wife, the young sculptor Barbara Hepworth; soon they were joined by their friend, the Russian sculptor Naum Gabo, a key figure in the constructivist movement.

The three artists began developing experimental abstract work that echoed the post-war modernist movements and were inspired by west Cornwall's shapes, light and landscapes. Hepworth, in particular, became fascinated with her adopted home, and her distinctive combination of stone, metal and sinuous forms was clearly influenced by the rugged Cornish landscape and its industrial remains and ancient monuments.

Attracted by St Ives' burgeoning reputation as a centre for abstract art, a new wave of exciting young artists, including Wilhelmina Barns-Graham, Terry Frost, Patrick Heron, Roger Hilton and Peter Lanyon, helped consolidate the town's position as a hub of creativity and experimentation throughout the 1950s and '60s.

Top Art Galleries

Tate St Ives (St Ives)

Leach Pottery (St Ives)

Newlyn Art Gallery (Penzance)

Penlee House (Penzance)

Barbara Hepworth Museum (St Ives)

THE ARTS PAINTING & SCULPTURE

ART & LITERATURE FESTIVALS

Port Eliot Festival (www.porteliotfestival.com; ☺Jul) Uber-cool fiesta of literature, music and funky fun, centred around a Cornish stately home.

Ways With Words (p80) Top-quality lit fest, at a gorgeous south-Devon medieval estate.

Fowey Festival (p175) Eclectic mix of literature and music, theatre and walks in this pretty harbour town.

Dartington International Summer School (p80) Month-long feast of musical styles ranging from early music and choral, via piano, to junk.

Animated Exeter (www.animatedexeter.co.uk; ☺Feb) Films include stop frame, puppetry and comics, plus talks and courses, too.

St Ives September Festival (www.stivesseptemberfestival.co.uk; ☺early Sep) A September celebration of music and the arts.

Recent Artists

Half a century on, west Cornwall remains an important centre for British art: Penwith claims a higher concentration of artists than anywhere else in the UK, at least outside London. Among the best known is St Just–based Kurt Jackson, who is famous for his expressive, often environmental-themed landscapes. He's also been artist-in-residence at the Eden Project. Work by Jackson and many of the area's leading emerging artists is regularly exhibited at the Newlyn Art Gallery and the Exchange in Penzance.

The abstract experiments of the 1950s and '60s continue in the work of contemporary Cornish artists, including Trevor Bell, Noel Betowski and Jeremy Annear. Meanwhile, in Devon, Damien Hirst is linked to Ilfracombe. *Verity*, his 20m statue of a naked, pregnant, half-flayed woman, towers over the harbour mouth and his installations dot the walls of his restaurant.

Plymouth also has strong connections with its own controversial artist, the bohemian Robert Lenkiewicz (1941–2002), who spent most of his life living and working around the Barbican. He specialised in large figurative portraits, and often used the city's more unsalubrious characters and locations, as well as controversial social issues, as inspiration for his work.

Rather less controversial was another Plymouth-based favourite, Beryl Cook (1926–2008), whose pictures of portly ladies tottering around in high heels became hugely popular with the public, and are often infused with a gently comic eye.

Unusual Art Spaces

Damien Hirst's Verity (Ilfracombe)

Broomhill Art Hotel (Barnstaple)

Tremenheere Sculpture Gardens (Penzance)

Roundhouse and Capstan Gallery (Sennen)

St Ives Society of Artists

Eden Project (St Austell)

Literature

Devon and Cornwall have inspired countless writers. Often they reflect the counties' characters in their work, and sometimes specific locations in their books can still be tracked down today. Devon-born crime-writing legend Agatha Christie wove many local places into her novels. You can visit her holiday home near Dartmouth, Greenway.

Another West Country writer inextricably linked with the landscape she loved is Fowey-based Daphne du Maurier. Best known for romantic, dramatic novels such as *Rebecca*, she also wrote the short story that became the Alfred Hitchcock film *The Birds*. Cornwall's bleak moors and tree-fringed creeks feature strongly in her writings. Another writer who was inspired by the countryside around the Fowey River was Kenneth Grahame, who supposedly dreamt up the idea for *The Wind in the Willows* while messing about on the river (he also supposedly used a local hotel, Fowey Hall, as the model for Toad Hall).

Other southwest literary connections include the popular poet and broadcaster Sir John Betjeman, who is buried near his Cornish home at Trebetherick on the River Camel; and the poet Charles Causley, who lived in and was inspired by Cornwall, especially the area around his home town of Launceston. Richard Blackmore's 17th-century epic *Lorna Doone* is based on Exmoor; its atmosphere infuses the book. Similarly, Henry Williamson featured the landscape of his north Devon home in *Tarka the Otter*. And then there's Arthur Conan Doyle's *The Hound of the Baskervilles*, set on, and still deeply evocative of, Dartmoor.

DH Lawrence was briefly based in the village of Zennor from 1915, but his stay there proved controversial. Lawrence's vehement anti-war sentiments and unconventional artistic lifestyle rankled with the locals – compounded by the fact that his wife Frieda was German and a cousin of Manfred von Richthofen (aka the German flying ace known as the Red Baron). The couple were later suspected of signalling to German submarines, and eventually ordered to leave the county in October 1917

Top Hula hoop performers at Port Eliot Festival (p257)

Bottom Minack Theatre (p216)

CORNWALL & DEVON ON FILM

Poldark (2015–) Locations from this rip-roaring period drama abound in Cornwall: Charlestown, Predannack Wollas, Kynance Cove, Porthgwarra and Gunwalloe have all featured. Visit Cornwall offers an Experience Poldark app.

War Horse (2011) Steven Spielberg shot his WWI epic amid Dartmoor's tors.

Alice in Wonderland (2010) Tim Burton filmed his Disney fantasy at Antony House, in east Cornwall.

Doc Martin (2004–) The north Cornish fishing village of Port Isaac doubles as Portwenn, home to grumpy medic Dr Ellingham (Martin Clunes).

Sense and Sensibility (1995) Ang Lee's version (starring Emma Thompson and Kate Winslet) was filmed at Plymouth's Saltram House.

Summer in February (2013) Dominic Cooper, Dan Stevens and the southwest Cornish coast star in this *plein-air* period drama about local painter Alfred Munnings.

Hound of the Baskervilles (1965) The BBC's classic version was filmed in the wilderness that inspired it. Dartmoor.

---

under the Defence of the Realm Act. Lawrence recounts the experience in his 1923 book, *Kangaroo*.

Another writer whose work has been rediscovered of late is Winston Graham, who penned a sprawling family saga set in Cornwall, documenting the fortunes of the Poldark family, who made their fortune from the mining industry. Supposedly modelled on the great family dynasties who once controlled much of Cornwall, the stories focus on the struggles of Ross Poldark, a brooding and troubled hero, torn between the conflicting demands of love, honour, pride and duty. Written between 1945 and 2002, the saga has recently been adapted for television for the second time, starring Aidan Turner in the hero's role.

Theatre

Despite being 200-odd miles from London's West End, the turnover of the Theatre Royal Plymouth is only bettered by the National Theatre and the Royal Shakespeare Company (RSC). The theatre's award-winning Drum performance space pioneers new writing.

In the Minack Theatre, Cornwall has a stunning and utterly unique performance space. Cut into the cliffs near Land's End, this amphitheatre was started by indomitable Rowena Cade in the 1930s. The season runs from June to September and features touring and local productions.

Cornish-based theatre company Kneehigh (www.kneehigh.co.uk) is one of the most innovative and exciting in the UK. Joyful, anarchic and highly acclaimed, its recent productions include *Tristan & Yseult*, *A Matter of Life & Death*, *946* and *Dead Dog in a Suitcase*. Every summer the company stages a new production inside its pop-up theatre, a geodesic tent dubbed The Asylum. For the past few years, it's been based at the Lost Gardens of Heligan, near St Austell, for around a month in July and August.

Landscape theatre is also a major focus of many Cornish companies: ex-Kneehigh alumni have gone on to form a new company, Wild Works (www.wildworks.biz), specialising in big, community-based outdoor theatre spectaculars. Another company operating in this sphere is Rogue Theatre (www.roguetheatre.co.uk), which stages several seasonal events in the woods of Tehidy, near Camborne.

Nature & Wildlife

For many people, it's the natural scenery that steals the show in Devon and Cornwall. The landscape here is astonishingly varied: cliffs, beaches, moors, hills, heaths, forests, farmland, islands, rivers and tidal estuaries can all be found here, each with its own unique, fascinating and often fragile habitat. It's an area rich with life, from basking sharks to butterflies, and choughs to kittiwakes – so remember to bring binoculars and a good telephoto lens.

Landscapes

Much of the West Country's landscape looks pristine, but in fact it's been worked and managed since the first human settlers arrived here some 10,000 years ago. Much of the peninsula was once covered by dense forest, but this was steadily cleared to make way for agriculture and industry. By the 19th century large swaths of Devon and Cornwall had effectively become an industrial landscape, pockmarked by slate and china-clay quarries, tin and copper mines, and numerous slag mounds and spoil heaps. Though much of the old industry has disappeared, you can still see traces of it in the old mining country around St Agnes, Porthtowan, Portreath and Camborne, where shattered rock and industrial spoil lie just a few inches beneath the topsoil.

Cornwall's granite rocks are rich in radioactive isotopes, including thorium, potassium and uranium. Some experts believe they could become a future source of geothermal energy.

The coastline is undoubtedly the region's most distinctive landscape, with a unique combination of sandy beaches, rock pools, dunes, tidal marshes, estuaries and clifftops. Generally speaking, the Atlantic-facing north coast tends to be starker and wilder, characterised by high granite cliffs and large sandy beaches, while the southern coast is gentler, with fields, meadows and valleys replacing the lofty cliffs. The south coast is also notable for several large tidal estuaries that punctuate the shoreline, including the Helford, Fal, Fowey, Tamar and Dart. These sheltered waters harbour unique subtropical microclimates that allow unusual plants, flowers and trees to flourish, and provide the perfect location for many of the region's great estates and landscaped gardens.

The southwest's other distinctive habitat is its moorland – notably the moors of Dartmoor, Exmoor, Bodmin and Penwith. These high upland moors are all located on the great spine of granite that runs directly down the centre of Devon and Cornwall, formed by volcanic processes around 300 million years ago. This hard granite is much more erosion-resistant than other forms of rock, and has worn away more slowly than the surrounding landscape, leaving behind the barren peaks and strangely shaped rock formations known locally as tors. Incidentally, the same volcanic activity was also responsible for forming the rich mineral deposits that later underpinned Devon and Cornwall's mining industries.

There are also plenty of patches of interesting woodland dotted around Devon and Cornwall. Wistman's Wood and Fingle Woods, both on Dartmoor, are the last remnants of the vast forest that once covered all of the moor, before it was cleared by human settlers. Across the border, the large forest of Cardinham Woods is worth visiting for its bike trails and tranquil scenery, as is Tehidy Woods further to the west.

National Parks & AONBs

The region has two designated national parks: Dartmoor, founded in 1951; and Exmoor, founded in 1954. Britain's national parks operate in a slightly differently way to those in many other countries: rather than being strict nature reserves, they are run more as areas of environmental protection and natural conservation, where human activity is allowed to coexist with areas of natural beauty in a managed way. Agriculture, forestry, residential housing and even some heavy industry (such as quarrying) are all theoretically allowed within the parks' boundaries, but strict rules on planning, land use and development ensure that the landscape remains largely unspoilt.

The parks are run by government-funded National Park Authorities who manage the landscape, ensure the welfare of the wildlife and natural environment, and oversee visitor activities within the parks' boundaries.

The area also has a number of Areas of Outstanding Natural Beauty (AONBs), which are protected in a similar way to the national parks, although the rules and regulations governing development, land usage and environmental protection are less rigorous. There are also many smaller nature reserves and Sites of Special Scientific Interest (SSSIs), established to protect specific habitats such as meadows, riverbanks, reed beds, moors and mudflats.

Large sections of the southwest coastline are owned by the National Trust, an independent charity that manages many important sites on behalf of the general public. The South West Coast Path (www.southwest coastpath.org.uk) allows hikers to follow a continuous trail all the way around the coastline of both counties.

Fossil Country

The Jurassic Coast in Dorset and east Devon is a popular spot for fossil-hunters, who often find archaeological treasures revealed by the fragile, erosion-prone cliffs.

Environmental Issues

A few decades ago some of the region's beaches were in a sorry state, and it wasn't uncommon to find raw sewage and industrial effluents being pumped straight into the sea just a few miles from the most popular swimming spots. Happily, thanks to environmental NGOs and local campaign groups such as Surfers Against Sewage (www.sas.org.uk), the southwest has cleaned up its act. Although pollution has sadly not been completely eradicated, the region's beaches are among the cleanest in Britain. Many hold the coveted Blue Flag award for water quality (for a full list, visit www.blueflag.org.uk). Dogs are banned on many beaches between April and October.

Other forms of pollution have proved more difficult to tackle. The region's agricultural industry has caused ongoing problems with pesticides and farming chemicals (especially nitrates and phosphates), which can seep into the water table, pollute river courses, poison fish and cause algal bloom. The problem is exacerbated by heavy rain, which washes topsoil into the rivers and seas. It's an especially big problem for shellfish farms, as oysters and mussels are filter-feeders, and as such can contain heavy concentrations of pollutants. Coastal erosion is another issue in many areas, especially along the southern coastline of Devon and Dorset, where landslips and rockfalls are a fact of life.

Traffic and air pollution are also growing headaches, especially during peak holiday periods. The vast majority of visitors – around 80% – travel to the region by car, with all the attendant problems of parking, pollution and traffic jams. It's not always the easiest option, but you might find you have a much less stressful time if you leave the car at home and investigate some other ways of exploring the region: bikes, buses and branch railways are all useful for dodging the tailbacks on a hot summer's day.

Wildlife

Cornwall Wildlife Trust (www.cornwallwildlifetrust.org.uk) and Devon Wildlife Trust (www.devonwildlifetrust.org.uk) manage many beauty spots and small wildlife reserves.

Birdlife

For a quick fix, the coast is the best place to start: you're bound to catch sight of common birds, including the razorbill, guillemot, gannet, cormorant and several types of seagull. Most common is the herring gull, distinguished by its grey plumage, light-coloured feet and black wing-tips; if you're being harassed by a gull for a bite of your pasty or you've just been blessed from above, chances are it's thanks to a herring gull. Less common are the slightly darker black-backed gull and the smaller common gull (which, despite its name, actually isn't all that common). Gulls have become a nuisance thanks to the growth in rubbish and street litter – don't feed them, as it makes them bolder.

There are also puffin colonies on the Isles of Scilly, Long Island near Boscastle and, in smaller numbers, Lundy. Inland, you might catch sight of a sparrowhawk, kestrel or buzzard hovering above farmland. By night keep an ear cocked for the hoot of the barn owl or tawny owl in remote countryside.

River estuaries are also good for a spot of birdwatching, especially for wading birds, and various species of duck, grebe and goose. The estuaries around the Tamar and Exe Rivers in Devon, Dawlish Warren near Exmouth and Hayle in Cornwall promise especially rich pickings for twitchers.

Animals & Insects

The region's most famous residents are probably the miniature ponies that roam wild across many of its moors. Best known is the Dartmoor pony, a stubby-legged, shaggy-maned steed that rarely grows much above 12 hands (4ft) high. Its cousins on Bodmin Moor and Exmoor are often slightly larger. Despite their diminutive dimensions, these hardy little ponies are astonishingly strong, and were originally bred as pack animals and beasts of burden.

Red deer are also fairly widespread on Exmoor and Dartmoor, although they're notoriously skittish creatures, so your best chance to see one is probably on a wildlife safari.

Wilder inhabitants include badgers, hares, many types of bat and, of course, several million rabbits. Foxes are also widespread, and since February 2005 have been protected (along with stags) by a ban on the traditional country pursuit of hunting with horses and hounds (much to the delight of animal activists and much to the chagrin of many country folk).

THE CHOUGH

The chough (pronounced 'chuff') was once a common sight around the southwest's shores. A member of the crow family distinguished by its jet-black plumage and orange beak, this elegant bird is a symbol of Cornish culture – legend has it that the chough embodies the spirit of King Arthur, and the bird even features on Cornwall's coat of arms. It suffered a huge decline in the 20th century due to intensive farming and habitat loss, but the first pair of choughs to nest in Cornwall for over 50 years arrived in 2002, and careful conservation efforts have resulted in choughs reestablishing themselves along several stretches of Cornwall's clifftops – the Lizard is one of the best locations.

Along the riverbanks you might glimpse the odd stoat, vole or, if you're very lucky, a playful otter, a species which is slowly recovering after decades of decline. Sadly, the once-common native red squirrel hasn't been so fortunate – it has almost disappeared over the last 50 years thanks to the introduction of the more aggressive grey squirrel from the United States.

The hedgerows, coastlines and meadows of the southwest are also great for spotting butterflies and dragonflies – some of the more common varieties you might see include the tortoiseshell, hedge brown, red admiral and painted lady, as well as more elusive species such as the orange tip and silver-washed fritillary. Rarest of all is the large blue, which became extinct from the British Isles in 1979 but has since been reintroduced to five areas around the southwest.

Look out, too, for grass snakes, slow worms and adders (Britain's only poisonous snake), especially on areas of exposed moor and heathland during warm weather.

Sea Life

The most spectacular visitor to southwest waters is the basking shark (the second-largest fish in the ocean after the whale shark), which can often be seen off the coast in the summer months. Despite its fearsome bulk – the average shark measures between 6m and 8m long – it's entirely harmless to humans, sustaining itself entirely on plankton and other forms of microscopic marine life. Some other species of shark, including the mako, porbeagle and blue shark, are rather less friendly, although you'll be unlikely to encounter them unless you happen to have hauled them up from the deep on a sea-fishing trip.

Grey seals are another common sight along the southwest coastline. You might occasionally catch sight of a grey head or two bobbing in the waters off the Devon and Cornish coasts, but most of the region's seal colonies tend to cluster on small offshore islands, especially around the coasts of Cornwall and Scilly.

Jellyfish are also common in the warmer months, and although poisonous or stinging species are unusual, it's best to steer clear if you see one.

Sightings of dolphins and porpoises are rarer, but you might find them accompanying you if you take a boat trip. The best places for land-based sightings are generally the far westerly coastlines around Land's End, Cape Cornwall and West Penwith. Very occasionally, whales stray into the southwest's waters – in 2017, a humpback whale lingered for several months off the south coast of Devon and Cornwall, briefly becoming entangled in fishing nets until being freed by conservationists.

Wildlife Reserves

Lundy Island

Looe Island

Dawlish Warren

Northam Burrows

Braunton Burrows

Hayle Estuary

Survival Guide

Directory A–Z

Accommodation

B&Bs

The great British B&B (bed and breakfast) is thriving across the West Country, ranging from larger, modern professional affairs to eccentric old-fashioned enclaves. Styles vary: you'll find crisp white linen in smart city streets, rustic rooms in remote villages, and clashing carpets in bucket 'n' spade resorts.

Some still have shared bathrooms but most are en suite (although bathrooms are often tiny). Most still serve the kind of belt-busting breakfast that means you don't have to eat until the evening.

Across the region, prices vary wildly. Expect to pay anything from £50 for a very basic double with shared bathroom, to £130-plus for a double, en suite room in a smarter guesthouse. Single travellers normally face a premium of anything between 25 to 50 percent.

Some further B&B tips:

➡ Booking direct, by phone is often cheaper because B&Bs have to pay an online transaction fee to third-party websites.

➡ Advance bookings are wise, and are essential in busy places during peak periods and in small villages, which won't have that many options.

➡ Some B&Bs don't take credit or debit cards and instead require cash or cheque.

➡ Rates rise at busy times, but some places cut prices for longer stays.

➡ When booking, check where the B&B actually is. In country areas postal addresses include the nearest town, which may be 20 miles away.

BOOK ONLINE

For more accommodation reviews by Lonely Planet authors, check out http://lonelyplanet.com/hotels.You'll find independent reviews, as well as recommendations on the best places to stay. And if you choose, you can book online.

BOOK YOUR STAY ONLINE

For more accommodation reviews by Lonely Planet authors, check out http://lonelyplanet.com/hotels. You'll find independent reviews, as well as recommendations on the best places to stay. Best of all, you can book online.

Bunkhouses & Camping Barns

Bunkhouses and camping barns are basic, budget places to bed down for the night. They're usually in gorgeously rural locations and aimed primarily at hikers and cyclists.

Individual places vary but bunkhouses tend to have more facilities. Expect dorm-style accommodation plus bathroom and cooking facilities, but you'll still need to bring a sleeping bag. Camping barns are more primitive – often just a sleeping platform, cold running water and a flush toilet – so bring all your camping kit except the tent.

Rates for both categories are around £7 to £17. The **Youth Hostels Association** (YHA; ☏ 0800 0191700; www.yha.org.uk) has a camping barn at Hound Tor on Dartmoor and a bunkhouse at Elmscott in north Devon. Other barns and bunkhouses are run independently.

Demand can outstrip supply during peak periods such as Easter and the school summer holidays – particularly if you're travelling on foot, so book well ahead to be sure of a space.

Useful information sources:

Dartmoor National Park Authority (www.dartmoor.gov.uk)

Exmoor National Park Authority (www.exmoor-nationalpark.gov.uk)

Visit Cornwall (www.visitcornwall.com)

Youth Hostels Association (www.yha.org.uk)

Camping
CAMPSITES

Devon and Cornwall's campsites have progressed far beyond tap-and-toilet sites in farmers' fields, although thankfully remote, basic sites do still exist. In more popular tourist spots and around key resorts expect to find family-friendly sites full of facilities such as bouncy castles and pools.

The trend towards glamorous camping (or glamping) continues and both counties bristle with uber-stylish Mongolian yurts, woodland eco-pods and retro caravans.

The prices we quote are per pitch, per night for two people unless otherwise stated. Expect to pay more for campsites near popular resorts in peak season. Region-wide costs range from around £9 to £30.

Summertime pitches at the more popular sites (especially those on clifftops or near beaches) can get snapped up very quickly. They'll also often require a two-night stay as a minimum during the school summer holidays, some require you book for a week.

Useful websites:

Camping & Caravanning Club (www.campingandcaravanningclub.co.uk)

Visit Cornwall (www.visitcornwall.com)

Visit Devon (www.visitdevon.co.uk)

WILD CAMPING

On Dartmoor you can experience wild or backwoods camping at its best. Pitching a tent on certain parts of the open moor is allowed, provided you follow some simple, but strict, rules. They're available from the Dartmoor National Park Authority (DNPA; www.dartmoor.gov.uk) and include the following:

➡ Only camp for one or two nights on the same spot.

➡ Don't pitch your tent on farmland, on moorland enclosed by walls, on flood plains or on archaeological sites.

➡ Pitch your tent at least 100m from any roads, and out of sight of them and any homes and farms.

➡ Use lightweight camping equipment – large family frame tents are not allowed.

➡ Camp only in areas outlined in the *Where To Camp On Dartmoor* map, and follow the Camping Code of Conduct (available from the DNPA website).

Hostels
Be they official or unofficial, the West Country is peppered with hostels offering a cheap and cheerful sleeping experience. The range is remarkable: recently revamped YHA hostels in towns and villages, converted clifftop cottages, funky backpackers

boltholes in resorts, and surfer crash pads in Cornwall. In the summer they're popular places, so book ahead, while in the winter some close – check before turning up.

YHA HOSTELS
There are around 20 hostels run by the **Youth Hostels Association** (YHA; ☑0800 0191700; www.yha.org.uk) and its affiliates scattered around Devon and Cornwall, making it perfectly possible to tour the region using them as bases. YHA hostels can have a more establishment feel than independent ones, but the 'youth' in the title is a misnomer; you can stay however old you are. Facilities are often modern and many offer en suite double and family rooms as well as dorms. Some specialise in activities. YHA membership is £20 for over 25s and £10 for those between 16 and 25. You don't have to join to stay, but members get a £3 per-night discount.

INDEPENDENT HOSTELS

With a distinctly backpacker vibe, the southwest's independent hostels are the place to revel in the region's chilled-out atmosphere. There's a good region-wide network; expect to encounter cool city-centre pads and hangouts with decks and beach views and noone bothering about sandy feet.

Dorms are quite often mixed-sex and prices average around £17 for a bed, but some peak at £30 in high season. Many have double rooms costing from around £45. Some have internet and laundry facilities. The Independent Hostels Guide (www.independenthostelguide.co.uk) is a useful resource.

Hotels

Devon and Cornwall's hotels tend to be posher, bigger and have more facilities than the region's B&Bs. There are the usual UK chains, plus independent, business-oriented, smooth, corporate affairs. Others are boutique beauties – the kind of luxurious coastal and country-house options that are travel experiences in themselves.

Demand can be high during the summer season – if you have a particular area, venue or budget in mind, it's best to secure a room at least several months in advance.

Pubs & Inns

The West Country's ancient inns offer fabulous meals, real ales and cosy places to sleep. They're also at the heart of community life – providing you with an authentic slice of local life. Accommodation is often stylish, but is occasionally seedy, with rooms a little too reminiscent of the atmosphere downstairs in the bar.

Prices vary considerably, from around £40/60 for a single/double to £90/150 and beyond. Inevitably demand is higher at weekend, so book well in advance.

Self Catering

Self-catering can be a supremely flexible option, especially if you're travelling with kids. The range of properties to rent is wide – all across the southwest there are snazzy flats, fisher's cottages and country retreats waiting to be booked. If you have a particular destination in mind, book early for stays in peak times. The following specialists can help you find your very own home-away-from-home:

Beach Retreats (☏01637-861005; www.beachretreats.co.uk)

Classic Cottages (☏01326-555555; www.classic.co.uk)

National Trust (NT; ☏0344-800 2070; www.nationaltrust holidays.org.uk)

Rural Retreats (☏01386-701177; www.ruralretreats.co.uk)

Stilwell's (☏0345-2680873; www.cottagesdirect.co.uk)

Unique Home Stays (☏01637-881183; www.uniquehomestays.com)

West Country Cottages (☏01803-814000; www.west countrycottages.co.uk)

Dangers & Annoyances

Compared to the world's trouble spots, England's southwest is a particularly safe place. But of course, crime can happen anywhere and you do still need to take care.

Climate

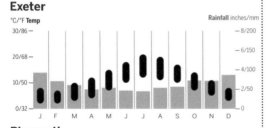

Exeter

°C/°F Temp   Rainfall inches/mm

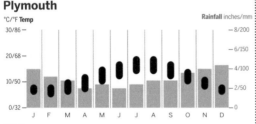

Plymouth

°C/°F Temp   Rainfall inches/mm

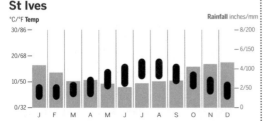

St Ives

°C/°F Temp   Rainfall inches/mm

→ Town centres can be rowdy on Friday and Saturday nights when the pubs and clubs are emptying.

→ It's always wise to keep money, valuables and important documents out of sight in cars, and not just in city centres – remote moorland and coastal beauty spots are sometimes targeted by thieves.

→ If you're in hostels, it's a good idea to take a padlock for the lockers and keep stuff packed away.

Beaches

The lifesaving charity, the Royal National Lifeboat Institution (RNLI; www.rnli.org. uk), has to rescue hundreds of people each year in the West Country and offers the following safety advice:

→ Use beaches that have lifeguards.

→ Read and obey safety signs.

→ Never swim alone.

→ Swim between red-and-yellow flags, and surf in water marked by black-and-white chequered flags.

→ Coastguards also advise parents not let children use inflatables – if they do, an adult should attach a line and hold onto it.

Some of the biggest tidal ranges in the world occur in the southwest, and the sandy route out of that secluded cove can soon disappear under feet of water – people regularly have to be rescued after getting cut off. Less dramatically, kit left on the sand when you go in to surf can be a soggy, scattered mess when you get back.

Times of high and low water are often outlined at popular beaches, as well as on local BBC TV and radio, and in newspapers. Small yellow booklets of tide times are available from newsagents and local shops (£1.40).

In recent decades, campaigners – particularly Cornwall-based Surfers

Against Sewage (www. sas.org.uk) – have battled (and in part succeeded) to improve water quality. 'Blue Flags' are awarded to beaches with high water-quality standards, and good safety and environmental records; see the latest list at www. blueflag.org. But note, some of Devon and Cornwall's best beaches don't qualify for the award, not because water quality is bad, but because they don't have specific features (such as toilets, bins and drinking water).

Walking

While stunning to hike, the region's moors are also remote, so prepare for upland weather conditions. Warm, waterproof clothing, hats, water and sunscreen are essential. Parts of Dartmoor are used by the military for live firing ranges.

Like the rest of Britain, the southwest's coastline is subject to erosion and occasionally rockfalls cause injury or even death. Unstable sections of the coastline are often fenced off and coastguards urge beach-users and walkers to obey warning signs.

Discount Cards

There are no region-wide, non-transport discount cards for visitors, but sometimes two or more attractions team up with joint tickets that allow entry to both.

Devon and Cornwall have a superb sprinkling of historic buildings and if you're visiting more than four or five properties it's usually worth joining a heritage organisation for a year. The National Trust (NT; www.nationaltrust. co.uk) has an excellent range of properties region-wide; members can park for free at their car parks, too. Annual membership is from £63 for an adult, £105 for two and £111 for families.

English Heritage (EH; www. english-heritage.org.uk) also has a good selection of prop-

erties in the southwest. Annual adult membership costs £52 (£44 for over 60s) and allows up to six children free entry; joint adult membership costs £93 (joint senior £76).

There are also regional passes for bus (p274) and train (p276) services.

Electricity

Type G
230V/50Hz

Gay & Lesbian Travellers

The southwest generally mirrors the UK's relatively tolerant attitude to lesbians and gay men. That said, you'll still find pockets of homophobic hostility in some areas. Gay (and gay-friendly) clubs and bars can be found in the cities and bigger towns (such as Exeter, Torquay, Truro and Plymouth), although there's often not a huge choice.

Gay accommodation based in Devon and Cornwall crops up in *Gay Times* (www. gaytimes.co.uk) and *Diva* (www.divamag.co.uk). The **Intercom Trust** (☎0800 612 3010; www.intercomtrust. org.uk) profiles the southwest's LGBT groups, and runs a regional helpline (9am to 4pm Monday to Friday).

Health

Adders

Britain's only venomous snake is not uncommon in the region's hills, moors and coast paths. Adders will only attack if harassed or threatened and, although their venom poses little danger to a healthy adult human, the bite is very painful and does require medical attention. If you are bitten, don't panic. Immobilise the limb with a splint (eg a stick) and apply a bandage over the site firmly. Do not apply a tourniquet, or cut or suck the bite. Get the victim to medical help as soon as possible.

Sunburn

The coastline and outdoor lifestyle in Devon and Cornwall are often blamed for some of the highest malignant skin cancer rates in England and Wales. Experts remind UK nationals they still need sunscreen even if they're holidaying at home. Stay out of the sun between 11am and 3pm, cover up, use water-resistant broad-spectrum sunscreen and UV sunglasses and take extra care of children.

Ticks

Ticks are increasingly common in the region's country-side, some carry Lyme disease – a relatively uncommon but potentially serious illness. To prevent bites, use insect repellent and wear long trousers tucked into socks and long-sleeved shirts. At the end of the day, check that you're tick-free. If you are bitten, remove the tick as soon as possible by grasping it close to the skin with tweezers and twisting anti-clockwise. Lyme disease may appear as an expanding, reddish round rash in the area of the bite, for up to 30 days later. Symptoms include influenza, mild headaches and aching muscles and joints. The condition is treatable with antibiotics but early diagnosis is best; if you think any of these symptoms may come from a tick bite, see a doctor.

Insurance

At the time of writing, if you're an EU citizen, a European Health Insurance Card (EHIC) – available from health centres or, in the UK, post offices – covers you for urgent medical treatment, including pre-existing medical conditions and routine maternity care. However, it will not cover costs such as being flown back home in an emergency, so private travel insurance will also be needed. Britain's vote to leave the EU may well see systems change – check for the latest before travel.

Citizens from non-EU countries should find out if there is a reciprocal arrangement for free medical care between their country and the UK. If you do need health insurance, make sure you get a policy that covers you for the worst possible scenarios, including emergency flights home.

Internet Access

➡ Both 3G and 4G mobile broadband coverage is good in large population centres, but limited or nonexistent in rural areas. However, beware high charges for data roaming – check with your mobile/cell-phone provider before travelling.

➡ Many hotels, B&Bs, hostels, stations and coffee shops (even some trains and buses) have wi-fi access, charging anything from nothing to £6 per hour.

➡ Internet cafes are surprisingly rare in England, especially away from big cities and tourist spots. Most charge from £1.50 per hour; it could be as high as £6 per hour.

➡ Public libraries often have computers with free internet access, but only for 30-minute slots, and demand can be high.

Maps

If you're heading onto the region's rural roads, a good regional atlas will save you frustrating diversions. Often you can't rely on signposts mentioning places you're familiar with, and GPS is notorious for directing drivers down unnavigable roads. Even Google Maps is far from infallible.

The most useful maps have a scale of about 1:200,000 (3 miles to 1in). Most road atlases cost £8 to £12 and can be bought at petrol stations and bookshops.

For walkers and cyclists the Ordnance Survey (OS; www.shop.ordnancesurvey-leisure.co.uk) Landranger series (£7) is good, with a scale of 1:50,000, but many prefer the detail of the Explorer range (£8), at 1:25,000.

Money

Visa and Mastercard credit cards are widely accepted, though other credit cards less so, and ATMs are widely available.

Currency Exchange

Banks and post offices in cities and larger towns will change money; exchange rates tend to be reasonable.

Tipping

Pubs and bars Not expected if you order drinks (or food) and pay at the bar; usually 10% if you order at the table and your meal is brought to you.

Restaurants Around 10% in restaurants and teahouses with table service, 15% at smarter restaurants. Tips may be added to your bill as a 'service charge' – it's discretionary.

Taxis Usually 10%, or rounded up to the nearest pound.

Opening Hours

Opening hours vary throughout the year, especially in rural and coastal areas where some places have shorter hours, or close completely, from October to March.

Banks 9.30am to 4pm or 5pm Monday to Friday; some open 9.30am to 1pm Saturday.

Pubs and bars Noon to 11pm Monday to Saturday (some till midnight or 1am Friday and Saturday), 12.30pm to 11pm Sunday.

Restaurants Lunch is noon to 3pm, dinner 6pm to 9pm or 10pm.

Shops 9am to 5.30pm or 6pm Monday to Saturday, and often 11am to 5pm Sunday.

Telephone

Mobile Phones

Mobile-phone coverage in the region's towns and cities is good, as are signals in many, but not all, rural and coastal areas. Geography also means different networks have different zones where they provide poor or no reception. Payphones are common in urban areas.

The UK uses the GSM 900/1800 network, which covers the rest of Europe, Australia and New Zealand, but isn't compatible with the North American GSM 1900.

Check roaming charges with your provider before you travel. Since June 2017, EU residents have benefited from the removal of roaming charges, although this may change depending on the outcome of Brexit negotiations.

Useful Numbers & Codes

Dialling to the UK Dial your country's international access code then 🖉44 (the UK country code), then the area code

(dropping the first 0) followed by the telephone number.

Dialling from the UK The international access code is 🖉00; dial this, then add the code of the country you wish to dial.

Mobile phones Codes usually begin with 🖉07.

Free calls Numbers starting with 🖉0800 or 🖉0808 are free.

Call charges Details here: www. gov.uk/call-charges

National operator 🖉100

International operator 🖉155

Toilets

➡ Public toilets are generally clean and fairly modern. Public-spending cuts mean some have closed. Some charge (20p).

➡ Regional railway station toilets rarely charge.

➡ Pubs and restaurants stipulate toilets are for customers only.

Tourist Information

Region-wide, tourist offices stock free town maps and have informed, helpful staff. Smaller offices have shorter opening hours. Some information centres are also run by national parks. Some sell walking maps and local books and can help book accommodation. Staff fluent in other languages aren't that common; French and, to a lesser extent, Spanish are the most likely specialities.

The official visitor websites for the region:

Visit Cornwall (www.visitcornwall.com)

Visit Devon (www.visitdevon.co.uk)

Travellers with Disabilities

New buildings have wheelchair access, and even hotels in grand old country houses often have lifts, ramps and other facilities. Hotels and B&Bs in historic buildings are often harder to adapt, so you'll have less choice here.

For long-distance travel, coaches can present problems, though staff will help where possible. On trains there's often more room and better facilities; in some modern carriages all the signs are repeated in Braille. There's normally a phone and a sign detailing how to request help.

Modern city buses tend to have low floors for easier access. Bigger taxi firms will have vehicles that can take wheelchairs.

Exploring the region's wilder spaces can present challenges, but efforts have been made. These include on the South West Coast Path (www.southwestcoastpath. com) where some more remote parts have been made more accessible – check the website's Easy Access Walks tab.

The Dartmoor National Park Authority (www.dartmoor.gov.uk) produces the *Easy Going Dartmoor* booklet for less-mobile visitors (available online). This outlines facilities and has a good range of accessible routes to explore.

Download Lonely Planet's free Accessible Travel guide from http://lptravel.to/AccessibleTravel.

Transport

GETTING THERE & AWAY

Devon and Cornwall sit, gloriously, at the far end of England, and getting there sometimes feels like it. At its worst, you'll experience traffic jams, long coach journeys or delayed trains – most of the time, though, it's a relatively easy, often scenic trip west. Internal UK flights, reasonable rail links and travelling off-peak all help ease journeys.

Flights, cars and tours can be booked online at lonelyplanet.com/bookings.

Air

➡ The cost of flying to Devon and Cornwall from the rest of the UK varies dramatically depending on when you book and when you want to fly.

➡ A return flight to the region from within the British Isles is around £60 to £140 for an adult, including tax.

➡ Many prices rise at peak holiday times and at weekends.

➡ Save money by booking far in advance.

➡ If travelling from outside the UK, you'll often need to come via one of the country's key international airports, but there are links with some European cities.

➡ Flights to the Isles of Scilly leave from Land's End and Newquay airports year-round, and from Exeter Airport between March and October.

Airports & Airlines

Exeter Airport (☎01392-367433; www.exeter-airport.co.uk) Routes from Belfast, the Channel Islands, Edinburgh, Glasgow, London City, Manchester and Newcastle, plus links from European cities.

Land's End Airport (☎01736-785231; www.landsendairport.co.uk; Kelynack, near St Just) This tiny airfield, 5 miles northwest of Penzance, offers flights to the Isles of Scilly.

Newquay Cornwall Airport (☎01637-860600; www.cornwallairportnewquay.com) Direct, year-round flights from London Gatwick, Manchester and the Isles of Scilly. Plus summer routes from London Stansted, Düsseldorf, Edinburgh, Glasgow, Liverpool and Newcastle.

St Mary's Airport (ISC; ☎01720-424330; www.scilly.gov.uk) Main gateway to the Isles of Scilly. Flights are Monday to Saturday only.

Bus

Travelling by bus to the southwest is cheap and reliable, but normally takes longer than the train.

National Express (☎0871-7818181; www.nationalexpress.com) A comprehensive network of services to Devon and Cornwall. Sample fares include London Victoria to Newquay (£20, 7½ hours, three daily) and Edinburgh to Exeter (£80, 13 hours, two daily). Special deals ('fun fares') can be a real bargain.

CLIMATE CHANGE & TRAVEL

Every form of transport that relies on carbon-based fuel generates CO_2, the main cause of human-induced climate change. Modern travel is dependent on aeroplanes, which might use less fuel per kilometre per person than most cars but travel much greater distances. The altitude at which aircraft emit gases (including CO_2) and particles also contributes to their climate change impact. Many websites offer 'carbon calculators' that allow people to estimate the carbon emissions generated by their journey and, for those who wish to do so, to offset the impact of the greenhouse gases emitted with contributions to portfolios of climate-friendly initiatives throughout the world. Lonely Planet offsets the carbon footprint of all staff and author travel.

Megabus (☎900-1600 900; www.uk.megabus.com) A smaller network, but fares are often cheaper.

Car

The vast majority of visitors to the southwest come by car, resulting in some serious traffic jams at peak times – try to avoid obvious Bank Holiday and school-holiday travel periods.

The 190-mile London–Exeter drive should take around 3½ hours; Birmingham to Newquay is 240 miles (five hours); Edinburgh to Penzance is 560 miles (10½ hours). Expect to add anything from half an hour to two hours (and beyond) for summer delays.

Sea

You can enter the southwest by sea through the port of Plymouth. **Brittany Ferries** (☎0330-159 7000; www.britta ny-ferries.co.uk; Millbay Docks) sails between Plymouth and Roscoff in France (six to eight hours; from two daily to three per week) and Santander in northern Spain (20 hours, one per week).

Prices vary dramatically; for cheap fares book early and take non-peak, non-weekend crossings. A 10-day, mid-week return in mid-August between Plymouth and Roscoff is £80 for foot passengers; £330 for a car and two adults. A similar Plymouth–Santander trip costs £200 for one on-foot passenger; £820 for a car and two passengers.

Off-season deals and special offers can bring the price down dramatically – the Plymouth to Roscoff return for a car and two passengers falls to £225 in mid-March. Off-peak deals can also bring 20% off journeys between Plymouth and Santander.

Train

Services between major cities and Devon and Cornwall tend to run at least hourly. National Rail Enquiries (www.nationalrail.co.uk) has information on times and fares.

Travel times and costs vary (the latter wildly); advance booking and travelling off-peak cuts costs dramatically. Sample fares include London Paddington to Penzance (£65, 5½ hours, nine daily) and Edinburgh to Plymouth (£130, 10 hours, every two hours).

GWR (www.gwr.com) Routes include those from London Paddington to Exeter, Penzance, Plymouth, Tiverton Parkway and Truro. It also runs services to Gatwick Airport and branch lines to Barnstaple, Exmouth, Falmouth, Looe, Newquay, St Ives and Torquay.

CrossCountry (www.cross countrytrains.co.uk) Links the southwest with the Midlands, and the north of England and Scotland. Stations served include Aberdeen, Birmingham, Bristol, Edinburgh, Glasgow, Leeds, Newcastle, Cardiff and the main southwest stations between Tiverton Parkway and Penzance.

South West Trains (☎0845 600 0650; www.southwest-trains.co.uk) Runs services between London Waterloo and Axminster and Exeter.

GETTING AROUND

Air

Flights within Devon and Cornwall are limited to those to and from the Isles of Scilly via Skybus and, in winter only, Lundy Island. Services are generally reliable and the safety record good.

Airlines

Skybus (☎01736-334220; www.islesofscilly-travel.co.uk) Run by Isles of Scilly Travel, Skybus provides year-round flights to St Mary's on the Isles of Scilly from Newquay (adult/child return £190/145, 30 minutes) and Land's End (adult/child £140/113, 15 minutes). Also, between Easter and October, it offers services from Exeter (adult/child £270/200, one hour). For all routes, flights are daily between Monday and Saturday, with no services on Sunday.

Lundy Helicopter (☎01237-431831; www.landmarktrust. org.uk) A seasonal, seven-minute, helicopter service that only runs in the winter (late-October to late-March), linking North Devon's Lundy Island with nearby Hartland Point on the mainland.

Bicycle

The southwest has an appealing network of car-free and cyclist-friendly routes; there are also hundreds of bike-hire outlets and hundreds of miles of National Cycle Network trails (p36). For info and maps, try the sustainable transport charity Sustrans (www.sustrans.org.uk).

The most enjoyable cycling weather tends to fall between spring and autumn. Because July and August are busy months, May, June and September make attractive alternatives.

Bicycles are banned from motorways, but are allowed on other public roads. Pedalling Devon and Cornwall's 'A' roads, though, can be both dangerous and frightening; some of the busier 'B' roads are also unappealing. Cyclists can use public bridle ways but must give way to other users. Be aware that you can't cycle on public footpaths, something that's a particular bone of contention on the southwest's moors and coast paths.

You can take a bike, for free, on the southwest's national train companies, but booking is now required and restrictions often apply at peak times.

Bike Hire

We specify bike-hire places throughout the guide. In general where there are well-used cycle paths, a good cycle-hire shop is often nearby. Expect to pay around £12 for a half-day rental.

Boat

Two key, reliable ferry services link the southwest's main islands with the mainland.
Isles of Scilly Travel (☑01720-424220; www.isle-sofscilly-travel.co.uk; Hugh St) operates the archipelago's emblematic passenger ferry (the *Scillonian III*) between Penzance and the main island, St Mary's (adult/child return £90/50, 2¾ hours). The service is seasonal – it doesn't run in the winter. Between March and November there are between two and seven sailings a week.

Once in the Isles of Scilly, a fleet of ferries shuttles between St Mary's and the smaller islands surrounding it. Services are operated by the **St Mary's Boatmen's Association** (☑01720-423999; www.scillyboating.co.uk) and run at least daily between April and October, leaving St Mary's in the morning and returning in the afternoon. Adult/child returns cost £9.50/4.50.

The passenger vessel **MS Oldenburg** (☑01237-431831; www.landmarktrust.org.uk) sails to Lundy Island from either Bideford or Ilfracombe, once a day between late March and late October. The journey time is under two hours for both crossings. Fares are the same from either port: adult/child/family day return £37/19/84; period return (ie: anything longer than a day return) adult/child £65/33.

There are also numerous car and passenger ferries, which shuttle across rivers.

Bus

The region's bus services are generally reliable, providing a safe, comfortable and cost-effective way to travel. Services are better in urban areas, but can dwindle to one a day, a week or even none, in rural areas.

Bus Passes

See the table below for standard bus passes, in addition consider the following:

PlusBus (www.plusbus.info) Adds bus travel around towns to your train ticket for £2 a day. Places covered in Devon and Cornwall: Barnstaple, Bodmin, Camborne & Redruth, Exeter, Falmouth & Penryn, Liskeard, Newquay, Newton Abbot, Penzance, Plymouth, St Austell, Totnes and Truro.

Ride Cornwall Ranger (adult/child/family £13/10/26) A day's off-peak travel in Cornwall on most bus services and GWR and CrossCountry trains.

Regional Travel

National Express (☑0871-7818181; www.nationalexpress.com) runs frequent services between the region's cities, major towns and resorts. Sample direct services include Penzance to Torquay (£20, four hours, one daily) and Plymouth to Torquay (£10, one hour, one daily).

Megabus (☑900-1600 900; www.uk.megabus.com) operates fewer services, mainly between Devon and southern and western Cornish resorts. Prices are often similar to those of National Express, but can be lower if booked far in advance.

Key bus firms include the following:

First Kernow (☑customer service 0845 600 1420, timetables 0871 200 2233; www.firstgroup.com/cornwall) Major operator in Cornwall.

BUS PASSES

NAME	COMPANY	AREA	DURATION	FARE: ADULT/ CHILD/FAMILY
DevonDay	Stagecoach	Devon	1 day	£8.50/5.70/17
Explorer	Stagecoach	Devon & Cornwall	1 day	£7.50/5.10/15.40
FirstDay	First Kernow	Cornwall	1 day	£12/6/24
FirstWeek	First Kernow	Cornwall	7 days	£26/13/52
MegaRider	Stagecoach	Exeter	7 days	£14*
MegaRider	Stagecoach	North Devon	7 days	£15*
MegaRider	Stagecoach	Torbay	7 days	£17.50*
MegaRider Gold	Stagecoach	Devon & Cornwall	7 days	£27

* Note: these items do not have child/family fares available.

Stagecoach (www.stagecoach bus.com) Devon's main cross-county operator.

In Cities

Devon and Cornwall's towns and cities have good bus networks, although routes tend to be winding down by 10.30pm. City day passes (with names like Day Rover, Wayfarer or Explorer) can be good value. Expect to pay around £1.20 to £2 for a single fare.

Car & Motorcycle

Devon and Cornwall can't claim an extensive motorway network – there are none west of Exeter. While many stretches of the counties' key 'A' roads are dual carriageway, some aren't, and the lesser 'A' roads are rarely so. They can become severely congested at peak holiday times.

'A' roads and many 'B' roads have plenty of petrol and service stations. But it's worth filling up before heading off these main routes into rural areas, onto the moors or along lesser-used coastal routes.

In the towns and cities fuel prices mirror those nationwide, but rise as you head into the countryside.

Bridge Tolls

There is a bridge toll for drivers leaving Cornwall on the A38 via the Tamar Bridge, near Plymouth. Rates are £1.50 for a car and £3.70 for touring vans over 3.5 tonnes. Charges apply eastbound only; you can pay by cash at the booths. The bridge is free for motorcyclists, pedestrians and cyclists.

Car Ferries

The deep rivers and wide estuaries that cut into the region's landscape sometimes make ferries the fastest, most scenic, route from A to B. At other times peak-period ferry queues make that 20-mile road detour seem like a better idea.

TRAINS WITH A VIEW

Some of the region's train routes offer superb coastal and estuary views. It's definitely worth looking out the window between the following places:

➡ Exeter and Newton Abbot

➡ Plymouth and Gunnislake

➡ Plymouth and Liskeard

➡ St Erth and St Ives

➡ St Erth and Penzance

The website Great Scenic Railways of Devon and Cornwall (www.greatscenicrailways.co.uk) has a wealth of information, plus details of local walks.

Some ferries take cars, people and bikes but some only carry foot passengers. The key car ferries run all year.

The following are one-way, combined car and passenger fares. Unless specified, charges apply when travelling in both directions.

Bodinnick to Fowey Ferry Links mid and east Cornwall, cutting out the detour to Lostwithiel; £4.60.

Dartmouth Higher/Lower Ferry Crosses the River Dart at Dartmouth in Devon, linking with Torquay; £5.60/5.

King Harry Ferry A shortcut to the Roseland Peninsula; crossing the Fal River from near Trelissick Gardens to Philleigh, a few miles north of St Mawes; £6.

Torpoint Ferry Shuttles between Devon and Cornwall, a shortcut from the city of Plymouth to the Rame Peninsula; £1.50; charges apply eastbound only.

Fuel

Fuel tends to be more expensive in rural areas, so it's nearly always worth filling up nearer to a major town.

Hire

Rates for a small car start at about £130 per week. The region's airports and cities, and many major towns, have car-hire outlets. Firms with a good presence in the region:

Avis (www.avis.co.uk)

Europcar (www.europcar.co.uk)

Hertz (www.hertz.co.uk)

Insurance

It's illegal to drive a car or ride a motorbike in England without (at least) third-party insurance. This will be included with all rental cars. If you're bringing your own car, you will need to arrange this.

Parking

Expect to pay from £1.40 to £1.80 for an hour and around £8 to £14 for the day. Be aware, in some towns you won't have to buy a ticket to park overnight on one road, but will on a neighbouring one.

Charges at beaches can mount up; some cost per two/three hours £2.50/3.70, or £10 a day.

Parking can also be at a premium amid the winding, cobbled streets of the region's fishing villages and tourist hot spots. Many have park-and-ride systems, with costs ranging from around £2.50 to £5.

Road Rules

Speed limits are usually 30mph (48km/h) in built-up areas, 60mph (96km/h) on main roads and 70mph (112km/h) on motorways and most (but not all) dual carriageways.

A foreign driving licence is valid in Britain for up to 12 months after entering the country.

Drink-driving is taken very seriously; you're allowed a

STEAM TRAINS

The West Country's privately operated steam trains ply some stunning routes:

Bodmin & Wenford Railway (📞01208-73555; www. bodminrailway.co.uk; rover pass adult/child £13/6; ⏱3-5 daily trains May-Sep, fewer at other times) Scenic journeys, skirting Bodmin Moor.

Dartmouth Steam Railway (📞01803-555872; www.dart mouthrailriver.co.uk; Torbay Rd, Paignton; adult/child/family return £17/10/46; ⏱4-9 trains daily mid-Feb–Oct) Links the Torbay resort of Paignton with Dartmouth.

South Devon Steam Railway (📞01364-644370; www. southdevonrailway.co.uk; adult/child return £15/9; ⏱Apr-Oct) Shuttles between Totnes and Buckfastleigh.

maximum blood-alcohol level of 80mg/100mL (0.08%).

Some other important rules:

➡ Drive on the left.

➡ Wear seatbelts in cars.

➡ Wear helmets on motorcycles.

➡ Give way to your right at junctions and roundabouts.

➡ Always use the left lane on motorways and dual carriageways unless overtaking.

➡ Don't use a mobile phone while driving unless it's fully hands-free.

Train

Services between Devon and Cornwall's towns and cities on the London Paddington to Penzance main line are generally good. Trains normally run at least hourly, sometimes more frequently. The National Rail Enquiries website (www.nationalrail. co.uk) details train timetables and fares.

Some sample direct, off-peak services:

Exeter–Penzance (£21, three hours, hourly)

Plymouth–Truro (£10, 1¼ hours, hourly)

Truro–Exeter (£18, 2½ hours, hourly)

Booking Sites

Sites selling tickets from all train companies to all national destinations:

➡ www.thetrainline.com

➡ www.qjump.co.uk

➡ www.raileasy.co.uk

Branch Lines

Branch lines fan out from the main London–Penzance intercity route. Some of the key lines:

➡ Exeter–Barnstaple

➡ Exeter–Exmouth

➡ Liskeard–Looe

➡ Newton Abbot–Torquay and Paignton

➡ Par–Newquay

➡ Plymouth–Gunnislake

➡ St Erth–St Ives

➡ Truro–Falmouth

Rail Passes

The following off-peak passes are accepted by all the national (but not private) train companies and can be bought either from them or at staffed stations:

Devon Day Ranger (adult/child £10/5) One day's unlimited travel on trains in the county.

Devon Evening Ranger (adult/child £5/2.50) Unlimited travel in Devon after 6pm.

Freedom of Devon and Cornwall Rover Three day's travel in any seven-day period across the two counties (adult/child £46/23); or eight day's unlimited travel in any 15-day period (adult/child £70/35).

Ride Cornwall Ranger (adult/child/family £13/10/26) Offers one day's travel on the county's buses and trains, off-peak.

Behind the Scenes

SEND US YOUR FEEDBACK

We love to hear from travellers – your comments keep us on our toes and help make our books better. Our well-travelled team reads every word on what you loved or loathed about this book. Although we cannot reply individually to your submissions, we always guarantee that your feedback goes straight to the appropriate authors, in time for the next edition. Each person who sends us information is thanked in the next edition – the most useful submissions are rewarded with a selection of digital PDF chapters.

Visit **lonelyplanet.com/contact** to submit your updates and suggestions or to ask for help. Our award-winning website also features inspirational travel stories, news and discussions.

Note: We may edit, reproduce and incorporate your comments in Lonely Planet products such as guidebooks, websites and digital products, so let us know if you don't want your comments reproduced or your name acknowledged. For a copy of our privacy policy visit lonelyplanet.com/privacy.

WRITER THANKS

Oliver Berry

As always, huge thanks to the many people who helped out with advice, suggestions and tips for new material, with an extra special shout out for Justin Foulkes, Sarah Bennett, Mark Sharham, Nigel Mortimer, Laura Hicks, Heidi Fitzpatrick and Another Place. Extra thanks to James Smart for captaining the ship, to Susie Berry for apple tree shopping and much-needed lunches, and to Rosabella for many happy days exploring Kernow with me.

Belinda Dixon

Researching a place is a real joint effort. It's the result of B&B, bar and hotel staff who share their recommendations; tourist office workers who share their knowledge; random strangers who share their time and countless kindnesses. Huge thanks to all. And, again, to James Smart for the gig, Lonely Planet's behind-the-scenes teams, and fellow authors and adventurers for humour, wisdom and travellers' tales.

ACKNOWLEDGEMENTS

Climate map data adapted from Peel MC, Finlayson BL & McMahon TA (2007) 'Updated World Map of the Köppen-Geiger Climate Classification', Hydrology and Earth System Sciences, 11, 163344.

Cover photograph: Salcombe, South Devon, Justin Foulkes/4Corners ©

THIS BOOK

This 4th edition of Lonely Planet's *Devon & Cornwall* guidebook was researched and written by Oliver Berry and Belinda Dixon. Oliver and Belinda also wrote the previous two editions. This guidebook was produced by the following:

Destination Editor James Smart

Product Editors Kate Kiely, Genna Patterson

Senior Cartographer Mark Griffiths

Book Designer Wibowo Rusli

Assisting Editors Janet Austin, Janice Bird, Andrea Dobbin, Rosie Nicholson, Susan Paterson

Assisting Cartographer Hunor Csutoros

Assisting Book Designer Jessica Rose

Cover Researcher Naomi Parker

Thanks to Carolyn Boicos, Kate Chapman, Catherine Din, Jeff Jacobs, Hannah Cartmel, Craig Kilburn, Tony Wheeler, Julie Woods

Index

LONELY PLANET IN THE WILD

Send your 'Lonely Planet in the Wild' photos to social@lonelyplanet.com
We share the best on our Facebook page every week!

Map Legend

Sights

- Beach
- Bird Sanctuary
- Buddhist
- Castle/Palace
- Christian
- Confucian
- Hindu
- Islamic
- Jain
- Jewish
- Monument
- Museum/Gallery/Historic Building
- Ruin
- Shinto
- Sikh
- Taoist
- Winery/Vineyard
- Zoo/Wildlife Sanctuary
- Other Sight

Activities, Courses & Tours

- Bodysurfing
- Diving
- Canoeing/Kayaking
- Course/Tour
- Sento Hot Baths/Onsen
- Skiing
- Snorkelling
- Surfing
- Swimming/Pool
- Walking
- Windsurfing
- Other Activity

Sleeping

- Sleeping
- Camping
- Hut/Shelter

Eating

- Eating

Drinking & Nightlife

- Drinking & Nightlife
- Cafe

Entertainment

- Entertainment

Shopping

- Shopping

Information

- Bank
- Embassy/Consulate
- Hospital/Medical
- Internet
- Police
- Post Office
- Telephone
- Toilet
- Tourist Information
- Other Information

Geographic

- Beach
- Gate
- Hut/Shelter
- Lighthouse
- Lookout
- Mountain/Volcano
- Oasis
- Park
- Pass
- Picnic Area
- Waterfall

Population

- Capital (National)
- Capital (State/Province)
- City/Large Town
- Town/Village

Transport

- Airport
- Border crossing
- Bus
- Cable car/Funicular
- Cycling
- Ferry
- Metro station
- Monorail
- Parking
- Petrol station
- S-Bahn/Subway station
- Taxi
- T-bane/Tunnelbana station
- Train station/Railway
- Tram
- Tube station
- U-Bahn/Underground station
- Other Transport

Routes

- Tollway
- Freeway
- Primary
- Secondary
- Tertiary
- Lane
- Unsealed road
- Road under construction
- Plaza/Mall
- Steps
- Tunnel
- Pedestrian overpass
- Walking Tour
- Walking Tour detour
- Path/Walking Trail

Boundaries

- International
- State/Province
- Disputed
- Regional/Suburb
- Marine Park
- Cliff
- Wall

Hydrography

- River, Creek
- Intermittent River
- Canal
- Water
- Dry/Salt/Intermittent Lake
- Reef

Areas

- Airport/Runway
- Beach/Desert
- Cemetery (Christian)
- Cemetery (Other)
- Glacier
- Mudflat
- Park/Forest
- Sight (Building)
- Sportsground
- Swamp/Mangrove

Note: Not all symbols displayed above appear on the maps in this book

OUR STORY

A beat-up old car, a few dollars in the pocket and a sense of adventure. In 1972 that's all Tony and Maureen Wheeler needed for the trip of a lifetime – across Europe and Asia overland to Australia. It took several months, and at the end – broke but inspired – they sat at their kitchen table writing and stapling together their first travel guide, *Across Asia on the Cheap*. Within a week they'd sold 1500 copies. Lonely Planet was born.

Today, Lonely Planet has offices in Franklin, London, Melbourne, Oakland, Dublin, Beijing and Delhi, with more than 600 staff and writers. We share Tony's belief that 'a great guidebook should do three things: inform, educate and amuse'.

OUR WRITERS

Oliver Berry

Cornwall Oliver is a writer and photographer from Cornwall. He has worked for Lonely Planet for more than a decade, covering destinations from Cornwall to the Cook Islands, and has worked on more than 30 guidebooks. He is also a regular contributor to many newspapers and magazines, including *Lonely Planet Traveller*. His writing has won several awards, including The Guardian Young Travel Writer of the Year and the TNT Magazine People's Choice Award.

Oliver also wrote the Plan Your Trip and Understand chapters. His latest work is published at www.oliverberry.com.

Belinda Dixon

Devon Only happy when her feet are suitably sandy, Belinda has been (gleefully) travelling, researching and writing for Lonely Planet since 2006. It's seen her marvelling at Stonehenge at sunrise, scrambling up Italian mountain paths, horse riding across Donegal's golden sands, kayaking down south Devon rivers, gazing at Verona's frescoes, and fossil hunting on Dorset's Jurassic Coast.

Belinda is also an adventure writer – which has seen her trek the Himalayas, scale Scottish mountains in a snow storm, climb Dartmoor crags, surf and swim in England's winter seas, become addicted to SUP and sleep out under the stars. See her blog posts at https://belindadixon.com.

31901062491305

Published by Lonely Planet Global Limited
CRN 554153
4th edition – January 2018
ISBN 978 1 78657 253 0
© Lonely Planet 2018   Photographs © as indicated 2018
10 9 8 7 6 5 4 3 2 1
Printed in China